RELIGION AND HUMAN NATURE

RELIGION AND HUMAN NATURE

KEITH WARD

CLARENDON PRESS · OXFORD
1998

Oxford University Press, Great Clarendon Street, Oxford OX2 6DP

Oxford New York

Athens Auckland Bangkok Bogotá Buenos Aires Calcutta
Cape Town Chennai Dar es Salaam Delhi Florence Hong Kong Istanbul
Karachi Kuala Lumpur Madras Madrid Melbourne Mexico City Mumbai
Nairobi Paris São Paulo Singapore Taipei Tokyo Toronto Warsaw

and associated companies in
Berlin Ibadan

Oxford is a registered trade mark of Oxford University Press

Published in the United States
by Oxford University Press Inc., New York

British Library Cataloguing in Publication Data
Data available

Library of Congress Cataloging in Publication Data
Religion and human nature / Keith Ward
Includes index.
1. Man (Theology) I. Title.
BL256.W37 1998 291.2'2—dc21 98-3194

ISBN 0-19-826961-7
ISBN 0-19-826965-X

1 3 5 7 9 10 8 6 4 2

Typeset by Hope Services (Abingdon) Ltd.
Printed in Great Britain on acid-free paper by
Biddles Ltd., Guildford & King's Lynn

ACKNOWLEDGEMENTS

Among the many people I have consulted in the writing of this book, I am very grateful, in particular, to Saunaka Rishi Das, of Iskcon, to Ram Prasad, who at the time was Gordon Milburn Research Fellow at Trinity College, Oxford, to Rabbi Norman Solomon, Hebrew Centre Lecturer in Judaism at Oxford, to Zaki Badawi, Principal of the Muslim College in London, and to Paul Williams, Reader in Indo-Tibetan Studies at Bristol University.

Needless to say, none of them bear any responsibility for the views expressed in the book, but talking to them has helped me to come to what I hope is a clearer and fairer understanding of the traditions to which they belong.

K.W.

CONTENTS

I
Introduction

There exists a wide range of views about human nature, about what human beings essentially are, and what their proper relationship is to other beings and to the wider universe in which they exist. The religious traditions of the world, which develop a number of communal interpretations of the insights of their originating prophets or teachers, enshrine distinctive views of human nature and destiny.

What seems to be characteristic of most religious views of human nature is that they relate human life in some way to a supra-material realm of spirit or mind, whether spirit is conceived as one or many, as substantial or as in continual flux. The major differences between religious traditions in these respects are about whether all human selves are essentially pure spirits, whether they are embodied and substantial selves, or whether they are composed of simpler, mostly spiritual (i.e. non-material) elements, which are either appearances of one non-dual reality or without any underlying substantial basis.

At one extreme, there is the view that human beings are essentially spiritual, indeed that they only appear to be individual souls and bodies. In fact, bodies are not essential to them, and even their individuality is an illusion or appearance. The non-dualistic school of Vedanta—Advaita—teaches that the Supreme Self, *Sat-Cit-Ananda*, unfolds into the illusion of separated and conflicting individuality. Spiritual practice consists in overcoming the illusion of separateness, and achieving a sense of non-duality, the pure unity of universal consciousness, which frees one from worldly desires into the liberated awareness of a wider 'ocean of blissful being'. The spiritual goal is to obtain release from earthly embodiment and from the illusion of distinct embodied individuality. These views are mostly found in some Indian religious traditions, though they are found in Plato and in strands of slightly heterodox Western religious thought which have Neoplatonic roots.

In a rather different interpretation of the spiritual practice of non-attachment, the Indian school of Sankhya-Yoga holds that each spiritual self will always remain distinct, without being absorbed into a 'greater Self'. One still seeks freedom from egoistic grasping, and from all the material hindrances which restrict and corrupt one's pure spiritual knowledge and freedom. But the goal is the pure consciousness of individual liberated existence, which always remains one's own consciousness, not that of some more inclusive self. In these traditions, there is agreement that the self is in bondage to ignorance and desire, and that the proper goal of human existence is to achieve freedom from that bondage, in a state of knowledge and unchanging bliss. Religious practice is the cultivation of attitudes and actions which lead to that goal.

Another main variant of this group of traditions is found in Buddhism, for which the analysis of the self and its motives leads to the conclusion that a sense of possessive ego and of selfish desire lies at the root of suffering. Accordingly, by a course of rigorous mental training, one seeks to eliminate selfish desire, and cultivate mindfulness, compassion, and equanimity. One's experiences will become less characterized by grasping, and one's actions will become less oriented towards personal gratification. The ideal goal is to transcend the sense of self altogether, and pass into a state in which all things can be enjoyed without attachment, simply for what they are in their transient and insubstantial flow. That state, nirvana, is beyond embodiment and the sort of action which is motivated by need or selfish desire. There is no individual immortality to be hoped for, but rather a dissolution of the elements that form personality and an entrance into a supra-individual state of being. Nevertheless, especially in Mahayana traditions, one may speak of this as a state of pure knowledge and of compassionate action for the welfare of all sentient beings. This, paradoxically, comes very close to the One Self teaching of Advaita, which sounds completely different. For release from embodiment to a state of 'no-self' is virtually indistinguishable from release into the state of 'one-only-self' of Advaita.

What is fundamentally important about human nature, for these views, is that agents can achieve liberation from bondage by a certain sort of mental training (which may include ritual activity (*karma*), meditation (*jnyana*), and devotion to gods or gurus (*bhakti*). Such training is seen as extending over many earthly lives. In each case, the goal is to achieve a state very different from that of individual personal consciousness as we know it. It is neverthe-

less an expansion, not a mere cancellation, of personal consciousness to a better state ('one self', 'no self', or 'pure self'), and it is
accomplished by personal effort. The individual personality, in so
far as it survives, becomes a vehicle and manifestation of spiritual
being, not a separate centre of autonomous action and enjoyment.

In opposition to these traditions, which see human nature as in
some sense essentially spiritual or non-material, is the view that
humans are nothing but material bodies, with no possibility of continuing after the death of those bodies. There are few religious
views of this type, though Carvakas in India adopted a ritual and
social code which involved no beliefs in a supernatural reality of any
sort, and some modern forms of Christian non-realism similarly
eschew any non-materialistic ontology. There is, however, an influential modern world-view, sometimes called evolutionary naturalism, which regards human nature as the chance product of blind
processes of natural selection. Its proponents are usually hostile to
religious belief and practice, and some of its proponents hold that
it is a scientifically established view which renders religious beliefs
about human nature obsolete. The situation is, perhaps, rather
more complex than that, and indeed evolutionary naturalism,
though it undoubtedly introduces important new perspectives to all
traditional beliefs, is not as much in conflict with some religious
traditions as it may seem.

The traditional view of the Semitic traditions, for instance, is that
humans are embodied souls, born from the material world and not
pre-existing it. They have a possible existence beyond this life, but
even that is not a purely spiritual existence. It will be either in a
reassembled material universe or in a different form of existence in
which both individuality and community will be retained. Such
views may take a dualistic form, insisting on the distinctness of the
spiritual and the material elements in human nature, even though
they are intimately related to one another. Or they may take a
monistic form, stressing that human beings are essentially embodied parts of the material universe, though they may have other
forms of embodiment in other forms of space–time. These views
are characteristic of orthodox strands of Judaism, Christianity, and
Islam, though they can converge on the *bhakti* traditions of India at
many points.

While Semitic views stress the embodied nature of human souls,
they also stress that human beings are not self-existent, but receive

their lives at every moment from God, and religious practice aims to help humans to realize this fact fully in thought and feeling. Prayer is the means of listening attentively to God, in order better to obey the divine will. In its purest form, prayer passes into the contemplation of the divine nature, and such contemplation forms in the mind the attitudes of reverence, gratitude, faithful obedience, repentance, and compassionate action, which characterize authentic human life.

For these traditions, human beings are parts of the material order, not separate from it. But what is important about them is that they are enlivened with the Spirit of God, given the possibility of relating in understanding, creativity, and love to the Creator and to one another, and the responsibility of nurturing the material order of which they are part. In this context, the material realm itself is seen, not as an inert, purposeless realm of impersonal laws, but as a dynamic and developing expression of the divine glory, containing already in its primal origin and constitution the potential for self-understanding and creative self-realization in a holistic and conscious community of being. Human beings are one growing-point in this development of the material towards fully conscious life, attracted and empowered by the absolute value of the divine Being.

For the Semitic religions, human persons are fully and unequivocally material beings. Yet in the end the importance of their lives lies in their interior experience, and in the creation of new values which can be understood and enjoyed. It is the capacity of matter for creative action and understanding that gives it value and purpose. Matter, in its original constitution, is without consciousness or purpose. Its elements interact in accordance with relatively simple laws, without any sense of aiming at value. Yet even in its simplest causal interactions, one may discern an adjustment of the inner states of material objects (spatially located foci of powers) to their environment, and an active expression of responsive powers projected into the future, albeit in very limited and determinate ways. In the increasingly complex organization of such objects into larger organic wholes, those inner states become conscious representations, and the responses become goal-directed actions within the wider environment. The mental may be seen as the inner pole of the physical, coming to understand and shape itself in accordance with conscious goals.

In so far as one speaks of a physical object as a centre of powers, which are expressed in accordance with various levels of organized complexity in the environment, one is committed to speaking of continuants, which have traditionally been called 'substances'. Powers are possessed by temporally continuing entities. Even if one says that objects consist of continuing collections of powers, such coherent collections must persist over time, if one is to have a physically ordered world at all. Mental powers are those which emerge gradually from organized physical complexes. So one has a continuing person when one has the organized complex physical structure of the brain, which reacts as a whole to its environment, representing it in perception and thought, and responding to it in feeling and action. That is when a material being can be said to possess a 'rational soul'.

In these matters, Christianity is in basic agreement with both Judaism and Islam, and is clearly a Semitic religion. Yet it also includes aspects more typical of Indian thought, particularly in its central notions of original sin, incarnation, and incorporation into the divine life. Humans are seen as in bondage to selfish desire and pride. This is not the result of past individual karma, but it is the consequence of a sort of social karma, according to which sentient beings suffer the karmic consequences of the acts of their ancestors. In incarnation, God enters into the material realm, and humans come to share in this divine life, as they become parts of the 'body of Christ'. The Spirit of Christ dwells within each person, and the ultimate goal is to become so united with Christ that one can say, with St Paul, 'it is no longer I who live, but Christ who lives in me'.[1] In this way, the whole world is destined to be united to the life of God, in a transformed and purified creation.

Perhaps the central distinctive teaching of Christianity is that the Divine shares in creaturely suffering, in order that the material order may be liberated from bondage to selfish desire, and transfigured to share in the life of eternity.[2] In this way, Christian faith unites the strong concern with the material and historical that marks the Semitic faiths, and the primary concern with liberation from desire and the attainment of a state of wisdom, compassion, and bliss that marks the Indian faiths.

[1] Gal. 2: 20 (all biblical quotations are from the RSV).
[2] 'The Word assumed humanity that we might become God,' Athanasius, *On the Incarnation* (London: Centenary Press, 1944), 45.

For Christians, the attainment of liberation is essentially a work of grace. It is the work of God, not of human effort, which cannot of itself unite humans to God. There is a difference between traditions that stress the necessity of personal effort to attain salvation, and those that stress the need for divine help. While this is true, however, I hope to show that this is not the huge gulf it sometimes seems to be. There is a great deal of scope for help from others even in the most severe Theravadin Buddhist schools, and very few Christian churches would deny that, while one is to rely wholly on divine grace, nevertheless, one must 'work out one's own salvation with fear and trembling'.[3] Here, as in so many cases, the realities of religious practice are more complex than the over-simplified oppositions which a focus solely on abstract doctrines can create.

Nevertheless, Christianity can undoubtedly be characterized as a religion of divine grace, and so contrasts with views which insist that all persons must accomplish liberation by their own power alone.

Whether they stress personal effort or divine grace, most religious traditions have developed doctrines of the destiny of the self beyond earthly death, and tend to see release (*moksa*) or salvation as a supramundane goal of earthly life. Thus the Indian traditions developed ideas of an endless cycle of rebirth, from which one could escape by religious practice. The Semitic traditions rather stressed the possibility of a more satisfying resurrection world in future, in which alone true human nature could be realized. Here too, however, the resurrection world—at least for those who are redeemed—is usually very different from the present physical universe, since it is without suffering, death, or conflict.

Such a concern is intelligible, when seen as arising from a basic insight into the unsatisfactoriness and imperfection of earthly life. Once it is postulated that humans are at least partly spiritual beings, it soon becomes clear that their spiritual nature is usually constrained and frustrated by their forms of material embodiment. If one also postulates, as most religious views do, that the universe is in some way morally ordered, it is natural to look for the possibility of a fulfilment of spiritual nature beyond the constraints of the present material world. Belief in life after death, and in the particular form it might take, seems to develop in religious traditions as an

---

[3] Phil. 2: 12.

extrapolation from beliefs about the nature of the human self, its impediments, and its possibilities of fulfilment. In this way, a consideration of the possibility of a fulfilment of human destiny beyond death is a natural corollary of a general analysis of human nature.

To help in analysing these views of human nature, I have taken two major living and easily accessible traditions, with leading teachers whom I could consult personally, from each of the main strands I have distinguished. From the 'pure spirit' strand I have chosen, to represent the 'many self' view, the International Society for Krishna Consciousness (ISKCON). To some people in the West, this may seem like a rather outlandish sect of young people who dance in groups along city streets, chanting 'Hare Krishna'. Such chanting is indeed central to the practice of this group, but the organization is part of a major Indian religious group, the Bengali Vaishnavas, or worshippers of the god Vishnu. The group is one of a number of *bhakti*, or devotional, groups, usually dedicated either to Vishnu or to Shiva. As such, it has a good claim to represent what is one of the most widely practised sets of religious beliefs in India. It is committed to the view that each individual soul has an eternal existence, without beginning or end, and that the supreme goal of every soul is to be released from the material world and achieve endless life in Goloka, a purely spiritual realm beyond birth and death.

To represent the 'one self' view, I have taken the Ramakrishna Mission, which sees itself as standing in the tradition of Sankara, the foremost theologian of Advaita, or non-dualistic, Vedanta. The Mission was founded at Calcutta in 1897 by Swami Vivekananda, to propagate the teaching of Sri Ramakrishna, an illiterate temple priest who was yet a great saint, ecstatic, and religious teacher. Ramakrishna was personally devoted to Kali, the 'great mother', but claimed to have realized in himself the teachings of the major religions, and to have seen that they all contain spiritual truth. Vivekananda took and developed the teachings of Ramakrishna, seeing them as a modern application of the teachings of Sankara, and an exposition of Advaita, which is at the heart, so he claimed, of all religions. The Mission provides an interesting example of the way in which an ancient tradition can be reshaped and revitalized in the modern world.

From the 'no individual self' strand I have chosen two rather different forms of Buddhism. One is the Theravadin school which is largely found in South East Asia, but now has many bases in Britain, and the other is the form of Tibetan Buddhism to which the Dalai Lama belongs. Both these schools deny that nirvana is sheer extinction or non-existence, and they deny that it is the survival of the earthly personality as we know it. To that extent, they do share the Advaita philosophy that the goal of human life is to obtain release from rebirth and individual existence, and to attain a state which cannot be straightforwardly spoken of either as continuance or extinction. The Theravadin school differs from Advaita in having no place for worship of Isvara, or a supreme creator god, or for the sacrificial rites of the Brahminical priesthood. The Mahayana school is chiefly distinguished by its doctrine that all sentient beings can, or will, become Buddhas, that innumerable Buddhas and *bodhisattva*s exist, who can help one to attain nirvana, and that the ultimate goal is not one of sheer non-duality, but rather one of compassionate action for the liberation of all sentient beings.

From the 'embodied self' strand I have chosen Judaism and Islam. They reject the distinctive Christian doctrines of original sin and atonement, as well as agreeing in seeing humans as created from material dust in order to bring the material universe to a perfect expression of God's glory. Judaism is almost unique in having very little interest in the existence of a soul after death. Instead, it tends to stress a hope for the existence of a perfected society, the Messianic kingdom, in the future of the earth. Islam, on the contrary, is essentially committed to belief in a Last Judgement and the resurrection of the dead. Its ultimate hope is not for the future of this earth, but for a new post-historical creation.

Since I write from a particular Christian viewpoint, I have tried to locate Christian ideas of the nature of the human person and its ultimate destiny in the context of this range of religious beliefs, and to develop a Christian view which is sensitive and responsive to the concerns which the other traditions express. In the Hindu, Buddhist, Jewish, and Muslim cases, I have taken care to speak to representatives who can interpret their own writings to me, and so convey authoritatively what at least some contemporary religious groups think and believe. In the Christian case, I have also been able to speak to Christians of various traditions. I make no pretence to neutrality. But I am certainly not aiming to use non-Christian views as a mere foil for my own. My interest is to formulate a Christian view about human nature, informed by other religious views which both contrast with it and, at many points, converge with it. Thereby I hope to extend Christian horizons and understand some of the limitations or distortions which others have perceived in the Christian tradition. The properly comparative theology to which this is meant as a contribution will only exist if members of many traditions contribute together to continue such a growth in understanding, each expounding their own tradition in the light of a genuine encounter with others.

2

Non-Dualism (Advaita Vedanta)

At the World Parliament of Religions in Chicago in 1893, Swami Vivekananda brought a new understanding of Advaita Vedanta to the Western world. 'He is undoubtedly the greatest figure in the Parliament of Religions. After hearing him we feel how foolish it is to send missionaries to this learned nation,' said a leader in the *New York Herald*.[1] In his introductory address, Vivekananda spoke briefly 'in the name of the most ancient order of monks in the world', and of 'the mother of religions'. That in itself perhaps changed the perceptions of those who had regarded Hinduism as a reactionary and fossilized jumble of empty rituals and idolatrous practices. The implicit claim was that, underlying the apparently riotous confusion of Indian religious life was an ancient and enduring doctrine, *sanatana dharma*, the eternal way, of spiritual depth, tolerance, and universal acceptance.

'We accept all religions as true,' he proclaimed, comparing different religions to different streams all leading to the one sea. That sea is the ocean of Advaita, of non-dualism, an all-inclusive unity which embraces all diversity and yet at the same time reduces it all to the level of appearance, or *maya*. At once the central paradox of this version of Advaita leaps into view. All religions are true: 'Unity in variety is the plan of nature, and the Hindu has recognised it.'[2] Christians are not, for example, to become Buddhists, but 'each must assimilate the spirit of the others, yet preserve his individuality'.[3] In this respect, the diversity of faiths, as of things and souls, is a real, proper, and valuable feature of reality, and is not to be undermined—for example, by attempts to make all people conform to one faith, or to deny the development of distinct individuality.

[1] *The Life of Swami Vivekananda*, by his Eastern and Western Disciples (Calcutta: Advaita Ashrama, 1993), i. 428.

[2] R.K. Dasgupta (ed.), *Swami Vivekananda, A Commemorative Volume* (Calcutta: Ramakrishna Math, 1994), 891.

[3] Ibid. 893.

On the other hand, there is higher and lower truth. Precisely when Vivekananda is speaking of the necessity of diversity in faith, he clearly ranks faiths: 'from the high spiritual flights of the Vedanta . . . to the low ideas of idolatry . . . all have a place.'[4] Even within Vedanta, he sees Dvaita (dualism) and Visistadvaita (qualified non-dualism) as steps towards the ultimate truth of Advaita (non-dualism). Religions might all be true, but there are many degrees of truth, and there is little doubt that non-dualism is the full truth. 'Every religion is only evolving a God out of the material man, and the same God is the inspirer of all of them.'[5] In this respect, the diversity of faiths, as of souls, belongs only to the realm of illusion, which is to be overcome in the realization of the ultimate truth that all is part of one divine undifferentiated reality. To know the truth is to know that one is divine, and to realize that divinity is far beyond the limited individuality of soul and body with which I mistakenly identify myself.

The paradox is that diversity is to be preserved, and yet undifferentiated unity is to be realized. In truth, there is only one reality, without distinctions or subject–object duality. And yet somehow the realm of *maya* exists, and there is the appearance of diversity and duality. This paradox applies with particular force to the doctrine of human nature. Am I Brahman, the one non-dual reality? Or am I a distinct individual soul, with particular duties to perform and a particular limited consciousness? It must be the case that I am both, but that the particular soul is only a transient appearance of the one enduring reality in which all dualities are transcended.

The teaching of Advaita is not that I simply do not exist, as an individual. Even if I am compared to a dream or illusion, such things exist in some sense, and cannot simply be denied. If I say that my life is a dream, I normally mean that there is some real world which is the causal basis of that dream. If I can become aware of that world, I may see more clearly the nature of the dream, and the possibility of waking to a different sort of experience. So the Advaitin asserts that there is a reality, other than this, which is the causal basis of our separate individuality. This life is not self-existent. It cannot be taken as independently existent, for it essentially depends on some reality beyond itself. If it is possible to

---

[4] Ibid. 891.   [5] Ibid.

become aware of that reality, I may see more clearly the nature of this samsaric existence, as dependent on what lies beyond it.

Yet, for the Advaitin, that word 'beyond' is misleading, as suggesting that the Real is another existent of the same sort as the dual existents we know in ordinary experience, or is a distinct and separate cause. The Real is not to be added to a list of existent separated and distinct beings, even as the greatest of them. On the contrary, it is the inner reality of all distinct beings, and they are its appearances. It would be wrong, for instance, to think of the Real as a distinct personal being, complete in itself, which gives rise to the universe by a contingent act of will. Vivekananda writes, 'God is not the monarch sitting on a throne, entirely apart . . . you are all Gods . . . Vedanta proposes . . . no God to be afraid.'[6] The Real is expressed in the finite universe, and is not apart from it. Yet the Real is beyond all distinctions and finite limitations, and universes arise from it by a process which is at the same time one of self-expression and self-concealment. All things express in a fragmentary way the unlimited nature of the Real. Yet all things pass into forgetfulness (*avidya*), and in their individuality the non-duality of the Real is concealed.

When Vivekananda teaches that 'you are divine', he does not mean that you are actually divine, just as the individual personality you are. If he meant that, no distinction could be made—as it is made—between *avatara*, physical manifestations of God, and ordinary human souls, or between *mahapurusas*, realized sages, and souls bound by materialism. He means that within each person there is a spark of divinity, which needs to be fanned and tended, so that it can illuminate and transform the soul. It is the true self, *atman*, which is one and the same in every distinct individual. It is not me, in distinction from anyone else. It is the 'me' which is identical with the 'me' in everyone else.

Again one runs up against a basic paradox. There is something in me that is identical with the heart of all beings, the ultimately real, and that in some way is truly me, although it is distinct from the bound and ignorant personality that I am. To realize my potential divinity and make it actual, I have to become aware of this true innermost self, and make my *jiva*, my individual soul, an expression and vehicle of it, so closely that I can then say it is my true self

    [6] *The Complete Works of Swami Vivekananda* (Calcutta: Advaita Ashrama, 1992), viii. 127.

which acts. The paradox here is that my soul must already be an expression of the true Self, since everything is. So how can I change it to make it such an expression?

'The apparent man', says Vivekananda, 'is merely a struggle to express, to manifest this individuality which is beyond.'[7] The realm of appearance is the realm of struggle, a struggle to realize God and unity with the One. But when that realization comes, it affirms that the unity of being is unbeginning and unchanging. So what has struggled, and what has been achieved that was not always the case? How could the immutably One 'become' a changing, struggling, many, or even the 'appearance' of such a struggling manifold?

Vivekananda never answers this question. Indeed, he explicitly refuses to do so, saying: 'I do not know how the perfect being, the soul, came to think of itself as imperfect, as joined to and conditioned by matter. But the fact is a fact for all that.'[8] This may seem rather lame, but there is a plausible explanation for this lack of knowledge: 'the answer can never be given in Maya, and beyond Maya who will ask it?'[9] In the realm of *maya*, we are hampered by ignorance, which makes us unable to answer such ultimate questions. When we achieve liberation from *maya*, we will have transcended all speech, name, and form, so there is nothing that can be said, and no individual personality to say it. Nevertheless, in one of his poems, 'A Song I Sing to Thee', Vivekananda gives some clue to an answer: 'The One, I become the many, to behold My own form.'[10]

It is clear that there is an ambivalence in the doctrine of Advaita. The world can be seen as just illusion, with no positive role to play, merely a fall into ignorance and suffering, to be escaped from through ascetic practice. Escape, *moksa*, is simply the recovery of true knowledge, a setting aside of illusions, which never had any positive role to play in human development. 'This universe does not exist at all; it is all illusion. The whole of this universe, these Devas, gods, angels, and all the other beings born and dying . . . are all dreams.'[11] Thus it is that 'when the Vedantist has realised his own nature, the whole world has vanished for him'.[12] Ultimate self-realization is the disappearance of the universe, together with the individual personality, mind, and body.

---

[7] Ibid. ii. 81. [8] Ibid. i. 10. [9] Ibid. vii. 67.
[10] Ibid. iv. 516. [11] Ibid. i. 402. [12] Ibid. i. 365.

Vivekananda speaks of the 'two birds sitting on one tree' of the Mundaka Upanishad 3. 1, and remarks: 'The lower bird never existed, it was always the upper bird, and what it took for the lower bird was only a little bit of a reflection.'[13] The upper bird, the Self, somehow is 'reflected' into the material world of *maya*, and takes the reflection to be the reality. It is not that the reflection does not exist in any sense, but that it is not a real bird, a real independently existing basis of change and experience. There is no independently existing 'I': 'None but I was God and this little I never existed.'[14] Each soul is God, who is under the illusion that it is a vast number of independently existing subjects. There really is an illusion. But it has no substantial reality.

The problem with this interpretation is that God (Brahman) is free from illusion and evil: 'Behind and beyond is the Infinite in which there is no more evil.'[15] Indeed, the goal of meditation is freedom from illusion and suffering, the realization of one's infinite reality. But if God falls under the illusion of plurality and limitation, realizing 'my' divinity will not free 'me' from the possibility of illusion. In fact, since the emanation of worlds is beginningless and endless, I will continue, as God, to be under illusion for ever. The individual soul that I take myself to be will not be liberated, for it will cease to exist. Atman/Brahman, that I truly am, will not be liberated, for it will continue to fall under illusion for ever. Thus in effect the goal turns out to be the cessation of attachment to this individual personality, the recognition of its unimportance, and the unimportance of all other individual souls, too.

What is the difference between the existence of souls under the illusion that they are distinct, and the creation of really distinct souls, which depend wholly upon God? The distinct soul will perhaps say: 'God is other than I am; I can relate to God in worship and devotion, and hope for endless life as a devotee.' The illusory soul, recovering from illusion, may say: 'God is not other than myself; so I should pass beyond worship, and hope for the disillusion of my individual ego.' For Advaita, I am God, temporarily under the illusion that I am a separate self. Such illusions will never cease to exist. But I, at least, can realize my true nature as the infinite God. Then, for me, the world will cease to exist, becoming like

---

[13] *The Complete Works of Swami Vivekananda* (Calcutta: Advaita Ashrama, 1992), vi. 25.
[14] Ibid. ii. 250.   [15] Ibid. ii. 144.

a dream which has little intrinsic significance. It is hard to see how one can have any positive concern for events or illusory souls, whether one's own or another's, which only exist in a dream.

That is the negative interpretation of Advaita characteristically given by non-Advaitic schools, who tend to refer to it as *mayavada*, in itself a slightly derogatory term. It is also, however, a reasonable interpretation of Sankara, who teaches the realization of absolute non-duality as the highest aim of the religious life, and who claims that when it is realized, all diversity fades away. On such a view, the realm of *samsara* has no positive role to play in the scheme of things.

But the world can also be seen as the divine play, in which the One, though remaining complete in itself, manifests in diversity so as to realize its infinite potential in endless ways, and to enjoy that self-realization. On such an interpretation, liberation is not seen as simply release from suffering and individuality. What matters is the realization of God-consciousness during earthly life, and the coming to awareness that *maya* has a positive part to play in the blissful self-realization of the Real.

There is little doubt that Vivekananda often, and more emphatically, takes the positive interpretation. He teaches that 'he who knows the Real sees in *maya* not illusion but reality'.[16] So things in their individuality are manifestations of the Absolute. Self-realization may be a positive part of the self-expression of the Real in human life. 'Vedanta . . . really means deification of the world . . . Deify it; it is God alone.'[17] On this interpretation, every part of the world becomes vitally important, as it is a positive expression of divinity.

THE SERVICE OF GOD IN OTHERS

The Ramakrishna Mission has from the first been concerned with social service as part of the way of life of its devotees. The practical import of the teaching is not that this life is simply to be renounced as worthless. It is that God is not to be regarded as an external being 'in heaven', but as within the self, in the 'cave of the heart'. Since God is within each soul, one can say that 'man is divine . . . each human being stands for the divine.'[18] It is intelligible for an

16 Ibid. vi. 92.   17 Ibid. i. 146.   18 Ibid. i. 388.

Advaitin to regard worship of an objective, external God as relatively unimportant, since each soul really is God, though it does not perceive itself as such. But Vivekananda gives this doctrine a new twist by saying that 'the only God to worship is the human soul in the human body.'[19] Instead of drawing the conclusion that worship is inappropriate to a fully enlightened soul, he suggests that worship is to be given, not to a God in heaven, but to human souls: 'The God of heaven becomes the God in nature . . . and at last becomes the soul and man—and there Vedanta reaches the last words it can teach'.[20]

Instead of each soul being an illusion, and therefore not an object of special concern, now each soul becomes a part of God, and therefore worthy of worship. Most members of the Ramakrishna Mission trace this change back to an ecstatic utterance of Ramakrishna, who said, 'It is not compassion to Jivas but service to them as Siva' which is important.[21] This distinctive docrine, which became central to the teaching of Vivekananda, is known as *Sivajnyane jive-seva*, serving man as Siva. It is appropriate to do this because 'You and they, the poor and the rich, the saint and the sinner, are all parts of One Infinite Whole, which you call Brahman.'[22]

Thus from the premisses of Advaita, Vivekananda derives a fundamental teaching of the equality of all human beings. This is not an implication which had been drawn by Sankara, who upheld the caste system in its classical rigour. Sankara saw the realization of non-duality as the preserve of a small spiritual élite. Advaita was for him compatible with great social inequality, and indeed with a very hierarchical view of society, in which the spiritually advanced should rule over the brutalized masses. Moreover, he held that *moksa*, release, is actually incompatible with action, which presupposes a duality between self and other: 'Action is incompatible with knowledge [of Brahman] . . . knowledge destroys the factors of action as it destroys the notion that there is water in the salt desert . . . for this reason action should be renounced by a seeker after final release.'[23]

---

[19] *The Complete Works of Swami Vivekananda* (Calcutta: Advaita Ashrama, 1992), ii. 321.

[20] Ibid. iii. 67.

[21] Swami Saradananda, *Sri Ramakrishna the Great Master*, trans. Swami Jagadananda (Madras: Sri Ramakrishna Math, 1991), ii. 939.

[22] *Complete Works*, iii. 432.

[23] Sengaku Mayeda, *A Thousand Teachings: The Upadesasahasri of Sankara* (New York: State University Press, 1992), I.I.12–15, p. 104.

The Ramakrishna Mission, while seeking to remain true to the Advaitic tradition of Sankara, introduces quite a new theme of social service and commitment to the life of religion. The objectives of the Mission, founded in 1897, include the sponsoring of medical research, training of teachers, and the establishment of ophanages, hospitals and other social welfare services and institutions. It is not an order of merely world-renouncing ascetics. As Vivekananda said, 'The fictitious differentiation between religion and the life of the world must vanish, for the Vedanta teaches oneness.'[24] He does not interpret non-duality as a secret truth, experienced by few, in a renounced form of life which is not open to householders or politicians. Rather, he interprets it as teaching that the life of the world, too, is part of the One Whole, so that all things must be respected as divine. Just as one would feed and clothe a deity in a temple, so one must feed and clothe the poor. 'It is now my firm conviction', he said, ' that it is futile to preach religion . . . without first trying to remove their poverty.'[25] To see God in all things is to serve God in all things. Indeed, Vivekananda wrote in one letter that 'altruistic service only is religion'.[26]

The major problem with such a view is that the very statement of the practical objectives of removing suffering, ignorance, and inequality seems to be odds with the affirmation that all things are already divine, or parts of the one divine reality. If all things are divine, how can one discriminate between them? If reality is non-dual, and has no parts, how can one prefer some parts of it to others (knowledge to ignorance, bliss to suffering)? Vivekananda's way of meeting this difficulty is to say that most things are potentially divine, but have not yet actualized their inner divinity: 'All differences in this world are of degree, and not of kind.'[27] The imperative for a Vedantin thus becomes, 'Manifest your Self in a high degree,'[28] and help others to manifest themselves in higher degrees, too.

For the classical tradition of Sankara, one cannot directly help others to realize the Self. One can only teach, whether by word or example, the way to realization, a way which each must follow

[24] *Complete Works*, ii. 291.
[25] Romain Rolland, *The Life of Vivekananda and the Universal Gospel* (Calcutta: Advaita Ashrama, 1970), 30.
[26] *Letters of Swami Vivekananda* (Calcutta: Advaita Ashrama, 1976), 338.
[27] *Complete Works*, ii. 299.   [28] Ibid. ii. 300.

alone. To manifest the Self is to transcend concern with individual personality and its acts, which implies non-attachment to any particular social or political programmes, which belong to the world of *maya*. Of course, for Sankara, one must do one's duty, but that is a matter of obeying various caste-based rules and regulations, and thus reinforces social hierarchies.

Vivekananda was vociferous in criticism of untouchability, the repression of women, and the social inequalities of traditional Indian society. He thereby reinterpreted Advaita in a socially radical way, as teaching that 'in all our actions we have to judge whether it is making for diversity or for oneness'.[29] Because all is One, we must aim at Oneness, and that means having a strong basic sense of equality and of the perfectibility of all beings. Moreover, 'the expression of oneness is what we call love and sympathy, and it is the basis of all our ethics.'[30] If one sees the unity of all beings, one will naturally love all beings as one loves oneself: 'According to Advaitism, love every man as your own Self and not as your brother as in Christianity. Brotherhood should be superseded by universal Selfhood.'[31] There is clearly a strong moral impetus in the thought that each person must be treated as divine, and in the thought that each other person is at the deepest level identical with oneself.

One must, however, disentangle a number of threads which are present here. If every person is divine, it would seem to follow that we must worship the murderer and rapist as much as the saint and hero, and treat them in the same way, garlanding them with flowers and showering them with gifts. In a letter of 1897, Vivekananda implies that he believes this: 'May I be born again and again . . . so that I may worship the only God that exists . . . the sum total of all souls; and above all, my God the wicked, my God the miserable, my God the poor of all races, of all species, is the special object of my worship.'[32] Swami cannot mean that he reveres and adores the wicked for his wickedness. It is rather that, even in his wickedness, the evil person carries the spark of potential divinity, which must be encouraged, so that the person may have faith in himself and strive to realize his true being. One should not view the wicked as simply

---

[29] *Complete Works*, ii. 304.   [30] Ibid. i. 389.
[31] Ibid. vi. 122. Of course, the Christian view is precisely that 'You shall love . . . your neighbour as yourself' (Luke 10: 27).
[32] *Letters*, 350.

condemned and destined for Hell. One should see him as still able to realize Heaven, by his own efforts.

By relying on the doctrine of degrees of divinity, one might say that a murderer is actually bound by ignorance and desire, but is still potentially divine. The murderer belongs to *maya*, the divinity to Reality. One can then seek to liberate the murderer from desire, and uncover the divinity lying hidden at the heart of his being, enabling it to be manifested in the world.

What is happening now is that *maya* is being seen as capable of both hiding and expressing the divine, and human action is able to overcome desire and progressively realize the divine, blissful, compassionate, and wise. One might describe the recommended path as one of discovering the God within, and manifesting it more fully in one's life. This undermines the thought that everything is an appearance of one changeless divine reality, and that everyone should be treated as equal. For human beings manifest Brahman to very unequal degrees, and must be treated accordingly. There is no way from the divinity of all humans to their equality, given the teaching that divinity is only potential in most humans, and is actualized to greater or lesser degrees.

A second strand of teaching is that each self is basically one, so that in loving others one is loving the true Self. One can literally love one's neighbour as oneself, when one realizes that one's neighbour *is* oneself! 'That man will love his greatest enemy who knows that that very enemy is God Himself.'[33] But what of those who torture children? Can one possibly see such torture as the work of God, or revere the torturer in the midst of his work? It is difficult for Advaita to have any strong sense of sin, evil, or injustice. 'Vedanta proposes no sin nor sinner.'[34] This teaching can make a refreshing change from the emphasis on human depravity that has characterized so much Christian preaching. If we think of ourselves as miserable sinners, it is all too easy to lack any sense of self-worth, and to view others in the worst possible light. How much better to see the good in everyone: 'The Hindu refuses to call you sinners. Ye are the Children of God, the sharers of immortal bliss, holy and perfect beings.'[35] Yet that is more plausible when said to an audience of basically well-intentioned but rather self-doubting seekers after truth, than when said to a rally of the National Socialist Party or the League of White Supremacists.

[33] *Complete Works*, ii. 286.   [34] Ibid. viii. 124.   [35] Ibid. i. 11.

What one wants to say to racial supremacists is that they are basically deluded about human nature, and in the grip of the passions of hatred and fear. One will not wish to encourage a sense that they are praiseworthy and heroic, perfect beings, just as they are. One might wish to say that delusion and passion is obscuring their true natures, which are meant to share in holiness, bliss, and perfection. One might look to encourage the good, not just condemn the evil. But delusion and passion exist, and cannot be condoned.

This is obscured when Vivekananda writes, 'Good and evil are but superstitions, and do not exist . . . it is all a manifestation of that Atman.'[36] Is delusion and self-love really a manifestation of Atman? Not even the most ardent Advaitin would say that they are manifestations to be sought or encouraged, as wisdom and non-attachment are. At this point, perhaps, the tolerance of Advaita may threaten to turn into acquiescence in evil, into an unconcern about injustice.

At one point Vivekananda writes, 'We have no theory of evil. We call it ignorance.'[37] Of course, that *is* a theory of evil, the theory that selfishness is due to an ignorance of the true unity of the Self in all things. What is needed is knowledge of that unity, and goodness will follow. So 'instead of telling them they are sinners, the Vedanta takes the opposite position, and says, "You are pure and perfect, and what you call sin does not belong to you. Sins are very low degrees of Self-manifestation; manifest your Self in a high degree" '[38]

This may be an effective psychological method in many circumstances, but it does not deny the existence of moral evil. Indeed, it seems to make it a self-manifestation of the Real, an expression of what the Real is. 'Do not think that good and evil are two . . . for they are one and the same thing, appearing in different degrees and in different guises.'[39] Is that description compatible with saying that 'sin does not belong to you'? Either sin manifests what Brahman is, or it does not belong to Brahman. Here one has a reflection of the ambiguity between saying that the *jiva* is a low manifestation of Brahman, and saying that it is an illusion, or not real. This in turn reflects a tension between saying that all things necessarily exist as they are, and that some things (selfishness and

---

[36] *Complete Works*, ii. 420.   [37] Ibid. v. 282.   [38] Ibid. ii. 300.
[39] Ibid. ii. 179.

ignorance) ought not to exist. If you ought to *become* pure and perfect, then it follows that you are not now pure and perfect.

Vivekananda's teaching does not stress the obvious imperfection of one's present nature, but the perfection of one's potential nature. It stresses that one's present nature (the individual personality) must be discarded, in favour of manifesting the true Self, which is changelessly perfect. But that is virtually identical with saying that the individual personality is a 'body of sin', destined for death; that is, that one is a sinner, and needs to be united to God to find life and health. Moreover, in view of the fact that I have agreed that some Christians seem to have an unduly pessimistic view of human nature, it should be pointed out, in mitigation, that a Christian view should hold that humanity is redeemed in Christ already, so that the true Self of Christ can live within each heart that accepts it. There may seem to be a fundamental difference between a Christian doctrine of 'human sinfulness', against which Vivekananda consistently protests, and a Vedantic doctrine of the divinity of humans. But on closer examination, it turns out to be a difference in emphasis and in what is regarded in each case as soteriologically effective teaching. For Vivekananda agrees that the individual self, bound to passion and ignorance, must be discarded. And most Christians agree that every human life is illuminated, in however hidden and potential a way, with the Spirit of God, which is in fact the Spirit of Christ, so that divinity does lie potential in every human heart.

There is, of course, a difference if one faith teaches that most humans are destined for eternal Hell, whereas another teaches that all will be released from suffering. But even here, it is quite compatible with Advaita to hold that many souls will not achieve release, but remain bound to *samsara* for ever, and it is possible for a Christian to hold that everyone will be, or at least can be, saved. Much depends on the interpretation one gives to doctrines. When Vivekananda says that Advaita does not call humans sinners, he is certainly not saying that all people are actually perfect, or that they have no obligations to be unselfish. In fact, he holds that virtually all humans are bound to suffering and ignorance, which is a fairly good depiction of 'original sin', in the sense of estrangement from knowledge of the truth.

The call to God-realization entails that God is not fully realized in actual human lives. Indeed, Vivekananda makes it clear that God

never will be fully realized: 'There will never be a perfectly good or
bad world, because the very idea is a contradiction in terms.'[40] So
the divinity of human nature will always remain largely potential,
an ideal rarely fully realized. For Sankara, that is necessarily true,
since finite individuality itself is an imperfection and illusion.
Perfect goodness, which is perfect knowledge, could only be realized in the Self without duality, which transcends all finite individual existence. For Vivekananda, the situation is less clear, since
maya manifests Brahman as well as concealing Brahman. But the
world manifests Brahman only in part.

If the world fully manifested Brahman, then one would not seek
to heal the sick or feed the hungry or liberate the poor from oppression, since there would either be none, or they would perfectly
express the nature of Brahman. Two different strands of Advaita
here stand in tension with one another, one implying acceptance of
all things as manifestations of Brahman, and the other recom-
mending changing reality to bring it more into line with a reality of
bliss and compassion. In so far as one wishes to change reality, one
cannot be happy with it as it is. But one is happy with the way God
is. Therefore one cannot be treating other selves as actually divine.
In fact, Vivekananda sometimes suggests that it is not another's
actual character and personality that one loves at all, but the usually very well hidden divinity within. 'This individualised self . . . is
to be given up,'[41] both in the case of oneself and of others. In fact,
'The Advaitists have no place for the individual soul. They say individual souls are created by Maya . . . in reality they cannot exist.'[42]
Strangely, it seems that one does not love others, as they actually
appear to us in all their individuality, at all. One has no place for
such concern for individualities, which do not really exist. What,
then, does one love, and who is it that is loving? It is the divine Self
which loves the divine Self, and that Self is 'homogeneous and
undifferentiated'. This is neither love of others nor self-love, in any
straightforward sense. It is simply the realization of unity, the
recognition of non-difference. But what ethical implications can
that have? None at all, it would seem, since 'I am the Soul, the ever
free; I never was bound.'[43] Once ultimate non-duality is realized,
there is nothing to be desired or done. Action has been transcended.

---

[40] *Complete Works*, i. 36.   [41] Ibid. i. 364.   [42] Ibid.
[43] Ibid. i. 502.

Vivekananda does not accept this conclusion, though it seems to follow from Sankara's Advaita. Oneness, for Vivekananda, is an ethical imperative, and the drive to love and harmony comes from realizing the oneness of all things. Here, too, one needs the supplementary doctrines of degrees of truth and the imperative of self-realization. Realizing the unity of being is realizing that there is a tendency towards unity at the heart of things. Incompletely realized or even wholly obscured by matter and imperfection, there is an indefectible drive towards unity and love. It is up to human beings to realize such unity, which is a recognition of the one divine life seeking expression in all the imperfection of *maya*.

EXPERIENCING THE REALITY BEHIND APPEARANCES

In what is usually called the Harvard Address, Vivekananda sets out his understanding of Advaita, as teaching that all things evolve by 'apparent manifestation' (*vivarta vada*) from the one homogenous and undifferentiated One. The One is not a distinct creator. It 'becomes' the many, and yet it only *seems* so to become. 'The whole universe . . . is unchanged, and all the changes we see in it are only apparent.'[44] One analogy he uses is that of a mirage, which only seems to be real, vanishing as one approaches it.

Such analogies are not very helpful. A mirage is a visual perception which differs from real perceptions in that it lacks the usual causal connections to other perceptions, including the tactile ones that would normally accompany it, and, of course, it disappears when approached, so it lacks the stability and predictability of normal perceptions. We can explain a mirage by showing how the refraction of light causes such visual information to occur in the brain. It may lead us to draw mistaken inferences about what to expect, but it is in itself a genuine perception, with an unusual set of causes. Moreover, mirages would not exist at all unless there were genuine perceptions of lakes and palm-trees. The existence of illusions is parasitic upon the existence of genuine sense-perceptions, which they misleadingly seem to be. At just this point the analogy fails, since there is no genuine perception of the sensory universe to which its illusory appearance could be compared. The appearance does not *seem* like anything genuine. On the contrary,

---

[44] Ibid. i. 363.

the appearance is quite unlike the reality—whereas mirages and dreams do seem to be something like genuine sense-perceptions.

In the case of the universe as we perceive it, there is an 'appearing' which is not like the reality that appears in that way. The mistaken inference that may lead us to draw is that the appearance is the reality, that it is self-existent or independent in being, and expresses the nature of things as they really are. As Vivekananda says, 'Maya is . . . neither existence nor non-existence.' It is not existence, because it is not capable of independent being, and it does not represent things as they truly are. It is not non-existence, because it does exist as appearance.

The world of many souls and things is a world of appearances, and as such they exist. But the reality that underlies appearances is very different from what appears. It is one undifferentiated unity, without distinctions or subject–object duality. That is the reality which I am, or of which I am an appearance.

How could I know that? For Sankara, it can only be known by revelation. It is, he thinks, a doctrine taught in the Upanishads, and so it must be accepted on authority. Vivekananda is rightly called a 'Neo-Vedantin', because he does not appeal in this way to the Shastras (Scriptures). Indeed, he explicitly says that the Veda are only to be accepted so far as they agree with reason, and that no ultimate authority is to be given to any book: 'Personally, I take as much of the Vedas as agree with reason.'[45] He takes the Vedas to be the spiritual treasury of knowledge in the Vedantic tradition as a whole, so his appeal is not to a particular interpretation (highly disputed among Vedantins) of the Vedic texts.

His appeal reflects in an Indian context the sea-change which occurred in European religious thought at the Enlightenment with Hegel and Schleiermacher. The growth of the natural sciences and the beginning of historical and critical approaches to Scripture undermined a straightforward appeal to propositional revelation, as directly written or inspired by God. When Immanuel Kant apparently demolished all rational arguments for God, and propounded his patently weak argument for believing in God as a postulate of morality, it seemed to many that the basis for religious belief had been removed. However, Kant left one blatant and fundamental lacuna in his critical philosophy. He distinguished between the world of appearance and the world of reality (the noumenal, or 'mind-world'), and argued that we can only know the world as appearance. We cannot know the nature of things-in-themselves at all. Such a completely unknowable reality is one that should not even be spoken of, so the basic Kantian error is to speak of it at all. In fact, it plays quite an important part in the critical philosophy. But those who generally followed Kant, seeing the contradiction, moved in one of two directions. Either they dropped the idea of a noumenal realm altogether—a trend of thought which culminated in scientific positivism and pragmatism. Or they denied that the noumenal was completely unknowable. Hegel was the leader of those who took the latter course. He argued that the whole historical process of the realm of appearance was precisely an appearing in time of what the Absolute reality in itself really is. There is no hidden reality, for the Absolute is realized in its temporal manifestations.

The Hegelian view gives a very positive view of history as the realm in which Absolute Spirit (*Geist*) necessarily manifests its nature. Yet it does see the whole of history as expressive of the self-evolution of one spiritual reality, and individual human lives as intruments of the self-expression of Absolute Spirit. Vivekananda was well acquainted with the work of European Enlightenment philosophers, and though he said that he had considered and rejected their philosophical views, the influence of Hegelian thought on Vivekananda's reinterpretation of Vedanta is clear. Sankara had seen the world as a realm of ignorance, from which to be liberated in an enlightened non-dual experience which would simply eliminate the illusion of apparent reality. But Vivekananda takes the much more positive view that the realm of appearance is the *lila*, the joyful play and self-expression, of Brahman, the supreme Self. Humans have a definite responsibility within the world, to try to make it conform more to the ideal of being a self-realization of Brahman. Each person must realize the divine in themselves, and seek to remove the impediments to its fuller realization in others. In this way, Vedanta is reinterpreted by an incorporation of the Hegelian theme of history as a progressive realization of the Absolute. It is not without irony that when the 'wisdom of the East' is proclaimed in modern Europe, it is very often a version of the European philosophy of Hegel, given a Vedantic religious dress, that is being brought back to those who have forgotten or are unaware of it.

Nevertheless, the Vedantic traditions of meditation and ascetic practice are quite foreign to Hegel's approach, and in Europe writers such as Kierkegaard vehemently criticized Hegel for failing to stress the intensely practical and experiential aspects of religious faith. To them, Hegel seemed to reduce religion to an all-embracing speculative system, and that was not much of an improvement on Kant's depressingly strenuous moralism. Vedanta, on the other hand, was never primarily a speculative system. Vivekananda's teachings are based on his acceptance of the ecstatic experiences of his guru, Ramakrishna, and on the importance of a personal search for the liberating experience of non-duality. However, even in this emphasis on the importance of individual experience, there takes place a certain reshaping of Vedantic tradition that owes much to another thinker of the European Enlightenment, Friedrich Schleiermacher.

Schleiermacher, in his influential book, *On Religion*, proposed a different approach to religious faith from that of Hegel. He disconnected religion from authoritative propositional revelation, intellectual speculation, and moral belief. Instead, he claimed to find an essence of religion, underlying all its many forms, doctrines and rituals, that was distinctive to religion and irreducible to anything else. This essence he found in experience, in what he called the 'feeling of piety', or 'the sense and taste for the Infinite'. 'To have religion', he says, 'means to intuit the universe.'[46]

He thus moved outside all particular religious traditions, and claimed to identify one common essence of all religion, the one important thing which could be found within every religion, but which was everywhere overlaid with particular doctrines, rituals, and cultural accretions. Moreover, this essence was to be found in a special sort of inner experience. Vaguely defined, it can be called 'God-consciousness', though it is perhaps wider than that, and speaks of a felt apprehension of a Totality or Absolute Being which somehow includes all other particular things, while not being identical with any of them. In his later work, the *Glaubenslehre*, Schleiermacher redefines this feeling as the feeling of 'absolute dependence', of being wholly dependent, even in one's most active

---

[46] Friedrich Schleiermacher, *On Religion*, trans. Richard Crouter (Cambridge: Cambridge University Press, 1988), 136.

moments, upon a reality whose existence is absolute, unconditioned and unchanged by any finite being.[47]

Schleiermacher's influence on subsequent Protestant religious
thought was immense. Through Rudolf Otto's 'Das Heilige', and
Martin Buber's 'Ich und Du', the idea that some form of personal
experience—whether of the Numinous, the 'Thou' which
addresses one in and through historical experiences, or of the
Cosmic Whole—is the essence of religion became widespread.
Revelation becomes, not the verbal utterances of God or particular
causal manifestations of the Divine in nature, but the occurrence of
a particularly intense or prolonged form of experience, which may
be passed on to others by personal influence.

The thought of neo-Vedantins such as Vivekananda reflects this
influence with remarkable fidelity. There is a downgrading of particular doctrines and practices in favour of one essential core of religion. That core is the experience of absolute non-duality, which Sri
Ramakrishna realized in himself, and which can now be at least
partly realized within the Ramakrishna Math, the community based
on his example and teaching.

RELIGIOUS EXPERIENCE AS A BASIS OF BELIEF

It is interesting to compare Schleiermacher, who was a Christian,
with Vivekananda, who was an Advaitan, in view of this similarity
of outlook. Schleiermacher interpreted that on which one was
absolutely dependent as the Creator God. He was, however, from
the first accused of pantheism, on the ground that he often referred
to God as 'the All' or 'the Whole', and that he seemed to regard creation as a necessary emanation from God rather than as a matter of
God's contingent choice. In his later work, he therefore stressed
that 'the Absolute' was not to be identified with anything relative or
finite, with anything in the universe or with the universe as a whole.
Schleiermacher saw Jesus as the supremely God-conscious human
being, sinless and uniquely united to God throughout his life,
though he rejected the classical Chalcedonian formulation of the
doctrine of incarnation. He saw each soul as part of the finite order
and as wholly dependent on God, though capable of apprehending

---

[47] F. Schleiermacher, *The Christian Faith*, trans. H. R. MacKintosh and J. S.
Stewart (Edinburgh: T. and T. Clark, 1989), 131.

God fully and in that sense of being to a lesser or greater degree one with God.

Vivekananda takes the essential religious experience to be one of non-duality. 'When he sees God, this universe vanishes entirely for him.'[48] He speaks critically about the idea of God as 'a father in heaven'. He calls it a relatively primitive idea compared to the idea of the God within. 'I am worshipping only myself . . . I am the Infinite,' he says.[49] Each soul is God, though it mistakenly thinks itself to be a distinct individual, or even a particular material body. His view of Jesus was that Jesus was 'a spirit, a disembodied, unfettered, unbound spirit'.[50] Together with Gautama Buddha, he is a great soul who, through many lifetimes of exertion and devotion, has become more than human, a messenger of God, teaching non-duality. There are many messengers from God, including Ramakrishna, himself divine, but their task is primarily to awaken the divinity that lies concealed in every human soul.

A crucial question to ask of both these thinkers is whether they can really derive their doctrines from the experiences they regard as important, whether the experiences they discuss are similar or different, and whether such experiences really constitute the essence of religion. In the first place, it is clear that a great deal of metaphysical speculation underlies their actual beliefs. Schleiermacher is indebted to Spinoza for his construal of divine omnipotence, and to a whole tradition of Christian doctrine for his general understanding of the dependence of the finite soul upon an infinite divine reality. Vivekananda accepts the Sankhya philosophy of *purusa* (spirit) and *prakriti* (matter), amending it in accordance with Sankara's teaching, and accepts the later Vedic teaching of reincarnation and of the cycles of cosmic evolution and involution. Such ideas may be true or false, but they do not derive from some special sort of personal experience.

Is the experience of 'absolute dependence', or of that awe and fascination which constitute the numinous feeling, the same as experience of undifferentiated non-dual reality? They are not experiences that have propositional content (words or thoughts expressed and communicated). They are also, on the accounts given, remarkably featureless—the experience of a homogeneous unity can hardly have various complicated features. How would an

---

[48] *Complete Works*, i. 363.   [49] Ibid. i. 501.   [50] Ibid. iv. 145.

experience of identity with the Self of All differ from experience of nirvana, and how would both differ from experience of the pure, unrestricted consciousness of one among an infinite number of selves, as in Sankhya?

It may seem that a feeling of dependence is very different from a feeling of absolute identity with the Self of All, and both are different from a mere feeling of unconditioned being. Yet if such experiences are undifferentiated, and thus virtually featureless, very little can be made of them, from a speculative viewpoint. It could be that to characterize such a very general feeling as one of dependence, rather than of identity, relies more on interpretation in terms of an already available conceptual scheme than on sheer introspection. So one might relate a way of obtaining such experiences, and show the attitudes and actions they seem to generate, and little more can be said. It does not seem that any substantial metaphysical positions could be built on them. This may lead one to question whether they are of such supreme value as to constitute the essence of religion. Such experiences are, after all, very rare and open to few. Could the whole point of religion lie in the cultivation of such infrequent experiences for a small élite?

It is not that experience is of no account in religion. Forms of consciousness and creativity, of understanding and attitude, are of central importance in human life. Religions do foster such specific forms. The question at issue is whether there is just one sort of intense and distinctive experience which is the entire goal of religious practice. An examination of the social reality of religion suggests that it is much more variegated than such a view would suggest. There does not seem to be just one goal of religious practice, or just one way of attaining a religious goal.

Vivekananda himself expands the three classical yogas of the Gita into four—*jnyana* (wisdom), *karma* (works, especially ritual), *bhakti* (devotion), and *raja* (ascetic practice). One could easily add to this list, if one takes seriously his declared view that there are many paths to the one God. Some people find it helpful to cultivate an intense devotion to a guru or teacher. Some are primarily interested in service of their fellow beings. Some find the divine in forms of social co-operation and friendship. Some wish for a set of ritual rules that can order their lives to God. Some like to reflect imaginatively on myths or doctrines, or to strive for speculative truth. Some strive for ascetic self-mastery and freedom from passion.

Some find in art an expression of the Divine. And some aim for the unitive experience of which Advaita speaks.

Is it necessary to rank these in a hierarchy of value, with unitive experience at the top? Might one not say that there are indeed many ways to seek and find God, in many forms of experience and action throughout the whole of human life? As a matter of fact, I doubt whether a strictly non-dual experience is as important to most members of the Ramakrishna order as they sometimes say it is. It is very remote from the actual experience of most practitioners. It belongs to a small élite, who are indeed revered and emulated as far as possible. What matters more to most are attempts to see divinity within oneself, to revere others as parts of the Divine, to overcome passion and anxiety, and to serve others with reverence and devotion. These are much less grandiose and recondite aims, which need not embody any claim to have apprehended the ultimate truth about reality.

I am suggesting both that the teaching of Advaita cannot be based on personal experience, and that strictly non-dual experience is not such a very central part of the Ramakrishna Math teaching as it may seem to be. It is, however, Sankara's speculative interpretation of the Upanishads that governs the basic teaching, now modified by a more positive stress on the Absolute as realizing itself in the historical process, and by an attempt to isolate a common core of 'mystical' experience in many religious traditions. While what is described as non-dual experience is very important both as an ideal and as a confirmation of faith, in itself it is theoretically underdetermined, and is amenable to many interpretations, ranging from that of 'absolute identity' Advaita to that of 'absolute dependence' dualism (Dvaita). One could hardly tell, from however close an introspection of an experience which is specifically said to be nonconceptualizable, whether it was an experience of absolute identity or of absolute dependence. In practice the key teachings of the Ramakrishna Math are its emphasis on realizing the God within, on sensing the presence of divinity in all things, on compassionate service of others, on meditation and renunciation as the true paths to knowing God, and on celebrating the good in all faiths and cultures.

These teachings do not necessitate, and indeed are in tension with, the theoretical position that the individual soul is an illusion to be overcome, and that true reality, the realization of which is the goal of the religious life, is one homogeneous and undifferentiated Existence, in the light of which the universe of plurality vanishes entirely. What they naturally suggest is that there is one divine reality which is present in all things, seeking to realize itself more fully through the renunciation and compassion of human souls, knowable through meditation as well as in the lives of the great religious teachers, and giving rise to an infinite number of different good and beautiful things, states, and processes. The 'illusion' of separated and distinct selfhood can be overcome, not by the vanishing of all duality, but by realizing the dependence and intimate communion of all souls with the Self of All.

Holding such a view, one can teach that within all religions are ways to the truth, though there are also elements which lead to undue dogmatism and exclusiveness of outlook. One can also teach that all should seek to realize the divinity within, though the selfish and competitive ego impedes and obscures that inner divinity. Each individual soul can become transparent to the presence and action of the universal Self, and will find its fulfilment in helping others in practical ways to freedom from hunger, pain, and ignorance.

EXCLUSIVE AND INCLUSIVE INTERPRETATIONS OF NON-DUALITY

This is the interpretation of Advaita Vedanta that is taught by the Ramakrishna Mission. It certainly does not seek to reduce all diversity to one monistic and impersonal Absolute, so that individual action and experience is of no value, and all that the enlightened soul seeks is release from rebirth and individual existence. It does affirm the existence of one non-dual Self, which alone is absolutely self-existent, and so independently real. This Self is not a distinct person, standing in need of or in contingent relation to other persons. It is a reality whose infinite fullness is beyond all conceptual grasp. Yet it can and does truly manifest in personal form, perhaps as Siva or Kali, and can rightly be worshipped as a supreme personal divinity. It manifests in human forms, in Ramakrishna and Sri Sarada Devi, to communicate God-realization to those who are ready for it. And it lies potential in every human soul, waiting to be realized in all who seek release from bondage to possessions and desires.

From it all universes emanate, without beginning or end, and by necessity. In their emanation, infinite possibilities of the divine Self are expressed, from ignorance, suffering, and passion, to worlds of wisdom, bliss, and calm. Individual souls become embodied in these worlds, by seeming to separate from the One Self, and take responsibility for their own futures. Such souls do not properly begin to exist, because their reality, the One Self, is without beginning or end: 'We cannot believe in such a monstrous impossibility as the beginning of the human soul.'[51] Yet they do begin to exist as individual souls, and no doubt cease to exist as such when they realize again their identity with Brahman. Somehow they fall into *maya* through their own actions: 'The soul in itself is perfect . . . Man lost his purity through his own actions.'[52] Through many lifetimes they learn to realize God again: 'Its primitive purity is to be regained by the knowledge of God.'[53] After many aeons, one cycle of the world comes to an end, and souls rest either in a state of completed unity with Brahman, or in an unmanifest state, waiting until another cycle begins to be manifested again. Thus the Self continually expresses itself and returns into itself, in unending creative action, throughout which it remains in itself, eternally unchanging.

In Vivekananda's interpretation of Advaita, the notions of 'identity' and 'otherness' become very stretched, both when considering the relation of Brahman to the finite universe as a whole, and when considering the relation of individual souls to atman/Brahman. It is Brahman who 'becomes' the universe, so Brahman and the universe are identical. Yet Brahman is unchanging, and is untouched by suffering and ignorance. So Brahman must be qualitatively other than the universe in which suffering and ignorance abound. I am divine, identical with the Infinite. Yet I am bound to the continual cycle of rebirth and death, and so am completely other than the unborn and undying Infinite.

There can be little doubt that the root metaphor for Advaita Vedanta is that of 'unity'. This metaphor can be interpreted either in an exclusive or an inclusive way. The exclusive interpretation holds that everything except completely changeless non-duality is illusion, and the insight that meditation can bring is to overcome all sense of duality, individuality, and temporality, in a blissful experience of non-duality, which is the goal of religious practice. The inclusive interpretation holds that the one Real expresses itself in individual souls and their history, so that the basic religious insight

---

[51] *Complete Works*, i. 320.   [52] Ibid. i. 319.   [53] Ibid. i. 322.

is to see Brahman as realizing itself within and through human lives, in an endless 'playful' manifestation of the infinite possibilities of Brahman. The soul is the instrument and finite experiencer of Brahman. The world is the place where Brahman realizes itself in greater or lesser degrees, and the responsibility of humans is to increase the realization of the divine, but also eventually to pass beyond all manifestation to the pure unity of the Real alone, 'One without a second'.

Both interpretations of non-dualism face major problems. If everything is the self-expression of Brahman, how can there be greater and lesser degrees of the realization of Brahman? It would seem that, if there is a low degree of Brahman's realization, there must be something other than Brahman which is also being expressed, and which restricts the full manifestation of Brahman. In particular, suffering, ignorance, and evil cannot belong to Brahman itself, which is pure and changeless. This 'something other' may be wholly dependent for its existence on Brahman, and it may be characterized as *maya*, and as not independently real. There is no ultimate duality of independent causal principles. But there is real duality of that ignorance and suffering which is to be overcome, and that knowledge and bliss which can be progressively actualized in the cosmos. When Vivekananda speaks of 'the deification of the world' through human action, he admits to the world its own level of reality, and gives the world a positive role to play in the progressive self-realization of Brahman, through human action.

Individual souls, moreover, are said to have lost purity through their own actions, by a fall from primal unity into the ignorance of individuality. But how can there be any individual responsibility, when all is undifferentiated unity? In order to be responsible for a fall, individuals would already have to exist, and yet individuality itself is said to be already a fall into illusion. Moreover, if the cycles of creation do necessarily express the *lila*, the joyful play of Brahman, individuality cannot be just an illusion or some sort of mistake. It must have a much more positive part to play in the cosmic story. One might even speak of there being a purpose to the realm of appearances, a purpose of realizing aspects of Brahman which otherwise would have remained only implicit or potential. In that case, the particular potential of individual souls may have intrinsic importance, since it will be a potential for manifesting a unique aspect of Brahman. This will not be a pure autonomy, or self-will without relation to Brahman. But it will mean that the realization of one's individual potential, in relation to Brahman, is a positive goal. Individuality is not merely something to be overcome and renounced, as the mirage image suggests. It is something to be transformed in a positive way, so as to become a unique instrument of universal self-realization.

The thought that the cosmos is a positive expression of Brahman also throws doubt on any claim that the personal form of Brahman, *Isvara*, the supreme Lord, is itself illusory, and to be overcome (as Sankara's doctrine of *nirguna* Brahman, Brahman without qualities, suggests). It may well be that the supreme Reality is, in itself, far beyond being encompassed by any conceptual framework humans can understand. But if it is indeed the highest form of reality, it cannot possess less than the personal aspects of knowledge, wisdom, and bliss. The expression of these aspects in a supremely personal form would seem to be a natural and necessary property of Brahman. In that sense, there is no higher perfection than that of a personal God, even though in God there are features which infinitely transcend all that we think of as personal.

Individual souls are not identical with the supreme personal God, since they are ignorant and filled with egoism. To that extent, worship is a proper expression of their relation to God, and Vivekananda is even opposing Advaitic tradition in holding that worship of an objective God has no place in non-dualism, since, he says, one 'is God'. As he himself makes clear, one is God primarily in the sense that one can and should realize God in oneself. But that very formula entails that one is not fully God as one actually is. One's whole being derives from and is sustained by God, but there is much in one's actual existence which restricts or even obstructs the realization of divine reality. One cannot worship those who do evil, for evil is a frustration of the divine reality. But one can love those who do evil, in that one can seek to release them from the power of greed, hatred, and ignorance, and help their fulfilment in goodness.

Such compassionate love is not love of the Self for itself. It is precisely love for an individual soul which is unable fully to express the supreme Self, but which is potentially able to do so. This is not, after all, a love which recognizes itself in all things. It is rather a love which recognizes what is other than itself, and wills it to find fulfilment in its own unique way. Otherness is as important to love as is identity, and in that way, too, individual souls must possess their own otherness and identity, if they are to be objects of genuine self-effacing love.

Vivekananda is wholly committed to service of others, and to realization of divinity in the self, as essential parts of religion. Yet he often uses terminology that belongs to a very different outlook, for which individual existence is illusory or non-existent, so that there is no one other than oneself to serve and no divinity remaining as yet unrealized. The simplest way to ease the tensions is to see the whole of creation as a field for the self-realization of the Divine through the compassionate action and growing knowledge of many individual souls, and to see all finite things as wholly dependent on a self-existent reality which is utterly simple and so beyond description. This, I suggest, is the most natural interpretation of Vivekananda's teaching, which is complicated, but not elucidated, by his espousal of Advaita, and by a reliance on a sort of meditative experience that is insufficient to be a firm doctrinal basis for a strict doctrine of non-dualism. In any case, the ultimate experience of non-duality is so far beyond the expectations of most humans that it plays little part in the spiritual lives of devotees. For them, it is enough to aim at some experience of union with a divine reality which is so close that one cannot psychologically distinguish human soul from divine reality. But that does not entail that the two are strictly identical, and the fact that the soul afterwards remembers such an experience as its own suggests that strict identity is not what is in question.

Advaita is often said, by its adherents, to be the 'perennial philosophy', the higher truth that underlies all religious doctrines. Ironically, in many of its contemporary forms, and especially in the teaching of Vivekananda, it already moves beyond strict Advaita, in its classical sense, towards a view that accepts the reality of many individual souls, but sees them all as parts of, or as wholly dependent upon, the One Real, which seeks to realize itself in and through them. Such views are more characteristic of non-Advaitic Vedanta, and were propounded by Ramanuja and by Madhva in different ways. Their views find one major religious expression in the *bhakti* sects of Vaishnavism, and by discussion of one of those sects further insight may be gained into the range of ideas of human nature in Indian religious traditions.

3
The Search for the Self
(Vaishnava Hinduism)

It has sometimes been thought that the most characteristic form of Hinduism is the sort of non-dualistic (Advaita) Vedanta propounded by Sankara, and that is the system that has received most attention in the West. It is true that Advaita Vedanta is widely regarded by Indian scholars as the outstanding scholarly interpretation of the *Sruti*, or revealed Scriptures—the Veda and Upanishads. However, much more widespread in Indian religious practice are the *bhakti* sects, a set of movements which are definitely dualistic in tone, and teach devotion to a supreme personal God. Among devotional sects, the best-known are the Saivites, who worship Siva, and the Vaishnavas, worshipping Vishnu, usually in the form of his main avatar, Krishna. The most important religious text for the Vaishnavas is the *Bhagavadgita*, which is used either as a primary religious text on its own, or as the key to interpreting the Upanishads and drawing out conclusions at which they only hint. A particularly important school is the Gaudiya (Bengali) Vaishnavism of the early sixteenth-century saint Sri Krishna Chaitanya. This school has become known throughout the world through the International Society for Krishna Consciousness (ISKCON), which propagates its teachings in a later form. Although it is regarded with suspicion by some traditionalists, and is only one subdivision of a sect which is itself only part of the vast stream of Indian faiths, nevertheless it is an authentic manifestation of a distinctively Indian tradition, which propounds an ultimate pluralism of spiritual selves, and has been influenced by the dualistic Vedanta of Madhva, though its teaching differs from his on some fundamental points.

Gaudiya Vaishnavas unequivocally teach the eternity of each individual self. As the *Gita* puts it, 'Never was there a time when I did not exist . . . nor in the future shall any of us cease to be.'[1] This is interpreted to mean that there is an infinite number of selves, each of which is without beginning and without end. The interpretation according to which there is only one eternal Self, of which all individual selves are only appearances, is definitely rejected. At the same time, the doctrine of the Sankhya school, that the infinite number of eternally existing selves are self-existent, is rejected. 'The living entities (*jiva*) in this conditioned world are My eternal fragmental parts (*amsah*).'[2] The eternal individual souls are parts of Krishna, the supreme Lord. They may be called 'separated expansions' of the Lord.

Their relation to the Lord, which is not one of identity and yet not complete difference, is called *Achintya bhedabheda*, or inconceivable identity-in-difference. There is an affinity at this point with the teaching of Ramanuja, who sees souls as parts of the cosmos, regarded as the body of the Lord, and thus they are in one sense part of the Lord, yet not to be identified with the Lord in his infinity and fullness. Gaudiya Vaishnavas are distinctive among Vaishnavas in regarding Krishna, the supreme Lord, as the creator of all things, seeing even Vishnu as an expansion of Krishna, and Siva and Brahma as created souls. It is a common Indian philosophical idea that the cause of all must contain all its effects, and that the effects are an unfolding of what is incipient in the cause. Thus the coming forth of a material universe is not, as in most Western traditions, a bringing-to-be out of nothing. It is rather an expansion of the Creator, a realization of its inner potentialities for being in infinite different ways. The Lord is the material cause of every universe.

The nature of the supreme Lord is infinite being, pure consciousness, and endless and untainted bliss. Individual souls are qualitatively identical with (of the same nature as) the supreme Lord, and their true nature is to be pure consciousness and bliss. In later Sankhya thought, each soul is identical in nature with every other soul. Each soul is intrinsically omniscient and perfectly blissful. There is no need of one supreme Soul, or God. The omniscient consciousness of each soul is said to be unchanging and infinite.

---

[1] *Gita* 2. 12. Quotations from the *Gita* are taken from *Bhavagad-Gita As It Is*, trans. and annotated by Swami Prabhupada (Los Angeles: Bhaktivedanta Book Trust, 1986). This is the version used by ISKCON devotees, and it contains translations of the Sanskrit which reflect their views.

[2] *Gita* 15. 7.

Vaishnava thought qualifies this view of the qualitative identity of souls, and denies their omniscience and uncreatedness. It insists that all souls are created by the supreme Lord. Individual souls have only a tiny part of the bliss and consciousness of the Lord. Their role is to serve the Lord, to do everything for his enjoyment and to desire nothing for themselves. As a part of a human body may exist to carry out the desires of the human soul, and to convey a particular sort of consciousness to the human soul, so each soul exists to serve the Lord and to convey to the Lord various sorts of enjoyment.

Krishna might then be said to be the true ultimate agent of all creaturely actions. The individual soul should seek to do only what Krishna wills, without motives and desires of its own. The Sankyha problem of how an infinite number of souls can be related to each other, and of what can make them differ from one another, is resolved by subordinating them all to one overarching plan of Krishna, and giving each of them an individual part to play in that plan.

But in what sense does Krishna act? According to the *Gita*, Krishna is ceaselessly active, but is not attached to the fruits of actions. 'There is no work prescribed for Me within all the three planetary systems. Nor am I in want of anything, nor have I a need to obtain anything—and yet I am engaged in prescribed duties.'[3] Krishna acts in sport (*lila*), not out of need or desire. There is nothing of which the Supreme Lord could possibly stand in need, nothing that could taint him, and nothing that could be a purpose for action. Why, then, should Krishna work to create and destroy universes at all? The best clue the *Gita* gives is that 'The learned may . . . act, but without attachment, for the sake of leading people on the right path.'[4] Krishna acts to lead people towards their own welfare, in pure disinterested action. That is, he acts so that other souls might have some share in his infinite goodness.

Thus Krishna can say, 'Although I am the creator of this system, you should know that I am yet the nondoer, being unchangeable.'[5] Krishna is the creator, yet he is also the non-doer (*akartaram*). In all creation, Krishna remains unchanging, and worlds spring from him without his changing at all. A further clue is given in the Upanishadic story of the self-sacrifice of the primeval person,

---

[3] *Gita* 3. 22.   [4] *Gita* 3. 25.   [5] *Gita* 4. 13.

Prajapati, to produce the cosmos.[6] The sacrifice of the supreme Person, which is a supremely non-attached action, is the gift of being to innumerable souls, who can live in pure consciousness and bliss.

THE RELATION OF THE SOUL TO KRISHNA

There remains a tension between the unchanging and the changing nature of Krishna. On the one hand, Krishna is eternally creative, since created souls are eternal. Indeed, the souls are 'separated expansions' of Krishna himself. Krishna loves all beings, is concerned for their welfare, and descends to deliver them from suffering in many incarnations. His devotees are dear to him—a statement made six times in the twelfth chapter of the *Gita*, verses 14–20. Not only that, in Gaudiya thought at least, Krishna is pleased by the love of his devotees, and is ever-increasing in happiness and bliss, because of the mutual devotion between them and him. On the other hand, Krishna says, 'I am ever detached from all these material activities, seated as though neutral.'[7] Krishna does nothing, is indifferent to what happens in the cosmos, and is therefore unaffected either for good or ill by anything that devotees may do.

Because of these tensions, there are various ways in which one may construe the nature of Krishna in relation to the cosmos. Since individual souls are qualitatively like the Supreme—or, in Advaitic versions, are identical with it—these ways will be reflected in different doctrines of the individual self. By stressing the immutability of Krishna, one can do full justice to the repeated statement that he is a non-doer. He contemplates his own perfection in supreme bliss, and so there is nothing he can do to improve this state or to change it in any way. His 'work' consists in the fact that the cosmos—in fact, an infinite number of universes—are expansions of, or overflowings from his essential being, which remains unchanged. Perhaps the individual soul can become unchanging, like the supreme Self, contemplating perfection in supreme bliss.

It is certainly possible to interpret *bhakti*—devotion—in this way. The injunctions repeatedly given in the *Gita* for the individual soul

---

[6] Maitri Upanishad 2. 6 (trans. R. C. Zaehner, in *Hindu Scriptures* (London: J. M. Dent, 1984), 221.

[7] *Gita* 9. 9.

are that it should seek to be indifferent to the dualities of pain and pleasure, good and ill fortune. It should do its duty with detachment from results, abandoning all desire, every purpose and every reward of action. It should renounce possessions, dwell alone, and perceive all things in the same way, without distinguishing between greater and less. It should control the senses by fasting, meditation, and rigorous self-discipline. In this way, it should strive to be wholly non-attached to the material world and its joys and sorrows, letting the 'three Qualities' of matter work without identifying itself with them.

So far, this sounds like an extremely rigorous ascetic discipline, pursued in the context of carrying out one's worldly duties without desire for their fruits. The element of devotion lies in the fact that, in being non-attached to the material sensory world, one becomes attached to the supreme Self. One is intent upon it, filled with it, devoted in loving service to it. Self-discipline does not lead simply to a 'blowing-out' of desires and a cessation of individual consciousness (as in some interpretations of Hinayana Buddhism). It leads to fuller consciousness and bliss, to a realization that one is part of the supreme Self, contemplation of which is itself supreme bliss.

In the Vaishnava tradition, there are said to be five *rasa*s, levels of devotion. The first two are adoration and service. The last three are the most significant, and are explicitly mentioned in the *Gita*,[8] reflecting the sorts of personal relationship that can obtain between individual souls. They are the relationship of child to parent, of friend to friend, and of lover to lover. It is in the final stage of loving union that it may become difficult to distinguish between the individual self and the supreme Self, since one shares so completely in the contemplation and bliss of the other.

One can see how Advaitins (whom Vaishnavas call *mayavadins*) can accept the teaching of the *Gita* that devotion is a possible way to union with the Supreme. For devotion is love of the Self, the desire to be completely one with it. As the Self properly loves itself completely as the best of all things, so it properly loves even those parts of itself which are separated by the illusion of distinct individuality. One can speak of a union of love between the individual self and the supreme Self precisely because it is an intimation, at a

---

[8] *Gita* ii. 44.

lower level, of that true union which is the complete identity of the apparently dual. For an Advaitin, the *Gita*, not being *Sruti*, or revealed Scripture, must be interpreted in the light of the Upanishads. Thus *bhakti* is finally subordinate to the way of knowledge, to the realization of the non-duality of Brahman. In the end, individual consciousness ceases to exist as anything separate from the Supreme. Even the individual avatar form of Krishna is an appearance of the higher non-dual Self. There is only one consciousness of supreme knowledge and bliss. If the individual soul achieves liberation it does not cease to exist. In becoming omniscient and perfectly blissful, through its liberation from the limitations of material form, it becomes, or realizes its identity with, the one and only omniscient and blissful Self. The supreme Self is not an enjoyer of anything other than itself, yet contemplation of its own being gives complete bliss. It is not an agent to bring about any change of itself, yet it is the support of its own self-subsistent being. It is not in relation to anything other than itself, yet it is related in perfect unity to itself in infinite being, consciousness of being, and blissful self-awareness.

If one accepts a Leibnizian principle of the identity of indiscernibles, then if there are an infinite number of individual souls, each of them qualitatively identical with all the others, it follows that there is in fact only one Self. The Advaitin view holds that it does not make sense to speak, as Sankhya does, of an infinite number of omniscient blissful souls, all possessing exactly the same liberated nature. There can be only one omniscient and omnipotent Self. Thus, when each liberated soul realizes that it is, freed from matter, omniscient and omnipotent, it also realizes that it is identical with the one and only supreme Self. The impression of a separated individuality is a function of immersion in karma and the material world. When the individual self is liberated from karma, it discovers itself to be the one and only Supreme and blissful Self, of which other individual selves are also separated parts suffering the illusion of distinct identity.

Vaishnavas completely reject this monistic interpretation. They insist that there is only one omnipotent and omniscient Self. I am not and will never be a supreme Self. There is an infinite number of centres of consciousness, eternally distinct, which are not omniscient or omnipotent, and whose function is to serve the supreme Lord in loving devotion. If the *jiva* is to be a non-doer, indifferent and detached, it may still work in the way Krishna works, who acts disinterestedly for the welfare of all beings, producing worlds out of the fullness of his own being while remaining untainted and unchanging. In the case of individual souls, their work will consist in letting Krishna work in them, and in contemplating at least part of the perfection of Krishna from their unique finite viewpoint. They will not be independent agents and self-regarding enjoyers. They will be perfect instruments and devotees, contemplators and worshippers of the supreme Lord. The living entity thinks it is agent and enjoyer, but in fact 'being part and parcel of the supreme Lord, it is neither the creator nor the enjoyer, but a cooperator.'[9] It is the Lord who is the enjoyer and the creator, and the individual soul exists as his servant and devotee. 'By worship of the Lord, who is the source of all things and who is all-pervading, a man can attain perfection through performing his own work.'[10] Work can then be offered as a sacrifice of love to Krishna, for it is in fact the work of Krishna himself: 'The Supreme Lord is situated in everyone's heart . . . and is directing the wandering of all living entities.'[11] The Lord lives in the individual soul, as *Paramatman*, or the Supersoul. When he controls the individual soul, then all actions become worship of Krishna, since they are able to express a tiny part of Krishna's own blissful contemplation of his own perfection, which is supreme worship. The devotee is taken up into the sacrificial yet unchanging work of the supreme Lord, which causes all universes to be, and to actualize finite reflections of supreme being. On this view, *bhakti* is the union of love by which the individual soul is filled with the life of Krishna and with consciousness of the beauty of Krishna, so that Krishna is seen in everything, as *Paramatman*, everything is seen in Krishna, as inclusive Brahman, and all thought and action is offered in devotion to Krishna, as supreme personality of Godhead.

The separated souls, however, have their own independence, which is necessary if they are freely to offer themselves as devotees of the Lord. With that independence, desire for pleasure and for the personal enjoyment of fruits of action becomes possible. Accordingly, the Lord creates a realm in which such desires can be actualized. That is the realm of *prakriti*, of matter. It is the 'separated inferior energy' of the Lord, the superior energy being the individual souls. Matter is also eternal, and into it the Lord 'seeds'

---

[9] *Gita*, Introduction, p. 13.   [10] *Gita* 18. 46.   [11] *Gita* 18. 61.

those individual souls which desire enjoyment for themselves—a very small minority of the total number of souls—so that they become conditioned and subject to karma. Material existence as such is a form of bondage, and liberation is to be sought from it. It can be analysed according to the twenty-four categories of Sankhya philosophy. These include the elements, the senses and their objects, mind (*manas*), the intelligence (*buddhi*), and the sense of self (*ahamkara*). The latter three form the 'subtle body' of the self, but it is important to see that they belong to the material order. They are not to be identified with the self. Wisdom consists in seeing the distinction of self from mind, intelligence, and ego as well as from the gross material body, and in seeking a final separation of self from all material elements.

It looks as if this affirms a very severe view of the self as a sort of impersonal intellectual consciousness and a bliss which is not associated at all with the pleasures and feelings of the mind. Since the sense of self is to be abandoned, it is easy to read this as saying that individual personality is to be abandoned, so that no sense of subject–object duality is to remain, and no distinctive capacities and dispositions which might mark out one person from another. Each soul might then be distinguished from others by the portion of finite knowledge it contains, by its content. But each one would be a 'pure objectless consciousness', a partial image of the supreme inactive Self, without purposes, intentions, sense memories, or feelings. If the liberation of the soul is indeed to be from discursive intelligence, sense-based mind, and personal ego, then it will be indifferent, detached, without desire or purpose, and wholly immersed in intellectual consciousness.

But what will the relation of such a soul be to Krishna, the supreme Soul? The 'supreme secret' of the *Gita* is to be found in the eighteenth chapter: 'Always think of Me, become My devotee, worship Me and offer your homage unto Me. Thus you will come to Me without fail. I promise you this because you are my very dear friend.'[12] One possible view is that devotion to Krishna is one means, or even the best means, to achieve liberation from suffering. 'Coming to Krishna' is achieving freedom from the material world, and eternal peace in pure consciousness, beyond action and suffering. Yet the statement that Krishna loves the devotee and holds him

[12] *Gita* 18. 65.

dear introduces a very different element. In a loving relationship, experiences and actions are shared and enjoyed. Each values the other for their unique and distinctive personal qualities and dispositions. Each contributes something to the other's experience or enjoyment that would otherwise not have existed. The ideal of pure consciousness is replaced by that of community of being, in which each partner achieves fulfilment by aiming at the welfare of the other, delighting in the other, and accepting the love of the other.

It is this ideal of devotional relationship that determines the Vaishnavite interpretation of the *Gita*. This requires a revision of much of the Sankhya philosophy and of the *jnyana* Yoga ascetic discipline which is so prominent in parts of the *Gita*. Within the *Gita* itself, atheistic forms of Sankhya are revised so that the eternal souls become creations of one supreme Lord. But it is not entirely clear that this Lord is finally adequately characterized as a loving person. For much of the *Gita*, it seems that the supreme Self is pure consciousness and bliss, without purpose and unaffected by anything in the material realm. In accordance with such a view, Sankara, the founder of Advaita, might be prepared to accept Vishnu as *Isvara*, supreme Lord, and Krishna as one of the main avatars, or earthly embodiments of Vishnu. But he would insist that beyond the personal form of Vishnu lies the impersonal or supra-personal *nirguna* Brahman, which is in itself without qualities and so is indeed beyond action and enjoyment as we understand them.

Vaishnavas turn this hierarchy completely on its head. Brahman is relegated to being an impersonal emanation of the personal supreme Lord Krishna, while the four-armed Vishnu himself is subordinated to the eternal two-armed form of Krishna, becoming a 'primary, personal expansion' of Krishna. Vishnu, like Brahma and Siva, is an 'individual identity' of the Godhead, but Krishna is the supreme personality of Godhead himself.

THE WAY OF DEVOTION

Vaishnavas thus affirm that the ultimate supreme reality is a person, Krishna, with a particular body, with hands, eyes, feet, and so forth. This person lives in a particular 'spiritual planet' or realm, Goloka, where his devotees are taken at death. The spiritual world in which he lives is a truly variegated world, with infinite specific forms and beauties. It is not some sort of undifferentiated oceanic unity. In the fifteenth chapter of the *Gita*, reference is made to the Banyan tree which has its roots in heaven, while its branches spread down to the material world. It is suggested that this tree is a reflection of a truly spiritual tree. 'This tree, being the reflection of the real tree, is an exact replica. Everything is there in the spiritual world.'[13]

In his spiritual world, Krishna is always acting and enjoying in specific ways. The true vocation of individual souls is to be in that spiritual world with him, to serve him with love and to share his 'transcendental pastimes', which are outlined in the famous tenth canto of the *Srimad Bhagavatam*. In that world there is no suffering or imperfection. Krishna enjoys the devotion of the individual souls, and they find their happiness in loving him. Vaishnavas, taking the 'supreme secret' verse,[14] with some justification, as their clue to interpreting the complexities of the *Gita*, go on to affirm that *bhakti* is the only way to achieve this supreme happiness.

Thus far, the Vaishnava system presents a picture of one supreme Person, who creates, without beginning or end in time, an infinite number of individual souls. Their destiny is not, as in Sankhya thought, to remain as pure consciousnesses, without individuality or sense of self. It is to enjoy endless bliss in loving the Lord and in being loved by him. Clearly, individual souls are not unembodied in any important sense. They have spiritual bodies, and spiritual forms of enjoyment that parallel those in this material world, though without suffering or egoistic desire. They have mind, intelligence, and ego, though in a true spiritual, not a perverted material form. In accordance with this view, *ahamkara*, the sense of self, is always translated by Vaishnavas as the 'false ego', or the identification of the self with the body. There is a true sense of self, which eternally remains, but which is non-possessive and wholly devoted to being the servant of Krishna.

For Sankhya, in this realm of material cause and effect, it is the three basic 'qualities', *sattva, rajas, and tamas*—goodness, passion, and ignorance—which cause actions and their consequences. 'One who can see that all activities are performed by the body, which is created of material nature, and sees that the self does nothing, actually sees.'[15] *Purusa* is the witness, and the three qualities are the real causes of all material change. The Lord creates the three qualities and sets them working, but is not involved with them and expects

---

[13] *Gita*, Purport to 15. 1, p. 713.   [14] *Gita* 18. 65.   [15] *Gita* 13. 30.

to achieve no personal purpose through them. The Lord remains detached and unchanging. The qualities begin to work when individual souls are embodied, and experience the joy and pain that the play of the qualities produces. In the Sankhya philosophy, all change and action comes from the qualities, while souls are the witnesses or enjoyers and sufferers of their interplay. A major problem is then that of explaining how souls, whose essential nature is changeless pure consciousness, become embodied, if it is not through some action of theirs. In an analogous way, it is hard to see how any soul can liberate itself through its own action, if souls are essentially non-causal. Sankhya has ways of dealing with these problems, which involve seeing embodiment and liberation as actions of matter, which do not properly affect the soul.

Vaishnavas, however, give souls a more active role to play in the process of bondage and liberation. It is because of desire for the sorts of pleasure the senses can give that souls fall into matter. They do act in the material world, giving rise to good or bad karma, which determines what sort of bodies they have in subsequent lives. It is by conscious discipline or freely given devotion that they can gain liberation from matter. And in the spiritual realm itself, they continue to act out of devotion to Krishna. Accordingly, they are said to be inactive only in that they cease to desire the rewards of sensual activity. Realizing that the bodies they have are the results of past karma, they understand that this karma will work itself out automatically, and that they are not fully in control of what happens to them. The three qualities are what they are because of the past acts of the soul. Now, the proper role of the soul is to stop creating more karma. This it can do by ceasing to desire sensual pleasure and the rewards of egoistic activity and purpose. The self should seek to become indifferent to all that happens to the body, to have no motives and no purposes, but to act without attachment or desires—'A person . . . who lives free from desires . . . he alone can attain real peace.'[16] This requires a hard discipline of emptying the mind of passions and attaining complete inner quietness. This is a sort of action, but its goal is the cutting-off of egoism. In this way one can 'become Brahman', and enter into pure bliss.[17]

This way of knowledge of non-duality by ascetic discipline, the way of *jnyana* Yoga, leads to liberation, but it is hard and lengthy.

[16] *Gita* 2. 71.   [17] *Gita* 5. 24.

There is another way to liberation, which is well established in Indian tradition, the way of karma yoga. This is the way of ritual works, and it is open to almost everyone. This includes sacrifice, devotion to the *archavatara* form of the Lord, who is embodied in a consecrated image, and the formal chanting of mantras or scriptural passages. Another form of the way of works is the keeping of one's moral obligations. The duties of one's caste are such that it is better to do the duties of one's own station badly than to do another's duty well.[18] There is a well-defined set of duties, which includes strict sexual abstinence or chastity in marriage, and many particular duties laid down in the codes of Manu.

The best way of all, however, is the way of *bhakti*: 'Those who worship me . . . having fixed their minds upon Me . . . for them I am the swift deliverer from the ocean of birth and death.'[19] One no longer desires to possess anything, since one is possessed by the Lord. One does not identify oneself with one's material body, since one is to live in a purified spiritual realm. One does not seek any sensual pleasure, because one is assured of eternal bliss. The goal is to be a non-doer, not to pursue one's own desires in passion, even the passion for goodness, snared by the still egoistic desire for bliss. It is to be a servant of the Lord, doing his work alone, devoted solely to him, thus allowing him to act through the soul for the welfare of all beings, and rejoicing in his free gift of grace. Vaishnavas hold that it is Krishna whose effulgence as impersonal *Brahmajyoti* is the goal of the ascetic. Krishna is the true recipient of all sacrificial action, both in ritual and in dutiful work. But Krishna in his supreme personality of Godhead can only be apprehended by devotion. It is in this sense that the only finally effective way is that of *bhakti*. Without devotion to Krishna, all ways of liberation are useless. With it, all ways become valid, and should not be wholly renounced.

Within the Vaishnava tradition in general, there are various understandings of how the grace of the Lord operates, though all agree that the liberation of the soul is by grace, and that it liberates one, not to an impersonal actionless nirvana, but to a realm of variegated spiritual delights. A divergence occurs between those (the *Tengalais*) who make the soul wholly reliant on the action of the Lord even for its acceptance of grace, and the *Vadagalais*, who give

[18] *Gita* 18. 47.   [19] *Gita* 12. 7.

the soul the independent power to turn to grace or to reject it. The former view deprives the soul of any independent responsibility for its actions, and thus seems to make the fall into material existence a matter of necessity rather than an exercise of individual moral freedom. The latter view faces the objection that a reliance on grace seems, on the face of it, to overthrow the whole theory of karma, that agents receive the deserts of their actions. For if the qualities act by an inherent law to generate and work out karmic consequences, how can these laws be affected by the act of love of some devotee? Is not the moral justice of the cosmic laws, which the theory posits, undermined by the mercy of the supreme Lord? How can one both say that the law of karma will ensure that all actions reap their due reward, and that the grace of the Lord will eliminate all karma if one makes an act of true devotion to him?

The *Gita* suggests that even the way of devotion requires hard discipline: the devotee 'achieving perfection after many, many births of practice, attains the supreme goal.'[20] Yet it also suggests, though not unambiguously, the possibility of an immediate release after death: 'Even if one commits the most abominable action, if he is engaged in devotional service he is to be considered saintly.'[21] For Gaudiya Vaishnavas, just chanting the *Mahamantra*[22] is sufficient to ensure entry to Goloka after death. Thus when they come to chapters in the *Gita* that stress the necessity of ascetic practice and meditation, especially chapter six, they follow the teaching of Chaitanya, that in the age of Kali, no one can attain Brahma by such difficult methods, and a simple chanting of the mantra is necessary and sufficient for all. Nevertheless, devotees are expected to renounce possessions, embrace celibacy, and devote much time to tending the images of Krishna and preparing the vegetarian food which is permitted to be offered to the god and shared by devotees. Both ritual works and a certain degree of ascetic discipline are thus required of devotees, though these things are said to follow from devotion to Krishna rather than to be independent means of liberation.

One tradition of interpreting the *Gita* stresses the immutability and dispassionateness of Krishna, the necessity of the laws of karma, and the path to release as one of ascetic discipline over many lives. Another tradition stresses that Krishna is one who loves

---

[20] *Gita* 6. 45.   [21] *Gita* 9. 30.
[22] The chant characteristic of ISKCON devotees: 'Hare Krishna, Hare Krishna, Krishna Krishna, Hare Hare; Hare Rama, Hare Rama, Rama Rama, Hare Hare.'

and is passionately related to his devotees, that the grace of the Lord can break the bonds of karma, and that pure devotion is the sufficient and the only final path to release. ISKCON devotees clearly belong to the latter tradition, and this leads them to emphasize the reality of a spiritual realm of continued personal existence, in which loving service to the Lord can be fully expressed.

As well as emphasizing the plurality of individual souls in relation to the supreme Lord, Gaudiya Vaishnavas radically qualify the Sankhya teaching that release from the realm of samsara leads to a wholly unembodied existence. For they see that a continued personal life of devotion will require some form of embodiment in which true service to the Lord can be expressed, and in whose experience and love the Lord can take pleasure. Such a deeply relational view of the self seems to follow from the concept of *bhakti*, but it has not always been explicit in Indian religious thought. Even the Vaishnava view is qualified by the crucial doctrine that the self is not to be identified with this material body. Though there is an infinite plurality of selves, they are all eternally existent. Most of them never come into contact with the material realm at all. Those that do must seek to free themselves from all attachment to both their gross and subtle bodies, and obtain release from matter.

Gaudiya Vaishnavism cannot, therefore, place a uniquely high value on the individual personality as it exists in this embodied world of human history. Such a value can only belong to the self which is never born and never dies, and which is not to be identified with any particular historical embodiment. However, the devotional doctrine of the reality of Goloka Vrindavana, the supreme home of Krishna, and of the transcendental delights which exist there, means that there exists a variegated world, without suffering or pain, in which souls find their highest fulfilment in loving devotion to Krishna. Such a view converges on the view often held in Semitic religious traditions that there will be a resurrection of the person to a transfigured spiritual world, without suffering. When the released self is not a purely disembodied consciousness of bliss and intelligence, as in Sankhya thought, there is not a vast difference from those doctrines of the resurrection of the body which stress how different and more perfect the resurrection body is from present material bodies. Surprising as it may seem, Vaishnava belief in the eternity of the soul is not vastly different from some Semitic beliefs in the resurrection of the body.

One major difference which does exist lies in the doctrines of karma and rebirth, which form the background to all Vaishnava views of human nature. The present material world, and present personalities and bodies, cannot have final significance for a view which regards material existence as in some sense fallen, and which sees each historical person as only one of a huge number of personalities which souls have assumed and will, in most cases, continue to assume. Yet the doctrine of rebirth can make a strong claim to provide a resolution to one of the major problems of any theistic view, the problem of apparently undeserved suffering. And, at least in some of its modern revisions, it offers the hope of a continuing improvement, through a number of earthly lives, towards a finally liberated life of bliss and love. It is important to make some assessment of the strengths and weaknesses of a belief which is so widely held, and which underlies most Indian and Asian religious views of human nature.

4

The Doctrine of Rebirth

Belief in karma and in rebirth is a basic feature of most Indian religions. It arises, no doubt, from a desire to find some sort of moral justice in human life. Self-discipline, application, and moral probity do, on the whole, lead to success, prosperity, and social esteem. Laziness, dissoluteness, and dishonesty do tend to lead to failure, poverty, and social disapprobation. However, it is not always so. Especially in times of social breakdown, it is the greedy who flourish and the good who are oppressed and persecuted. The world seems to be indifferent to human goodness and evil, and fortune distributes her benefits with little regard to human moral endeavour.

For anyone who believes in a spiritual basis to reality, who believes that the material world is an expression or product of an underlying spiritual reality of supreme power and value, this situation is unacceptable. Dutifulness and self-discipline must be appropriately rewarded. Deceit and gratuitous violence cannot be allowed to succeed. That does happen to some extent in this life, but in any universe governed by a being of supreme power and value, it does not happen often enough. There must therefore be another life or lives in which rewards and deprivations can be allocated justly to those who deserve them.

If this life is itself seen as a place where rewards and deprivations due to some past life can be allocated, that will explain why there are such huge differences of fortune between people, which do not seem to depend on their conduct in this life. And it will enable one to postulate that in future lives the consequences of conduct in this life will in turn be worked out. The theory of rebirth and of life as a realm in which rewards and deprivations are allocated in accordance with past conduct is rather an elegant way of reconciling the existence of a supreme Lord with the perceived injustices of human life.

The notion of 'desert', upon which this theory rests, is more complex than may at first appear. It is most often seen as a forensic concept, one which belongs to proceedings in a court of law. Particular crimes are described and specific punishments are attached to them. Then one can say that if a person commits a particular crime (or performs some meritorious act), then that person deserves a particular punishment (or a particular reward), at some future time. It may be possible to add up rewards and punishments, and come to some overall reward or punishment due, which can then be loaded into the conditions of some future life.

In human lawcourts, punishments are graded according to the responsibility of the agents, their knowledge and freedom to act, and the seriousness of the offence (the amount of harm done, perhaps). Given a complete set of crimes and punishments, it is a quasi-mechanical operation to calculate the amount of punishment (or reward) due. Thus it is easy to see karma as an impersonal law of moral cause and effect, which requires no personal interaction of a supposed lawgiver, once the system is set up.[1]

Precisely because the system is mechanical, however, the specifically religious point of it may seem to have been lost. It sees human life as a sequence of performances to which specific rewards and penalties are attached. Each soul becomes an isolated moral atom, pursuing its private game of moral profit and loss, until the game is ended, and the final score added up. Or, on the theory of rebirth, the game never ends, and one just goes on endlessly, unless one can find a way out of the game.

One can see that this model does not, at least for theists, adequately express the religious perception which underlies it, when one considers what the religious idea of the final goal of human life is. Even in the Semitic traditions, where there is one life followed by a Judgement which adds up one's moral accounts, it does not seem that one receives the due reward or punishment of one's acts at all. No actions, however good, can merit eternal bliss. No actions, however bad, can merit eternal punishment. Unless the punishments and rewards are grossly disproportionate, the system does not function to achieve the religious goal. In the Indian traditions, too, the goal is not to achieve the best score, and thus the highest rewards. Even rebirth in the realm of Brahma is subject to karma, and from it one will return to lower realms eventually. The

---

[1] 'The law of karma is seen as a natural law . . . like a law of physics. It is not operated by a God', Peter Harvey, *An Introduction to Buddhism* (Cambridge: Cambridge University Press, 1990), 39.

goal is to get out of the game, which obviously cannot be done by good moral conduct alone. In both traditions it seems that a concentration on a forensic notion of desert misses something basic to the religious perception.

What is missing is the idea (formulated in Vaishnava terms) that the goal of human life lies in a relationship of devotion to the supreme Lord. A mechanical and forensic model, concentrating on individual moral success or failure, misses this element of personal relationship, which lies at the heart of devotional faith.[2] There is another model available, which one might call a soterial model, which construes the spiritual state of the human self primarily in terms of analogies to disease and health. The healthy soul is one that is in a state of devoted loving service to the Lord, that is transfigured by the beauty of the Lord, and empowered by the Lord's love. The sick soul is one that withers and atrophies because it is incapable either of giving or receiving the love that alone gives life.

Using the soterial model, one will not see human life as a moral proving-ground for individual success. One will see it as an opportunity for learning love, for learning to attend to the Lord, or for falling under the sway of the desire-led qualities of goodness, passion, and ignorance. This choice has important moral dimensions. No one can love the supreme Lord without reflecting his love, joy, and wisdom, without seeing him in all things and serving him without personal desire. No one can turn aside from such love without falling progressively into that sickness which sees all things as objects to be used and discarded, which finds joy in nothing, and which fails to discern the spiritual nature of being.

Seen in this light, one can see that even earnest moral striving and self-discipline, the ways of works and knowledge, are still bound by the quality of goodness (*sattva*). They can easily give rise to self-righteousness and the feeling that one 'deserves' a just reward. The forensic view of karma still binds the soul to the wheel of desire, even though that desire is for the noblest of pleasures. The true devotee does not desire any reward for goodness, but serves the supreme Lord out of pure love. On a soterial model of karma, such service will unite souls to the Lord for ever, thus delivering them from rebirth. Those who renounce the notion of

[2] Peter Harvey, from a Buddhist standpoint, objects to the term 'mechanical', but I use it to make the point that there is no personal element in its operation, for a non-theist.

retributive desert, desiring no reward, will receive an eternal reward.

As long as such love for the Divine does not exist, the soul will be bound by the sickness of self-love, and the forms such bondage takes will be determined by the sorts of egoistic desire to which the soul falls prey. It is not that individual bad acts deserve a specific amount of pain, which can be cumulatively added up. Rather, if, for example, one sees other persons primarily as means of sexual gratification, one will gradually lose the perception of their spiritual nature and freedom. One will come to see them as instruments of pleasure or as obstacles to pleasure. Real personal relationships will become impossible, and so one will become isolated, filled with the sickness of solitude, unable to relate in love to anyone, and thus self-excluded from the loving community which it is the divine will to create.

If one sees the world as a means to one's pleasure, one will cease to be able to revere it for its own beauty and sublimity. One will destroy one's own body by the pursuit of excess and be driven by a constant dissatisfaction with the present, and a desire to possess the world. So one will fall to the sickness of possessiveness, unable to share with or give to others, and thus unable to share in the selfless love of God which is the health and life of the soul.

If one sees others as competitors to be defeated or destroyed, one will become unable to trust or to co-operate with anyone. One will be infected with the sickness of hatred, unable to accept love from others for fear that this will give them power over one. So one will be unable to accept the love of God for fear of falling under divine power, even though that love is solely for the welfare of all beings.

For a forensic view of desert, each evil act has a specific penalty attached to it, and this penalty is exacted with precision. The penalty will probably do the offender no good. It is not primarily meant to reform or to deter similar acts by others. It is just the application of an objective measure of retributive justice. For a soterial view, there is no such calculus of harm done to pain deserved. Egoistic acts build up habits and attitudes which will isolate one from the love of God, and trap one in a vicious circle of isolation, possessiveness, fear, and hatred. There is no specific penalty, the same for all, since each self shapes its own future in personal and particular ways. There is no automatic end to the penalty, when it has been paid, whatever the offender thinks or is like. Souls do not shape their futures in isolation. They can be influenced by their co-operation with or rejection of the influences exerted by others, including, most importantly, the all-pervasive influence of the supreme Self. The process is not designed simply to cause pain for an equivalent amount of harm done. It is designed by the Lord so that selves who choose egoistic desire may come to realize the harm that such egoism causes, both to others and to themselves, and so that selves who choose to accept love from others and from the Lord may find that love to be supremely liberating.

There are two possible futures for such egoistically trapped souls. Perhaps they will sink so low in the cycle of rebirth that they will never escape. Being born as beetles or even as trees, their chance of ever again achieving a human existence, in which liberation might be possible, is virtually non-existent. Thus they are destined to be reborn for ever, as each universal creation comes to be and passes away, without beginning or end. It is not that liberation is impossible, even for them. But they have fallen so far from health that their sickness corrupts their vision, and makes even the thought of liberation abstract and remote.

The other possible future is that the bound souls, whether in the demonic realm or in Brahma heaven, will come to realize how egoistic desire binds them to material existence, which is inevitably filled with suffering. They may come to formulate a wish for liberation from such existence. At that point, in Vaishnava belief, the Lord becomes incarnate in the material world—indeed, he becomes incarnate in every form of material being, and in every age, in an appropriate way. He does so in order to teach the way to liberation, 'To deliver the pious and to annihilate the miscreants.'[3]

Thus karmic suffering is potentially reformative in intent. It aims to bring souls to such a realization of their suffering and of their sickness and inability, that they will be ready to turn to one who offers health and liberation. Just as there is no end to the penalty if they do not change their inner attitude, so there is the possibility of an immediate end if they can reorient their deepest motivation from egoism to loving devotion.

The objection that justice will be undermined if the mercy of the Lord breaks the karmic chain can be seen to depend on a forensic

---

[3] *Gita* 4. 8, from *Bhagavad-Gita As It Is*, trans. Swami Prabhupada (Los Angeles: Bhaktivedanta Book Trust, 1986).

view of desert, which the Vaishnava tradition rejects.[4] Justice, on a soterial view, consists in love finding its realization in a community of sensitive and creative agents, and in egoism finding its fruits in a world of agents trapped in isolation, hatred, fear, and greed. Injustice exists when love does not find such realization, and when egoism brings pleasure that is not seen to carry its associated defects of suffering. The supreme Lord brings justice by creating a community of purified devotees, on the Goloka planet, and by involving the egoistic souls in forms of material being which are calculated eventually to bring them to see that suffering is the inevitable consequence of all egoistic desire.

When a bound soul comes to such realization, and sincerely turns to seek liberation, the situation if there is a loving personal Lord is very different than if karma is an impersonal causal mechanism. If one takes the latter view, as is arguably the case in Theravada Buddhism, all that can happen is that one must begin a long process of discipline, aimed at extinguishing egoistic desire and 'blowing out' the karmic chain of cause and effect.[5] This will probably take many lives, until eventually one passes beyond both desire and fear. Lust, greed, and hatred is extinguished. One can pass beyond rebirth to a state of pure non-dual consciousness, which can be characterized neither as the continuance of the person nor as complete annihilation. Because the process is quasi-mechanical, one has to work it out to the end, however long it takes. It is not surprising that ultimate liberation plays little part in the hopes of most lay Buddhists, who find it enough to desire a better life as a result of their meritorious acts in this life.[6]

If, however, as in Vaishnava belief, there is a personal Lord, then what happens is more like a reorientation of love from the individual self to the supreme Self. Instead of seeing others as objects of lust, for the gratification of egoistic desire, one sees them as vehicles of *Paramatman*, the supreme Self, and thus as objects of respect

[4] The terms 'forensic' and 'soterial' are mine, but they have been accepted by Ravindra Svarupa Das of ISKCON.

[5] Richard Gombrich points out that this severe doctrine is mitigated in a number of ways. Nevertheless, he says, 'The doctrine of *karma* places full responsibility for his fate on the shoulders of the individual', Richard Gombrich, *Theravada Buddhism* (London: Routledge, 1988), 125.

[6] 'The most widespread Buddhist goal nowadays can be seen in this light; one hopes for rebirth as a man in the time of the coming Buddha Metteya', Steven Collins, *Selfless Persons* (Cambridge: Cambridge University Press, 1982), 151.

and devotion. Instead of seeing the world as an opportunity for personal greed, one sees it as owned by the supreme Lord, and thus as a field of loving service. Instead of seeing others as competitors and enemies, one sees them as eternally existing souls bound by desire, whose proper nature lies in loving service of the Lord. They are fellow servants of one Lord, lost in ignorance, and are thus subjects of present compassion and ultimate friendship.

As an avatar, the Lord enters into the material world, remaining untainted by its suffering and evil, so that, seeing him, our loving devotion may be aroused by his beauty and power. At once, as long as this loving devotion is aroused, we are released from lust, greed, and hatred, simply by our love of the Lord. Of course this is not a magical transformation, as if our long past of bondage could be overcome in an instant (though there are views which tend to say that). But there does not remain some fixed penalty which is either to be paid or remitted. It is the formation of the self in habits of lust, greed, and hatred which is to be unfixed. This is effected, not by rigorous self-discipline (though one must discipline oneself in loving the Lord), but by fixing one's whole attention on the Lord, by achieving Krishna-consciousness—which, in this age, according to the Gaudiya Vaishnavas, is best done by chanting the Krishna mantra.[7] It is then divine grace or loving power that will complete the transformation of the bound self into a self of loving devotion. This will probably be a gradual and partial process during this earthly life, but it will liberate the soul to the Goloka realm at physical death.

THE COSMOS AS A REALM OF FALLEN SOULS

Vaishnavas do not see karma as a mechanical process, but as a soterial path leading to acceptance of the grace of Krishna. This may seem to deprive the theory of rebirth of its rationale as a working-out of impersonal laws of cosmic justice. Nevertheless, the belief that eternal souls are born repeatedly in different bodies is central to Gaudiya Vaishavism. It seems clear that love of Krishna does not, for most people, find complete fulfilment in this life, and also that people whose lives are dominated by lust, greed, and hatred do

---

[7] 'In this age of Kali there is no other religion but the glorification of the Lord by utterance of His holy name', Swami Prabhupada, Introduction to *Srimad Bhagavatam* (London: Bhaktivedanta Book Trust, 1987), i. 35.

not always suffer more than the saints. Some form of life after death is therefore required, to enable love to be fulfilled in fuller knowledge of the supreme Lord, and to ensure that souls in bondage come to a realization of the full extent of their estrangement from the Supreme, and have the possibility of 'returning home to God', when they realize their estranged situation, and if they resolve to seek liberation from the egoism which causes it.

The hypothesis of rebirth can be seen as one way of achieving these aims. It possibly originated in India with the *Brahmanas*, in about 800–1,000 BCE, as an extension of the idea that the performance of sacrificial rites could assure a life after death in the world of the *deva*s, or gods.[8] If the rite was not powerful enough, that afterlife, too, would end in death. Then the soul would fall back to earth, either as a human or as an animal. As the idea of a soul without beginning or end developed, so the series of rebirths was extended backwards and forwards to infinity. This earth came to be seen as just one place of birth and death. There are many others—the Hell and ghost worlds below, the heavenly and bliss worlds above. Souls are born time after time, without beginning or end, rising and falling in the cycles of birth and death.

At that stage in the development of early Indian cosmogeny, the process of endless rebirth came to be regarded as unsatisfactory. Whereas the early Vedic cults looked for a blissful life with the gods, the Upanishads take the view that even the lives of the gods must end. They too must fall back to lower cycles of existence. Thus suffering of every conceivable sort becomes the lot of every soul that is bound to the cycle of rebirth. The ultimate religious goal is to achieve release from rebirth itself, and in Sankhya philosophy, to return to a pure objectless consciousness of immaterial existence, beyond time, birth, and death.

Ironically, the developed view threatens to undermine the *bhakti* ideal of loving union with the Lord, since such union seems to belong to the heavenly world of the gods, rather than to pure spiritual existence. Vaishnavas avert this threat by conceiving the liberated realm as one of delight in the presence of Krishna, and by speaking of release as into a spiritualized creation rather than a purely immaterial liberated existence. The ideal of liberation from rebirth qualifies any view of earthly life as in itself intrinsically good,

---

[8] Cf. Collins, *Selfless Persons*, 41–53.

or of human nature as essentially good. For each soul is eternal, and at any point in time no embodied soul is without suffering. This means that at every moment of material existence every being is liable to suffering, and this is because of a (previous) free choice of egoistic desire. Each being is responsible for what it is, at every moment of time. And since each being is in bondage to desire, it seems that each being in the material world has always made the egoistic choice. The material realm is, as such, a realm of fallen souls. Vaishnavas accept these implications, and accordingly stress that the material world is a place of temporal imprisonment for eternal souls,[9] and that only the love of Krishna can turn them from egoism to seek liberation.

There are some major disadvantages with such a hypothesis. One difficulty arises from the Vaishnava belief that the universe—and, indeed, an infinite number of universes—is endlessly repeated in a series of vast cycles of existence, punctuated by ages when there is a *pralaya*, or reversion of the material universe to a state of potentiality in Brahman.[10] It is believed that all souls are eternal, and that liberated souls will be taken to the Goloka 'planet' at death, never to be reborn. It seems that there will always be a huge number of bound souls, and therefore that it cannot be the case that all souls will be liberated.

If all souls are eternal, new souls cannot come into existence. If the material world of bondage exists without beginning or end, and if liberation is final (liberated souls never being reborn in any material universe), it follows that there must be some souls (a huge number) which are never liberated. If there is an infinite number of souls existing in a pre-material state, and they successively fall into the material world before achieving final liberation, then one might say that every soul that becomes embodied can be liberated. It will still be true that, at any time, there must be a vast number of unliberated souls, in fact, an infinite number, since the succession of universes is endless. That in turn entails that some, indeed, an infinite number, will never achieve liberation. For at any given time, an infinite number of souls must be waiting for material birth in one of an endless succession of universes.

---

[9] 'The living entity has by chance fallen into this material existence', *Bhagavad-Gita As It Is*, 670.
[10] Cf. ibid., Purport to 8. 19, p. 435.

What is the situation of such waiting souls? It is not one of liberation, for there is no material birth for liberated souls. It is not one of material embodiment, since they will be required to fill the gaps left by liberated souls in cosmic cycles. If they are in a state of pure consciousness, it seems hard to guarantee that just the right number of souls will fall into the material world at the right time, so that the universe can be reconstituted by Vishnu in each new cosmic cycle. Of course, it is a relatively small amendment to abandon the doctrine of eternal recurrence, and just assert that, out of the total number of eternal souls, some fall into the material world through desire for sensory pleasure. From that world they can either be liberated, or continue for ever. In the latter case, there will always be a material universe, though it will not repeat itself in the same way for ever. On this view, the material world has itself become a sort of Hell, though one from which liberation is possible.

If the material universe is, as such, a realm of suffering and desire, do souls fall into it by freely desiring material pleasures, or do they simply find themselves in it from the first? The latter view, that one exists beginninglessly in Hell, is hard to square with the existence of a loving Lord—which is perhaps why Buddhists do not usually posit such a Lord.[11] Further, it undermines the argument that all personal sufferings are deserved, since one does not deserve material existence itself. To that extent, the idea of rebirth is less appealing. One might hold that material existence is the condition of achieving liberated existence, and thus of a great good for those who learn to love. But it is hard to see why it should be such a condition, when souls are essentially non-material. In any case, Vaishnavas cannot maintain such a view, since for them most souls never fall into the material world.

The most satisfactory view seems to be to say that souls exist in an immaterial realm, and some of them choose material embodiment, of which there are various types, with many degrees of relative happiness and suffering. As a soul orders its life by love or egoism, it moves up or down the series of worlds, progressing towards liberation or total suffering. This planet is an intermediate one, in which some souls are moving up and others down, in which final liberation is possible but rare, but in which it is always possible to make some progress towards God.

[11] For this reason, Peter Harvey says, 'There is no theological problem of evil in Buddhism': Harvey, *Introduction to Buddhism*, 36–7.

This view implies that people with fortunate births have done sufficient good things to deserve them, and that the unfortunate—including, presumably, the handicapped, the poor, and the oppressed—have acted badly in previous lives. If that were so, one would expect to find that the poor, ugly, or handicapped were more disposed to evil than the rich, that the wealthy were souls habituated to goodness, and the poor were souls habituated to evil. There is something morally distasteful about such a thought, and it does not seem to be supported by a study of the moral habits of the rich and the poor, respectively. It is tempting to argue that the very reverse is the case, and that it is better not to be born rich if one wants to be good. What seems most offensive, however, is the thought that physical handicap gives evidence of undue egoism in a past life, which egoism would normally be expected to continue in the present one.

What one might expect, if the rebirth hypothesis is true, is that loving people would progressively become more loving, and would inhabit forms of social reality in which love became easier and more fully reciprocated, and less subject to the misfortunes which evil brings on good and bad alike. The unloving, however, would be less and less able to love, and would exist in societies of other fearful and greedy souls, which made the undesirable consequences of desire more and more apparent. In other words, one would expect an increasing separation of the loving and the unloving, even though it would always be possible for the unloving to reorient their lives towards goodness, and begin the path to release from their social worlds.

This is not how the world appears to be. Good and evil are mixed together in ways which continue often to make evil flourish and good come to nothing. Even if this is an intermediate world, between more loving and more hate-filled worlds, the morally upward-movers do not seem to correlate with the physically favoured, and the down-goers fail to correlate with the physically or economically disadvantaged. In short, it does not look as though the conditions of human life can be explained in terms of past-life activity and desert in a very plausible way. The theist wants there to be a separation of loving from egoistic souls, but that does not ever seem to happen on this planet. It rather looks as though each soul is called to a moral choice, in a life whose physical and social conditions are largely due to laws of physics or social and economic circumstance, and not to past individual moral activity.

This suggests that the 'moral separation' occurs after death, in other non-physical worlds, rather than in some future earthly life. Such a possibility is given by the proposal that rebirths may be in heavenly or hellish worlds. But that proposal makes any idea of earthly reincarnation less necessary or plausible, and largely replaces it by a hypothesis of different, and perhaps progressive, realms of human existence after death. The rebirth hypothesis in the end gives an unsatisfactory explanation of the great inequalities of human birth, and has a morally questionable tendency to blame the disadvantaged for their own condition. Nevertheless, the rebirth hypothesis emphasizes the possibility of a continued development of individuality beyond death, and the possibility of liberation in the life beyond death. This may be thought to contrast favourably, from a moral point of view, with some traditional Semitic views, which have tended to insist that all crucial moral decisions must be made before physical death, and to deny that further development and liberation are possible after life on this planet. The developmental view is much more consistent with the idea that souls are created for an existence of loving devotion to a supreme Lord, and that, I think, is the fundamental belief that underlies the Vaishnava interpretation of rebirth.

DIFFICULTIES WITH THE IDEA OF REBIRTH

Vaishnavas press the idea of development over a number of lives to its logical limit. They see the whole of the material world as filled with souls. The supreme Lord is present, as the Supersoul, within everything from an atom to the god Brahma.[12] And each entity, from atom to Brahma, is an individual *jiva*, or soul. If one falls prey to lust during one's life as a human being, one may be embodied as a tree, or even as a rock. There are no purely material entities, since (in another major revision of Sankhya doctrine) matter only acts when it is vivified by individual souls. The cycle of rebirths includes everything from rocks to gods, and unless one is liberated, one will ascend and descend the chain of being endlessly.

The theory of karmic desert, whether in its forensic or its soterial form, supposes that souls can learn to love or fall prey to egoistic desire. They must be free to do either, and so they must know

---

[12] 'The Lord, as Supersoul, pervades all things', *Srimad Bhagavatam*, I. 2. 32, p. 137.

what they are doing, what in general the consequences will be, and have the capacity to intend and initiate actions. They must have knowledge, foresight, and some degree of intellectual competence—they must have the ability to analyse, infer, intend, and act. This implies the possession of quite a high degree of reflective self-consciousness. Without it, there can be no question of souls progressing or regressing through their own merit or demerit.

As far as one can tell, only the higher animals possess reflective self-consciousness. Trees, rocks, and beetles do not show any signs of doing so. How, then, is one to envisage a soul's embodiment as a tree as part of its karmic destiny? What can a tree do that can liberate it from rebirth, or even improve it's chances of a better birth? One obvious move is to limit karmic rebirths to the human or higher animal realm. Birth as a tree might be seen simply as a punishment, to be followed by birth in the human realm again. However, it can hardly be considered a punishment, unless some pain or distress is suffered. Even that is hardly sufficient, if one does not know why the pain is being suffered, and that it is a consequence of some previous act.

If an animal feels pain, but is not aware—and is not even capable of being aware—that the pain is a result of past acts which have made one such an animal, can the pain properly be considered a punishment? The soterial punishment for egoism has been seen as membership of a group of beings as greedy, fearful, and aggressive as oneself. But to see this as punishment, one would have to remember one's relevant past acts, see how they have led to this condition, and accept that one could have chosen otherwise. In this way, punishment is potentially reformative, as one perceives the consequences of egoism, though such potential may not be realized if the egoist remains unwilling to repent.

The occurrence of animal pain, or of human pain in a different earthly life, fails to fulfil these conditions. The sufferer does not see it as freely chosen, or remember any relevant past acts, or see how the pain follows naturally from them. So one does not see it as punishment. Animals cannot do so, and humans will only do so if someone else tells them it is, i.e. on authority. Nevertheless, it could be that animal pain is a punishment, even if the animal could not see it as such. A criminal can be punished, even if he does not remember committing a crime. Presumably there must come a time, between births, when the soul comes to see why it has been so embodied, and when it sees what it must do in future to avoid such rebirths.

Each life is lived in ignorance, in forgetfulness of one's past lives. So it seems to each soul as if it is newly born, suffering and enjoying various things which come to it by accident or fate, and challenged in the present to make a decision for either love or egoism. When it leaves the body, the soul realizes that it has lived before, that it suffered and enjoyed the consequences of its past acts, and that the decisions it has just made in its last life will bring further consequences in future births. Then it will again be plunged into the river of forgetfulness, and live out a new life, needing to make new decisions in circumstances it has itself largely caused.

It is implausible to think that, during earthly life, I can acknowledge the sufferings of my present life as a just punishment for past acts, since I cannot remember those acts, or what their consequences were for other people, or see why this suffering should appropriately follow from them. I only find out those things in a postulated afterlife. It is only then, when I remember what I have done, see it in its true context, and remember the skills and cognitive capacities that I have built up during my past life, that I can begin truly to learn from my past acts, and begin to build a better future in the light of that.

An afterlife which can be seen as one of punishment and of possible reform seems to depend upon my having memory of past acts and of past accumulated skills or habits. I can only believe that this earthly life is one in which my sufferings are punishments for past acts if I am told so on authority. Even then, since I do not recall the acts in question, I cannot be quite sure of what I have to do to make amends for them. It looks as though I can only acknowledge the justice of the system, and can only usefully learn from my experiences between rebirths, when I am in possession of the necessary information. In that case, however, the real moral work of punishment and reformation (the aims, presumably, of cosmic justice), is done in a realm beyond this earth. To that extent, the hypothesis of rebirth on earth seems to add little to a hypothesis of judgement and spiritual progress in the world to come itself, which is needed in any case to enable one to see things as they are.

In addition, there is a certain moral unrealism in the thought that everyone really deserves all that they get. There seems to be a lot of sheer luck in life, as any winner of a lottery will testify. To say that, however hard one tries, one cannot evade the law of moral reward and punishment, is to introduce a moral rigour and neatness into human existence that does not seem to be there. An afterlife has been posited partly to compensate for the inequalities of luck or mischance that are so evident on earth. It seems implausible that further lives, in which the same inequalities will still seem so evident, can be used precisely to eliminate such inequalities. The supposition that all lottery winners have done immense amounts of good in some past life, and that cancer sufferers have done evil, is unfalsifiable. But, if a general assessment of their character or degree of spiritual discernment is in question, it seems implausible to establish any correlation of good or bad fortune and spiritual eminence or poverty, however far in the past one goes.

To the extent that one allows chance or circumstance to play a part in governing the sorts of things that happen to one during life, the hypothesis of rebirth becomes more plausible. But the price is that it also becomes less necessary. The more things in life it is not needed to explain, the less one needs to postulate it. Some modern defenders of rebirth (such as Vivekananda) try to dismiss its punitive aspects as unhelpful, and concentrate on the positive teaching of possible advancement in the future, and the importance of making moral choices in the present.[13] Once again, however, this lessens the explanatory power of earthly rebirth, as compared with views of an afterlife in spiritual realms. That this life is the result of forgotten past choices does not affect its character as a place for making decisive moral decisions. One has to act as though one is beginning with a more or less blank moral sheet, and can decide for oneself what one's future will be. But if those decisions are to work out in future lives which involve a consciousness of the appropriateness of reward or punishment, in some sense, they will have to be in conditions very different from those foreseeable on this planet. What the model suggests is a succession of future lives in different, spiritual realms, where the consequences of earthly actions can be worked out and perhaps developed further.[14] Reincarnation on earth is not ruled out as one possibility, but it

[13] This is even clearer in Aurobindo: 'If we could grasp the essential cause . . . of error, suffering and death . . . we might hope even to eliminate them altogether:' Aurobindo Ghose, *The Life Divine* (Calcutta: Arya Publishing, 1939), 69.

[14] Such a view is defended in John Hick's classic work, *Death and Eternal Life* (London: Macmillan, 1976).

would not seem likely to be the normal pattern for every human soul if either real spiritual advance or consciously experienced punishment are to exist.

A further difficulty with the hypothesis of rebirth is that it threatens to undermine the fact of human community and relatedness, the way in which persons affect one another for good or ill by their acts. I may well be born in a society where others seek to oppress and use me, and where I therefore suffer because of what they do, not just because of what I have done in the past. It may be because of my past choices that I am born in such a society, but once I am in it things will not work out with great moral fairness. Just as I have to assume that I am free to help or to harm others, so I have to assume that others are free to help or harm me. They will not act in obedience to some foreordained karmic law. Consequently, whether they harm or help me, they will be causing things to happen to me, good and bad, which are not karmically ordained.

If my karma must play itself out, then any alleviation of my suffering by another—God or creatures—can only postpone it to another life. Of course, one could be so born that it is destined that one's suffering is to be relieved by another. Yet if that other is a free agent, they may not relieve it when they should. I will then suffer more than I should. This could be compensated by a great deal of bliss in another life, I suppose. Karma requires specific rewards and punishments, and other people can always complicate the process by hurting or helping an agent. If I hurt you, and it is not your karma to be hurt, then this must be compensated. Over many lives, this could all be worked out, so that at the end of each life one would have a certain amount of merit or demerit to carry over to further lives. I do not get what I deserve in any one life, but things will work out over future lives.

This does entail, however, that agents will not get perfect justice in any one life. They may reap undeserved benefit from the altruistic acts of others, or undeserved harm from the egoistic acts of others. I will not be able to say of anything that happens to me, 'I deserved this.' I can say, 'I will be compensated for this, or will pay for this later!' At that point, however, the postulate of previous lives loses some of its explanatory force. Things will, after all, happen to me which I do not deserve, because I am born into a community of free agents who can help or harm one another.

In a society of free agents, what happens to one person will depend, in a largely unpredictable way, on what others do, in their freedom. This is not only the case with present actions, for the actions of people in the past will have consequences which reverberate through societies for many years. If I injure another person, that will perhaps have serious implications for the bringing up of their children, and for their children in turn. Thus I will suffer because of the past acts of others as well as (on the hypothesis) because of my own past acts. Such unfairnesses, both for good and ill, will multiply, as humans seek to oppress or help others.

In a world in which real communities exist, it must be possible for individuals freely to help and harm others. In such a world, the innocent will often suffer, and we will all often receive benefits that we do not deserve. Thus the existence of communities of moral agents is in tension with any strict application of a law of karma, which must tend to work in an individualistic way. One might even say that, in so far as one is concerned with the flourishing of community, and thus in so far as one is truly altruistic and has escaped from egoistic selfishness, one will be less concerned with matters of strict individual desert.

REBIRTH AND THE LAWS OF PHYSICS

Paradoxically, in so far as I manage to turn from egoism, it will not particularly matter to me whether what happens to me is the result of *my* past acts or of the past and present acts of others, with whose lives mine is closely bound up. For I will be more concerned that all should have the chance of liberation, than that I should get exactly what I deserve because of my past acts.[15] What will matter is whether it is possible for everyone now to enter a path of growing devotion to the Lord. Real altruists will have transcended any concern that they themselves should receive any rewards due to them. They will have transcended any concern that the sufferings they undergo should be no more than they have personally deserved. For if, by their free acceptance of undeserved sufferings, they are able to strengthen a sense of community and to encourage others to become devoted to the Lord, they will count that a cost worth accepting. One might say that a truly altruistic being would take the risk of suffering undeservedly, if that risk was a condition of

[15] This is particularly clear with, and may be a main source of, the Buddhist doctrine of 'no-self', treated in the following chapter.

opening up the possibility of eventual liberation from suffering and entrance into a loving relationship with the Lord, for every soul in bondage. If that is so, then the transcending of egoism, which is the goal of Vaishnava practice, stands in contrast with a commitment to a strict application of karmic law. It may be therefore of no great consequence to me whether I, this very self, have lived before and now gain the consequences of my past acts, or whether I am suffering or enjoying the consequences of the acts of other selves, and have the opportunity to act in ways which may help to accomplish liberation from the sufferings and injustices of existence for all.

In addition to complicating factors based on human freedom in community, the theory of karmic law also stands in tension with much modern scientific understanding of physical causality. Physical and biological laws produce their effects without reference to moral considerations. If I step off a cliff, the law of gravity will draw me to the ground, whether or not I deserve it. My character may not be determined by genes, but it is certainly strongly influenced by genetic factors, which again introduce a strong element of moral randomness into my situation. The genes that go to make up my individuality are products of a random shuffling of the genes of my parents, and their order and character seem to depend primarily on the working out of physical laws, which are not determined by moral considerations.[16] Unless the mixing of genes is in fact spiritually determined in detail, which seems highly implausible, it will not be possible to guarantee that a particular personality can be born of a particular pair of parents. Gender, bodily structure, and general personality will be inherited in accordance with physical laws. Moreover, the activities of the parents, their success or failure, will influence the social position and prospects of children to a great degree, as will the geographical and cultural position of the society into which they are born.

The simplest explanation of the inequalities of birth is given by reference to laws of mutation and inheritance, to physical factors of temporal and spatial location, and to social factors of the position in society into which one is born. The laws of the material universe do not seem to be karmic laws which the physical order simply expresses. Chance, physical necessity, and emergence are all features of the material world, and they support the view that souls are

---

[16] The role of chance and law in biological nature is elegantly sketched in Arthur Peacocke, *Theology for a Scientific Age* (London: SCM , 1993), cf. ch. 3.

emergent from particular material complexes.[17] Souls are not trapped in an alien realm of matter, but represent the gradual unfolding of the self-conscious and self-directing capacities of matter. They originate in a particular time and history, and that origin marks them as finite and unique, historically, genetically, and culturally particularized individuals.

It complicates the situation enormously if one adds that there is a 'subtle body', a habituated personality (*manas*) and an evaluating intelligence (*buddhi*), together with a distinctive sense of self (*ahamkara*) which needs to find an appropriate material body. If two humans mate and an ovum is fertilized, a human being will develop naturally, and a soul will have to be found to fit it. It seems that there will be a waiting list of souls looking for appropriate bodies, and their birth will be contingent on the chance genetic mix of fertilization.

If the brain is what stores information, a developed soul will require a formed brain, with an exceedingly complex structure, which has been built up over many years of experience. Infant brains are obviously not formed in the appropriate way, and they need to be developed slowly through experience and practice before they successfully store the information natural to an adult human. A believer in reincarnation therefore has to hold that there exists a developed soul, with a rich information content, which is not able to convey all this information to the brain in which it is to be incarnated. So one has to maintain a strong dualism, according to which the soul is only partly incarnated in a particular brain, and plays an important causal role in determining the structure of the brain.

Ian Stevenson, an American psychiatrist, has researched into a number of cases of claimed memories of past earthly lives, and regards rebirth as the best hypothesis to explain their occurrence.[18] Among the phenomena he records are the occurrence of physical birth-marks at points on the body where a previously living person was injured or wounded. This would entail that there is a definite—and physically inexplicable—causal shaping of the physical body by a non-material causal component—usually called the 'subtle body'.

[17] This view is more fully expounded in K. Ward, *God, Chance and Necessity* (Oxford: Oneworld, 1996).
[18] Ian Stevenson, *Twenty Cases Suggestive of Reincarnation* (New York: American Society for Psychical Research, 1966).

If enough evidence of this sort could be collected, I think that it might be reasonable to regard rebirth as empirically established, whatever the theoretical difficulties. As with so many claims, however, the nature of the evidence is highly disputed, and much stronger evidence would be needed to carry scientific conviction. Nevertheless, the claim that people are reincarnated is a factual claim, susceptible in principle to scientific investigation. In this discussion, I am bringing out theoretical problems with the claim, either as an explanation of injustice in people's lives or as a coherent and plausible account of the form of individual survival of death and the possibility of attaining an ultimate religious goal. In these respects, I regard it as a prima-facie plausible and elegant hypothesis which on closer examination, however, turns out not to carry the benefits it seems to offer, nor to have the explanatory force it seemed to have.

The major problem with the rebirth theory is that it is at odds with most results of modern genetics and the neurophysiology of the brain. This would, of course, turn out to be a major advantage if the best-attested scientific claims in these areas are incorrect. This is an area where the conflict of science and religious belief is a real and living issue. If reincarnation is true, a great many modern scientific theories on the nature and functioning of the brain and the development of the human embryo must be false.

This is not impossible, but it raises in a marked way the difficulty that has always been felt with strongly dualistic views of human nature, that consciousness seems not to be wholly independent of the brain, but to be supervenient upon the existence of a developed brain and central nervous system. If such a brain exists, then it seems that consciousness also comes into existence. As the brain develops, so does consciousness. If the brain is damaged, the functioning of consciousness is impaired. That implies that consciousness is not a wholly independent ontological entity, but comes into being whenever a particular complex physical structure exists. It is a new property or quality, such that it emerges from the material realm in predetermined conditions. It is emergent from physical structures, and causally dependent upon them for its functioning. In the light of these facts, it may seem more plausible to say that individual souls are genetically and physically unique individuals, emergent from the physical complex of a particular body and brain. Conversely, it seems less plausible to think that an already complex structured soul can be incarnated into a genetically unique and physiologically developing brain.

REBIRTH, EVOLUTION AND THE SEMITIC TRADITIONS

The rebirth hypothesis contrasts quite strongly with an evolutionary view, for which souls are generated by emergent material processes, and the purpose of creation is the existence of a community of creative agents who are parts of the material world and can understand and appreciate it, and shape it to new forms of beauty. If souls are eternal, they are not generated through a process of evolution. On the contrary, they enter into a material world which has been specifically formed to provide an arena for expressing their desires.

Consequently, Vaishnavas reject the scientific hypothesis of evolution, proposing quite a different history for humanity.[19] Human beings do not evolve gradually from other species. Rather, eternal souls descend into matter, over millions of years. If anything, things are getting worse in this age of Kali, which will end in a great conflagration. After that will come the *Satya-Yuga*, a new golden age. But that will not last for ever. It will in turn be succeeded by further ages of degeneration. At the end of a vast cosmic cycle, the whole process will start over again. There is a noticeable antagonism in the movement to technological invention—for instance, in space exploration—on the grounds that it is spiritually pointless.[20] The material world exists as a realm of sensuality, competition, and greed. Some souls sought such things out of a desire for mastery and new experience, even though suffering inevitably resulted. That suffering becomes much worse as souls become entangled in selfish desire. It is good for the Lord to permit such a world to exist as long as it is freely chosen by souls. But there is no positive purpose in the material world as such, and the goal of spiritual existence is liberation to the Goloka planet, going 'home to God'.

The Vaishnava view is that each soul chooses its own path through the material world. It has chosen to exist in this world, but its true home and its goal is the spiritual world of the Lord Krishna. On a Semitic view, I have not personally chosen to be born into this

---

[19] The outline is given in the Purport to *Gita* 8. 17, *Bhagavad-Gita As It Is*, 433.
[20] '*Bhagavad-Gita* does not advise us to go to any of the planets in this material world', ibid. 22.

world. I, as the precise individual I am, can either be born into this world, with all its injustice and corruption, or not at all, since I am an emergent agent and enjoyer, generated by physical processes. My personality is shaped by my evolutionary inheritance, by my social context, and by the history of my community. I have no choice about that, but theists are logically committed to the view that all selves would have chosen to be born rather than not exist. For it contradicts the idea of a just God that any self could exist without its choice, when it would have chosen not to do so, when its existence is worse than its non-existence. Many people do, unfortunately, judge their earthly lives to be not worth living. The theist would say that this judgement is due to ignorance of the true possibilities of human life, an ignorance which death will remove. In the life of the world to come, it can be supposed that it will be possible for all to come to a state in which they clearly see that it is better to exist than not. If they do not in fact come to such a state— if they continue to choose self-destruction—it will be by their clear and unequivocal choice.

Whereas for Vaishnavas every soul necessarily exists eternally, for most Semitic faiths each soul begins to exist on earth, and there is no necessity that life beyond death should be endless. Faith requires only that in the world to come one should experience the fulfilment of what one has begun to shape oneself to be on earth. If one achieves a loving relationship with the Lord, it does not matter how long that lasts. Nevertheless, it is plausible to think that the longer a good relationship lasts the better, so that, by grace, God may extend my life without end. On a typical Christian view, I do not 'deserve' the sort of suffering I may have to endure on earth. But neither do I 'deserve' the endless bliss of a fulfilled loving relationship with God. The idea of forensic justice is subordinated to the idea of soterial justice, which decrees that souls should originate in a sick or diseased world, in order that they may help to heal it and may eventually themselves be brought to a limitless fullness of health, through the self-sacrificial healing ministry of the others, and especially of the Lord himself, in which they may to some extent participate.

Vaishnavas have a strong belief in the grace of the Lord, and of the liberated life as consisting in personal loving service to the Lord. They thus have a soterial rather than a forensic interpretation of cosmic justice. In some ways it might be said that the doctrines of the eternity of the soul and of rebirth make the Vaishnava view more rather than less difficult. The hypothesis of rebirth, with its emphasis on individual merit, makes it more difficult to take the social nature of the self seriously. It makes it more difficult to regard grace as a crucial element in human liberation. In somewhat the same way, its emphasis on the eternal spirituality of the soul makes it more difficult to take the specific individuality of a particular human life, and the continuity of that same life in the presence of Krishna, seriously. Each soul has existed without beginning, in a seemingly infinite number of bodies. When this human body and personality is only one out of an infinite number that a soul has had, its particularity is of infinitesimal importance. When 'I' have been infinitely many people in the history of the cosmos, it would seem unreasonable to identify myself with any one of them in particular. It is not surprising if Indian religious views tend not to talk of the fulfilment of an individual personality, but of its renunciation and overcoming.[21] This life may be important as a stage on an infinite journey, but it is only one stage, after all. It is unlikely to be of utterly decisive significance.

The ultimate stage, that of *moksa* or release from rebirth, transcends the temporal order completely. In it, the whole succession of individual personalities in which the liberated soul was once embodied is left behind. The hypothesis of rebirth has little place for a full actualization of the potentialities of this individual personality, of the community of which it is a part, or of its wider material environment. This is not necessarily a negative point. It may express a better understanding of human nature to see that materiality, community, and individual personality must all be transcended before the soul can realize its true, eternal, liberated nature. But it is a very different assessment than one which looks for the possibility of some fulfilment of this precise personality, in a community of co-operating and coexperiencing individuals, and in an environment which allows creative action and new cognitive experience to occur.

What is interesting about the Gaudiya Vaishnava view is that it combines these assessments, by holding that the present form of

---

[21] 'A person in the divine consciousness, although engaged in seeing, hearing, touching, smelling, eating, moving about, sleeping and breathing, always knows within himself that he actually does nothing at all', *Gita* 5, 8, *Bhagavad-Gita As It Is*, 282.

bodily existence must be transcended, but only in order to enter into a higher, 'spiritual' form of embodied life, where one can dance and rejoice in the presence of Lord Krishna for ever.[22] It would be disingenuous to claim that the hypothesis of rebirth is not central to Vaishnava belief. It is central to the understanding of the material body as inessential to the soul, to the understanding of this human life as part of an unceasing round of rebirths, and one stage in a pilgrimage to spiritual enlightenment, and to the doctrine of the many avatars, or earthly appearances, of Vishnu (or Krishna, in ISKCON belief). Nevertheless, in teaching that the ultimate religious goal is devotion to Krishna, and in conceiving this goal as one in which both individual and social life are still present in a higher form of embodiment, the school has moved a long way from Sankhya belief in the ultimate liberation of non-individual souls of pure discarnate intelligence and unmoving bliss.

I have considered three major interpretations of rebirth within Hindu orthodoxy, which correspond to some extent with the three paths of wisdom (*jnyana*), works (karma), and devotion (*bhakti*) in Indian tradition. The Advaita view is that there is one non-dual self which, through the mysterious power of maya comes to see itself as many individual selves. The individual is composed of the gross body of matter and the senses, and the subtle body of mind (*buddhi*, sense-integrating consciousness), intellect (*manas*, analytical and inferential reason), and ego (*ahamkara*, sense of self). It is the subtle body that transfers from one gross body to another, in rebirth. Each subtle body is implicit in the potencies of maya, and is necessarily manifested in each new cosmic cycle. If it achieves liberation, it ceases to exist, and only the pure consciousness of Brahman remains. The self as agent and enjoyer must cease to be, once it is seen to be a restriction on and dream-like concealment of the unlimited consciousness of Brahman.

The Sankhya view is that each self is qualitatively identical to every other, but there is an infinite number of selves, which all exist without beginning or end. Some of them become immersed in matter, which is an independently existing reality, and come to identify themselves, falsely, with particular material bodies. Liberation consists in destroying all links with matter, including the particular personalities of embodied selves, and in returning to a state of pure

---

[22] Cf. *Gita*, Purport, 15. 7, *Bhagavad-Gita As It Is*, 720.

isolated consciousness. Again, the self as agent and enjoyer ceases to be, though each soul remains eternally distinct.

The Vaishnava view is that the material body is a reflection of a spiritual body, so that each soul has a distinct personality in the spiritual world, and liberation consists in being freed from the limitations of 'false ego', and relating in loving devotion to the supreme personality of Godhead. The agent and enjoyer will always exist, though not as a self-controller. Instead, it will be an instrument of the supreme Lord, and seek to possess nothing of itself.

Human beings are 'fragmented parts' of Krishna, and their true nature is pure consciousness and bliss. Yet some form of embodiment is a natural expression of that nature, and they remain eternally distinct from, and in a relation of obedient devotion to, the supreme Lord. The Vaishnava school forms a bridge between the ascetic traditions of Indian spirituality and its popular practices of devotional personalism. However central the idea of rebirth is in Vaishnava cosmogeny, it loses most of its power to explain earthly inequalities (since divine grace undercuts the laws of merit), and to provide the vast time-span needed to attain release from rebirth (since that is accomplished by a simple act of loving devotion). Nevertheless, the idea of rebirth does enshrine a hope for the possibility of spiritual progress and development, even for those whose earthly lives seem to make such a hope impossible. That is a hope that must be basic for any religion of devotion to a truly gracious and loving God, and there must be some way of providing for it in any religion of grace. Even if the hypothesis of rebirth is rejected, that hope is one of the things that Gaudiya Vaishnavism has to teach the Christian tradition.

5
Buddhism and the Self

The views of human nature considered so far have assumed that there exists a substantial, eternal self, the essential nature of which is knowledge and bliss. Human beings are either illusory appearances of this self, or are individual selves existing in relation to it. Within the complex of Indian religious traditions, however, there is one that explicitly denies the existence of eternal selves, whether one or many. While it accepts many elements of Indian cosmogeny, including the hypotheses of karma and rebirth, it stands outside the orthodox traditions by its rejection of the Brahminical priesthood and of the inspired nature of the Veda. It gives a very different account of the essential nature of human being.

'He who goes for refuge to Buddha, to Truth and to those whom he taught, he goes indeed to a great refuge. Then he sees the four great truths: sorrow, the cause of sorrow, the end of sorrow, and the path of eight stages which leads to the end of sorrow.'[1] The teaching of Buddhism is traced back to Sakyamuni, the fifth-century BCE Indian sage of whom it is said that 'an undeluded being has arisen in the world, for the wellbeing and happiness of the multitude, out of pity for the world'.[2] Sakyamuni was undeluded in that he attained, at his enlightenment, a 'purified divine eye transcending the human', with which he was able to recollect a thousand former births, and see the passing away and arising of all beings. It was in that suprahuman state that he discerned the four noble truths, personal appropriation of which leads to the freedom which destroys rebirth and to the ending of suffering.

The central claim is that a fully enlightened being, a Buddha, possesses a supranormal insight into the nature of things, which enables him to see 'what is the satisfaction of worldly pursuits, what

---

[1] *The Dhammapada*, 14. 190–1; trans. Juan Mascaro (Harmondsworth: Penguin, 1973), 63.

[2] *Majjhima-Nikaya*, i, discourse 4, in *Discourses of Gotama Buddha*, Middle Collection, trans. David Evans (London: Janus, 1992), 8.

the disadvantage, what the escape from them'.[3] The insight of a Buddha is unique. 'The Exemplar . . . recognises all things for what they are, and has no attachment to any of them.'[4] He is 'the originator of a way not (previously) come into being, the parent of a way (previously) unconceived, the teller of a way (previously) untold.'[5] There is not even one monk who wholly possesses the things possessed by Gotama. As he says, 'I alone am truly enlightened.'[6] There may be other Buddhas for other world-periods and in other worlds. For Mahayana Buddhism, there is indeed an infinite number of Buddhas. Yet Gotama stands unique in this world-period, 'the Lord, *arahant*, truly enlightened, proficient in knowledge and conduct, adept, seer of worlds, matchless charioteer of men to be tamed, teacher of *deva*s and humans, Buddha and Lord'.[7]

From his supranormal insight, born of complete liberation, the Buddha tells us the most important thing about the human condition: that it is characterized by greed, hatred, and delusion, that such things arise from craving for sensory pleasures, and that what is required is 'an abandonment of the delight and intoxication with (worldly pursuits)'.

There are five (often said to be six) strands of worldly pursuit, corresponding to the five senses which offer pleasure and excitement.[8] But with such pursuit of pleasure come inevitable disadvantages. For 'if it fails to gain its object there is distress, if it gains its object there is the worry of protecting what has been gained. And because of it there is quarrelling, exploitation, and death'. The Buddha does not claim that there is no pleasure in existence. Far from it. In the *deva*, heavenly worlds, there is very great pleasure. Yet the craving even for such pleasure brings suffering in its train, and the only way to end suffering is to end craving and attachment.

Such an ending is itself said to bring a unique form of happiness. The Buddha says that he could, with an unstirring body, and without uttering a word, experience nothing but happiness for seven nights and days.[9] He compares the attainment of *nibbana* to bathing in 'a lotus-pond, with water that is clear, sweet, cool, and limpid', 'experiencing feelings that are altogether happy'.[10] There are two forms of *nibbana*, one 'with substrate' (with the aggregates

---

[3] Ibid., Discourse 13, p. 36.
[5] Ibid., Discourse 108, p. 336.
[7] Ibid., Discourse 85, p. 262.
[9] Ibid., Discourse 14, p. 42.

[4] Ibid., Discourse 1, p. 1.
[6] Ibid., Discourse 26, p. 77.
[8] Ibid., Discourse 14, p. 40.
[10] Ibid., Discourse 12, p. 32.

of body, feelings, perceptions, mental formations, and consciousness), which is an experienced cessation of craving and a limpid happiness, and the other 'without substrate', which occurs at death, and of which nothing can be said. From that state there will be no return, but it is contrasted in the texts both with eternalism (the view that there is a substantial and eternal soul, continuing to exist roughly as it now does) and with nihilism (the view that nothing survives the extinction of desire).[11]

Remarkably little is said about the state of *nibbana*, though it is the ultimate goal of meditative practice. The Buddha apparently discouraged speculation on its nature, though he said of it, 'Destroyed is birth, fulfilled the good life, done what was to be done and (there will be) no more return to this world.'[12] Further than that, he recommended holding no view on issues about the ultimate state of liberation. The texts give three main reasons for this. First, holding such a view is not conducive to overcoming egoism and achieving equanimity, compassion, and mindfulness. It tempts one to speculate on matters which can have no direct soteriological import. It may even lead to a form of long-term egoism, if it encourages desires for quasi-sensory pleasures (as in some ways of thinking of heaven). It is enough to know that there is a goal which is beyond suffering. It is actually an impediment to progress in meditation to speculate about it, since it is far beyond one's present understanding, and might seem unattainable or even undesirable to a desire-bound mind. Second, to hold such a view may lead to grasping, obsession, and attachment, to quarrels with others, and defensiveness. Where no way of settling disputes is available, they are particularly idle. Third, any such views would be theoretical constructs, not capable of being immediately experienced by meditators, and so would distract from the path to release.

The Buddha said, 'This too is a fixed opinion, (namely) this is the world; this is the self; after death I will become stable, continuous, perpetual . . . (is not that opinion) complete and utter foolishness?'[13] All such speculations, he says, are 'not useful, not conducive to disenchantment, dispassion, becoming tranquil, cessation, gnosis, enlightenment, *nibbana*'.[14] Against all such views,

---

[11] *Majjhima-Nikaya*, i, discourse 4, in *Discourses of Gotama Buddha*, Middle Collection, trans. David Evans (London: Janus, 1992), Discourse 11, p. 27.
[12] Ibid., Discourse 11, p. 28.   [13] Ibid., Discourse 22, p. 64.
[14] Ibid., Discourse 63, p. 186.

the Buddha says, 'I proclaim simply suffering and cessation.'[15] The practical urgency of liberation is too great to wait for speculative answers about the nature of reality.

At the same time, the Buddha's teaching is that 'all compounded things are impermanent, all states are devoid of self'.[16] There are some true views. Indeed, the first limb of the eightfold path is the holding of right views, so the teaching can hardly be that one is to hold no views whatsoever. There are what most would call speculative assertions about the non-existence of the self and the existence of rebirth. Yet they must not be held in a disputatious or obstinate way, or for their purely speculative attraction. They are to be held because they are necessary for the establishing of the right view, which leads to the path of liberation.

The doctrine of no-self in Buddhism is thus not primarily a speculative doctrine, but a soteriological one. It does not encourage speculation on the ultimate nature of the self, but seeks to free humans from that sense of self which binds them to the world of suffering. In that world it is natural—though it is born of ignorance—to think, 'This is mine. I am this. This is myself.' The sense of self is a sense of possessiveness and of attachment. Wisdom comes when, freeing oneself from attachment, one achieves the realization: 'empty is this of self or of what belongs to self'.[17]

Liberation comes when one achieves insight into experience as 'empty of self', as not able to be possessed by 'me', as not to be separated into what is 'mine' and what is 'not mine', and as not to be made an object of pride or self-satisfaction. Suffering results from such a sense of exclusive possession, which gives rise to egoism in all its forms, and which arises from the conceit of the self-subsistent existence of the self. To be born as a human is already to carry with one many negative karmic traces, resulting from such a conceit, which need to be overcome. Through right views, moral action, and meditation, they can be overcome, though it will almost certainly take many lives to achieve that.

THE ELIMINATIVE VIEW OF SELF

On the popular view of rebirth, both within and without Buddhism, one is a continuing self, and as such one suffers for one's own past

---

[15] Ibid., Discourse 22, p. 65.   [16] Ibid., Discourse 35, p. 102.
[17] Ibid., Discourse 106, p. 330.

misdeeds, and exerts mindfulness in order to achieve release from suffering in future and enter into a state of bliss beyond suffering. This cannot, however, be considered as a finally adequate statement. Steven Collins writes, '[Buddhist] ultimate thinking refers solely to collections of impersonal elements, the sequence of which provides continuity both within "one lifetime" and in the process of "rebirth".'[18] On the Buddhist view there is no inherently existing self, so it is not strictly true that 'I' will be reborn. One seeks to be 'freed of every bias towards, "I the doer, mine the deed" '.[19] What happens is that the collection of aggregates which constitutes the empirical self gives rise to a karmic continuation in another physical form, which may be seen as a 'continuation of the self', though it is more accurately seen as the continuation of a series of continuous, transient, and causally connected states. The seeker for enlightenment strives to bring this series to an end by 'the quieting of all tendencies, the giving up of every attachment, the rooting out of craving, dispassion, cessation, *nibbana*'.[20]

This eliminative interpretation of the human person holds that there is nothing permanent or stable that endures through all experiences. There is only a collection of five *skandha*s, or a series of transient and ever-changing elements. The five aggregates are: matter (the physical body), feeling, sense-perception, disposition (or mental capacities), and consciousness, (or memories, thoughts, and ideas). The human self is a bundle of these aggregates, bound together by an illusory sense of 'self' (*ahamkara*). It is as if one thought that a haystack was something that continues to exist as one and the same thing, even if all the individual pieces of hay are gradually replaced by other pieces. In a sense, of course, one can say that it is the same haystack. It is not non-existent.

It is clear that, on such a view, personal identity is a matter of degree. At some time far in the future, I will be more or less the same person as I am now. Perhaps all my thoughts and feelings will have changed, and I will remember little or nothing of my present life. Then I might say, 'I am not really the same person', even if I have the same material body—that is, one continuously but slowly changing structure of atoms in space-time. But if I then have capacities and habits which are the result of present activities and disci-

---

[18] Steven Collins, *Selfless Persons* (Cambridge: Cambridge University Press, 1982), 160.

[19] *Discourses*, Discourse 72, p. 210.   [20] Ibid., Discourse 64, p. 188.

pline (perhaps I will play the violin well, as a result of practising hard now), and if I remember much of my present life, I will probably say, 'I am the same person.'

The more there is a common mental content and a continuous spatio-temporal and gradually changing causal path between two sets of aggregates, the more I am likely to think of these two sets as belonging to 'the same person'. However, one can easily think of circumstances in which such continuity breaks down. One can imagine the same body suddenly coming to have the memories, thoughts, and intentions which used to belong to some other body. Or—more relevantly to Buddhist theory—one can imagine a set of memories, thoughts, and dispositions being removed from one body and inserted into another one. We might not know whether to say this was the same person in another body or not. So it is understandable that the Buddha teaches that it is not strictly 'I' who am reborn, yet nor is it another.[21]

As the *Visuddhimagga* puts it, 'While nothing whatever moves over from the past life to this life, nevertheless aggregates, bases and elements do not fail to be produced here, with aggregates, bases and elements in the past life as their condition.'[22] There is no enduring 'I' which passes from one life to another. '[The wise man] sees no doer beyond the doing, no experiencer of the result beyond the occurrence of the result . . . elements alone occur, that is right vision.'[23]

It is essential to the Buddhist view, however, that there are causal links between the aggregates of elements which constitute living beings, links based on desire and attachment. Actions and even intentions occurring in one series of aggregates will inevitably produce karmic fruits in a later series of aggregates. Those fruits will be produced, whether in a series that one would be tempted (with an unenlightened eye) to call 'mine', or in a series that one might naturally say belong to 'someone else'. Thus present actions have results of happiness or suffering, and it does not matter whether those results will accrue to a series which contains (probably repressed, but recoverable in principle) memories of this series or not. It is because of this that action for the sake of accruing merit in

---

[21] *Milinda-Panyha*, 40.

[22] *Visuddhimagga* 19. 22, trans. Nanamoli Bikkhu, as *The Path of Purification* (Ceylon: BPS, 1975).

[23] Ibid. 19. 19.

some future life is not, as it might seem, mere long-term self-interest. The merit will accrue to one who is neither the same as nor different from the agent. Such action is, strictly speaking, neither egoistic nor altruistic. It is simply action that produces future states of happiness or future states of suffering.

On most accounts of rebirth, it is the 'subtle body', the mental dispositions to act in certain ways, and the accumulated merit or demerit of a certain sequence of actions, which transfers to another gross, or material body. Memories and thoughts are also transferred, but remain almost entirely repressed or implicit. There is not usually an awareness that I am the same person who once lived in a different body. So rather than saying that I will be reborn, it may be more accurate to say that my actions in this body will have karmic consequences for some sentient being in the future, who is connected with me by various causal continuities and overlaps of mental content.

For the purpose of getting people to act well and seek liberation, it can be said that they will be reborn, and will reap the consequences of their present actions in a future life. But this is a 'skilful means', rather than a strictly accurate portrayal of how things are. Their acts will build up karmic consequences, which will accrue to some future sentient being. If one is released from egoism and one is compassionate to all beings, one will naturally seek to avoid suffering for any future being as far as one can, and so one will strive for liberation. Strictly speaking, however, it is not 'oneself' who will be liberated, since there is no such continuing self, and it would ironically be egoistic to desire its liberation in preference to the liberation of another. It is rather that one chain of suffering will be terminated. As Poussin puts its, 'If a Buddhist undergoes the discipline which leads to *nirvana* . . . it is in order to diminish by one the number of living and suffering beings.'[24]

The scholastically developed doctrine of Theravada Buddhism often asserts this strong interpretation of selflessness. But even if it technically avoids nihilism, by saying that there never was a self to be annihilated, it is still nihilism in the perfectly clear sense that there is no experience of a finally liberated state-without-substrate by any being. There is just the stopping, or blowing out, of a chain of karmic causation. This is rather an odd soteriological aim, when

[24] L. de la Vallée Poussin, *The Way to Nirvana* (Cambridge: Cambridge University Press, 1917), 50.

one realizes how much effort is needed by so many beings to end just one tiny chain of causation, when so many other chains are continuing that the extinction of one will hardly be noticed. Just to rub the point in, so few humans achieve liberation at any time that the difference liberation makes to the karmic realm is negligible.

One may wonder whether even rigorous Theravadins mean to make the attainment of *nibbana* quite so miniscule in its consequences. Is it not true that, precisely in achieving such a liberation, a sentient being is released from the sense of individual self and personality, and enters into a conscious state which is limpid, clear, cool, and limitless? Is it not true that this is a goal for all sentient beings? Beyond the sense of false ego there is the deathless, and the realization of it is the goal of the eightfold path, which all sentient beings may tread.

There is a tension at the heart of Theravada between the strongly motivating sense of an ultimate goal of meditative practice and the doctrine that there is no self to attain such a goal. One traditional way of easing this tension is to distinguish between two levels of truth, the conventional and the ultimate, or, as Spiro does, between what he calls nibbanic and kammatic Buddhism.[25] Kammatic Buddhism is the faith of most ordinary lay Buddhists (and even of most monks), who hope to achieve a better rebirth, especially in the time of the coming Metteya (Maitreya) Buddha, by their acts. Nibbanic Buddhism is the faith of the virtuosi, who achieve exalted meditative states, and who hope to leave the samsaric realm altogether. There are certainly desirable future goals, in better worlds, for selves who will exist there in much the same sense that they exist now. But ultimately the goal, conceivable by few, is of the cessation of desire even for existence. There are, one might say, many temporary goals of religious practice, to be experienced in future by present selves. But the ultimate goal will never be experienced, is conceivable as a goal only by the few, and is a goal at all only in a paradoxical sense.

In this way, meditation functions, for most Buddhists, as a way of achieving release from egoistic possessiveness and progressing in realizing the four 'divine abidings'—loving-kindness, compassion, sympathetic joy, and equanimity. At this level, the doctrine of *anatta* functions as a sort of asymptotic ideal for meditation practice. It is

[25] M. E. Spiro, *Buddhism and Society* (New York: Harper & Row, 1970), 70.

what Collins calls a 'soteriological strategy' for countering egoism and encouraging mindfulness in everyday life.[26] It also forms a clear conceptual opposition to the Brahminical religion, with (from the Buddhist standpoint) its priestly hierarchy and magical view of sacrifice as a system of rituals which causes beneficial karmic consequences. In Buddhism, the sacrificial ritual is internalized so that the life of ascetic practice becomes itself the ideal sacrifice. It is universalized so that the priestly functionary is replaced by the ascetic virtuoso. And it is moralized so that good karma is caused by good intentions and mental dispositions, and not by ritual correctness.[27]

The basic intention in kammatic Buddhism is to obtain release from suffering for oneself and one's family, and to implore the help of enlightened beings or various gods in achieving better births in future. It is only at the level of the meditative virtuoso that the doctrine of *anatta* requires the complete renunciation of the idea of self, together with the renunciation of any desire for further existence, good or bad. At this level, there is no one to obtain release, and there is no goal to be attained or experienced by anyone. There is simply the cessation of desire, the ending of one sequence of aggregates. It is in that rigorous sense that there is no agent and enjoyer, no self at all.

There is a certain philosophical similarity in this ultimate view to the official philosophy of David Hume, who also denied the existence of any continuous self over and above the impressions and ideas that exhaustively constitute human consciousness. What Hume did not accept was the view that there is such a thing as causality by desire, the particular theory of Dependent Origination characteristic of Buddhist thought. And he did not think that impermanence has the nature of suffering, from which release is to be sought. The conclusions Hume drew from his denial of self are therefore quite different from those of Gautama. Hume sought an urbane existence, in which culture and friendship were to be desired, and of which one had to make the best one could. It is only if one sees one's desires as inevitably causing suffering for sentient beings, through the chain of Dependent Origination (*pratityasa-mutpada*), that one can intelligibly aim at entirely cutting off the

---

[26] Collins, *Selfless Persons*, 12.

[27] It is interesting to see in Christianity a similar process, wherein the Temple sacrifices of Judaism are replaced by the life of Jesus, seen as a perfect, selfless renunciation, in which disciples can participate.

roots of desire. It is thus essential for 'ultimate' Buddhist thought that the sequence of Dependent Origination gives a correct analysis of the coming-to-be of things in the world, and that particular chains of states formed within such a sequence can be ended by the attaining of higher meditative states. These are the right views without which Buddhist soteriology has no basis in reality.

THE NON-DUAL VIEW OF THE SELF

The eliminative analysis of human being, which eliminates everything except the elements and the series to which they belong, seems to imply that nirvana is, as its linguistic root suggests, just the cessation of a particular series of elements: 'That by which he can be talked about is no longer there for him; you cannot say that he does not exist . . . all ways of description have also been removed.'[28] But there is a rather different analysis which this text might seem to imply. For it states that there is a sense in which 'he', the same self, exists, though he is now beyond description. This is implied in the very fact that it is the self that is liberated: 'I shall go beyond change, I shall go beyond formations . . . you may consider this as mind released.'[29] 'I' go beyond all form and becoming. So one must understand that the subject is no longer identified with any particular form. Yet it is 'perfect, balanced mindfulness';[30] it is tranquillity and perfect knowledge. The subject is then beyond birth and death, and will never return. The individual does not cease to be, and yet does not go on existing as the same series. One seems forced to say that there is a continuant, though it is not the same personality that continues in the liberated state.

There is something which returns through various births. It identifies itself with desires and uncompleted projects. There is something which goes beyond birth, and never returns. It is freed from such identification with a particular set of mental contents, existing in deathless wisdom and tranquillity, without desire, consisting of pure intelligence and bliss. This state can be attained during earthly life: 'this Way is one which can be known here and now'.[31] But in its fully liberated reality it is beyond form and description. Many scholars have interpreted the Buddhist view in this way, perhaps

---

[28] *Sutta-Nipata*, trans. H. Saddhatissa (Richmond, Va.: Curzon, 1994), v. 1076 (p. 123).
[29] Ibid. 1149 (p. 133).   [30] Ibid. 1107 (p. 128).   [31] Ibid. 1053 (p. 121).

most notably Christmas Humphreys and Mrs Rhys Davids, but it does qualify a purely eliminative analysis of human being, positing beyond the transient reality of the individual person a non-dual reality, which is pure bliss and wisdom. That is tantamount to saying that there is a continuing, stable existent, an element which, according to the *Abhidharma* (further teachings), is the eighty-second *dharma* (element), nirvana, free from ageing and death.

Presumably that element is always present in human life, though hidden and covered over by the false sense of self, which identifies the self with transient elements of personality and sensory experience. On this interpretation, the way of liberation is a way of disentanglement from identification with transient states, and an entrance into pure non-dual consciousness, which, being beyond description, one can neither describe as the persistence of an individual soul nor as the extinction of the soul. This is what became known in some East Asian traditions as the Buddha-nature, which exists in all sentient beings, whose full realization is the goal of meditation practice.

Eliminative theorists such as Steven Collins object to this interpretation that it is virtually indistinguishable from the 'pure Self' theory of Advaita, which should be the very opposite of a no-self theory. It must be remembered, however, that the Buddhist teaching pre-existed Advaita by hundreds of years, and that Sankara's Advaita probably arose precisely as an attempt to defuse the Buddhist threat to Hindu social life by incorporating its teaching into Vedanta in what was then a new way. Sankara's view has often been called crypto-Buddhist, and though that is an oversimplification, there is little doubt that Sankara was deeply influenced by Buddhist ideas.[32] It is plausible to think that before the time of Sankara, Vedanta was closer to the Sankhya philosophy of many eternal souls, existing as stable, continuous and perpetual selves, in relation to or as parts of one supreme Self, who is the creator and *Isvara*, or supremely auspicious Lord of the world.

If this is the case, the Buddhist doctrine of no-self is primarily a denial that the real essence of human being is an individual and eternal soul, which isolates every self in an ultimate and indissoluble way from every other, and which may give rise to thoughts of competition between selves, and therefore of grasping and posses-

[32] The issue is sensitively discussed in Friedhelm Hardy, *The Religious Culture of India* (Cambridge: Cambridge University Press, 1995). Cf. pp. 453–5.

sion. This would, of course, be a corruption of the Sankhya view, which is as committed to non-attachment to matter as is Buddhism. But selfishness might nevertheless be seen as a natural, if unintended, consequence of a view which gives ultimate reality to individual and distinct selves, a tendency which could be checked by the teaching that there is no self which could accumulate and possess the transient elements of experience.

The Buddhist teaching also constitutes a denial that the non-dual consciousness, which is nirvana, is properly thought of as a supreme Lord or creator and providential ruler of the universe. For Buddhism, there is no such creator, for how could a creator produce a world of greed, hatred, and delusion? No providential ruler is needed, since all sentient acts produce their natural causes and effects by the impersonal law of karma, and not even a god can with justice intervene to change that law. Non-dual consciousness is the goal, but it has no causal influence on the realm of samsara, and is thus quite different from the supreme Self of Vedanta, even in its non-dual forms.

Later forms of Mahayana do manage to find a place for the providential or beneficial acts of *bodhisattvas*, and even, in the *Karandavyuha Sutra* and in the Lotus Sutra, apparently speak of a Buddha as creating a world at the beginning of its cosmic cycle. Such complications, however, do not exist in Theravada, which can consistently teach a doctrine of no-self, while preaching the goal of a state of supreme knowledge and bliss which lies beyond the realm of birth and death and is the ultimate calming of all passions in the limpid tranquillity of nirvana.

BUDDHISM AND REBIRTH

The Buddhist account of rebirth raises a major problem of how karmic consequences are supposed to accrue to causally connected series of aggregates. In the previous chapter, I suggested that non-theists might naturally interpret karma in a forensic way, in terms of a concept of 'moral desert'. If I cause great pain to another, then it is natural to feel that I deserve an equivalent amount of great pain as punishment. If I sacrifice much to help others, then I deserve an equivalent reward, in terms of happiness, recognition, and so on. The trouble is that desert is not a physical property which can be accrued and then passed on to some other body. It does not seem to be a property at all. If I am to get what I deserve, this seems to require some being of vast knowledge and power, who can see the inner secrets of my heart, so as to know what I really deserve, and then order things so that I get what I deserve. Karma is supposed to proceed, however, without any such being, as a law-like and impersonal process. In any case, if the universe is, as Buddhists generally suppose, a realm of suffering to such a degree that it could not have been created by a good God, then how can one have any assurance that it contains such impersonal, unconscious, and yet absolutely just laws as those required by karma? There seems to be no physical mechanism by which desert could be stored and passed on, and no reason, in a universe of suffering, to think that desert has any significance in the scheme of things at all.

The very notion of karma moves one towards an idea of a morally ordered universe. One posits it because it is what justice requires. But the first holy truth of Buddhism seems to deny that the universe is just, in any absolute sense. As a realm of suffering, it could not have been created by a just God. One may think, therefore, that karmic laws could only exist if there is a personal God. If there were such a personal Judge, however, he or she might not act in the strictly retributive way that karma seems to imply, but might be more concerned with reform and discipline than with imposing suffering for past deeds. The introduction of a God undermines a quasi-mechanical or automatic interpretation of karma, and tends to replace it by the soterial idea of disciplinary and reformatory 'punishment', which will be tailored to an individual's responsiveness, and will thus lack much of the generality of law.

The doctrine of *anatta*, however, may suggest another interpretation of karma. Perhaps the idea of desert must ultimately be rejected, since it depends on the idea of a continuing self, which can later receive what it has now deserved. It may be more a matter of building habits, like practising the violin, which will, by natural processes, cause certain abilities to exist which otherwise would not have existed.[33] I can habituate myself to egoism or to compassion, and thus create a subtle body which comes to have egoistic or compassionate inclinations. In this life, I can build up ignorance and bondage to desire, or I can eliminate ignorance and desire, and that will affect the future of some sentient beings. Now the stress on per-

---

[33] Peter Harvey seems to suggest such a view, in *An Introduction to Buddhism* (Cambridge: Cambridge University Press), 41–2.

sonal liability has disappeared, and one is speaking of the way in which present actions affect future beings—and, analogously, of the way in which the acts of many past beings have caused me to be as I am.

The price of this move, which is wholly in line with Buddhist eliminative theory, is that the explanatory power of the theory of rebirth to deal with questions of human injustice and inequality is undermined. 'I' do not suffer in this life because of what 'I' did in a past life. There is suffering in this bundle of aggregates, because of past acts which were part of some past bundle. Is it morally significant that such a past bundle is causally continuous with this, or contains some items which are closely similar? Why should this bundle not be caused to be what it is by many past bundles, each more or less closely connected to me by causality and similarity? But if that is so, the rebirth theory collapses into a theory of the solidarity of consciousnesses, and the effects of their actions for good and evil upon one another.

At that point, the idea of rebirth is superfluous, since all one needs is the insight that I (one bundle of aggregates) am born with particular sorts of habit and a proneness to certain sorts of suffering largely because of the past acts of others, who are causally connected with me to various degrees. Once the enduring self drops out of the picture, no appeal to just retribution as an explanation of differing circumstances will have force. So perhaps on this issue all Buddhism needs is the acceptance that my acts will have future consequences for (someone's) suffering, and my meditation can end those consequences. The story of personal rebirth is a myth for those who cannot achieve the sophisticated understanding of the no-self theory. In this sense, Buddhism can afford to be agnostic about rebirth—that may turn out to be a speculation which is not necessary to the primary task of perceiving the nature of suffering and the way to its ending.

However, this will not quite do. One of the revisions to the doctrine of karma which Buddhism made was to see intentions, not just actions, largely of a ritual nature, as of final moral importance.[34] It is intentions which have karmic consequences, rather than actions which have causal effects in the physical world. An intention is a purely mental event, which may have no physical realization. It is

---

[34] Cf. Richard Gombrich, *Theravada Buddhism* (London: Routledge, 1988), 67–8.

intelligible that such a mental event may change the mental dispositions of the agent. What I intend today will probably affect the sorts
of things I intend in future, since it will begin to build up a habit or
disposition of my mind. Buddhist theory, however, requires that
such mental dispositions continue to have causal effects in future,
even where no apparent physical causality is involved (after the
death of the physical body). Even if literal rebirth is a myth, the
forms of mental causality required by Buddhism are not just those
of physical or social influence. They must make it possible for continuous series of aggregates (rebirths) to issue progressively in states
converging on Buddhahood (the ending of rebirth). It is hard to see
how liberation could be proclaimed as a goal if such chains of mental causality did not exist. In that fairly sophisticated sense of mental causality, rebirth is a necessary postulate of Buddhism, even
though there is no continuing self to be reborn.

This brings the deepest difficulty of Buddhist analyses of the
human person to the fore. Intentions may, on occasion, be mental
events. There can be occasions when I formulate an intention to do
something, which 'places' the intention as a background disposition to subsequent mental activity. But are intentions like pieces of
hay, which can be added to other mental events to form a 'self'? In
the case of a haystack, I can take pieces of hay from one stack and
transfer them to another, or leave them on their own, apart from
any stack. Can I do anything analogous with an intention? Suppose
I say, 'I hereby intend to write a book.' Such a thought could be had
by innumerable other persons. But could this particular intention
be had by any other person?

It belongs in a very rich and interconnected context of mental
events. The 'I' who speaks is one who has learned English, attained
a certain facility in its use, practised to achieve a certain style; who
has gained relevant information and knows what sort of book to
write and how to get it written. The intention involves a great deal
of past activity and learning, a complex array of knowledge of how
to write books, and specific ideas as to what sort of book to write
and how it might take shape. It is not an isolated thought which
could be the same thought in a very different context. If Ronald
Reagan has the intention, 'I hereby intend to write a book', that
mental event will be different, by virtue of the different background, memories, abilities, interests, and aims which are presupposed by the intention.

Each mental event grows out of a complex of past events, which are reflected in it, and is projected towards a future which involves a complex understanding of the environment, the possibilities for action it contains, and the abilities which can realize them. Mental events are internally related to many other past, present, and projected mental events. They would not be the same in another context.

So far, this account seems in accordance with the Buddhist idea of conditioned co-origination, though it heavily qualifies any 'haystack' view of human persons. But an intention is not just a mental *event*. It is a mental act. A mental event is something like having a feeling, which happens to one whether one wishes it or not. A mental act is something over which one has some control. One chooses it to occur, when there is usually an alternative: I need not intend to write a book. Such choices are (more or less) carefully considered, made as a result of knowledge and desire, but they involve a real element of decision. Can one really eliminate the notion of an agent, a subject which causally initiates such choices, and which does so in the light of knowledge which it possesses, feelings and past experiences which guide its choices, and processes of reflection and inference which it freely and consciously undertakes?

The Buddhist account, of course, accepts that there are mental phenomena called 'decisions', which have causal effects, and which are themselves dependent on many previous and concurrent mental phenomena. But it insists on seeing each decision as a momentary, though richly interconnected and manifoldly dependent phenomenon. The account also accepts that decisions will build up dispositions and habits within a particular sequence of aggregates, which affect its future. What happens within such a sequence at a particular time will largely be a result of what has occurred in it at previous times. At each moment, a new set of aggregates comes into being, the whole nature of which is causally dependent on what immediately preceded it. That set contains decisions, actions, and thoughts which will have a positive causal role in bringing about a coherently connected immediately future state of the sequence. So in what significant sense is a self being denied?

If one takes two successive states of a sequence, call them A and B, which are virtually alike in content, one may say that B is neither the same as nor different from A. 'There is neither identity nor

difference in a sequence of continuity.'[35] It is not the same, for
every element in it has ceased to be and has been replaced by
another. Yet it is not different, for the replacement is almost qualitatively identical, except for differences which have an immediate
causal basis. Because of this, it can be said that 'The perception of
impermanence, when developed and increased . . . wears down and
destroys the conceit "I am".'[36] But of course it will not destroy the
idea that there is a succession of causally connected states, whose
future partly depends upon those voluntarily exercised states which
exist in the present. It only destroys the Sankhya idea that the self
is separate from all the contents of consciousness, as something
contentless: 'In Buddhism the concept of a self, *atta*, is taken to
postulate something wholly free from phenomenal determination,
an entity independent of the process of karmic conditioning.'[37] The
agent, as continually changing and being changed, as part of the
chain of causal conditions, is not denied. The eliminative interpretation denies that there is any continuing agent, throughout one
chain of conditions. But it is possible to argue that there is such a
continuing, though constantly changing, self, which makes it possible to speak of one agency throughout a chain of conditions. This
provides a third interpretation of the doctrine of no-self, different
from both the eliminative view of Steven Collins and from the non-
dual consciousness view of Humphreys and Rhys Davids.

A BUDDHIST PROCESS VIEW OF THE SELF

Steven Collins, in arguing for the eliminative interpretation, says
that there is a very obvious continuity among the aggregates which
constitute 'one self'. As Collins puts it, 'Although consciousness is
said to change constantly, and is not thought of as a unitary or personal "soul", still it is the element whose evolution is the thread on
which continuity and the series of lives-in-*samsara* are woven.'[38]
There is something which gives continuity to a specific sequence,
and enables one to speak of 'one consciousness'. He later states that
there is 'simply a string of beads—some of which are moments of
consciousness functioning, some of which are "unconscious" *bha-
vanga*-mind—which have no underlying connecting thread.'[39] The
elements are, however, united in one consciousness, within which

---

[35] *Visuddhimagga*, 17. 17.   [36] *Samyutta Nikaya*, 155–6.
[37] Collins, *Selfless Persons*, 95.   [38] Ibid. 214.   [39] Ibid. 248.

they have well-defined causal relationships, and it is these that give to notions of responsibility and desert their meaning.

When one says that one must punish the same person as the one who committed a crime, one is not committed to the view that there is some literally identical element, existing unchanged between the two states. Such a thing is strictly impossible by definition, since the states will be different in at least one property, the time at which they exist. Yet one does not want to punish a person who has no connection with the crime. If one causes a harmful state within a sequence of aggregates—a physical body; dispositions to feel, perceive, act, and think; memories and beliefs; feelings and perceptions—all of which are quite different from those of the sequence in which a voluntary crime was committed, then one can say that one would be punishing a different person from the criminal. There must be some differences, but there must be limits to those differences. The question is what those limits are.

Steven Collins suggests that for the Buddhist view it is consciousness, itself a continuously replicating set of momentary states, which in some way provides the factor of continuity which is required. Leaving aside the body for the moment, all the other aggregates are what might be called mental elements. Mental elements fall into sequences, within which they have relations with one another that they do not have to similar elements in other sequences. One of 'my' feelings is related to other mental events in 'my' consciousness in ways in which it is not related to 'other people's' thoughts and feelings. The pronouns are put in inverted commas to remind one that what is being spoken of is not discrete selves, but sequences of mental elements. Just as many physical events are bound together by being in one continuous space-time, so mental events are related as members of some consciousness. A spatial relation is a particular relation that can have boundaries. So a consciousness relation may have boundaries, but connect all events 'in' it in a particular way. But in what way? One may just have to say that 'being members of one consciousness' is a logically primitive relation, not capable of being further analysed or defined. Though there is no separate agent, as an immaterial substance above the flux of causality, change, and dependence, still there are many momentary free and voluntary acts, closely correlated with distinctive perceptions of intending and acting. Such acts are inseparable from perceptions and beliefs, and stand to them in the relation of being members of one sequence of mental elements, one consciousness.

Within that stream of consciousness, the two elements that are central to the idea of continuing identity are those of character and memory.[40] It is memories which provide the similarity of content between conscious states that helps one to identify them as states of the same consciousness. It is character, comprising all those sets of capacities and dispositions to act, normally modified and shaped over many years, that provides the similarity of causal base between conscious states of the same person. During one earthly life, continuity of body is also important to personal survival, but that is not a feature which can obtain throughout a series of earthly lives. So it is not an essential part of the Buddhist analysis.

If one thinks of personal beings who become trapped in greed, hatred, and delusion, it is easy to think of them as progressively degenerating into selves for which connectedness of memory and character, of mental content and its causal base, is lost. They may sink to a state in which disconnected fragments of memory coexist with aimless and unfocused habits of uncontrolled action. They may begin to dissolve into disconnected bundles of passions and desires, the whole personality losing its central coherence. One may say, at that stage, that they cease to be persons, rational self-shaping unitary agents, and thus at last they cease to be, leaving only incoherent desires and obsessive mental states in increasingly fragmentary co-conscious sequences, not even fully remembered or consciously recognized any longer. In this way, wholly evil persons, if there are any, may eventually cease to be, by progressive self-annihilation.

On the other hand, one can also envisage what is needed for the healing of such disintegration and for the establishment of greater self-control and fuller personhood. A sequence of conscious states needs to be brought to fuller self-awareness and insight, to be brought to comprehend its nature, control it, and unify the personality around a coherent set of long-term projects, undertaken in full awareness of the conditions which make those projects possible and desirable. One may be helped on the path to such integration by compassionate teachers who understand the factors which conduce

---

[40] A good discussion of these issues—though I do not agree with the conclusions—is found in: Derek Parfit, *Reasons and Persons* (Oxford: Clarendon, 1984), Pt. 3.

to greed, hatred, and ignorance, and the way to liberation from their influence.

Personhood, on this view, is a matter of degree. It can be impaired or lost, and it can be brought to greater perfection. That perfection will include complete mindfulness, knowledge of the arising and passing away of beings, freedom from egoistic desire, and transcendent bliss. On such a view, the self which is denied is not a continuing subject of action and experience, as such, but the linkage of this self with a possessive attachment to a particular physical life and body. 'There is a greed that fixes on the individual body-mind.'[41] One sees oneself as a particular body, with desires and anxieties, bound to a particular set of worries and concerns. To see oneself as a 'self', in this sense, is to identify with a set of desires and possessions that define what one is. What enlightenment brings one to see is that there is no fixed immutable content to this self, but a continuing flow of desires and actions. If the subject is freed from its imagined identification with some particular set of pleasant feelings or some states which it thinks it can possess for ever, then it has 'gone beyond all the states of being and of becoming'.[42]

Rahula writes: 'What in general is suggested by Soul . . . is that in man there is a permanent, everlasting and absolute entity, which is the unchanging substance behind the changing phenomenal world.'[43] If this is the case, then the soul that the Buddha, in his historical context, rejects is either the uncreated, eternal, and immutable atman which is one with Absolute Reality, Brahman, or an entity which is not involved intrinsically with matter, and finds its truest reality in isolation from matter. Such a self would not account for the dynamic flow and causal interconnectedness of all elements. Even the subject is in continual dynamic change. It continues as a flow of actions and experiences, and is either bound to greed, hatred, and delusion, or liberated in omniscience and universal compassion. The 'flow' may continue beyond samsara, but in a way that is purely other-orientated, to the welfare of all beings. Such a self, the subject of a continuing dynamic stream of elements, whether attached to birth and death by desire or acting in compassion beyond rebirth, is not that which the Buddha denies.

It fits well with this Buddhist outlook to say that all sentient beings are what might be called process-selves, in this sense.

---

[41] *Sutta-Nipata*, 1100 (p. 127).   [42] Ibid. 1133 (p. 131).
[43] W. Rahula, *What the Buddha Taught* (Bedford: Gordon Fraser, 1967), 51.

Human beings do not have a special 'soul' that all other animals lack. Yet the form of subjectivity in humans is such that it makes liberation possible, in a way that it is not for most other animals. It is humans who can learn the truth of *dukkha*, who can practise right thought, action, and meditation, and who can achieve the desire-less state. That is because the degree of conceptual understanding, self-knowledge, and mental control possible for them is much greater than for most animals, which are largely bound by sense-perception and instinct.

It is natural to envisage a hierarchy of selves, and Buddhist cosmology often thinks of a series of *loka*s or realms (conventionally six), from hellish and ghost worlds, through the earth, to heavenly bliss-realms of the gods and *bodhisattvas*. In the lowest realms there are beings which have virtually no conceptual understanding, who are wholly immersed in sensory desires, whose personalities are divided and uncontrollable, and whose memories are incoherent and focused on pain and resentment, causing age-long bitterness. In the highest realms are beings who understand the causes of all things, who are free of desires, perfectly self-controlled, with perfected memories, transfigured by the bliss of being, untroubled by desire and decay. Beyond the six realms there is the state of complete liberation, unimaginable by us, beyond the possibility of suffering and death, which is the ultimate human goal.

This enables one to construct the idea of a person as a discrete succession of free acts, cognitive states, and dispositions, closely correlated, in continual flux, and united to one another by the logically primitive relation of co-consciousness. The Buddha teaches that such succession is driven by desire or attachment, and inevitably results in suffering of three main kinds—bodily and mental pain, and the realization that impermanence and bondage to causal conditions are as such imperfections.[44] When desire is blown out, suffering ceases, and the flow of experience can be seen in a very different way, even in this life. After life, it can expand to embrace knowledge and experience of more expansive and radiant realms of being, and it comes to have that character of freedom and bliss which can be characterized as nirvana.

The notion of a succession of co-conscious mental acts and states is certainly different from any idea of the self as a permanent and

[44] *Visuddhimagga*, 16. 34.

unchanging substance. But does it not presuppose the idea of the self as a subject of action and experience? Does the belief that there is unconditioned awareness and freedom not presuppose that there is something more to human being than just a bundle of nameable aggregates, a 'more' which is a subject, either of transient, sensory states, with which it wrongly identifies itself, or of an unconditioned awareness, which is its essential nature? This subject can be thought of as being continually replicated or replaced by a similar subject in successive moments, and as constantly changing in content, but it is not wholly reducible to the elements taken as items of consciousness. The subject only exists as the agent or experient of specific contents, but the acts and states require a unitary agent in order to form elements of one rational conscious life.

Even at one temporal moment of conscious life, there is a uniting agent, who concentrates, recalls, recognizes, enquires, and understands more or less well. This sense of activity, and therefore of an agent, is essential to the most primitive form of experiential knowledge. It will thus exist in every form of being in which experiential knowledge exists. As one thinks of a succession of overlapping moments in time, this noetic activity will extend through memory and anticipation, so that one has to think of one agent which continues from moment to moment (or which is continually re-created in each successive moment). That agent, the subject of action and experience in every noetic being, is the process-self. Its continuing noetic activity is what makes co-conscious states apprehensible as members of one consciousness.

While there is no distinct, enduring, immutable substantial self, it can be said that I, the agent of knowledge, remember, intend, and feel, and thus I actively connect various events within one consciousness. Even when a relatively passive emotion occurs, the way I interpret it depends on past cognitive activity. I cannot, for instance, feel guilty, if I have no idea of having done an act which I know to be wrong, and need not have done—a very complex set of beliefs, imported into the interpretation of the feeling. In every consciousness, I must connect a mental event to others, remember many past events, recognize present ones in terms of them, and anticipate the future outcome to some extent. Conscious experience is essentially active, and requires a discriminating, recognizing, and evaluating agent, which is the subject of all events which are members of one consciousness.

It is false to say that one can never apprehend this subject, since one can apprehend it as causally active in every reflective activity. Of course, one can never observe it enduring, as one can a physical object.[45] But if I apprehend myself as an active element in every one of a series of mental acts, then I must conceive of myself as the same agent, to the extent that mental acts are members of the same consciousness. If I have long-term intentions—say, to write a symphony—then that intention is spread out over a long time, and it is the same subject who first forms the intention, then sustains and at last completes it in finished action. To the extent that mental acts overlap, in guiding the development of one consciousness, one must speak of the same subject of experience and action as continuing.

In so far as Buddhism works with the idea of a process-self, it should not be seen as a view which holds there is no self at all, over against a view which holds there is one immutable and indestructible self, beyond the temporal flow. The process-self which lies between these extremes is a dynamic, ceaselessly active subject, its content in constant change. It is prone to egoistic attachment, but can also be free to participate in the flow of ideas and perceptions without such attachment, acting with compassion and without self-regard. Nirvana can be experienced even within the flow of samsara, when the subject experiences without anxiety or obsessive desire, and when it acts without desire for personal gain or aggrandisement. The Buddhist theory of *anatta* does not, in this form, hold that there is nothing to be egoistic about, no ego—which would make egoism incoherent. It holds that there is no isolated and enduring receptacle of sensory pleasure, which can possess and retain such pleasure for ever, ignoring all others. There is no permanent, inherently existing, isolated self. There is only the transient flow of interdependent selves-in-relation, process-selves in ceaseless change and dynamic interplay, free to move into the future by continual interaction and exchange of information—or bound by attachment to the past, by mutual hostility and isolated secrecy.

There is here a third interpretation of nirvana, in addition to the eliminative view of cessation of desire, and the *Abhidharma* view of non-dual consciousness. It is one form of the Mahayana view,

---

[45] This is the point made much of by David Hume, *A Treatise of Human Nature* (first pub. 1738), i. 4. 6.

shared in different ways by Madhyamaka and Yogacara schools, of a 'non-abiding nirvana', attained by the Bodhisattva path of liberating all sentient beings from suffering.[46] This also involves a form of non-dual consciousness, which is not conceptually describable, but that consciousness is consciousness of the unceasing flow of experience, now a 'pure radiant flow'.[47] It is not consciousness of some absolute reality, or some reality which is inherently self-existent. The Mahayana doctrine of emptiness teaches that no element of experience or of reality is self-existent. All elements are caused and conditioned by other elements, and rest on no unchanging foundation (such as Brahman). Even the 'mind only' school of Yogacara does not regard mind as an unchanging substratum. Mind is precisely the flow itself: 'Even nirvana, I say, is like a magical illusion, is like a dream.'[48] There is nothing but the flow of experiences. The division of the world into subjects and objects, as polarized realities, is illusory. Samsaric experience is the making of such a division, and the formation of a concept of Self, which mistakenly thinks that it can possess elements of experience as its own. When this conception is overcome, there is nirvana, the non-attached comprehension of the radiant and purified flow.

One undertakes the *bodhisattva* path for the sake of all sentient beings, undertaking a way of giving, patience, effort, concentration, and wisdom. As one approaches and eventually attains Buddhahood, one attains infinite awareness and compassion, and finds oneself in a world of infinite Buddhas and Buddha-realms, all interpenetrating and engaged in compassionate action, in purifying their Buddha-fields, and resting in unlimited awareness and omniscience.

From such views arise the Pure Land cults of Buddhism, which aim to visualize living Buddhas in their pure lands, and find rebirth in those lands, worlds of flowers and music, where all is beauty and wisdom. While an Absolute Self is denied, one has infinite numbers of omniscient and compassionate enlightened beings, and the material universe becomes the seed-ground for generating and bringing to maturity countless Buddhas, often with the help of *bodhisattvas* such as Maitreya or Amitabha.

---

[46] Cf. Paul Williams, *Mahayana Buddhism* (London: Routledge, 1989), 52–4.

[47] The phrase is from Williams, ibid. 94.

[48] *Prajna-paramita Sutra, The Perfection of Wisdom in 8,000 Lines*, Eng. trans. E. Conze (Bolinas: Four Seasons Foundation, 1973), 99.

From this perspective, instead of thinking of 'perfect selflessness' as not being really related to anything else, being beyond dualities of every kind, one might think of it as being selflessly, compassionately, related to everything that is. The perfected person would extend its mind to all finite beings in kindness and compassion, and would seek to bring them to the highest perfection possible for them, in ways that enhanced, and did not impede, their freedom. Thus it would desire all beings to be related to one another by compassion, and to be helped by awareness of its creative power, unlimited wisdom, and unrestrictedly sympathetic joy.

LIBERATION IN BUDDHIST AND HINDU TRADITIONS

There are thus at least three diverse interpretations of the self in classical Buddhist thought. The first is the eliminative view, that the self consists in nothing but the flow of aggregates, which enlightenment will bring to an end. The second is the non-dual consciousness view, that the bound self wrongly thinks it is a particular mind and body, whereas the liberated self knows itself to be an unconditioned state of bliss, knowledge, and compassion, beyond all dualities of subject and object. The third is the radiant flow view, that one may speak of an agent and experiencing self, not as an unchanging substratum, but as a continually changing process of agency and experience which, in the liberated state, is to be experienced as the pure radiant flow of a universally related pattern of action and experience.

The first or second view tends to be favoured by Theravadins, who are primarily concerned with release from the unsatisfactoriness of attachments here and now. They typically refuse to speculate about what might lie hereafter. To do so is taken to be a sign of egoistic self-concern or of obsessive desire for intellectually correct views. That is not conducive to enlightenment, which lies in attaining cool limpidity of mind in this life. The third view is mostly found in Mahayana traditions, which have a much greater commitment to positing some form of existence for the liberated self, because of three distinctive doctrines which developed in those traditions. First, there are innumerable Buddhas who can help suffering beings in this life, and who thus obviously exist in some sense. Second, it is said that all beings can become Buddhas, so that there is a sort of personal immortality held out as a (non-egoistically) desirable goal. Third, each being contains the 'extremely subtle body' of the Buddha-nature within it, as the heart of its being. It is that which exists as hidden in the conditioned state and as free in the liberated state.

In Mahayana belief, when a sentient being becomes a *bodhisattva*, it acts over a vast field of action for the welfare of beings, has knowledge which transcends external sense-perception, and enjoys a bliss which is not dependent on transient events. The self that does not exist is this cramped ego, in its disintegrated personality and crumbling body. The self that most truly exists is the liberated subject of knowledge of all worlds, the agent of endless compassionate acts, and the enjoyer of supreme bliss. On the way to final liberation, the self, with its subtle body of dispositions, repressed memories, and accumulated merit, takes material existence in many physical bodies, in each of which it is more (or less) easy to achieve final liberation. When, in this tradition, it is said that 'All will become Buddhas',[49] the thought is not that these dynamic selves will cease to exist, but that they will transcend their physical forms completely, and exist in a state of expanded knowledge, compassion, and bliss which is virtually impossible to describe in presently available concepts.

The doctrine of no-self, in all its interpretations, is held to be primarily practical in import, being concerned with overcoming selfishness, rather than with engaging in speculation. That practical concern is very salutary, and I have some sympathy with the view that commitments to speculative dogmas can lead to argumentative and divisive attitudes. I have suggested, however, that Buddhist doctrines of liberation cannot be wholly free of speculative views, including especially that of rebirth. Moreover, one might well wonder if it is really the case that belief in the existence of an eternal self is quite as harmful as some Buddhists seem to hold. Rahula holds that 'the idea of self is an imaginary, false belief . . . which produces harmful thoughts of 'me' and 'mine', selfish desire, craving, attachment . . . to this false view can be traced all the evil in the world'.[50] It does not seem to be the case, however, that any of the varied ideas of self to be found in the great Indian religious traditions can be held responsible for such effects. Advaita, for example, certainly

---

[49] *Scripture of the Lotus Blossom of the Fine Dharma* (Lotus Sutra), trans. L. Hurvitz (New York: Columbia University Press, 1976), stanza 2.

[50] Rahula, *What the Buddha Taught*, 51.

asserts the existence of one unchanging substance beyond the phenomenal world, but it is hard to see how this might generate egoism. On the contrary, it aims to bring embodied souls to see that they are all parts of one reality, and that divisions between souls are unreal.

Sankhya, though it holds that there is an infinite number of distinct souls, teaches that the true self of each person is to be distinguished from the body and from the desiring subject. The true self can only be released from bondage by desireless action, and so this belief, too, can hardly be accused of encouraging egoism. Vaishnavas certainly hold that every soul is eternal, and they look for a continued existence in a spiritual realm in which there are at least analogies of sensory experiences, which are finally good and desirable. But one can only enter that Goloka realm by completely transcending desire for this material realm and putting oneself wholly at the service of the Lord. It is hard to see how such a belief in an eternal self leads to egoism. Indeed, there can be a certain initially surprising convergence between the Buddhist insistence on the renunciation of the idea of self and the Vaishnava doctrine that the finite self can only be fulfilled in devotion to the supreme Self. Both insist that the self lives falsely in so far as it thinks that it can gain enjoyment for itself, as an isolated experient. Liberated existence is the orientation of the self beyond its individual existence to a suprapersonal state of knowledge, compassion, and bliss. Vaishnavas identify this state with Krishna, the supreme Self, whereas Buddhists tend to view it as an impersonal state of being, beyond duality.

The Buddha teaches that whatever comes to be is of a nature to cease, and whatever becomes conscious of its own transient and dependent being is liable to grasp at permanence and inherent existence. Thereby arises the delusion of the inherently existing self, concerned for its own pleasure through the stimulus of feeling, in competition with all others, and constantly fearing its own injury or cessation at the hands of others. Liberation comes by giving up this craving for permanence, and the doctrine of no-self exists primarily to aid the process of giving up.

For Vaishnavas, it is also a delusion to believe in an inherently existing, permanent, and self-sustaining self. That illusion can be overcome, however, by cultivating a strong sense of utter dependence on the supreme Self, source of all being and goodness. Seen in this light, these are different ways of overcoming egoism and attaining supreme wisdom and compassion.

There is no doubt that devotional theists such as the Vaishnavas have a stronger sense than Theravada Buddhists of 'the uncompounded' as exhibiting active compassion. The Buddha does, however, exhibit universal compassion, and the monk aims to 'live pervading the entire world with a mind like the Ganges, abundantly, boundlessly, unrestrictedly, peaceably, benevolently'.[51] The Buddha spreads thoughts joined to compassion, to gladness, to equanimity. He turns the wheel of dharma, for the liberation of all sentient beings. Because of this, Buddhists rightly object to the frequent accusation that their path of liberation is selfish, concerned paradoxically only with personal freedom from the bondage of self. Yet in the end all persons are responsible for their own destiny, and the Buddha can do no more than teach and show the path by example. It is always good to help others in material ways. But the highest way is to renounce all worldly ties and become a forest-dweller, thereby showing the way to release for all sentient beings. A doctrine of unitive, divine love which might actively co-operate in bringing humans to release from suffering sits uncomfortably with Buddhist dharma, especially in its Theravadin form.

There, the path to liberation is one of strict moral and meditational training, bringing the mind to a state of 'energy, joy, repose, concentration, equanimity'.[52] The true brahmin, says Gotama in one text, is one 'who has and holds to nothing . . . strong in patience . . . without anger . . . not stained by worldly pursuit . . . deep in wisdom, intelligent, knowledgeable . . . who is immersed in the deathless . . . emptied of doubt, unattached and cool'.[53] If the dharma is a raft for bringing one to such a state, for crossing over and not for holding onto, then it is a method well designed to bring one to know 'what is unborn, ageless, disease-free, immortal, unsorrowing and incorruptible—the matchless haven from bondage, (that is) *nirvana*'.[54] This is a method which leads to a state which theists might well see as at least part of the meaning of union with God, free of the anthropomorphic limitations which so often disfigure popular ideas of God. But it is certainly not a path which leads to an ecstatic relationship of love with a personal God.

[51] *Discourses*, Discourse 21, p. 59. [52] Ibid., Discourse 2, p. 5.
[53] Ibid., Discourse 98, p. 305. [54] Ibid., Discourse 26, p. 75.

In traditional Buddhist teaching the path of liberation is only possible within the *sangha*, the community of monks or nuns. In the ideal *sangha*, the monk is assured of enlightenment in no more than seven lives. In those lives, he must gradually ascend through the stages of meditative insight, through the four levels of absorption, the awareness of infinite space, infinite consciousness, nothingness, the realm of neither perceiving nor not perceiving, and finally to nirvana, the cessation of all attachments. He must be wholly committed to celibacy, poverty, and membership of the *sangha*. For the lay follower, what is to be hoped for is a better birth, perhaps into a Pure Land or heaven-world. For the householder, nirvana must be a distant goal. But that is not a distressing matter, since even Gotama required many lifetimes before he achieved enlightenment, and, given good intentions and the accumulation of merit, final enlightenment is assured.

For theists who believe in a loving God who is able actively to help human beings, it is easier to develop a view that release can be achieved in just one lifetime, not by ascetic heroism, but by an action of divine love. The soul has become trapped in a humanly constructed realm of attachment and suffering. The only way to liberation is by undermining the structures of attachment. Since these are created by human souls, however, what must be destroyed are the self-regarding desires that create them. How can they be destroyed, without destroying the souls in which they are rooted? Souls must come to wish for self-regard to be destroyed in them. They must come to see the consequences of self-regard—suffering for sentient beings—and wish to renounce them. Sincere renunciation certainly entails resolute striving for perfection. At this point the possibility is formulated that one may rely on a power not one's own, which can transform self-regard into selfless compassion. This requires a union of trust and faith with a power which can renew the roots of human motivation and action, which can shape the pliant self into a channel for universal beneficence.

While that may seem to be a pre-eminently theistic belief, the doctrine of the compassionate *bodhisattvas* exists to meet the same requirement.[55] The *bodhisattvas* are beings of unlimited compassion. They have themselves suffered through innumerable past lives

[55] An exposition of the development of devotional cults in Buddhism which are based on the *bodhisattva* doctrine can be found in Williams, *Mahayana Buddhism*, ch. 10.

in the realms of rebirth. They have undertaken a vow to dedicate many lifetimes to liberating all sentient beings. In that sense they can be said to have freely accepted suffering for the sake of sentient beings. In a rather similar way, a creator god could choose to bear or permit the sufferings of sentient beings patiently, so that god may persuade souls to the path of liberation. Such persuasion would require that the supreme Lord in some way makes clear the suffering caused by attachment, and acts to make clear the path of liberation from suffering, by manifesting its own divine nature as the true object of self-renouncing love. The suffering of the *bodhisattva* is, similarly, the patience of supreme compassion, which never ceases to strive for the turning of all sentient beings towards the true source and goal of their being.

Such turning is never instantaneous and complete. Beings can be established on the path, can become enterers on the stream, by their repentance and faith in the power of the Buddha to bring them to nirvana. Beings can be united with the one who will bring them to their proper fulfilment of being; they can see what that fulfilment will be; they can catch glimpses of it in their own lives. But they remain always dependent on that power that promises fulfilment, by its patience and by its demonstration that there is release and there is a way to release, established in the realm of imprisoned selves, completed through the power of grace, which is established in the world through the presence of the Liberator in the realm of samsara. In this way, Mahayana developed the idea of the compassionate *bodhisattva*, who defers final nirvana for the sake of all sentient beings, and who is the object of faith and trust for beings unable to achieve liberation by their own power. This parallels the theistic portrayal of a compassionate God.

As has been pointed out, there is a tension between the idea of strict karmic causality and the idea of merit, by which unskilful acts can be wiped out by, for instance, giving robes to the monks, with the right intention. Like most religions, Buddhism can give rise to rather mechanical notions of moral causality, according to which wrongdoing builds up an accumulation of bad karma, which can be wiped out by the ritual repetition of mantras, by calling on the name of Avolekitesvara, or by ascetic practices. Wrong is seen as being like dirt, which can be wiped away by various means. On a more sophisticated view, wrongdoing traps the soul in greed, hatred, and ignorance, and what is needed to counteract its effects is renunciation, compassion, and wisdom. What is important in the recitation of mantras, for example, is the right intention, which is to follow the path of renunciation of self. For this, disciples need faith in the three refuges, the Buddha, the dharma, and the *sangha*. Such faith does not replace the necessity for good deeds, but it makes the performance of such deeds easier. It is a small step to suggest that faith in the Buddha allows him to act, out of compassion, to unite the soul to his own truth-nature, not only to teach but to help the soul's progress towards enlightenment.

BUDDHIST AND HINDU VIEWS OF THE IMPORTANCE OF INDIVIDUALITY

Nevertheless, there remains an almost complete lack, at least in Theravada Buddhism, of an ideal of ultimate individuality, diversity, and community. The goal seems to be, not a creative community of agent-subjects, but the calm of the limpid pool wherein all sense of individuality has been long transcended, and all activity has ceased in complete freedom from desire. There is no enduring individuality, and the succession of thoughts, feelings, and sensations that we call a 'self' comes to an end with the realization of pure, objectless bliss.

Personal happiness is not rejected by Buddhism: 'One does not stain one's unstained mind [by ascetic suffering] nor reject rightful happiness. (Yet) one is not intoxicated with that happiness.'[56] In the end one must renounce all attachment to what is finite and compounded. 'It cannot be, that a man of (right) view should treat any compounded thing as permanent, should treat any compounded state as happy, should treat any compounded thing as self.'[57] The attainment of final nirvana is a passing beyond the compounded. Thus, 'the Exemplar is freed from the designation of (physical) form. Deep, immeasurable, unfathomable as the great ocean, neither "arises" nor "does not arise", nor (both) nor (neither) is applicable'.[58] What is renounced is a self that was always a delusion. What is found is a state beyond the finite, 'transcending logic, subtle, intelligible (only) to the wise'.[59]

There is an obvious difference between the Vaishnava assertion that there is, in the Goloka realm, a form of finite experience which

---

[56] *Discourse*, Discourse 101, p. 316.
[58] Ibid., Discourse 72, p. 211.
[57] Ibid., Discourse 115, p. 357.
[59] Ibid.

is finally good and desirable, and which will endure for ever, and the Buddhist assertion that 'from the arising of delight comes the arising of suffering . . . from the ceasing of delight comes the ceasing of suffering', so that eventually all individual delight must cease.[60]

Vaishnavas cannot say that finite existence is in itself unsatisfactory, inevitably giving rise to suffering and attachment. Even if this material world is created for beings which have somehow fallen from divine grace, the creation of a finite Goloka realm itself is good, and it is to such a realm that the soul proceeds at the time of liberation. It is true that the material world is a realm of suffering, and to be transcended. But it is a corruption or shadow of a realm of true individuality, where interpersonal love can flourish.

For Buddhists, suffering seems to be inevitable in all individual existence as such. For Vaishnavas, the existence of suffering in this material order is explained as due to the genesis of desire in some created souls, which leads to attachment to the material world, and subsequently to ignorance of their true spiritual nature. When that attachment is overcome, there can be a form of individual existence without suffering.

There is one sutra in the Buddhist canon which seems to suggest a similar view. The *Agganna Sutta, Digha Nikaya* (III. 80–98), does suggest that this universe began when a group of radiant beings became greedy to taste the pleasures of the material realm, and so fell into the earthly life of greed and selfishness. Richard Gombrich, however, thinks that this account is satirical, and so does not offer a serious account of how suffering begins.[61] Even if it did, the existence of the radiant beings, and of the material realm with all its suffering, remains unexplained. These are just ultimate, brute facts. How, a Buddhist may say, could a God help, since God, too, must be an ultimate brute fact? There is clearly the possibility, in Buddhist tradition, that this earth itself is a realm into which previously existing beings fall by desire for worldly pleasure, and such desire is something that tends to arise wherever there is consciousness. But there is also the possibility that sentience simply arises for no particular reason; and when it does it brings suffering and attachment inevitably in its train. Either way, it seems that there is

[60] Ibid., Discourse 145, p. 435.   [61] Gombrich, *Theravada Buddhism*, 85.

after all an unresolved problem of suffering in Buddhism. But a Buddhist might say that there is simply no explanation, and cannot be one, for ultimate brute facts, and that at least Buddhists do not have to complicate the story by introducing an allegedly perfect creator of the whole process.

If samsaric existence intrinsically has the nature of suffering, and if suffering is caused by attachment, Buddhism seems committed to a doctrine of original evil, if not original sin. 'Uncertainty, habits [or conventions], impulse towards worldly pursuits and ill-will are innate in [a small baby].[62] Those who come to birth as humans are already in thrall to the threefold bondage of greed, hatred, and ignorance. It takes many years of striving to achieve release. This will continue to be true, as long as humans continue to be born. So it seems clear that, while earth continues, suffering and evil will continue.

This raises special difficulties for the Mahayana view that all beings can become Buddhas, since there will always be an infinite number of future beings who are not yet Buddhas. So *bodhisattva*s, who take a vow not to enter nirvana until all suffering beings have achieved release, will never be able to enter final nirvana, and there will never be any Buddhas at all. There will always be an infinite number of *bodhisattva*s and an infinite number of suffering beings.

However, one can turn this difficulty into the positive proclamation that there will always be more beings to become *bodhisattva*s, and in fact the *bodhisattva*-stage of joy and compassion may be the highest one would wish to attain. In the Mahayana tradition, one can distinguish at least two sorts of nirvana. There is the sort of nirvana attained by *pratyekebuddha*s, those who aim at liberation from sorrow by a life of solitary meditation and renunciation (those, of course, who belong to the non-Mahayana traditions!). But there is a higher sort of nirvana, non-abiding nirvana (*apratisthitanirvana*), which is altogether beyond the duality of samsara and nirvana. In it, one attains freedom from suffering without abandoning those in samsara. Then, one will not think of *bodhisattva*s as 'postponing nirvana', but as embarked upon a path of meditation and purification which culminates in entering into what is in fact a higher form of nirvana, characterized by compassion for all beings, and associ-

[62] *Discourses*, Discourse 64, p. 187.

ated with the vow: 'I will lead to Nirvana the whole immeasurable world of beings.'[63] The nirvana to which all beings are led is precisely the nirvana of universally compassionate beings, who exist in infinite realms and in infinite interpenetration, forever engaged in acts of compassion, and emanating innumerable further Buddhas and *bodhisattva*s, who continue endlessly to lead many from suffering to compassionate bliss.[64]

For this developed Mahayana view, each life is surrounded by an infinite number of compassionate and well-wishing beings, ready to help one to achieve liberation. One can turn the apparently pessimistic view of everlasting samsara into the more optimistic thought that all suffering creatures, however many there are, will become beings of joy and compassion. So Mahayana can adopt a very positive and optimistic world-view which, while being extremely reticent about the liberated state, offers much more scope for speaking of community and activity. Even in Mahayana, however, there is a drawing-back from speaking of liberation as a fulfilment of the potentialities of a present embodied self. The Buddhas are 'oceans of virtues with unlimited aspects',[65] yet there are no enduring minds, and, for the Madhyamaka school, the ultimate truth is emptiness (*sunyata*). This may, of course, connote some inconceivable interpenetration of all liberated beings in a dynamic and ever-changing series of wise and compassionate activities. If the life of the liberated soul is interpreted by Vaishnavas as a transformation of egoistic personality into a wholly loving union with a divine being of supreme compassion and bliss, there is a possibility at this point, also, of a significant convergence between the traditions.

Theravadins, virtually the only surviving non-Mahayana school, are mainly distinguished by not having a doctrine of compassionate *bodhisattva*s or of ever-living Buddhas. They are not generally committed to the view that all sentient beings will become Buddhas, so they are not faced with the Mahayana paradox of holding both that there is endless suffering and that there is universal final release. They stress the necessity of achieving liberation by 'own-power',

---

[63] Conze (trans.), *The Perfection of Wisdom*, 163.

[64] This view is taken by the Hua-yen, or 'flower-garland' school, and is expounded in the *Avatamsaka Sutra*, trans. T. Cleary, as *The Flower Ornament Scripture* (Boulder, Col.: Shambhala Press, 1984–).

[65] Santideva, *Bodhicaryavatara*, 6. 116, trans. Kate Crosby and Andrew Skilton (Oxford: Oxford University Press, 1996), 60.

and see the process of liberation as continuing through many lives of suffering. Yet they strongly deny Mahayanist objections that their view is 'negative', since they are aiming at an achievable goal of final wisdom and the highest sort of happiness there is. Similarly, they object to being called 'selfish', since by their teaching and example they show others the only way to release. After all, they claim, that is all that alleged *bodhisattva*s can actually do that is of value to anyone. They agree, however, that there is a goal for human existence, and that the goal is attainable. It is a goal of supreme wisdom and bliss, and such wisdom and bliss can be experienced, to some extent, even in this life. Thus earthly life is not just a realm of suffering. It is the arena in which endless bliss can be won, by a path of resolute human striving. Theravada may be at a very different point on a continuum of beliefs about the self, its bondage and liberation, from both Mahayana and Vaishnava schools, but it is on what is recognizably the same continuum.

This discussion has brought out a range of oppositions between Vaishnava and Theravadin religious beliefs. Vaishnava theists hold that there is a created realm of individual and communal existence which is good and intrinsically desirable, whereas Theravadins hold that all conditioned existence is unsatisfactory and not to be desired. Vaishnavas hold that individual souls are eternal and some of them fall into egoism by rejection of divine love, whereas Theravadins hold that there are no eternal souls, that individual existence intrinsically has the nature of suffering, and that it must be transcended. Vaishnavas hold that liberation is attained by the grace of a compassionate Lord, whereas Theravadins hold that liberation is attained by resolute striving over many lifetimes.

There are convergences as well as oppositions, however, and these become much stronger when Mahayana Buddhist traditions are considered. After all, Vaishnavas do think that this material universe is not to be desired, and Pure Land Buddhists hope for rebirth in Buddha lands of beauty and bliss. Vaishnavas believe that one should not identify the self with this particular earthly body and personality, and Mahayana Buddhists hope, not for extinction, but to become enlightened beings of infinite knowledge, compassion, and bliss. Vaishnavas believe that even the love of Krishna requires prolonged meditation, ascetic practice, and discipline, and many Mahayana Buddhists pray for the aid of the compassionate *bodhisattva*s, who can release them from the bonds of karmic justice.

Oppositions exist in religion in abundance, and as soon as one set of oppositions dissolves, another set arises. What would be misleading would be to regard different traditions as locked into an unchanging and definite set of oppositions, with no possibility of development or convergence in and between traditions. One of the things that this discussion shows is that there do exist very different analyses of human nature within the Indian religious traditions. But any particular tradition has a certain fluidity and varying degrees of responsiveness to changing contexts and to other traditions. One can draw distinctions between doctrines. One cannot insist that such clear distinctions will continue to correlate with unchanging religious traditions. On the contrary, one can show by historical investigation that interpretations of doctrine are in constant change, as traditions continue to redefine themselves.

It does seem to be the case, however, that Buddhist analyses of human nature share with most Indian traditions a theory of mentalistic causation which underlies the possibility of karma and rebirth. Such a theory is common to virtually all forms of Indian religion, whether they are one-self, many-self, or no-self in form. The Indian traditions contrast, in this respect, with the Semitic traditions, which have no doctrine of rebirth, and which regard material, bodily existence as having much more causal importance in their analysis of human nature.

From this point of view, Buddhist analyses seem particularly hard to reconcile with scientific views of the human mind and brain. In particular, it would be difficult for a Buddhist to accept the evolutionary account of the emergence of mind from a material substratum which typifies the scientific world-view. The Semitic traditions, which typically tie human identity much more closely to particular material states, do not have such severe difficulties, though of course they were formed in cultures which had no idea of evolutionary theory. Indeed, some have argued that no religious view is compatible with an evolutionary account. For, they claim, modern science relies on a materialist view of human nature that eliminates consciousness—denying not just an eternal self, as Buddhists do, but thought, feeling, and consciousness as independent elements of human nature. Thus it eliminates any meaningful idea of a 'soul' or spiritual self at all. That is an extreme view, but it is one that should be assessed in any attempt to see the plausibility of a religious account of human nature in the light of modern science. One needs to assess the extent to which such a view would in fact make a religious account impossible. Consequently, it is one such interpretation of the data of evolutionary natural science that will be examined next.

6

Evolutionary Naturalism

THE THEORY OF NATURAL SELECTION

Opposed to the mentalistic trends of all religious views is perhaps the most powerful image of the human condition to spring from the European scientific Enlightenment. This image is encapsulated in Charles Darwin's bold hypothesis of 'natural selection' as the basis for the origin of human life. In Darwin's own view, this was not an atheistic hypothesis, though it made belief in a providential God difficult. In the hands of some of his later disciples, however, natural selection becomes an alternative theory competing with theism.[1] On this interpretation, no God is necessary to explain the genesis or development of life, and there is no moral structure to the universe that would make it somehow pliable to human desires and intentions. Human beings are biological organisms which happen to have been selected for survival in a blind and purposeless shuffling of genetic possibilities. They succeeded in becoming dominant through their lust and aggression, and they are destined either to become extinct or to evolve in further ways as the weak die and the strong survive.

The selfishness and greed of human beings needs no supernatural explanation in terms of a fall from a higher spiritual condition, for this form of strong Darwinism. Lust and aggression are the natural condition of human beings.[2] The problem is one of goodness. How can such beings come to have a moral sense at all? How can they retain it, once they see that it is probably a survival mechanism manipulable by chemical or genetic means? The imperious 'ought', which Immanuel Kant thought was so obvious and inescapable, comes to be seen as a relic of the biological past, which is not rationally justifiable, and probably needs to be severely mitigated by a more realistic assessment of human capabilities.[3]

---

[1] e.g. cf. Richard Dawkins, *The Blind Watchmaker* (London: Penguin, 1988), esp. Preface.

[2] Cf. Konrad Lorenz, *On Aggression* (London: Methuen, 1966).

[3] This argument is made in: Michael Ruse, *Evolutionary Naturalism* (London: Routledge, 1995), ch. 8.

Darwin states his view succinctly:

Owing to the struggle for life, any variation, however slight and from whatever cause proceeding, if it be in any degree profitable to an individual of
any species . . . will tend to the preservation of that individual, and will generally be inherited by its offspring. The offspring, also, will thus have a better chance of surviving, for, of the many individuals of any species which
are periodically born, but a small number can survive. I have called this
principle, by which each slight variation, if useful, is preserved, by the term
of Natural Selection.[4]

Four elements are essential to Darwin's theory. First, there must
be continual slight variations in inheritance, which make offspring
different in slight degrees from their parents. Second, organisms
must multiply at a tremendous rate. 'Each species', he says, 'tends
to increase inordinately.'[5] Third, there must be a desperate struggle for existence, constantly eliminating the unfit. There is, Darwin
writes, 'One general law, leading to the advancement of all organic
beings, namely, multiply, vary, let the strongest live and the weak-
est die.'[6] Fourth, there must be enough time for the continual elimination of the unfit to produce more and more efficiently adaptive
organisms, each carrying a slight evolutionary advantage, building
up cumulatively over many generations. 'As natural selection works
solely by and for the good of each being, all corporeal and mental
endowments will tend to progress towards perfection.'[7]

Darwin himself calls his view Malthusian, after T. R. Malthus,
whose *Essay on Population* (published in 1798), claimed that population growth will always outrun food supplies unless checked by
war, famine, or disease. The vision of evolution as a ruthless struggle for survival is a brutal and depressing one, all the more so when
one reflects that Darwin opposed any thought of necessary progress
or improvement in evolution (despite the last quotation cited).[8] He
proposes it simply as a descriptive theory, that it is random variation plus the struggle for existence that has caused organic beings
to evolve by imperceptible steps to their present complexity. It has
all happened by chance, and there is really no guarantee that it will
continue. The most efficient reproducers may turn out to be preda-
tory insects or viruses, and intelligence, moral sensitivity, and cul-

---

[4] Charles Darwin, *The Origin of Species* (Harmondsworth: Penguin, 1968), 115.
[5] Ibid. 325.   [6] Ibid. 263.   [7] Ibid. 459.
[8] 'I believe in no law of necessary development,' Darwin, *Origin*, 215.

ture may have little survival value in the war of all against all which is the natural world.

'We may console ourselves with the full belief', writes Darwin, 'that the war of nature is not incessant, that no fear is felt, that death is generally prompt, and that the vigorous, the healthy, and the happy survive and multiply.'[9] Can one be so sure that it is not disease-ridden spreaders of plague, incessantly copulating to alleviate their perpetual misery, who will inherit the earth, by efficiently killing off the tender-minded and compassionate, who feel an inefficient reluctance to exterminate members of other species?

Of course, one must just accept a brutal and depressing theory if it is true. But, while Darwin's theory is undoubtedly an elegant and economical explanation of many of the facts of organic variation and diversity, it is clear that it embodies a highly metaphorical vision of nature, derived from reading Malthus and from an increasing disposition in Darwin (possibly, it has been suggested, due to the death of his daughter) to distrust any talk of particular divine providence or oversight of nature.

Darwin draws attention to three key facts of the biological world. Organisms exhibit frequent and continued replication, mutation, and competition for scarce resources in a largely hostile environment. These three facts together give rise to the principle of natural selection: that slight advantages are preserved. But do these facts give any idea of what sorts of organisms may develop, much less suggest that organisms will tend towards perfection? What the theory comes down to is that mutations which give better survival and replication rates will come to predominate in any ecosystem. That is, of course, a very obvious truth. The force of Darwinian theory does not lie here, but in the claim that replication, mutation, and competition alone can account for the development of all the animal species we now have from a simple common progenitor.

What one might predict from Darwin's theory is that successful organisms will reproduce fast enough to take over the environment, but not so fast that they exhaust its resources. They must be able to survive well in many environments, but not so well that they do not die, to be replaced by new mutations. They must dominate other organisms, but not to the extent of exterminating them completely and eliminating their possible usefulness. One might reasonably

[9] Ibid. 129.

expect that the dominant survivor will be a fairly simple parasitic organism with a very high replication rate, coexisting with a number of similar but complementary organisms, which can check its growth in an unending struggle for dominance. If it continues to mutate, it will continually change its character, so there will be no permanently dominant species. There will be a continual replacement of species, as fast-replicating mutants supplant slower replicators or less well-adapted species.

When one says that a species has an 'advantage', one means simply that it will be better at obtaining scarce resources or at replicating or at eliminating competitors. It is decidedly not a matter of 'improving', in any valuational sense. Is there a limit on mutational advantage? If an organism obtained total dominance, how could any mutation improve on that? It is already replicating as fast as possible. It has eliminated competitors and established a monopoly on resources. Perhaps its fate is, sooner or later, to generate its own devourers. If the process continues long enough, there may result an organism maximally efficient at producing mutations which eliminate competitors and are able to survive in a number of environments. They in turn however will produce their own exterminators, in the unending struggle for life. The likely result of natural selection, it seems, is something like a perpetually self-destroying organism, continually mutating its forms into more resistant strains which in turn fall victim to new forms of virulent attack from its own offspring.

If that is a likely consequence of the principle of natural selection, how well does it account for the development of animal life as we now have it? One can invent a just-so story, postulating that, for instance, any mutation which gives a power of motion will possess a great advantage over a stationary plant, in obtaining energy resources. So if one can get a mutation for movement, animals will dominate plants. Of course, that is to suppose that the plants will not develop by mutation a poison which will eliminate the animals. Then some animals may develop an antidote to the poison; new poisons will be developed, and so on. The fact is there is not much reason to suppose that the 'advantage' of motion possessed by animals will outweigh the 'advantage' of poison produced by plants. Slight advantages need not be cumulative at all, since they can be defeated at a subsequent stage by mutations of much simpler organisms. Indeed, they are likely to be so defeated, since complex organisms are more prone to breakdown than simpler structures.

On the principle of natural selection, there is no reason to expect that the process will ever get beyond the mutant plant, unless there is some inbuilt disposition, in the mutational process, favouring the development of sentient agency. It is not obvious that conscious agents, like the higher mammals, will tend to become dominant in the struggle for survival. They could be eliminated overnight, as the dinosaurs were, by some natural disaster which left other species intact, or by some virulent strain of primitive virus. This is just to emphasize the point that there is no movement towards the perfection of species implied by the principle of natural selection. One could by no means predict the emergence of conscious agents as probable.

In fact, such emergence remains highly improbable on the theory,[10] and in that sense the Darwinian theory is not a wholly satisfactory explanation of the emergence of animal species on earth. No explanation is wholly satisfactory which makes the events it explains highly improbable—though, admittedly, it may be the best explanation one can get. It could, of course, happen that, by chance, plants fail to poison animals, which then do become dominant. But to say that is rather like explaining why Napoleon lost the Battle of Waterloo by saying that somebody had to lose, and the reason the English won was that the English possessed a slight military advantage. That remark fails to give an explanation, and we still want to know just what the advantage consisted in, other than winning the battle. So, with evolution, we want to know why animal forms developed at all by mutation, and why they established themselves successfully. To say it was just an accident, as the principle of natural selection does, is a very weak form of explanation.

There are at least two major areas in the Darwinian account which stand in need of further explanation. One is how it comes about that genetic mutations give rise to forms of complex animal life culminating in conscious agency. Darwin himself had no idea, and we are not much better informed today, even though we know the structure of DNA in some detail. The other is how it is that conscious agents became dominant in the struggle for life on this planet, when they have always been so prone to destruction by accident, disease, and internal malfunction. It hardly seems enough to

---

[10] Even Dawkins says, 'Does it sound to you as though it would need a miracle to make randomly jostling atoms join together into a self-replicating molecule? Well, at times it does to me too,' *Blind Watchmaker*, 158.

talk vaguely about selfish competition for scarce resources, when in fact what is required is an extremely complex adaptation to a whole ecosystem of great complexity, which itself develops in a way conducive to the development of rational life-forms. Almost everything remains to be done, in discovering what complex balance of interacting environmental forces needs to be in place before organic life can develop towards sentience and agency, in harmony and co-operation as well as in competition with other forms of life.

In short, Darwin establishes a powerful picture of organic life as developing from simple forms to all the species there are in the world at this time. But the principle of natural selection is only the beginning of an explanation of this process. It gives no explanation of why mutations occur as they do or of why particular life-forms have come to be dominant. It relies on a basic Malthusian picture of evolution as a 'struggle for life' which is much too one-sidedly individualistic, anthropomorphic, and adversarial to fit the complex reality of the beautiful, integrated and symbiotic planetary totality of which we are now aware.[11] To some extent it rests on a questionable Malthusian picture of a process which, to any dispassionate observer, is a much more holistic and goal-directed one than Darwin, at least in his gloomier moments, allowed.

THEISTIC EVOLUTION

Despite the claims of many neo-Darwinians, the evolutionary hypothesis is quite consistent with a much more positive theistic interpretation of those facts that Darwin so brilliantly elucidated. The theistic hypothesis is that there is a God of supreme creativity, wisdom, and bliss, who wills to create this universe for the sake of the distinctive values it can realize. One distinctive sort of value—one that could not exist in any other sort of universe—is value that is developed by emergent striving and growth from an initial state of many transient, unconscious, and relatively simple identical elements. For such emergence to take place, there would have to be some way of binding the elements into stable structures, of giving such structures some form of relatively independent causal agency, of organizing them to become vehicles of consciousness, and of uniting them into co-operative social wholes. There would be a

---

[11] The more integral view is well set out in: James Lovelock, *A New Look at Life on Earth* (Oxford: Oxford University Press, 1979).

long process in which the creator builds up such complex and integrated wholes out of the simple elements with which the process begins. This process could not be deterministic, for that would render the subsequent development of creaturely freedom and autonomy impossible. There have to be alternative futures, some of them constructive and harmonious and others destructive and disharmonious, between which free creatures can later choose. But if God cannot determine these futures in every detail, God can certainly determine the available alternative possibilities, and can exercise a causal influence (which creatures may reject, when they achieve that capacity) giving the process a propensity towards actualizing some of the more constructive possibilities.

How can one envisage such a causal influence? A fully theistic view would reject as inadequate any idea that nature could proceed on its own, unaffected by the divine presence and intention. It must be the case that the divine intention influences how things go in definite ways. On the other hand, divine influence need not and probably should not be seen as a series of interferences with purely natural processes. The truth must be that there are no purely natural processes, that all causal processes are continually influenced by the divine intentions.[12] There is a causal input by God which draws physical elements in the direction of greater intensity of consciousness and control of the environment. In other words, God exercises a selective pressure favouring features which tend towards the personalization of nature. When consciousness comes into existence, God can become a partner in conscious dialogue with finite sentient beings.

It is this hypothesis which neo-Darwinians reject as both superfluous and undesirable. It is, they say, superfluous, for natural selection alone is, they suppose, capable of explaining any amount of variation and 'improvement', given enough time. It is undesirable because it introduces a doctrine of 'final causes' into biology, which is unscientific, indemonstrable, and useless as an explanatory device.[13]

The hypothesis of God is not superfluous if it contributes elements to an explanation which would otherwise not be present. In

---

[12] This view is elaborated in A. N. Whitehead's *Process and Reality* (London: Macmillan, 1929), and is dissociable from the 'pan-psychist' interpretation which has sometimes been given to it, and which Whitehead denied.

[13] Cf. Dawkins, *Blind Watchmaker*, 316–18.

considering what such elements might be, one might first consider
that if natural selection is to operate in the way Darwin desires, one
needs a set of instructions ensuring that physical elements will organize themselves into patterns of interaction which are suitable for
increased complexity and stability of operation, sensitivity, and
responsiveness to their environment. A very precisely integrated set
of instructions is necessary. They will produce changes which are
certainly not random, in the sense of being uncontrolled or wholly
unpredictable. What appears to be random at the biological level is
law-like at the more basic level of fundamental physics. And the
existence of physical laws that are so well tuned as to produce the
biological complexity that consciousness requires is more likely on
the hypothesis of an ordering creative mind than on the hypothesis
of pure chance.[14]

This may seem like introducing a 'God of the gaps', using God
to explain something which may later be explained in purely physical or scientific terms. But this explanation functions at a metascientific level, to enquire as to the best explanation for why the basic
physical laws are as they are. At this level, the postulate of God is
not a competitor with any properly scientific explanation. But it is
a competitor with other metaphysical theories, such as materialism
or the Buddhist theory of *sunyata*.

Even the suggestion that God acts as a 'lure', ensuring that conscious beings emerge from natural physical processes, does not
claim to fill a gap in some physical or biological explanation. If such
a lure exists, it will (like human free acts) have a causal influence on
the way things go, but all physical explanations will remain intact at
their own level. It would be a rash physicist who claimed that laws
of physics explained absolutely everything that happens. Such laws,
however, work very well with regard to those physical properties
with which they deal. The theist is claiming that there are other,
non-physical, levels of reality.

There is a huge difference between saying that there is some
inadequacy in e.g. the laws of mechanics which God might remedy,
and saying that the laws of mechanics explain everything without
remainder. Theists can consistently deny the former and assert that
there are things the laws of mechanics cannot explain—among
them the existence and purposes of God. It is not that there is any-

---

[14] This probability argument is elegantly formulated by Richard Swinburne, in
The Existence of God (Oxford: Clarendon, 1979).

thing wrong with scientific theories, it is just that they do not explain everything.

Both the claim that they do, and the claim that they do not, are metascientific theories about the nature and limits of science and of human knowledge. One would not expect physics to explain the existence and will of God. In so far as the divine purpose makes a difference to the world, physics will not even attempt to explain that. There may be no gap in scientific explanations, but there are limits to them. To point that out is not to subscribe to the view that there is a God of the gaps. It is simply to point out that, if there is a non-physical reality, God, then physical explanations will not deal with it.

So the theist will claim that God provides a good explanation for the existence of the fine-tuned laws of physics which make evolution possible. But do those very laws not exclude God having a causal role in the universe? They do not, if there are elements of the physical process which are not wholly and sufficiently determined by previous physical states and physical laws alone.

One indication that there are such elements is found in the consensus among quantum theorists that there are basically undetermined events at the subatomic level, to which a precise probability, but no more, can be assigned.[15] One expects probabilities to even out in the long run, so as to form virtual certainties. If there is a 50:50 chance of a coin landing on a particular side, then it is pretty certain that in the long run 50 per cent of coins will land on that side. However the run could be very long indeed, and in any particular finite system, very improbable sequences may well occur (the smaller the system in relation to the possible length of the run, the more likely this will be). In a closely interconnected web of systems, the occurrence of very improbable sequences may trigger off a set of events which are very different than they might have been if other sequences had occurred. Quantum uncertainties do, in the right circumstances, lead to macrocosmic differences. They do not always simply cancel out to leave things as they would have been anyway. A combination of quantum theory and chaos theory, which shows how, in dynamic systems far from equilibrium, small causes can have major effects, allows for many alternative futures in a quantized physical system.[16]

---

[15] A readable account is given by Ian Barbour, in *Issues in Science and Religion* (London: SCM, 1966), ch. 10.
[16] Cf. John Polkinghorne, *Science and Providence* (London: SPCK, 1989), 28–35.

Thus one can set up a physical system which is mathematically specified, and which allows for many alternative futures. Which futures result will depend on the precise determination of probabilistic events and on the total structure which governs the sorts of macro-effects that will ensue. The process will not be random, but it will not be determined either. The Heisenberg Uncertainty Principle, assuming that there are no 'hidden variables' as yet undiscovered, is just one example of the way in which a degree of indeterminism may exist in a law-like universe. There may be many other causal factors at work in complex physical processes, which cannot be captured completely by the general quantifiable regularities which the 'laws of nature' describe. But the Heisenberg Principle shows how one might not be able, in principle, to establish a deterministic account of physical processes. In addition, it is generally accepted that one could never specify initial conditions precisely enough to enable wholly accurate predictions to be made. If this is so, one cannot exclude the possibility that factors other than those specified by the known laws of physics enter into the bringing about of future events and states.

There could be non-physical causal factors unknown to us which determine, or influence, what seem to us at the physical level to be probabilistic events. It is quite conceivable that God could exert such a causal influence which, being non-physical, would be physically undetectable. Theistic belief in a causal influence exerted by God is in this way quite consistent with present knowledge in physics. Theists would expect God to play some causal role in the process of evolution, giving to natural processes a propensity to complexity and responsiveness to environment which a wholly Darwinian account would not be able to provide.[17]

If one adopted such a view, one would see the evolutionary course of nature, not as an unceasing and ruthless battle of species, but rather as a slow-developing process of seeking an integrated harmony of connecting organic forms. Disharmonious and radically defective elements would tend to be discarded, but it would not be a matter of eliminating the weak and preserving the strong.

---

[17] Dawkins writes, 'Mutation is not systematically biased in the direction of adaptive improvement', *Blind Watchmaker*, 312. And in *The Selfish Gene* (Oxford: Oxford University Press, 1976), 16, he says that the formation of replicating molecules is 'exceedingly improbable'. Neither statement sits easily with believing in a propensity for sentient life-forms to emerge through natural selection.

It would rather be a matter of including all that could be included in a harmonious whole, and eliminating only what was inimical to survival. At lower levels of life, consumption of others as food is necessary. But at higher levels, requirements of harmony and altruism become more important, and care for the sick becomes more natural than their elimination. This would not be an inefficient by-product of a ruthless system. It can plausibly be seen as the goal of a system of energy-exchange which gradually and naturally develops greater degrees of rational control of feelings and behaviour, and compassion for and disinterested delight in others.

THE POSSIBILITY OF A PURPOSIVE VIEW OF EVOLUTION

Darwin was vehemently opposed to the idea that any species could develop for the sake of the good of others. Every evolutionary advantage had to be for a selfish good, for greater survival. The 'hidden hand' of Adam Smith, which uses selfish action to bring about improvement, is at work in Darwin also. If one builds morality into the system, however, the aim will be to move from a concern for simple survival towards a concern to realize and appreciate beauty and value as such. 'Natural selection will produce nothing in one species for the exclusive good or injury of another,'[18] writes Darwin. Perhaps so; but what that may suggest is that natural selection is not the only principle of evolution. Selective divine pressure could be what moves the whole development of the natural order towards the goods of rational and moral consciousness.

The Darwinian metaphor is of a ruthless struggle of individuals for survival. The metaphor is not very appropriate, since it has been convincingly demonstrated that altruistic behaviour is, on principles of natural selection, likely to be widespread in populations.[19] Animals which sacrifice themselves for their young will enhance the propagation of genes (present in their offspring) which reinforce such self-sacrificial behaviour. Thus co-operation is as important as egoism in the evolutionary process.

There is a temptation to reinstate selfishness at the level of the gene, and argue that the whole process exists to replicate 'selfish genes', which seek their own survival by the most efficient means.

[18] Darwin, *Origin*, 232.
[19] W. D. Hamilton, 'The Genetical Evolution of Social Behaviour', in *Journal of Theoretical Biology*, 7 (1964), 1–32.

This ploy cannot succeed. Genes are clearly not selfish, since they aim at nothing; nor do they survive, as physical entities. What happens is that some pieces of DNA replicate more prolifically than others. For that to happen, however, a great deal of co-operation with other genes is necessary. Moreover, the biological function of genes is to build the proteins which form bodies. So if one is going to use an anthropomorphic metaphor at all, it seems more appropriate to think of 'altruistic genes', giving their lives for the sake of greater wholes. But it is probably better to avoid such metaphors, and simply register the fact that even a pure process of natural selection gives rise to altruistic and co-operative behaviour as much as to selfish and aggressive behaviour. So, at the biological level, the metaphor of a struggle for life gives a very one-sided view of the evolutionary process.

Darwinism is a scientific theory, with both elegance and explanatory power. But it is not only that. The scientific theory asserts that species mutate, that many become extinct, and that they adapt to their environments as some mutations prove more successful than others at surviving and procreating. But when this is spoken of in terms of a struggle for life, or of the survival of the fittest, a deeper metaphorical picture is at work. Malthus and Adam Smith are used to paint this picture. The hand of individualistic capitalism is not so hidden.

Is there an alternative picture, which may include the scientific aspects of Darwin's theory in a different perspective? Clearly there is. One may think of a more purposive account, for which the 'higher forms' of consciousness and moral action provide desirable goals towards the realization of which nature is purposively ordered. And one may think of a more holistic morality, for which integration, beauty, and harmony are the goods for which individuals strive and sacrifice themselves. Instead of the metaphor of the survival of the fittest, which seeks to eliminate the weak and survive at any cost (though it is doomed to fail, since every organism must eventually perish), one might picture a striving to generate new and more creative forms of life, out of the sacrifice of individual parts to a greater whole, which endures and thrives even as they perish.[20]

---

[20] Such views have been developed most notably by F. R. Tennant, *Philosophical Theology* (Cambridge: Cambridge University Press, 1930), ii, and Alister Hardy, *The Living Stream* (London: Collins, 1965).

Of course, this too is a pathetic metaphor, that is, one which attributes aims and motivations to material events. Behind the metaphor, for a theist, lies the hypothesis of the mind of God, moving the world towards a goal, to which the births and deaths of innumerable particles are essential means. One might then see nature as an organic whole, moved by God through time from simple unconscious plurality, by a constant interchange of energies and a continual development of organization, towards one integrated complex, conscious, and self-directing community, or set of communities.

How could one decide whether this was true? Darwin seemed to think that anything, even mental and physical perfection, could be explained simply by indefinitely repeated mutations and selection by competitive struggle. On the other hand, he also saw that this mechanism could not guarantee any development at all, since it is blind and without purpose. That tension remained in Darwin's thought, between nature as remorselessly progressing and as stumbling from one mutational mistake to another. The predictive power of the theory is, in short, extremely weak, since it can equally well predict the perfecting of life and the extermination of life.

In considering the adequacy of a pure natural selection theory, one might first take note of the extreme improbability of having a process of reproduction with slight variability at all. To have nucleotide sequences capable of replicating themselves requires a very closely co-ordinated set of physical constants and laws of regularity. To add the characteristic of just enough variation to give rise to differential survival rates without destroying the structure of organisms altogether would require superb mathematical skills, were it consciously designed.

Then one might note that such mutations, while they appear to be probabilistic, nevertheless do issue in more complex and efficient structures. It is not the case that every mutation is an improvement. Nevertheless, it is plainly true that a sufficient percentage of them are advantageous to ensure that, given natural selection, development does occur. This is by no means necessarily the case. It looks very much as if the nature and number of mutations is exactly, perhaps uniquely, such as to preserve a probabilistic character to fundamental physical laws, while ensuring that, given certain other facts which are themselves guaranteed by the same physical laws, development will inevitably occur.

Thus far, then, one has a set of fundamental laws which facilitate the development of self-replicating structures. Such structures will evolve by laws which, while probabilistic in nature, yet determine that a sufficient number of these structures will grow more sensitive to their environment, and so evolve increasingly effective survival strategies. Now one has to ask: is the struggle for sheer survival a sufficient explanation of the course of evolutionary development? One might simply be asking: *could* it bring about the results we see on this planet? Any answer to this question is bound to be highly speculative, based on vast extrapolations from very few observations in rather different circumstances. If everything tries to exterminate everything else, and some things get more efficient at this while others get less, because of slight mutations, then it does at first seem obvious that the more efficient will soon predominate. However, it is possible to be too efficient at exterminating, and leave oneself without future means of survival (humans may be in this position). What is actually needed is a very delicate and intricate balance—in other words, not a war of each against all, but a development of ecological networks which encourage developmental mutations and discourage regressive mutations.

There is no reason why continued reiteration of processes of graduated mutational replication and eliminative competition should produce any organizational development at all. Many factors could prevent such development. Mutations could prove universally harmful. The most effective predators could be relatively simple forms, like viruses, which inhibit any development. Increased organization of living forms is in fact likely to produce more breakdowns and defects, leading to an expectation that highly diversified forms are not likely to develop. On strict natural selection principles alone, there is thus very little likelihood that highly specialized life-forms will develop, much less an expectation that the process will lead towards greater physical and mental perfection.

Such forms could develop by chance, because conditions just happen to favour them. But there comes a point at which the appeal of reductionism (employ the least number of the most primitive principles) is outweighed by the appeal of predictive power (employ a principle which most efficiently predicts what actually happens). In the case of the development of organic life forms, if the process is natural selection alone, the probability of conscious self-directing organisms resulting is extremely low. But suppose one introduces a principle that organisms will tend to develop the most complex, environmentally sensitive, sustainable forms. Then mutations will be such that, while not precisely predictable in detail, they will tend to build up complex and relatively stable forms, in relation to their particular environment. Those mutations will be selected which offer the best possibility of evolving towards the goal of complex conscious existence. They will be selected, not by a simple competition to see who reproduces most quickly and eliminates competitors most effectively—though that will be part of the process—but by a tendency to generate organisms that show the greatest integrated complexity and potential for further development.

The principle of natural selection maintains that it just happens that some replicating forms eliminate competitors and replicate most efficiently in their environments. The fact that in the process conscious rational agents are produced is quite incidental. But the facts as we observe them might well suggest a principle which can ensure the production of conscious valuing agents from primitive replicating organisms. It would then not 'just happen' that some forms—it does not matter which—eliminate others and replicate best. On the contrary, the process would be set up so that conscious rational forms emerge, for the sake of the values they embody.

The materialist will ask, what mechanism could bring about this result? Is it not a return to a discredited vitalism, the postulation of an occult and undetectable force which organisms are supposed to possess, the 'ether' of biology? Committed materialists will be unwilling to entertain the idea of a goal-directed selection mechanism, since goals cannot exist without minds, and no minds exist until evolution is very well developed. The theist is not, however, committed to the existence of any occult vitalistic force in organisms themselves. On the contrary, the theist accepts the existence of a supreme Mind which has created the universe precisely for the sake of a goal. It is the cosmic Mind which selects those organisms for survival which play a positive part in forwarding this goal. Instead of natural selection, this could be called goal-directed selection, and it involves no vital force within organic life-forms.

I am not here attempting anything so grandiose as a refutation of evolutionary naturalism by theism. I am suggesting, minimally, that the processes of evolution as we observe them are compatible with the existence of a creator God. More strongly, the hypothesis of a

God who intends to create responsible rational agents obviously makes the evolution of such beings much more probable than the hypothesis of blind chance.

EVOLUTION AND RELIGIOUS BELIEFS

So, on the one hand, evolutionary naturalism is not a strict implication of Darwinian theory. On the other hand, the postulation of God, far from being superfluous, enables one to give the actual evolutionary process a much higher probability than would blind natural selection alone. Any postulate which raises the probability of an occurrence clearly has content, and is therefore not superfluous. It is another question whether there actually is a God. But the theory of evolution does not imply that there is not. On the contrary, it makes the postulate of God quite a reasonable one—though it is important to note that it may suggest revisions to some religious ideas of God (for instance, a very literal account of the biblical book of Genesis).

But how is the selection achieved? The Darwinian model is that in a desperate struggle for survival, the fittest (the best reproducers) are selected, and all others go to the wall. Suppose one replaces the metaphor of a struggle for life with the metaphor of a creative and communal realization of value. Instead of a struggle for survival, one may have, with a small but immensely significant change, a striving for life, for more valuable and dynamic life.[21] Instead of individuals seeking to dominate, with values emerging incidentally, by a 'hidden hand' process, one would have a holistic process tending towards the emergence of values, with individuals playing their part in maintaining a complex, integrated, balanced, and emergent ecosystem. There would be striving to excel. There would be the extinction of species which could not adapt and develop. The struggle would be not for sheer survival, but for greater creativity and awareness of intrinsically worthwhile states. Death would be an inevitable concomitant of the birth of new values, but co-operation and harmony would be as important in the process as competition and destruction.

In old, Paley-style design arguments, God is thought of as wanting a certain sort of entity to exist, and simply bringing it into exis-

---

[21] This line of argument is pursued in Keith Ward, *God, Chance and Necessity* (Oxford: Oneworld, 1996).

tence, as conceived.[22] This model ignores the creative and emergent character of evolution. It fails to account for the obvious blind alleys and harmful mutations in the evolutionary process. That process seems to be both probabilistic and yet to lead towards greater value, so that the most apt model is that of a creative striving towards goodness, towards consciously enjoyed existence. One may think of a plant reaching towards the light of the sun. Some existent reality of great and intrinsic value draws insensate matter towards itself, so as to embody reflections of infinite value in largely self-created finite forms.

This model requires a replacement of the machine-model of physical laws as deductive premises by a different, more organic model of a gradual expansion of dispositional powers, by progressive interaction, to generate new forms of holistic relationship. If one thinks of dispositions as evoked from entities by interactions with their environment, then one can think of God as the ultimate environment. The final causality of God and the creative causality of finite entities combine to form a process which is both expansive and creative.[23] God sets up the basic powers of material substances, and draws them towards perfection. But they actualize their powers by creative response to the final causality of God.

Properly scientific theories are accepted largely because they have high predictive power, because they make the existence of the facts as we see them highly probable, as an outcome of their application. The irony is that the theory of natural selection has virtually no predictive power. It makes the existence of presently known facts highly improbable, rather like the outcome of the National Lottery. It could all have happened by chance, but it is an outcome of extremely high improbability (as any outcome would be, on the theory). The theistic hypothesis, on the other hand, postulating that there is a consciousness which intends the existence of finite rational agents as the outcome of a process of emergence from simple basic physical elements, provides a high probability that things should now be as they are. It predicts that there will be sentient beings capable of knowing and loving God. This is a very general prediction, though no more general than the Darwinian theory, but it is an elegant and substantial explanation, precisely because it makes it likely—indeed, makes it certain—that sentient beings will

---

emerge from the evolutionary process. What theistic explanation adds to the Darwinian theory is a great increase in the probability of sentient life coming to exist as it actually does. It is therefore (given the important assumption that the idea of God is itself a coherent and plausible one) a better explanation, at a metascientific level, of the process of evolution than the hypothesis of a purposeless process of reiterated replication, mutation, and competitive elimination.

Evolution, for the theist, is not a blind process of eliminating the unfit but a goal-directed process of actualizing emergent values, through creative and explorative striving. The theist is committed against purely natural selection, as a non-purposive process indifferent to the realization of value. The alternative is not to think of God as directly producing exactly what God intends, without any need for evolution. Theists can think of God as instituting a process of the emergent actualization of dispositions, evoked by interaction with the environment. God, as the ultimately environing reality, will then interact with all finite entities, seeking to evoke their creative response as they shape values proper to them.

What sort of interaction will this be? One must conceive a form of divine influence which will encourage positive values and impede destructive forces. The most natural and directly known form of causality is intentional causality, bringing about states that a conscious agent desires. We are familiar with the fact that such causality is not always fully and easily efficacious. We may have to try hard to climb a mountain, using the resources available to us. We may have to contribute our effort to a communal endeavour, so that many individual powers may be added together. Agents, as we know them, have limited capacities, and live in a world of many mutually interacting and limited powers. Each agent is able to direct some range of powers. With the co-operation of others, fairly large changes may be brought about in an environment which is stable and predictable on the whole.

Suppose that a creator God brings about a universe which operates in accordance with stable (if not inviolable) principles, and brings about agents with limited powers in that universe. God may assume a limited power to bring about changes, either in co-operation or in conflict with the powers of finite agents. What will define the limits of divine power? One possibility is that God will exercise the greatest power for good compatible with the existence of general regularities in nature and with the freedom of finite agents. This will involve a sort of self-denying ordinance on God's part, to restrain the exercise of divine power so as to permit regularities of nature and free finite actions. This means that the regularities must be such as to permit both free finite actions and some divine actions, which usually operate within the parameters of the probabilistic regularities of nature.

When one speaks of God influencing genetic mutations for good, this will be action within the parameters of physical probability which ensures that mutations in general conduce to the generation of more sensitive and creative forms of life. The physical laws will, of course, be set up so that they make it possible for creative forms to be generated. But they will also allow many alternative possibilities within which God's action can make choices. Such choices must leave the general probabilistic structure intact, while they will cause the process to move in ways it otherwise would almost certainly not have done.[24]

It is always possible for someone to claim that things might have evolved this way by chance. But this seems to be a much less probable hypothesis than that the process is being directed towards the actualization of value, within the probabilistic structure of basic laws of emergence. The simplicity of eliminating mental direction from the process is in this case outweighed by the overwhelmingly greater probability of accounting for the process in goal-directed terms.

On this view, when consciousness emerges, there is the possibility of a consciously interactive relationship between God and the universe, wherein free finite choices can either impede or increase the creative influence God exerts universally. The religious sense of response to divine revelation, and of experience of a divine reality, is a natural development from the universal relation of God and the universe, not a sudden and unexpected interruption of God into the material realm. In humans, the world begins to make a conscious response to the God who has always been drawing the world towards the realization of value. Evolution can be seen as the means by which the material order is raised to the capacity of conscious co-operation with the purposes of the supreme Mind. Theism provides a good explanation of evolution, and evolution provides a new insight into the nature of theism.

---

[24] The coherence of this view if expounded in David Bartholomew, *God of Chance* (London: SCM, 1984).

The Darwinian vision has succeeded in establishing a high probability that sentient life-forms evolved from a single simple biological source, that there is a branching tree of life, of which humans are a part. What it does not do is to eliminate the probability that this process is purposively instituted and guided by a cosmic intelligence. It does not eliminate the important distinctions in value between organic and non-organic, sentient and insentient, morally self-directing and non-responsible life-forms. In particular, it does not undermine the belief that human persons are capable of what is, on this planet, a unique form of relationship to the Creator, which requires responsible knowledge and love.

Humans, on a theistic view, have largely turned away from a properly creative response to God, but their natural inclinations are originally ordered towards good, and their fulfilment lies in returning to full responsiveness, to knowledge and love of God. The theistic hypothesis predicts that such a return will be actualized, since the goal of the creative process will be achieved, though the hypothesis remains unspecific about how or when this will be, and different theistic traditions offer different accounts of that.

The hypothesis of evolution gives a very different perspective on human nature from that found in virtually all traditional interpretations of religion. For many traditional religions, humans had once existed in a state of goodness, but fell into a world of illusion and egoism. For others, humans have existed for innumerable lifetimes and in beginningless cycles of cosmic existence, which will be repeated endlessly. On an evolutionary view, humans are material forms of being, complex integrated structures which have developed over millions of years from simpler material forms. They actualize consciousness and rational understanding, and so move towards conscious relationship with the Creator. While theism gives a good explanation of the apparently progressive nature of evolution, the theory of evolution, if it is accepted as scientifically well-established, compels one to reinterpret traditional religious views of human nature.

I think that such a reinterpretation can be given. Indeed, illuminating reinterpretations already have been given, mostly within the Semitic strands of religion, which have had a greater emphasis than the Indian traditions on the material basis of human life, and on the nature of human history (if not of the history of all organic life) as moving towards a decisive goal or end-point. In many ways, an evolutionary view can be seen as a very natural development of a view of human beings as created for a purpose, and of historical existence as having a significance which is unique and irreplaceable. But the Semitic traditions still face problems with the hypothesis of evolution. For they have traditionally seen humans as fallen from a prior state of perfection, which is in tension with the evolutionary account. And it is not easy to see just how belief in a soul or spirit fits into an evolutionary view, which normally assumes that consciousness is an emergent property of a complex central nervous system, not a supernatural creation. In moving on to consider the Semitic religious traditions, it is these problems that will first be considered.

7
The Embodied Soul

CONCEPTUAL AND CONTINGENT MATERIALISM

The theory of evolution is, I have argued, compatible with a theistic world-view, and is in fact an enrichment of such a world-view. It holds that finite minds and spirits emerge from a developing material world, and do not 'fall into it' from some non-material realm. But one of the greatest problems of modern scientific understanding is how mind and matter relate to one another. Many philosophers and scientists hold it implausible to regard mind and matter as completely independent sort of things, which just happen to relate to one another. They are attracted to some form of materialism, a view that there is only one basic sort of existent, matter, and that spiritual existence is explicable as an admittedly sophisticated form of materialism.[1] It is worth exploring the extent to which this may be the case.

It may seem that materialism is wholly incompatible with religious belief. In one obvious sense, I think that it is. Theists are committed to the view that the one self-existent reality upon which all other realities depend, God, is non-material. They are usually committed to the view that the material realm is not capable of existing on its own, but must depend upon a spiritual reality transcending it. Even theistic traditions which do think of matter as eternally existing (as in Sankhya schools of thought), regard the non-material realm as the more important, with which religious practice is mainly concerned. Buddhist beliefs, while not theistic, also teach the possibility of non-material forms of existence. Whatever liberation is for a Buddhist, it is beyond the changing and conditioned nature of matter, and so Buddhists hope for an ultimate form of being beyond the material, as well as many intermediate forms of being which are not in this physical realm.[2]

---

[1] Cf. the essays collected in C. V. Borst (ed.), *The Mind/Brain Identity Theory* (London: Macmillan, 1970).

[2] Cf. Paul Williams, *Mahayana Buddhism* (London: Routledge, 1989), ch. 9.

Religious believers in general accept that there are purely spiritual forms of existence, and also forms of existence which are very unlike the material form we now experience, with its specific three-dimensional space and causal laws. They usually believe that they, or at least some people, have experienced such spiritual realities—even within this material realm there is the possibility of experience of God, or of some liberated spiritual state. Materialists deny that such entities as God exist, and they sometimes deny that God could possibly exist.

The denial of the very possibility of spiritual existence is hard to defend. It seems to commit a materialist to saying that it is a necessary truth that everything that exists must exist in space, and even perhaps in the very three-dimensional space in which we exist. Even if no one could imagine something that exists, but is not in space, that would be a very long way from proving that no such thing could exist. It would only show how limited human imagination is.

It seems plausible to think that things could exist which are not in the three-dimensional space in which we exist. Suppose that space is, as most physicists think, a certain sort of relationship between objects. Such a relationship can be conceived to obtain between two sets of objects which are not related to each other by that relationship. That is, in the very idea of space as a relation, there is implicit the possibility that there can be different spaces, not spatially related to one another. Cosmologists almost routinely talk of different space-times, and there seems to be no great difficulty in thinking of there being spaces other than this one.[3]

Nor need such other spaces have the same sorts of properties this space has. Again, cosmologists tend to talk of ten or more dimensional space-times, out of which this space-time is one selection.[4] Space, for a physicist, does not have to be the sort of three-dimensional structure we move around in. It can take many different forms, which mathematicians delight to explore in imagination. If we can imagine such different sorts of space, we can certainly think of them as being filled with objects very different

[3] Cf. the discussion of many-universes theories in Paul Davies, *The Mind of God* (New York: Simon & Schuster, 1992), 225–30.

[4] Cf. C. J. Isham, 'Quantum Theories of the Creation of the Universe', in R. J. Russell, N. Murphy, and C. J. Isham (eds.), *Quantum Cosmology and the Laws of Nature* (Notre Dame, Ind.: Vatican Observatory Press, 1993).

from the ones we know, governed by laws very different from the ones in this universe.

For most physicists, it is not an unduly weird thought that there can be different spaces from this one, and different sorts of spaces from this one. The determined materialist, therefore, should not say that everything must exist in this space, but just that everything must exist in some sort (perhaps a very different sort) of space. This assertion does not exclude very much, unless one can place a definite limit on the sorts of space that can exist. Angels can exist in angelic space. Even God can exist in Divine space, a space where there may be room for only one existent.

It may seem very odd to talk about divine space. Karl Barth, however, points out that if one is going to speak of coexisting elements or modes of the divine being, one may speak of 'divine space' as that set of co-ordinate relations which makes coexistence possible.[5] Of course it will be nothing like the three-dimensional space that physical objects inhabit. But that three-dimensional space is just a set of transitive and symmetrical relations, in which each element is related to every other in a uniquely definable way. One can accordingly speak of a 'space' wherever one has a set of transitive relations ordering items as uniquely coexistent. If, in God, there coexist things analogous to thoughts, feelings, or different states, then one may speak by analogy of divine space, as that set of internal relationships in which the divine elements are ordered.

Virtually no theist thinks that God is in, or is confined to, the same space in which creatures exist. One cannot get to God by travelling in any direction from any point in this space-time. Nor does God share the divine space with any creature. It is a space which is internal to the divine Being. But once the possibility of different spaces is accepted, there is nothing very odd about that. It thus surprisingly turns out that any sort of materialism which is sensitive to the plasticity of the concept of space is wholly innocuous, from a religious point of view. When the concept of space is clarified, the theist can simply say that divine space is different both in kind and in number from the space-time in which the earth is situated.

The materialist may now try to tighten the requirements of possible existence by holding that everything that exists must have some material property, such as mass. But that will not do either.

[5] Karl Barth, *Church Dogmatics*, ed. G. W. Bromiley and T. F. Torrance (Edinburgh: T. and T. Clark, 1936–77), ii. 1. 463–8.

There are physical particles, such as photons, which have no mass. Nor can it plausibly be held that all existents must have gravitational, electro-magnetic, or nuclear force. How can one possibly know that there are not other forms of force, unknown to us? Procrustean materialism, when analysed, just amounts to the arbitrary decision that every possible thing must conform to some set of requirements of physical things in this universe. As such, it can justifiably be ignored.

A reasonable materialist must accept that there could possibly be forms of existence which are not spatially extended in the way that physical objects in this universe are, or which do not possess the sorts of physical forces such objects possess. But such bare possibilities, it may be said, are not the real point at issue. The fact is that everything we know about, every actual thing, is a form of energy existing in one shared transitive set of spatial relations. This is no longer an a priori assertion about the possibility or impossibility of certain sorts of thing. It is a contingent hypothesis about the characteristics of all the things that humans know. It could be false, but, it is claimed, as a matter of fact it is true—at least, one would have to add, it is true so far as we know. This sort of view may be called contingent materialism, since it only asserts that, as a matter of contingent fact, there exists nothing that is not in this space-time universe.

Contingent materialism turns out to be a very dogmatic view, since it denies the existence of things it admits to knowing nothing about. Any theist will have good reason to deny contingent materialism, since God is not a form of energy existing within this space-time, and theists typically claim that God can be known. It should be apparent that the existence of God cannot be ruled out by materialism, since materialism is now precisely the hypothesis that there is no God, or that no God is experienced. Any hypothesis of that sort must be predicated on the facts. It would be absurd to use it to rule out any facts. A good hypothesis must cover and account for all the facts. If there is a God, materialism is false. So the truth of materialism must depend upon whether or not there is a God. The existence of God cannot depend upon whether or not materialism is true—that would be to put things completely back to front. Materialism could only be asserted as a plausible hypothesis after it has been independently discovered that as a matter of fact there is no God. It is extremely difficult to establish such a negative existential assertion. To that extent, materialism must remain at best a probable hypothesis rather than a certain or uncontested one. It is a hypothesis the truth of which depends upon showing to be illusory many claims made by well-informed, intelligent observers. So it does not have the sort of certainty possessed by a well-established scientific hypothesis. Its status is that of a controversial attempted conceptual simplification of our conceptual scheme. As such, it must be tested against some obvious counter-examples, which resist assimilation to the materialist paradigm.

The most obvious counter-examples are the phenomena of consciousness, the perceptions, sensations, images, feelings, and thoughts which form the starting-point of human reflection. It is agreed on all sides that such things do not *seem* to be forms of energy in one public space-time. For example, if I hum a tune 'in my mind', there is nowhere in public space that I can locate that tune. The materialist may say that, nevertheless, what is happening is a locatable event in my brain.[6] The mental humming is in public space, even though it does not seem so to the hummer.

All mental properties can be interpreted in this manner as dispositions of the physical brain to react in certain ways. The whole inner life of a person will then be the history of the activity of a particular brain. It may seem obvious that, when that brain ceases to exist, that person will cease to exist. A person just *is* a brain, and begins and ends when the brain does.

This suggests that materialists cannot believe in personal survival of bodily death. Strangely, however, two of the best-known and most vocal materialists, David Armstrong and Daniel Dennett, allow the possibility of survival. Armstrong points out that, though the perception of a colour (say, red) is identical with the occurrence of a specific brain-state (or a rather complicated disjunctive set of brain-states), such identity is itself contingent.[7] It could have been the case that a different brain-state correlated with the seeing of red. There is no logical tie between the colour perceived and the brain-state.

But if phenomenal states and brain-states can be moved around in this way, it is logically possible for the phenomenal states to exist

---

[6] 'The various phenomena that compose what we call consciousness . . . are all physical effects of the brain's activities', Daniel C. Dennett, *Consciousness Explained* (London: Penguin, 1991), 16.

[7] D. M. Armstrong, *A Materialist Theory of the Mind* (London: Routledge, 1968).

without any brain-states at all. Although Armstrong does not think that they do, phenomenal (mental) states could exist, he says, even in the absence of brains. On this view, it is just a contingent fact that mental states are correlated with brain-states. After brain-death, mental states may continue, and survival is perfectly possible.

Dennett is more intransigent. He takes the ruthless step of denying that there are any phenomenal states that could be correlated with brain-states. There are only the brain-states, and the dispositions of brains (connected to vocal chords) to make utterances about how things seem to them when their brains are in certain states. He likens these dispositions to computer programmes that cause the brain to operate in specific ways. A disposition is a sort of programme which, loaded onto a suitable piece of hardware (a brain of a certain sort), brings about actions in the world. Following this analogy through, he offers the thought that such programmes could be extracted and run on different hardware (in different brains), so that a form of survival is again possible.[8]

Programmes have to be compatible with their hardware, but any good computer engineer can adapt a programme to new hardware, so it is possible that a significantly similar programme could be run in a very different sort of physical environment. The sets of reactive dispositions that make up persons could be run in very different brains, bodies, and environments, after the destruction of the brain which had been their original operating environment. In view of the possibility of there being different sorts of spaces, it is possible that a programme developed in a physical brain on earth could be run on a piece of hardware of a very different sort, in a very different sort of space. Dennett does not explore just how different such an environment might be, but the main point, that a person could exist in a very different embodied world, is remarkably like some religious doctrines of the resurrection of the body.[9] For such doctrines, human bodies and personalities will be recreated in a new and superior sort of material world, long after the original bodies had decomposed and disappeared. Dennett remarks that this is quite conceivable for a materialist, and in that sense the survival of the self after the death of its physical body is possible, though he thinks it is highly unlikely. Surprising as it may seem, then, a theist could be a contingent materialist with regard to the nature of the human self.

[8] Dennett, *Consciousness Explained*, 430.
[9] Cf. the classical Christian source, 1 Cor. 15: 35–8.

MATERIALISM AND THE SOUL

Any materialist who does not simply ignore the facts of consciousness and intentional action will need a view of matter that enables it to become conscious and to exhibit purposive behaviour at a certain stage of complexity. One may see material things as extended parts of space which possess various powers to interact with other things in space. It is impossible to put a priori limits on the sorts of powers of interaction which material things can have. When one is dealing with relatively simple structures existing in isolation from other physical systems, one need consider only a limited range of interactive powers. For instance, Newtonian laws of mechanics provide an adequate account of the motions of most planetary bodies. In the light of quantum mechanics and relativity physics, we know that there are a great many complex forces at work in such situations, but they can usually be ignored. It is sufficient for most purposes to measure such factors as mass, velocity, size, and location, and to regard objects such as planets as related solely by fairly simple mathematical relationships involving those factors. The astronomer works with an ideal abstraction, plotting the relation of a few measurable powers or forces. That is enough for purposes of prediction in most cases (the perihelion of Mercury being one outstanding exception).

When one considers more complex physical structures, a greater range of forces needs to be considered. In solid-state physics one needs to take quantum effects into account, and other powers, such as weak and strong nuclear forces, will become relevant in accounting for the behaviour of objects. At the level of human consciousness one has to introduce the concepts of information-theory to understand what is going on. The powers of physical objects include the capacity to react to higher-level representations of the environment (perceptions), and the capacity to act to preserve complex physical structures (intentions). The powers of material objects include the power of environmental awareness and control. That power can only be realized in an incredibly complex and highly structured physical environment, but it is a natural and perhaps inevitable unfolding of the potentialities of matter that it should come to exhibit consciousness and control in some form.

One of the transformations of outlook that has been brought about by evolutionary theory is an acceptance of a continuum of development in organic life-forms. There may, as Stephen J. Gould has argued, have been sudden jumps (saltations) in evolution—as, for example, from the pongid to the hominid brain.[10] Even so, the saltation builds on the basis of previous evolution, perhaps transforming it by including it within a new holistic structure, but not simply starting again with a quite new form of life.

At each stage one can see a new set of powers coming into being. Before the genesis of organic life, chunks of matter interact in repetitive and regular, almost mechanical ways, without forming unities which are more than accidental agglomerations of atoms and molecules. In plant forms of life, there begin to exist within the plant holistic responses to stimuli such as light and water, and behavioural patterns of growth, flowering, and seeding. In elementary forms of animal life, the development of specialized senses increases perception of the environment, and 'instinctive' behaviour of moving, fighting, mating, and nesting becomes established. In the higher animals, one has clear evidence of consciousness of the environment, and of intentional behaviour, guided by inborn mechanisms or by immediate external stimuli.

As organic life develops through these increasingly complex stages, consciousness becomes more sensitive, defined, and specialized, and the set of behavioural dispositions also increases in complexity, range, and specificity of response. The process seems to be one of a gradual flowering of potentialities, made possible by more complex forms of physical organization, which realize new potentialities in an environment which is suitable for their actualization. One does not need to think of consciousness and dispositions to act as coming from outside the physical realm, as though there was some pre-existing set of spiritual powers which is then matched exactly to a physical structure. The situation is more like one in which the physical realm develops powers of consciousness and action from its own complex structuring and interaction.

Physical objects have an interior aspect, developing from the unconscious and routine behaviour of inorganic solids, through the slow and dimly responsive life of plants to the conscious perceptual states and goal-directed behaviour of the higher animals.[11] Human

---

[10] S. J. Gould, 'Epidosic Change Versus Gradualist Dogma', in *Science and Nature*, 2 (1979), 5–12.

[11] Such a view is expounded in A. N. Whitehead, *Process and Reality*, corr. and ed. D. R. Griffin and P. W. Sherbourne (New York: Free Press, 1978).

beings are parts of this continuum of a developing interior life of the material realm. In an evolutionary saltation made possible by the rapid growth of the neo-cortex, humans develop linguistic ability, the capacity for abstract and reflective thought, and a sense of moral responsibility for their actions. At this stage, consciousness becomes able to distance itself from its immediately embodied situation. Most animals are conscious of and respond to immediate stimuli in their environment, and pursue fairly immediate goals, such as fighting, food-seeking, or mating. But human animals can stand back from immediate stimuli, consider possible situations, and evaluate them. They can formulate goals to be pursued, and evaluate the efficiency of their own acts in pursuing them. They can frame general ideas of worthwhile states and policies of obtaining them. They can have an intellectual grasp of the nature of their environment, an appreciation of its beauty and order, and frame long-term intentions to modify that environment in accordance with imagined goals. They can, in short, frame general ideas of truth, beauty, and goodness, and order their behaviour in accordance with them.

This is certainly a qualitative evolutionary leap, from an organism which is immersed in the immediate environment to an organism which is capable of formulating abstract general ideas and pursuing reflectively constructed goals. But that is not a very good reason for thinking that humans uniquely possess spiritually preformed souls inserted into physically receptive brains, while animals do not. It is a reason for seeing human souls as a fuller development of potentialities always present in the material world, which are realizable only after a long process of developing integrated organic structure and complexity has been completed. The immediate perceptual responses and instinctive behaviour of the lower animals are on the same continuum of being as the abstract thought and responsible decision-making of *Homo sapiens*.

The human soul, on this view, develops as the inner aspect of the human brain. But it need not be thought of as a passive epiphenomenon, as though it was a mere by-product of an activity of the brain which is explicable in terms of laws of physics alone. The principles that govern physical changes in the organism are modified by the emergence of the soul/brain as a higher-level organizing and initiating centre of the organism. The soul/brain operates in accordance with laws of logic and intention as well as in accordance with laws of neuro-chemistry. It is not satisfactory to think of these two sets of laws operating in two different parallel realms, the mental and the physical. When a person thinks, the brain moves through a series of connected physical states. One has to regard the causal impetus as coming from the directed thinking, and not simply from a prior physical state of the brain, in accordance with laws of momentum and so on.

One might say that the brain can direct itself in accordance with laws of logic. It does so by modifying the physical programmes, wired into the brain, which would otherwise operate in a purely physically directed way. Responding to stimuli from the environment, it is able to organize and modify its responses to change that environment, and in doing so it moves beyond the regularities with which physics deals into a realm of creative freedom. The brain is a physical organ that transcends the machine-like regularities of mechanics, and thereby reveals that mechanism never was the whole story even about atoms and molecules. Matter always contained the potentiality for sensitive inner response and creative action, and the evolution of the human soul is the gradual realization of that potentiality.[12]

This is a form of 'identity theory', identifying the mind (or soul) and the brain. But it is not a reductive theory, which would account for all brain activity in terms of laws of physics or chemistry alone. It stresses the potentiality of matter for coming to awareness of itself and for consciously directing its own future, and thus tends to see the elementary laws of physics as structuring a basic substratum of matter, which is to be built on and modified through evolution. Laws of physics, on this view, do not determine everything that happens, but lay the foundation for the evolution of matter towards conscious self-direction.

When one reaches the human stage of evolution, the sorts of powers that physical objects can actualize have been rapidly expanded. At the earliest stages only routine powers such as gravitational attraction or electro-magnetic force are actualized, in relatively simple environments in which other powers can be ignored. The human world is a complex biological environment, in which complex physical objects can actualize powers of conscious

---

[12] Such a 'theory of emergence', which distances itself from the pan-psychism of some Process thought, is expounded in A. R. Peacocke, *Theology for a Scientific Age* (London: SCM, 1993), esp. ch. 12.

attention, subjective evaluation, and creative response. The inner aspect of the material realm has increased enormously in importance and causal efficacy. What looks from outside to be a sequence of electro-chemical processes in the brain is experienced by that brain as a sequence of experiences, decisions, and intentions, organized and directed by a continuing subject of consciousness. The subject is, of course, the brain, but the brain as a subjectively experiencing and partly self-directing entity. That subject is what has been traditionally referred to as the soul in Christian theology.[13]

THE SOUL AND DISEMBODIED EXISTENCE

Whereas in the early stages of evolution the inner aspect of matter has little causal efficacy, as the brain develops, its inner consciousness becomes richer and its causal input to the environment becomes greater. The subject of consciousness and action *is* the brain, but the brain as developing new and astonishing powers of sensitivity and creativity. The subject cannot exist at all without some environment to provide content to its awareness and an interactive field for its actions. But the possibility arises that the inner aspect may achieve a content which is not limited to what is given by immediate sensory stimulation, and a set of goals that are abstractable from the immediate sensory environment. At that stage, it becomes theoretically possible for the inner aspect to split off from the outer.

One can see this happening to some extent in the imaginative and dream life of higher animals, when sensory images occur without external sensory stimulation. Of course the brain is still active, and may be the main cause of the occurrence of such images. But if that image-life could take on greater autonomy, and come under conscious control, it could in principle continue to exist without the brain that first caused the images to occur.[14]

More significantly, a person may at first engage in linguistic behaviour, then be taught a language by others, and finally begin to use that language creatively, modifying the original and natural behaviour patterns in consciously directed ways. The more that thinking becomes causally initiating in the sequence of brain-

---

[13] Cf. the classical discussion in Thomas Aquinas, *Summa Theologiae*, I q. 76 a. 1 (London: Blackfriars, 1964).

[14] This possibility is elaborated by H. H. Price, *Essays in the Philosophy of Religion* (Oxford: Clarendon, 1972), 105–17.

events, and the more that thought-processes become removed from a direct concern with immediate problems of food-gathering or defence, the easier it is for the rich mental life of thinking, feeling, and willing to exist without the physical brain which generated it.

In this sense, the evolution of matter naturally tends to transcend the limits of its external mechanisms, and to generate forms of being which can disengage from their material environment. When inner conscious life is no longer confined to direct depiction of its immediate environment, or to direct concern with immediate problems in that environment, then it can take on a reality of its own. The soul (the subject of experience and action) is the inner aspect of the brain, and cannot exist without objects of experience and action. But the soul can in principle disengage from the brain, and find objects of experience and action in new ways.[15]

To take an example, the power of walking upright is one that is naturally possessed by human beings. It is a natural physical power, though it has to be learned and practised before it can be properly actualized. As humans grow, they learn to exercise this power intentionally. They are not simply subject to instinct or to immediate response to stimuli. They can decide to walk to get to specific places when and how they want to. Most humans will be able to abstract, from their ability to modify their walking behaviour, the general intention to be in a particular place at a particular time. Once such a general intention has been formed, it is possible that one could realize the intention without walking, if some other means of locomotion can be found (one can ride or drive).

A perfectly ordinary and obviously physical power has generated the abstract intention to be directly aware of a particular place by any appropriate means. That intention, with a set of associated desires and other purposes, could exist without any physical brain or body, if it was possible to have direct awareness of an environment without a body. Whether such a thing is possible is a question of fact. There are many reported cases of environmental awareness, which is not obtained through ordinary sensory organs. Patients undergoing serious operations sometimes report seeing the operating theatre from a point outside their own bodies.[16]

---

[15] This view is elaborated a little in K. Ward, *Defending the Soul* (Oxford: Oneworld, 1992), ch. 7.

[16] Accounts are given in David Lorimer, *Survival?* (London: Routledge, 1984), ch. 10.

Clairvoyants claim to describe scenes at which they are not physically present.

Whether one gives much credence to such reports or not, it seems that they present coherent possibilities. To investigate them is not just to investigate the logically impossible. One can see how disembodied existence is possible in principle, even for an identity-theorist who accepts that the identity of inner and outer aspects of the soul/brain is a contingent one. Such an existence beyond the death of the body will be possible only for beings which do develop a fairly rich imaginative and causally efficacious conscious life. This would seem to include what are called the higher animals and human beings. It suggests that the Christian tradition has been roughly correct in granting possible immortality to 'intellectual souls', or souls capable of abstract understanding and responsible activity, but rather too restrictive in its understanding of 'intellect' as a purely human and overtly linguistic attribute.[17]

This view may be characterized as a sort of very soft materialism, since it allows not only that physical bodies possess mental characteristics (soft materialism), but that such characteristics could in principle exist in different forms of embodiment, or even in a disembodied way, however unsatisfactory that might be. It may be felt that the difference between this view and that of soft dualism is vanishingly small. Dualists hold that souls are distinct spiritual substances that are contingently connected to material brains. Thus Richard Swinburne suggests that 'the soul is like a light bulb and the brain is like an electric light socket'.[18] This analogy implies that the soul is a fully formed structure, which requires the brain for its operation, but comes to that brain as an external and subsistent entity. The trouble with such a dualism is that it makes the connection between soul and brain quite mysterious: 'We cannot say what it is about the brain which gives rise to mental events, nor what it is about the soul which requires a brain to sustain it'.[19] Indeed, it seems that mental events could originate very well without a brain, and the existence of a brain seems oddly superfluous.

Swinburne describes himself as a 'soft dualist', by which he means that the functioning of the soul normally requires the func-

[17] A discussion of the status of non-human animals in this regard is given by Andrew Linzey, *Animal Rights* (London: SCM, 1976), ch. 7.
[18] Richard Swinburne, *The Evolution of the Soul* (Oxford: Clarendon, 1986), 310.
[19] Ibid. 195.

tioning of some body. It is a small step from here to saying that it is
the functioning of the brain which *is* the functioning of the soul,
even though the soul can later develop so that it can function in a
different sort of embodiment. On the soft dualist view, the soul is
complete in itself, but (contingently) needs to be switched on by the
brain. On the soft materialist view, the soul originates and develops
as the brain does, and its proper form of being is to bring to consciousness the properties of the material world in which it is
embodied, and to shape those properties in accordance with reflectively formulated goals, rooted in the natural desires and behaviour
of the physical organism. It is possible for the soul, the inner aspect
of the brain, to be separated from the brain, but one might suspect
that such is not its natural and proper condition.[20] One might hope,
in other words, for a resurrection of the body rather than for a disembodied immortality of the soul.

The topic of consciousness is one of the greatest mysteries of
human thought. I do not rate my chances of formulating an adequate account of it very highly. What I am sure of is that, on a theistic view, God is a conscious and creative being who acts to realize
and appreciate states and processes of intrinsic value.[21] Humans, as
made in the divine image, are conscious and creative beings, and
they can act freely and responsibly to realize and consciously appreciate values. What it is important to preserve, in any theistic
account of human nature, is the capacity for free creative action and
for conscious appreciation of value. It is important to preserve the
possibility of a positive relationship to God, in which one can
apprehend the infinite source of all value, and co-operate with the
infinite source of all creativity. To speak of 'the soul' is to speak of
that, in the created order, which acts freely, appreciates consciously, and relates in awareness and action to the Divine.[22] This
requires a non-reductive account of human nature, an account
which does not reduce free action to imprinted behaviour, consciousness to organic response, or knowledge to purely sensory
data.

The difficulty is to give an adequate account of freedom and
awareness which is consistent with the best scientific knowledge of

---

[20] Aquinas, *Summa Theologiae*, I q. 76 a. 1.
[21] Cf. the second vol. of this project, *Religion and Creation* (Oxford: Clarendon,
1996), 341–6.
[22] Cf. Ward, *Defending the Soul*, 151–2.

the development and nature of the human brain. Dualists tend to the view that freedom and awareness lie outside the causally conditioned material realm, in a separate substance, which must interact with the material through the brain.[23] That, of course, implies that the material must be open to spiritual influence, and so perhaps it is not quite so causally conditioned as may have been thought. Non-dualists emphasize that point, and see free action as a natural increase of the creative power that exists in all physical objects, but is restricted at low levels of physical complexity to rather simple and routine behaviour. They see awareness of the environment as a natural increase of the responsiveness of all objects to external stimuli, which again develops in richness and complexity as matter becomes more organized and structured. Non-dualists do not deny freedom and consciousness, but see it as developing out of the material structure itself, perhaps as it is drawn towards its proper fulfilment by the attracting causality of God.

The soul, on either account, is the subject of free action, conscious understanding, and mutual relationship. It is embodied, and that is its proper form, since it requires an environment to provide content for its consciousness and to be the field of its actions. It is not confined to this earthly body, and may, at least once it has developed, be embodied in various forms. The non-dualist, impressed by a view of the evolutionary continuum of organic life, and by evidence from neurophysiology of the way in which mental activities can be mapped onto brain activities, will identify the soul, in its origin and development, with the inner aspect of a complex brain of the sort found in hominids. The non-dualist theist will accept that the inner aspect of the brain can split off while the brain itself ceases to exist, and that inner aspect can be re-embodied in other forms.

One may well feel that the proper fulfilment of the soul is to be able to express its powers positively and creatively in a material body, so there is good reason to hope for resurrection. Even the idea of a disembodied state will in fact introduce some analogous form of embodiment, if souls are to communicate with one another

---

[23] The classical exponent of such dualism is Descartes, in the *Méditations* (1641), but his position is more subtle than is sometimes supposed: 'I am not just lodged in my body like a pilot in his ship, but am . . . so confused and intermingled with it that I and my body compose . . . a single whole', trans. A. Wollaston (London: Penguin, 1960), Meditation 6, p. 161.

or learn from and interact with an environment. It is not accidental that most religious accounts of disembodied states (such as Purgatory) in fact speak of bodies of some sort, even if they are in some ways more like the bodies we sometimes seem to have in dreams, shaped by our desires and not fully substantial, than like the bodies we now have. Such relatively disembodied states are not usually seen as finally satisfactory states of the soul, but as preparations for forms of embodiment which may be free of some of the restrictions imposed by the moral and physical limitations of earthly existence.

With a degree of tentativeness, therefore, I suggest that a soft identity theory provides one of the most plausible accounts of the human soul, and is compatible with the main Abrahamic traditions on the subject. What a theist will wish to maintain is that the ultimate reality, God, is not limited by the set of space-time relations in which we exist, that God creates the universe for a purpose, and that the purpose can be achieved, at least after bodily death. Materialism, as a philosophical theory, is often asserted as an attack on such religious beliefs. It is not, however, in a non-reductive form, incompatible with the beliefs just mentioned.

First, materialism is not in a position to deny that there logically could be a non-spatially extended reality, God. In so far as it accepts the view of many physicists that there are, or may be, many different space-times and many different forms of space, it is even able to allow for a divine space, not spatially related to this space-time. This can, strange as it may sound, permit a materialist notion of God. Just as some brain-states give knowledge or apparent knowledge of objects in the environment, so other brain-states could give apparent knowledge of such a God. Therefore a materialist account can allow both for the existence of God and for the occurrence of brain-states which give veridical knowledge of God. If God and knowledge of God is denied, it will not be on the ground of a materialist theory alone.

Second, many materialists assert their theory because they want to say that the existence of the universe is a matter of blind chance. But again that does not follow from a materialist view. Even the most hardened materialist must accept that human beings formulate conscious purposes and bring things about in accordance with such purposes. A materialist view insists that the existence of such purposes is compatible with a physicalist account of what is really going on. In other word, materialism does not eliminate human purpose. Reductive materialism hazards the guess that a complete physical account can one day be given of such purposes, but even that in no way implies that human actions are in fact all due to blind chance. Non-reductive materialism is quite compatible with the assertion that human behaviour is genuinely purposive. So there is no special problem about the idea of a divine purpose for the universe. The reductive materialist will assert, on faith, that a complete physical account could in principle be given of the universe. But even that will not show that there is no purpose in the existence of the universe. Any such account, to be successful, will have to be compatible with the existence of such a purpose, if there is one, and cannot simply eliminate it. Non-reductive materialism can assert that the true nature of matter is only seen when one perceives its development towards the final goal of the realization of its inner potentiality for complete self-awareness and self-directedness, and for the actualization of apprehended value.

To use a favourite example of contemporary materialism, the fact that a complete physical account can be given of the workings of a computer does not at all imply that computers work by blind chance, and not by design. On the contrary, the more complete the physical account, the more likely it is that the whole thing has been amazingly designed. So it is with the universe. That the universe as such has a purpose, or that there are particular events within the universe which may be called 'intentional acts of God', are claims as compatible with materialism as is the claim that there are particular physical events which may be called 'intentional human acts'. The question of whether such a compatibilist account is coherent, and of whether a complete physical account of the universe could ever be given, in principle, are different questions. As a matter of fact, I believe, on general philosophical grounds, that the answer to both questions is 'no'. But even if the answer is 'yes', a fully paid-up materialist could believe that the universe is intentionally created by God, and that it contains many divine purposes.[24]

---

[24] Maurice Wiles, while far from being a materialist, provides an account of divine action in the universe which is in fact compatible with a materialist account, in *God's Action in the World* (London: SCM, 1986). The insufficiency of a purely physicalist account of the universe is defended by R. Taylor, *Action and Purpose* (Englewood Cliffs, NJ: Prentice-Hall, 1966), and by K. Ward, *Divine Action* (London: Collins, 1990), esp. ch. 5.

Third, a materialist can believe in the possibility of life after the death of a particular body, simply by supposing, as Dennett suggests, that the information-bearing programme which constitutes a body as a personal agent is inserted into a different body, even a different sort of body, as long as it is capable of running the programme. That different body may even be better suited to actualizing the dispositional powers of the programme than was the original, which may have been damaged or defective in some way. Thus the theory of materialism is not as such incompatible with the existence of a creator God, of a purpose for the universe, and of a resurrection life, probably in a different space-time, for those who have died in this space-time.

It is nevertheless obvious that most of those who call themselves materialists are opposed to religious belief. They wish to deny the existence of objective values or an objective moral law, of an authoritative God, and of the truth of religious experience-claims. They often wish to reduce all forms of understanding and explanation to some sort of mechanistic explanation in terms of brute physical laws, and to see human life as a vastly improbable accident in a purposeless and uncaring universe.

Theists will naturally oppose such claims, pointing out that they are at least as undetermined by the facts and as speculative as most theistic claims. But theists can accept a more limited materialist claim that brain-states are contingently identical with mental states, or that the soul is a sort of informational programme which must be operated in complex physical environments. That is a theory that must be judged on its merits. In any case, the Abrahamic traditions, at least, can accept a form of materialism. They are not as such committed to mind–body or soul–body dualism, especially not in a strong form.[25]

The relation between the Abrahamic traditions and materialism is accordingly quite a close one, and much depends upon what sort of interpretation one gives to 'materialism'. Certainly, the Abrahamic theist would accept that humans are essentially embodied beings, living in a common public spatial world, that such a world

---

[25] Cf. Oscar Cullmann, *Immortality of the Soul or Resurrection of the Dead?* (London: Epworth, 1958). This view is now almost standard in contemporary theology: 'The concept of humankind as animated bodies rather than incarnated souls is generally characteristic of Hebrew thought', Church of England Doctrine Commission, *The Mystery of Salvation* (London: Church House, 1995).

really exists, and that it has a positive part to play in realizing the divine purposes. Nevertheless, the Abrahamic traditions need to insist that the material exists for the sake of the values and purposes that it realizes. In that sense, a reductive materialism, which makes consciousness and purpose accidental by-products of purposeless laws, must be eschewed. But a more expansive materialism, which sees matter as a vehicle and expression of consciously enjoyed values and goal-directed activities, is one possible metaphysical articulation of a doctrine of human nature.

BIBLICAL AND TRADITIONAL VIEWS OF THE SOUL

In the Hebrew Bible, the close connection between such an expansive materialism and belief in the existence of the soul is clear. Genesis 2: 7, part of the second creation account in the book of Genesis, states that 'the Lord God formed man of dust from the ground, and breathed into his nostrils the breath of life; and man became a living being'. Humans are formed of dust, of material energy, and they will return to dust. They are given life by the breath of God, which can be given and taken away by God. The Hebrew word used here for breath is *neshamah*, but in Genesis 6: 17 the same thought, 'the breath of life', is expressed by the word *ruach*, which can be translated as 'air' or 'spirit'. So humans are pieces of matter formed and given life by the spirit of God, or by spirit which emanates from God, as breath emanates from a living being.

Another important element in the biblical creation stories is given in the first creation account, which states that 'God said, "Let us make man in our image, after our likeness" '.[26] Humans image God, like reflections in a mirror or sparks from a fire. They are given 'dominion' over the natural world. Just as God creates and cares for all creatures, so humans are to share in this Lordship, by caring for the natural world and ordering it to the glory and service of God.

The Genesis creation stories express the belief that the material universe is created for the sake of the forms of goodness it makes possible. Humans do not exist eternally, but originate as parts of the material universe. They have a special role in the universe,

----

[26] Gen. 1: 26.

which is to shape it to express the glory of God. They also share in the Spirit of God, and so are able to relate in friendship and love to God. They can be seen as mediators between the material and spiritual realms, ordering matter to become a manifestation of spirit, and offering the material realm, through their consciousness and actions, as a sacrifice of praise to God.

Early Hebrew thought does not make a great distinction between humans and other animals. Presumably every living thing, not just humanity, is filled with 'the breath of life'. If humans are uniquely in the image of God, this uniqueness lies in their role as stewards of the created world and as the 'priests of creation', who offer it in worship to the Creator. It does not lie in any ontological uniqueness (in being a soul-substance, for example), except in so far as responsible stewardship and worship of God both require reflective thought and fully intentional action. One might fairly say that, on the biblical view, humans are complex structures of matter which have become capable of self-consciousness, reflection, and purposively self-directed action. They lie at one end, on earth, of a continuum of living things, with a responsibility for the well-being of the material order of which they are part.

It is not surprising, then, that there is little sign of a belief in the immortality of the soul in the thought of the Hebrew Bible. But there are factors pulling in another direction. The Creator is pure Spirit, with consciousness and will. Thus hard materialism, the theory that there cannot exist consciousness without a material brain, must be false. According to the prophets, God has a desire for relationship with created personal beings. This cannot be a relationship between material beings, so again the possibility, and indeed the fact, of an immaterial, spiritual, personal relationship is asserted by the Bible. For early Hebrew belief, humans are material beings which yet contain the possibility of a purely spiritual relationship.

This is the basis of what became the classical Christian idea of the soul as the Form of the body. The idea comes from Aristotle,[27] but was modified to make a place for the Jewish and Christian belief in the essential relation of the soul to God. In Aristotle's view, Forms are universals or defining natures which are given actualization and individuated by matter. The soul is the Form of the body, a particular instantiation of a defining nature. However, Aristotle seems to

[27] Aristotle, *De Anima*, 2. 1, trans. J. L. Creed and A. E. Wardman, *The Philosophy of Aristotle* (New York: Mentor, 1963), 246.

think of a soul, not merely as an abstract definition, but as an actual power that enables a body to act in a certain way. Nutritive souls cause plants to grow and multiply. Animal souls cause animals to perceive and move. Rational souls cause humans to think and intend. Humans are distinctive in having rational souls, which are those properties of bodies which enable them to think and intend.

The Aristotelian idea of a Form includes both the idea of an essential nature and of a final cause, or proper goal of activity. So, in speaking of a Form of the body, one would be speaking of its essential nature, which can be actualized as the goal of a process of activity. In the Aristotelian world-view, matter has a teleological aspect, a goal towards which it moves. In the case of the human body, that goal is the actualization in the body of the full nature of an intellectual being, a conscious and self-directing agent. It is natural for a theist to accept this account, since theists believe that God creates for a goal, and that matter is the proper vehicle of realizing and expressing that goal. In this sense, hope for the resurrection of the body is a reasonable consequence of the doctrine of creation. But the universe may need to be re-created before that becomes a possibility, and souls may need to be prepared in forms of intermediate existence for life in such a renewed universe. Christian tradition thus speaks both of a resurrection of the flesh, and of an intermediate state, in which souls born into a corrupted and alienated world can be refashioned into their proper, or divinely intended, forms.

In traditional Catholic theology, a basically Aristotelian account of the soul is accepted. Thomas Aquinas's account, for example, maintains that the soul is the Form of the body. But he also holds that the intellectual soul is a substantial Form. It is capable of existing on its own, though in 'an unnatural and imperfect way'.[28] In the case of plants and animals, such souls are material properties, and are not separable from the bodies that manifest their activity. This may be true of humans as well, but Aristotle canvasses the possibility of the agent of thought being immaterial, since understanding, he supposes, is not a material activity, and thus possibly has some sort of existence without the body. Aquinas amplifies this view, and asserts that the rational soul is a spiritual principle of thinking and intending which can exist without a body, but whose

---

[28] Aquinas, *Summa Theologiae*, I q. 76 a. 1.

proper function is to animate a particular material body, to which it is intrinsically fitted.

Thinking, after all, is closely dependent on sense-activity to provide objects of thought. Intending is dependent on a body which can act in the world. So the soul is that which gives a particular complex material body the capacity for reflection and rational agency. It is the subject of the experiences and actions of a particular body. This view can be developed in two different ways. One gives a hard materialist interpretation (which was probably Aristotle's own), so that talking about the soul is simply a way of talking about the properties of a material body which enable it to think. To say that humans are rational souls is just to say that they are animals that can think. The thinking cannot exist without the body, the matter, which makes that activity possible. But one can also give a soft materialist interpretation (which appears to have been that of Aquinas), so that the thinking subject can exist substantially. If it does, however, it exists 'unnaturally' or 'improperly', since each soul or substantial intellective Form is meant to be the active principle of a material body, and indeed of a particular material body.

Aquinas maintained that the developing human embryo naturally develops first a vegetative or organic, and then a sensitive or animal, soul. At 'the completion of man's coming into being', about six weeks after conception, this soul is destroyed, and God creates in its place an intellectual soul which possesses the new power of understanding. That soul is naturally immortal or incorruptible, because it does not consist of parts, and so cannot decay. It naturally survives the death of the body.

Aquinas was thus able to develop a view of the soul, the subject of thinking and willing, as able to exist after death in a 'disembodied' state, by the grace of God. In that state, development or purification of the soul is possible (in Purgatory), preparing it for eventual resurrection. But it will not form a complete person until the resurrection of the body, when it will once again have its proper organ of perception and action in a public, communal world. The resurrection, for Aquinas, was to be of this earthly physical body, with all its physical attributes, though in a perfected form.[29] At the Last Judgement, when earthly history has come to an end, all souls

[29] Cf. the useful discussion in Brian Davies, *The Thought of Thomas Aquinas* (Oxford: Clarendon, 1992), 215–20.

will receive their own bodies, and will enter into their eternal destiny, for final union with or exclusion from the presence of God.

Disagreements on this subject between Catholic and some Protestant theologians are fairly minor. They mainly arise from the fact that some Protestants insist that the soul never exists in a disembodied state, and so 'sleeps' between death and the General Resurrection. This makes any thought of development of the person after death, or of possible repentance after earthly death, virtually impossible to conceive. The traditional Catholic view, however, also denies the possibility of repentance after death, and the doctrine of Purgatory, as officially formulated, seems more like a time of expiatory punishment than of positive development. So many theologians, probably most, feel that the traditional views need to be restated in some way.[30]

The traditional Christian view holds that each soul is naturally immortal, and is directly created by God,[31] which can give the impression of a series of supernatural interventions that, strangely, seem to be dictated by developments in the central nervous system. It is hard to think that a brain may develop and start functioning in the normal way, but will have no soul if God does not specially create one. It is more plausible to think of the soul as emerging by natural processes of development. The traditional idea, however, is restatable in a way which takes account of this point.

The idea that God directly creates each human soul is meant to oppose two ideas. One is the idea that the soul is simply a product of material forces, that it is a material entity in a reductive sense. The other is that the soul is solely a product of its parents, and not a unique individual in its own right. One can rephrase this in contemporary terms by saying that the soul is a truly emergent entity, carrying quite new properties of understanding and intentionality. It has a unique individuality. It is capable, as the inner aspect of the brain, of existing without that brain, though it is a natural part of its perfection to be embodied in a public world of interacting persons. And, since it is essentially capable of conscious relationship to God, it is rational to hope that God will cause it to exist in a form in which such a relationship can be properly actualized.

[30] Such a restatement is attempted in the final chapter of this book.
[31] Cf. *Catechism of the Catholic Church* (London: Geoffrey Chapman, 1994), para. 366, p. 83.

There is no doubt, for a Christian, that God causes every soul to exist, as a new and unique entity which is both properly embodied and properly meant to be consciously related to God, and that God will hold each soul in being until the possibility of such a relationship has been fully placed before it. These are the essential elements meant to be safeguarded by the traditional doctrines of the direct creation of each soul by God and the natural immortality of the soul. They are compatible with a greater stress than has been usual in the tradition on the continuity of human and animal life, on the natural genesis by emergence of new entities within a non-reductive material order, and on the total dependence of the soul on divine grace for its existence beyond physical death.

Jewish, Christian, and Muslim views of the soul are compatible with scientific accounts of the emergence of consciousness through a long process of evolution, and of the contingent dependence of mental activity upon the functioning of a complex central nervous system and brain. In speaking of the human soul, these religious traditions do not necessarily mean to introduce a separate and distinct spiritual entity, related in some external way to the human brain and body. They do, however, mean to stress the importance of freedom and dignity, of the search for goodness, beauty, and truth, and of relationship to God, as distinctive features of developed conscious life. They mean that the whole evolutionary system is properly seen as directed towards the goal of bringing into existence such developed forms of consciousness, and cannot therefore be regarded as a mere mechanism, with no significance or purpose. Such forms of consciousness may not be confined to the human species, but we are at least sure that the human species normally and properly exhibits such a form of consciousness, so that its existence is a goal of the divine activity, not an accident of blind nature.

This does, however, raise a major religious problem. If human beings can be properly viewed as goals of divine activity, which activity is directed to the realization of intrinsic goodness in the universe, how does it come about that human lives are so often, in Thomas Hobbes's words, 'nasty, brutish and short'? The traditional Christian answer to this problem is that the first members of the human species sinned, and corrupted human nature. Judaism and Islam do not have a doctrine of 'original sin', but they do traditionally share the view that humanity fell from a condition of original perfection into a state of suffering, wrongdoing, and death.

The ideas of original perfection and of a fall from it are not easily compatible with evolutionary theory. These ideas may have to be discarded or revised in the light of modern scientific knowledge. The next chapter will consider whether or to what extent this is the case.

8
Original Sin

The biblical narrative of Adam and Eve in the Garden of Eden may seem to be completely outdated by the evolutionary account of human genesis. After all, if one takes the Genesis narrative literally, humans were directly created by God in about 4004 BCE, and lived in a state of bliss and knowledge of God in a world without death or suffering. When they disobeyed God they were punished by having to cultivate the earth in hardship and bear children in suffering, and so death entered the world. This contrasts sharply with the evolutionist account of humans evolving from other species, and achieving their dominant position on earth by the exercise of a lust and aggression which become necessary conditions of their survival in a competitive environment. Death and suffering existed for millennia before humans arrived on the scene, and the first humans were probably ignorant, barbaric, and religiously primitive. The idea of a 'fall' from grace seems to have been replaced by the idea of a hesitant, ambiguous, and only partly successful 'rise' towards moral and rational action.

The contrast is not in fact as great as this suggests. The Genesis narrative is usually interpreted in recent theology as primarily symbolic of the human situation, rather than as literally descriptive. It is most plausibly taken in the same way that one takes myths of origin from other primal traditions, as an imaginative and putatively inspired symbolization of the fundamental elements of the human situation. If one does that, Adam, which can simply mean 'person' in Hebrew, becomes the symbol of humanity, and Eden, 'bliss', is the ideal intended state of human existence. Humanity is intended to know and love God, and to care for the earth in harmony and joy. When Adam takes the fruit of the tree of knowledge against God's command, what is being pointed to is a basic flaw in human knowledge and understanding. Humans seek knowledge before they are ready for it, they seek knowledge without responsibility, and use it for self-regarding purposes. Their misuse of knowledge leads to profound spiritual death, separation from knowledge of and friendship with God. It leads to the institution of work as drudgery, to the creation of forms of social oppression and to a sense of estrangement from the environment and from other sentient life.

This is a profound analysis of the human condition, and it is quite compatible with the evolutionist account of human biological origins. As is common in primal origin stories, the concern is not with what happened at the beginning of human history, but with the condition of every human being in relation to the environment and to God. The 'beginning' is the intended ideal and the 'Fall' is the flawed human condition, which makes that ideal apparently impossible of achievement, though it remains the true human goal.

Nevertheless, it is hard to resist the question of whether humans could ever have achieved the ideal without flaw, and of how that flaw came into being. Was the Fall necessary, and was it in any sense a historical event? One might just say, as Buddhists tend to do, that these are unanswerable and unprofitable questions. We can see the ideal and the flaw, and what is important is what one can now do about it. It is unimportant to know exactly how and when humans originated. But I do not think this is quite satisfactory. If one believes that humans were created by God, that God is a being of perfect goodness who wills fellowship with humans, and that humans are apparently trapped in a world of corrupting self-regard and estrangement from God, some account is needed of how such a situation is possible.

The first stage of such an account is to understand the nature of the universe as a realm of integral and emergent creativity. It is a universe of interlocking energies, such that the creation of the new is made possible only by the replacement and destruction of the old. Destruction and death are built into the universe as necessary conditions of its progress to new forms of life. All things are ephemeral and co-dependent, and the perpetual perishing of all things gives rise to the genesis of the new. Out of the destruction of primordial energy the basic subatomic particles were generated. Out of the destruction of stars the molecular elements of carbon were generated. Out of the mutation, and thus the destruction, of patterns of DNA, new and more complex forms of life were generated. Out of the feeding of one form of life upon another, animal species of more sentient kinds were generated.

Thus when humans first came into being, they were already locked into a world in which competition and death were fundamental to their very existence. In this long process of the emergence of consciousness, there was a first moment at which a sentient animal became aware of moral obligation. At some point, animal life emerged from a stage of what Hegel called 'dreaming innocence',[1] at which moral considerations were irrelevant, since animals simply acted in ways natural to their species. At that point, a sentient consciousness discerned, or thought it discerned, an obligation to act in one way rather than another, an obligation which it was free to respond to or ignore. It seems to me plausible to say that it was at that point that truly personal consciousness first began to exist.

Two elements seem to be axiomatic about moral obligation. One is that, if a moral obligation truly exists, then it must be possible to meet it; otherwise it is not an obligation. The other is that it must also be possible to ignore it; otherwise it is not a matter of morality. It therefore seems to me beyond dispute that there must have been a first sin in the history of this planet. There must have been a moment when a conscious being decided to ignore an obligation, when it need not have done so. It is not an antique fable, it is an indisputable fact, that sin entered into the world through the free action of a conscious being which chose to do what it should not and need not have done.

In the biblical narrative, the first sin is associated with knowledge, obtained in defiance of a divine command.[2] A human being sensed that it ought not to pursue a certain sort of knowledge, and it ignored that obligation. Throughout the mythologies of the world, this theme of forbidden knowledge is to be found. Such knowledge is forbidden because it gives power and self-determination to the knower. It in some way attacks the prerogatives of God—a theme also to be found in the Tower of Babel story. This is the sin of Prometheus, to take what belongs to the gods, and use it for oneself. It is not wrong to know or to seek to know. It is wrong to seek knowledge born of pride and self-will, knowledge obtained for the sake of obtaining personal superiority or power over others.

The sort of knowledge that Genesis speaks about is a 'knowing-how', a knowing-how to grow in understanding of the universe and

---

[1] G. W. F. Hegel, *Phenomenology of Spirit*, trans. A. V. Miller (Oxford: Oxford University Press, 1977), ch. 7C, p. 467.
[2] Gen. 3: 6.

in the capacity to shape one's own further development. When this power exists without love, that is, in disobedience to the commands of the God who is love, then it becomes demonic and destructive. While there is no possibility of ever knowing just what, exactly, the first sin was, the Genesis narrative seems entirely right in pointing out that one of the basic elements of sin is the attempt to gain knowledge as a form of power without love, without the conquest of self-regard.

It is also right to point out that the consequence of such an attempt is 'death', an estrangement from God which leads first to a destruction of others and of the environment, and then, inevitably, to a destruction of self. Again, in trying to conceive such an estrangement from God, I do not think one should take a literalist view that the first humans knew God as a clear and distinct personal presence, as if 'knowing God' was just like knowing another embodied person. It is rather a matter of an unreflective unity with the Divine, a non-thematic consciousness, as Rahner calls it, of the origin and goal of creation, the only real basis of existence.[3]

The most appealing account of these matters in early Christian thought is perhaps that of Irenaeus, who spoke of the first humans as infants, made in the image of God, who were meant to grow by their own co-operation with divine grace into the likeness of God.[4] The Fall consisted in the loss of the sense of a felt unity with the sacred root of being, in the inability to co-operate with its gracious guidance, and so in the growth of that sense of solitude and estrangement which becomes the lot of humanity in a state of sin. The 'banishment from Eden' is the sense of human solitude and weakness that is the consequence of the human attempt to grasp at power without responsible love. The human desire for self-determination becomes a human determination towards self-regard. Therein lies the paradoxical tragedy of human existence, that it is precisely self-regard which leads to the destruction of the self. Human society is a society set on a course of self-destruction, and unless self-regard can be eradicated at its root, there can be no health either for individuals or for society. That is the heart of the doctrine of 'original sin'.

---

[3] Cf. Karl Rahner, *Foundations of Christian Faith* (New York: Crossroads, 1995), 21–2.

[4] Irenaeus, *Against Heresies*, bk. 4, chs. 37 and 38, in *The Ante-Nicene Fathers* (Grand Rapids, Mich.: Eerdmans, 1956), vol. 1.

An evolutionist account of human origins in some ways makes the doctrine of original sin more intelligible than it has been on some traditional accounts. A frequent objection to some traditional understandings of the first sin was that, if humans had clear knowledge of God, they could not possibly choose to disobey God, who is the only source of their being and happiness.[5] Sin then becomes a wholly irrational choice. How could a being faced with the choice of either good or evil, seeing all the unpleasant consequences of evil, possibly choose anything other than good? Sin becomes virtually impossible to account for.

If, on the other hand, one sees human persons as having become a dominant species by being more efficient at replicating, obtaining scarce energy supplies, and eliminating competitors in the struggle for life, then it is perfectly understandable that they should have strong drives to sexuality, possessiveness, and aggression. Instead of sin being almost impossible to account for, it may seem that it is goodness which now becomes virtually impossible. Lust, greed, and aggression are the natural inheritance of every human being. How, then, could anyone wholly escape their power?

This consideration, added to the thought that it must be possible to do what one ought, leads to the conclusion that it cannot have been an obligation for the first proto-humans to be wholly free of lust, greed, and aggression. At the point of the origin of moral obligation, it must have been possible for the natural desires of procreation, possession, and aggression to come under conscious control to some extent, however small. The obligation would be to mould such desires gradually towards a state in which sexuality could become an expression of personal commitment and love, ownership could become stewardship of goods for the sake of the whole community, and competitiveness could become an expression of creativity and striving for fuller life.

The theist will naturally think that these would not be abstract moral obligations, suddenly becoming apparent to conscious agents. To some extent it is misleading to speak at this stage of purely moral obligations, as though what was at stake was a stark choice between good and evil. Rather, what might be felt is the pressure of the divine nature, a nature of supreme love, justice, and creativity, upon emerging human consciousness. The ultimate

---

[5] Cf. John Hick, *Evil and the God of Love* (London: Macmillan, 1966), 314.

human choice, from a theistic viewpoint, is not so much a choice between good and evil, abstractly conceived, as a choice between relationship with God, as the source of love and power, and a form of self-determination which inevitably leads on to self-regard. The process to which the first humans were called was one of growing knowledge of and interaction with the source and goal of their being. It is friendship with God that transforms lust into love, possessiveness into stewardship, and aggression into creativity. Yet this process is not automatic. It requires the conscious and continuing assent of the finite mind to the pressure and call of the divine mind. To assent to primal obligation is to assent to God. To refuse the transformation of one's natural desires into expressions of spiritual life is to turn from God, and from the power of the Divine to transform the material into the spiritual.

One should probably think of the first creatures who were moral agents as having very limited knowledge and understanding and a largely tacit knowledge of God as the supranatural source of their being. That knowledge and understanding should have grown, correlatively with growth in the mastery of desire. At every stage, the axioms of moral freedom entail that knowledge of the divine presence and access to the divine power were sufficient to sustain and nourish such growth. Yet it would never become irresistible. It would always allow the egoistic choice to seek self-regarding experiences and self-determination.

MORAL FREEDOM AND EXISTENTIAL ESTRANGEMENT

The evolutionary account sets out the intelligible background for such a basic choice between objective goodness and egoistic pleasure. Sin is not an arbitrary choice between abstract good and abstract evil, with a clear knowledge of all their consequences. As F. R. Tennant put it in one of the first attempts to address the problem of the origin of sin in an evolutionary context, sin is 'the survival or misuse of habits and tendencies that were incidental to an earlier stage of development'.[6] These tendencies are not evil in themselves. 'No natural impulse is itself sinful, unless present through our volition.'[7] What is sinful is the conscious refusal to

[6] F. R. Tennant, *The Origin and Propagation of Sin* (Cambridge: Cambridge University Press, 1908), 96.
[7] Ibid. 104.

direct these tendencies towards a higher goal: 'Man's moral evil would bespeak . . . the present non-attainment of his final goal.'[8]

On Tennant's account, humans are obligated to progress from a premoral stage ruled by animal impulses, towards an ideal stage of moral attainment by a gradual moralization of those impulses. Moreover, he holds that this is an arduous process: 'It is with difficulty that our natural, non-moral tendencies are moralised . . . every failure in the attempt . . . is sin.'[9] Because of this difficulty, sin is virtually inevitable. It is, he says, 'empirically inevitable', but not 'an absolute necessity'.[10]

The acute problem raised by this account is that, if sin is empirically inevitable, it is hard to see how we can be held accountable for it, and how it can really be sin, in any meaningful sense. Indeed, he says, 'Sin universally arises amid the stress of the moral problem assigned to us by our Maker.'[11] In that case, the Maker is responsible for giving us the problem, and for the universality of sin. Dr Tennant speaks of 'the antinomy between the inalienable sense of responsibility which the individual feels for his own evil and the fact that sinfulness seems at the same time inborn and prior to any action'.[12] Surely the antinomy ought to be resolved, on his account, by insisting that, in so far as sin is inevitable, it is not our responsibility and is not truly sin. We can only be held responsible for what is fully under our control—that is a principle that the eighth-century BCE prophets enunciated with hard-won clarity, and that should not be renounced.[13]

Nevertheless, Tennant seems to be right in saying that goodness is very difficult, and perhaps 'empirically impossible'. The fact is that we do not have the sure knowledge of God that might give access to divine power to release us from self-regarding desire. We seem to be in bondage to desire, and to be unable to do what we know to be right. On a traditional Christian account, such bondage is not the natural and proper condition of personal life. It is due to a massive and calamitous choice of self-regard early in the history of humanity. It must have been possible for the early humans to do what they ought, and the presence and power of God, however non-thematic, would presumably have made such a course much easier than it now is.

---

[8] Ibid. 11.   [9] Ibid. 84.   [10] Ibid. 113.   [11] Ibid. 39.
[12] Ibid. 54.   [13] Ezek. 18: 20.

The human race could always have remained in the love of God. They would not thereby have lost their freedom in any way. They would in fact have had a surer grasp of true creative freedom, the sort of freedom that belongs to the divine Being. God is free in being able to act creatively without limitation, choosing to realize particular sorts of value and to share action and experience with others. But God is not free to sin, to fall prey to self-regarding desires and to ignore the needs of others. God is creatively free but not morally free.[14]

Humans are naturally limited by their capacities and by their environment, but they can still exercise creative freedom in choosing to realize many sorts of value in community and co-operation with others. By participating with others in the creative power of God, freedom to bring about endlessly new states of value can be increased and sustained. However, humans who possess such creative and co-operative freedom are also emergent biological organisms with all the biological drives that implies. Moral freedom arises from the fact that the human situation offers many possibilities for pleasurable experiences, which can lead to competitive and egoistic behaviour. The creative freedom to realize communal values can be supplanted by the egoistic freedom to do whatever one pleases. The former freedom may seem limited by its relation to communal concerns and interest, but in fact it opens out new creative possibilities. The latter freedom seems to offer total freedom, but in fact it limits one to a circle of desires which increase in their addictiveness and personal isolation.

Moral freedom as we know it is thus a function of beings which have a limited, individual, and material nature, and which need to learn to shape that nature towards transcendent, communal, and spiritual goals. Had humans not lost the gift of the knowledge of God's presence and access to God's power, such shaping could have resulted in the gradual but sure transformation of an unconscious and biologically driven material nature into a conscious and unrestricted expression of its underlying spiritual reality and goal. That, one may postulate, is the intended purpose of creation.

It follows that moral freedom does not exist below the level of evolutionary development at which beings can be conscious of a spiritual goal and capable of attaining it. Moral freedom will not

---

[14] K. Ward, *Religion and Creation* (Oxford: Clarendon, 1996), 216–19.

exist at a point at which beings have shaped their lives fully to co-operative love and creativity—as it does not exist in God. Creative freedom will then exist, more fully than before. But moral freedom is a property only of those who are still learning to love, and who may conceivably fail to do so.

At the stage of moral freedom, a whole range of alternatives is possible for a society of moral agents. All may accept and embrace the divine help. The vast majority, but not all, may do so. A very small minority may do so. Or conceivably all may turn from God to the path of selfish desire. It is hard to tell what would be the case in all these different scenarios, and it is not very important to try to guess. The import of the Genesis story is that our world is one in which at a very early stage all humans rejected God. It is that original and massive embracing of desire that has drastically altered the moral situation of all subsequent human descendants.

It may seem as if the present miserable condition of humanity is vastly too great a punishment for the sin of some group of proto-humans. And it may seem puzzling that *all* humanity should apparently be involved in that sin and its consequences. What is required is a rejection of the oversimple picture of God as a particular person who hands out a formidable punishment on all the descendants of a human being who has just performed one wrong act. Sin must be seen as a rejection of moral responsibility, as a grasping at power without the control of love. Humans have moral obligations. But in a way to see them as obligations, as duties which one would rather not undertake, is already to have lost that sense of a natural and gladly accepted action which follows from the unity of love. The first failure to accept an obligation is therefore much more than a matter of one isolated act. It is, as Kant pointed out, a subversion of the whole personality and will,[15] a subversion which turns love into duty and turns pleasure into something that opposes dutiful action. It is that turning of the will towards self that constitutes sin, and it corrupts the motive of every individual act.

Nor should such a turning to self-regard be seen as a purely individual choice, which leaves the wider group unaffected. Marx held that 'the real nature of man is the totality of social relations',[16] and

[15] Immanuel Kant, *Religion Within the Limits of Reason Alone*, trans. T. M. Greene and H. H. Hudson (New York: Harper, 1960), 25: 'wicked acts reverse the ethical priority among the incentives of a free will'.

[16] *Selected Writings*, eds. T. B. Bottomore and M. Rubel (London: Penguin, 1961), 83.

while this is an exaggeration, it points to an important truth. I am the person I am as part of a particular culture and history, and nothing that one person in my culture does leaves me quite unaffected. Moral choices are not atomic and isolated decisions, which can be quarantined from the rest of society. Humans are bound together in such a way that each individual action affects the whole, and influences the possibilities for action which exist. If at some time a group of people chooses self-regard, this will so structure subsequent society and those who are brought up in it that it may make the temptations of desire virtually irresistible. Deprived of empowering relationship with God, the natural drive to sexuality, freed from the restraints of instinct, will devalue personality by regarding others as means to pleasure, and so lead to a lack of respect for personhood. The drive to territorial possession, freed from the limits of tribal life, will lead to unlimited acquisitiveness. The drive to aggression, extended by the invention of weapons, will lead to the subjugation of possible competitors. Falling from unity with the love, wisdom and creativity of God, humans come to exhibit a grossly distorted perception and vitriolic hatred of others, together with a seemingly boundless personal greed. Greed, hatred, and delusion become the passions which control the lives of human beings, driving them to cause pain and suffering to countless sentient creatures, and to destroy their own environment and ultimately themselves.

It is not just that humans are less far-sighted than they might be. They see the world in such a distorted manner that life becomes a struggle of each against all, and others become enemies whom one must destroy or placate. It is not just that humans fail to love God as much as they might. They are motivated by deep hatred for the goods that others enjoy, for the goods they cannot control, and for any alleged authority which threatens to curb their self-aggrandisement. It is not just that humans are unable completely to achieve the good at which they aim. They see all good as a means to their own short-term pleasure, and ruthlessly use all others to achieve their aims, discarding them when they have served their ephemeral purpose.

Thus incapacity becomes corruption, and the world becomes a battleground of mutually destructive desires. For anyone born into such a world, the choice of good and evil is no delicately balanced, dispassionately contemplated decision. In a world of greed, hatred, and delusion, one must either be an oppressor, a victim, or a resister. One will be born as a child within one of these groups, and one's habitual responses and learned activities will be shaped accordingly.

The oppressors, if successful, will conceal the nature of their oppression of others, but will rear children to a standard of living that can only continue with the perpetuation of inequality. Hidden greed will underlie the accepted standards of living, and its hidden character will produce delusion about the interests and needs of the oppressed, even about whether they are oppressed. It will produce hatred of those who attack the status quo, who will be seen as barbarians threatening culture and civilization. It will produce a self-image of strength and security, which needs to be protected by the discrete exercise of force.

The victims will know the sense of injustice and helplessness, and will rear children in an atmosphere of unspoken resentment, envy, and frustrated rage. This will produce delusions, often of a religious or quasi-religious character, about compensatory revenge for the poor in an afterlife, or about the moral rightness of subservience and of a lack of self-respect. But it will also produce secret hatred of the oppressors, of the privileged and wealthy, which is a source of great destructive power, often directed, uselessly, against the victims themselves. It will produce a self-image of deference and complaisance, which needs to be reinforced by a continual masochistic self-punishment.

The resisters will live in a state of continual defensive conflict, seeing themselves as always threatened and needing to take pre-emptive counter-measures. This will produce delusions of a paranoic character, for which everyone is an enemy to be resisted, no one is to be trusted, and life is matter of the triumph of the will to power. It will produce hatred of others as perpetual threats, a tendency always to draw sharp lines of disagreement and conflict, and to defend one's own views to the death. It will produce a self-image of heroic solitude, which requires that all 'outsiders' are seen as dangerous intruders, to be treated with caution or outright hostility.

If these are the social contexts in which young humans are reared, from which they learn their perceptions of the world and appropriate ways to act in the world, one does not need to appeal to heredity to explain human fallenness. Virtually every human being will grow up with a distorted perception of the world, a disordered affective attitude to others, and an excessive attachment to the beliefs and values of its own class. How, in such a state, could impartial judgement, sincere love of others, and calm self-control be found? I think one has to say, only with extreme difficulty. Perhaps only by entering a 'religious' society in which mindfulness, compassion, and self-control (wisdom, love, and temperance) were valued above all, and which was in some way distanced from the world in which greed, hatred, and delusion reign. But even such societies cannot exist out of all relation to the wider society of disorder, and so they too will be flawed, holding out intimations of an ideal human life that cannot actually be realized.

This is not to say that 'original sin' is a purely social phenomenon. It arises because of an existential lack, a lack of positive relation to God. It is not hereditary, as though it were carried by the structure of DNA, or, as Augustine thought, by the physical act of procreation.[17] But it is a universal estrangement from God, caused by past human turning from God, and thus a condition into which every child is now born. The cultural training that children receive is a result of and reinforces this estrangement.

MORAL AUTONOMY AND PERSONAL RELATIONSHIP

Among modern theologians, it is Paul Tillich who most consistently develops a view of original sin in terms of the idea of alienation or estrangement, which was most clearly formulated by Hegel. Tillich rejects the 'essentialism' which he finds in Hegel, which makes estrangement a necessary part of the process of the self-realization of Absolute Spirit, part of 'the process of the divine self-realisation'.[18] For such a view, he says, there is 'no gap, no ultimate incertitude, no risk, and no danger of self-loss'. At least on one, rather controversial, interpretation of Hegel, there is no real finite freedom, which may realize itself, or fail to realize itself, in various ways. The Fall is an essential part of the objectification of Spirit, and independent human freedom plays no part in it.

Tillich wishes to give to an 'irrational' use of human freedom a great role than that. Yet he insists that one must take 'the Fall as a

---

[17] Augustine, *On The Trinity*, 13. 10. 16, in M. Wiles and M. Santer, *Documents in Early Christian Thought* (Oxford: Oxford University Press, 1975), 115.
[18] Paul Tillich, *Systematic Theology* (Welwyn: James Nisbet, 1968), ii. 26.

symbol for the human situation universally'.[19] 'It is not an event of the past.'[20] It expresses the transition from essence to existence. This involves a 'break', a 'self-contradicting power of human freedom'. Existence does not just realize essence; it is estranged from essence. Adam comes to stand for the undecided potentialities of the essential structures of being, not a historical state. Tillich's account is vitiated, however, by the fact that he continues to speak in temporal terms. He says that the possibility of a transition from essence to existence 'is *experienced as* a temptation'.[21] But by whom could it be experienced? Anxiety, he says, is one of the *driving forces* towards the transition. But again, how can one give this a non-temporal interpretation? Man *decides* for self-actualization. But when?

It is a standard criticism of Tillich that the only non-temporal way to interpret this is to see it as a necessary estrangement, which precedes every actual choice. It is a 'transition from dreaming innocence to actualisation and guilt'.[22] And that is 'a universal quality of finite being'. This account retains the moral problematic of the classical view of original sin, for 'it must simultaneously acknowledge the tragic universality of estrangement and man's personal responsibility for it'.[23] Tillich stresses the way in which freedom is a total and centred act of the personality, so that it is limited by the fallen world. 'Actualised creation and estranged existence are identical.'[24] Yet 'existence cannot be derived from essence'; this is a leap and not a structural necessity.

But who makes the leap? Only an already existing being can decide. So a transition from essence, which is pure potentiality, to existence cannot be a decision. All decisions must come after the transition has been made, though they may indeed be made in an already flawed situation. Against Tillich, therefore, it must be insisted that the transition to existence is not a decision—unless of course it is a decision of God's, in which case God would be creating a fallen world. Consequently, humans cannot be held responsible for their fallen state, though their situation may well be tragic. Tillich has left himself unable to account for the fallenness of the world in terms of past finite decisions, since he denies any such temporal element in the doctrine of the Fall. So, despite his denials, he does seem committed to ascribing to God a fallen creation, or

---

[19] Ibid. 33.   [20] Ibid. 42.   [21] Ibid. 39.   [22] Ibid. 42.
[23] Ibid. 45.   [24] Ibid. 50.

affirming the necessity of some negative surd element in finite existence as such. This differs from the Idealism he rejects only in not being able to see estrangement as a positive developmental power which is necessary, but will be inevitably overcome by reconciliation in history. And it leaves him in the untenable position of holding both that estrangement is necessary, in the fall from essence to actuality, and that it is not necessary, as Idealists are alleged to hold.

The idea that sin is inevitable sooner or later springs from our sense that obligation is difficult, and selfish pleasure is easy and attractive. Sin must always be an option for moral agents, but it need not be such a very easy and attractive option, by comparison with virtue. If one had a keen sense of the suffering of others, a strong sense of integrity and of kinship with the God who calls one to keep divine law, wrongdoing would be a much less attractive option. It is not too hard to imagine a society of persons of such sympathy and self-control, and such a sense of God as a supremely desirable reality, that wrongdoing would become a practical impossibility. But the society we live in is one which encourages greed, ambition, and conflict, which wholly lacks a real sense of the presence of God, and so makes rightdoing a practical impossibility. One may suppose that the earliest human or proto-human society was not yet determined in either of these ways, but could grow towards either possibility. It is a contingent, regrettable, yet undoubted fact that, if this supposition is correct, our earliest ancestors chose the path of self-centred desire, and in doing so determined the tragic course the lives of their descendants would thenceforth have to take.

Just as creative freedom enhances the possibilities for co-operative human development, so corrupted moral freedom restricts such possibilities. Humans are no longer morally free, in the sense that they can choose in a wholly undetermined way between the objective good and egoistic desire. In creative freedom, humans would be overwhelmingly influenced by the divine presence, so that evil would be in practice impossible. But in corrupted moral freedom, humans are overwhelmingly influenced by their initial formation in motivations of greed, ambition, and aggression, so that a consistent choice of the good becomes in practice virtually impossible. What one would naturally do, if creatively free, becomes a matter of obligations which one can only fulfil with great difficulty, if at all. And the proper goal of moral activity, the realization of a community of creative wisdom and love, becomes impossible to achieve.

The very existence of morality as we know it is a symptom of a corruption of nature, a fall away from God towards the finite self. What should be a natural and fulfilling co-operation with an infinite source of love has become a matter of being confronted with a set of difficult obligations requiring strenuous effort to fulfil. We are born with an inclination towards egoistic desire which radically impairs our moral freedom. It may be possible to do all that we ought, in the sense that we may do all that is within our power as corrupted agents. But that will no longer ensure the realization of the moral goal of human life. Moral freedom still exists, but it cannot achieve its goal and the reason for its existence, which is the complete moralization of natural impulses by empowering relationship with God, the supreme spiritual value and power.

In the ideal human situation, one would know God, or the nature of being as gracious, creative, and unitive. One would respond in love to God, in reverence for the divine perfection and in gratitude for one's own existence. One would obey God out of a natural trust that divine commands were for good, out of confidence that human fulfilment would be accomplished thereby, and out of natural love for the source of one's being. The notion of obligation, as what one ought to do in distinction from what one is inclined to do, would hardly arise, since no inclination could seriously compete with the love of a perfect God. Thus the idea of obligation arises only when inclinations are divorced from love of the good, and when God is seen as commanding resistant and reluctant wills. In that sense one cannot have a sense of obligation without already having a sense that one is estranged from God, as the source of obligation. The primal sin is not disobeying a perceived obligation. It is turning aside from the natural good towards the self; it is such a turning which brings obligation into being. Once obligation exists, one is already in a position in which it has become difficult to achieve perfection, since to be obligated is already to have fallen away from love.

On a Kantian view of human nature, all the dignity of humanity lies in its capacity for free moral action, which is the self-legislation of Reason over nature.[25] Morality, as a set of commands of Reason,

---

[25] 'Morality, and humanity as capable of it, is that which alone has dignity', Immanuel Kant, *Fundamental Principles of the Metaphysic of Ethics*, trans. T. K. Abbott (London: Longmans, 1959), 64.

stands supreme, and by it all human lives are assessed. The Christian view is significantly different. It is God, a being of over-flowing love, creativity, and bliss, who stands supreme. The human goal is not to allow Reason to legislate categorically over nature. It is to enter into loving, creative relationship with God—a conception conspicuously absent in the work of Kant. The dignity of humanity thus lies in its capacity for relationship with God, with the creative co-operation and shared experience that entails. The human possession of the *imago dei* is not the possession of autonomous reason and will, as though humans were little autonomous gods. It is the capacity to participate in the creative wisdom and love of God, and in that way to attain human fulfil-ment. Community and relationality take precedence over auton-omy. The moral life is not so much conformity to purely rational and universal principles as it is the transformation of the individual self to enable it to become a vehicle of creative and loving action, by its inward relationship to God and to other finite creatures.

It is that which the corruption of the will renders impossible. Even if one sets out a list of specific obligations and fulfils them, being innocent of any moral offence, one can never escape from self-regard so as to be completely open to the creative love and wisdom of God. Beyond the fulfilled obligations lies the unattained goal of loving God with all of one's being, and of participating in the divine love itself. It is that goal which is unfulfillable, since it requires a reorien-tation of the inner springs of human motivation and being. So even if I fulfil all my obligations, I cannot attain the divinely intended human goal. It is much more likely that I will fail to keep the obliga-tions I have; but whether I fail in this strictly moral obligation or not, complete devotion to God remains impossible. The incapacity of my nature which isolates me from God will inevitably result in loss of contact with the only source of being, and so in spiritual death.

It is because of this that morality as we experience it is both flawed and ultimately futile. It is flawed because it first substitutes an impersonal moral law for the personal presence of God, and then it makes success in keeping that law a criterion for judging the conduct of others, and dividing the 'good people' from the 'bad people' in oversimple ways. It is ultimately futile, because it cannot realize the goal of a truly just human community, and cannot be fully justified either on long-term prudential grounds or on grounds of its contribution to the general happiness. Morality remains important and imperative. It is true that we ought not to kill, steal, or lie. Nevertheless, the existence of such a moral imperative is a standing reminder of the rupture in being which results from the human rejection of relationship with God. Moral success cannot remedy that rejection, and moral failure only intensifies it. The ultimate existential contrast is between openness to divine power and insistence on individual self-determination. Strangely, then, moral success may be a barrier to the human goal, as it may express the highest point of human autonomy, precisely in its proclamation of the possibility of human moral perfection—a tragic perfection, which is destined, as Immanuel Kant saw, to fail to achieve the complete good at which it aims.[26]

FORENSIC AND SOTERIAL ACCOUNTS OF SIN

The Christian hypothesis is that sin occurred on a massive scale early in human history. This caused that corruption of social structure and moral training that results in a marked weakening of the will and the loss of a strong sense of God. This is what traditional Christian theologians call the loss of 'original justice', the ability to do right easily, and 'the sense of Divine sonship', the experiential knowledge of the presence and power of God.[27] The doctrine of original sin is a Christian idea, not shared by Judaism or Islam. They see the 'sin of Adam'—sin occurring on a large scale early in human history—as indeed incurring the 'punishments' or disadvantages of ignorance of God, lack of self-control, and short-sighted restriction of moral concern. But they insist that all persons must be free to choose and to realize goodness or evil, and will be held responsible for their choice. Christianity has a more tragic sense of the impossibility of goodness in a world trapped in evil. While traditionally these views hardened into mutual opposition, there is the possibility of a mediating view. The axiom of moral freedom must be upheld— that each individual has a choice for or against objective goodness. But one can combine this with a sense of the impossibility of fully realizing the goodness that agents may choose. To choose the good

---

[26] 'What we are able to do is in itself inadequate', Kant, *Religion Within the Limits of Reason Alone*, 40.
[27] Defined at the Council of Trent (H. Denzinger, *Enchiridion Symbolorum*, 23rd edn. (Fribourg: Herder, 1963), 1511). Cf. *Catechism of the Catholic Church* (London: Geoffrey Chapman, 1994), 85.

expresses one's moral will. To recognize its impossibility admits the corruption of that will, located as it is in a web of corrupted social and environmental relationships. The only hope of wholeness for the corrupted will is that it might be placed in a new set of positive relationships, inwardly oriented to God. The covenant community of Judaism, the *Umma* of Islam, and the Church of Christianity are all attempts to establish such a divinely ordered community of relationships. In all of them the establishing of personal moral innocence is less important than the redemption of the community from the disordered world of greed, hatred, and delusion. In all of them, forgiveness and divine mercy become central concepts which need to be articulated in various forms, if such redemption is to be possible. And in all of them, the divine community exists for the sake of bringing the whole creation back to God, rather than for providing an escape route for a favoured few. There is not necessarily a great divide between the Christian view that all need to be redeemed from original sin, and the Judaeo-Islamic view that all individuals must finally account for their own actions.

A mediating view between the three Abrahamic traditions is to think of original sin as more like a disease or an incapacity than like a crime. One's ignorance of God, one's subjection to strong passions, one's incomplete grasp of the excellences of human being, seem like defects of nature, which make it impossible for us to live a fully authentic human life, one that is in close and loving relationship with God. This may be tragic, but it is hardly a matter for which one can feel, or be, personally guilty. Indeed, if blame is to be assigned, it may be to someone else—God or our ancestors or whoever is to blame for our present situation. The forensic concepts of praise, blame, punishment, and forgiveness are perhaps not finally adequate terms in which to describe the human situation. Rather, one may think in terms of inability and ideal, bondage and release, as a non-moralistic, more soterial description of the human condition, which yet captures the tragic sense of human impairment and slavery, and the possibility of liberation and healing. The forensic account sees humans as bound by guilt, which must be punished, perhaps even by eternal torment. The soterial account sees humans as impaired by incapacity, which results in final loss of being, in spiritual and then in real death.[28]

---

[28] The forensic/soterial distinction is made in Ch. 3 of this volume.

The forensic account faces a number of conceptual difficulties. First of all, where there is guilt, there must be the possibility of innocence. Judaism and Islam would have little problem with this idea, since at the Day of Judgement the guilty will be punished, while the innocent will be rewarded with a share in the life to come.[29] Christians have traditionally held that all humans are guilty, but how this could be known in advance, while retaining the axiom of moral freedom, it is impossible to see.

On a soterial account, there is little difficulty in holding that all humans are incapable of participating in the divine nature, and that this incapacity is the result of repeated actions of people in the past, rejecting relationship with God. There can be no personal fault then imputed, but it can readily be seen that the result of such incapacity, if not remedied in some way, will be a failure to reach the divinely intended goal of human existence. For Jews and Muslims, too, Heaven is not something anyone can strictly deserve, since one can do no more than one ought, and thus cannot deserve a reward for doing right. It is undoubtedly true that evildoing is so widespread, and righteousness is so rare, that the divinely intended goal of a community of creative love and wisdom cannot be realized in this world by human effort. It will have to be realized in the resurrection world, however that is conceived. If there is a share in the life to come for the just, it is purely by divine gift, and the human acceptance of that gift requires trust in God's self-revelation as well as moral striving. So there is not a deep disagreement in Judaism and Islam with a soterial interpretation of the Christian view, that human moral effort cannot achieve fulfilling relationship to God, and that one can participate in the life of God only by unmerited grace.

The forensic account is committed to a doctrine of strong retributivism, which holds that good or bad conduct strictly deserves rewards and punishments, whatever the consequences may be. This view is in danger of reducing moral decisions to decisions of long-term prudence, leading people to act for the sake of reward or to avoid punishment. It is also questionable whether punishment without hope of remission or reformation is truly just in the long

[29] 'That day you shall be brought to Judgment . . . then he that will be given his record in his right hand . . . will be in a life of bliss . . . and he that will be given his record in his left hand will say . . . "Ah, would that [death] had made an end of me"', Qur'an 69: 18–27, trans. Jusuf Ali (Leicester: Islamic Foundation, 1975).

run. Particularly where the punishment is unending, one may feel that it is disproportionate to the crime, and it ought at least to offer the possibility of repentance and reform. One can respond to these points by stressing that God's aim in punishing is reformative, so that Hell is only eternal if a person is irrevocably impenitent. But it is plainer on a soterial account that the natural consequence of human incapacity will follow only if that incapacity is not remedied, and that a loving God will offer whatever remedy is appropriate to all who stand in need of it.

The main problem for those who insist on a strict accounting for one's moral conduct as the condition for having a share in the life to come, is that so few can claim to be morally innocent, and that so many will deserve punishment. Presumably those who are judged righteous at the Final Judgement will be so because they have realized selfless love, as far as it has been possible for them to do so. In that case, they will continue to desire the welfare of those who have been judged wanting. They will not be content to accept their reward until everything that can be done to reclaim sinners has been done. They will themselves rely for their share in the life to come wholly on Divine mercy, which they will ask to be given to those who have turned from God, so that they may have time and opportunity to see the wrong they have done, and help to make amends in some way. In other words, the righteous will pray for God to have patience with wrongdoers and to give strength to the penitent. They will want to ally themselves with God's patient and strengthening mercy and love, to become channels, so far as that is possible, of the divine patience and mercy. Thus all the Abrahamic traditions have a place for the prayers of the righteous, for divine mercy and for the free gift of endless life with God.[30] It is not just a matter of individuals balancing their own moral accounts, without help from others and without concern for others. Each person is responsible for their response to the divine concern for their ultimate well-being, but the self-giving prayers of the righteous and the limitless mercy of God ensure that moral incapacities and failures can be mitigated and forgiven.

It is a mistake to think that life on earth is a series of moral tests for individuals, which are completed when that life ends, and which terminate in the wicked being punished for ever and the good being

---

[30] 'The Apostle of God will pray for your forgiveness', Qur'an 63: 5.

rewarded for ever. Life on earth was intended to realize communities of creative wisdom and love, in which finite persons could share
in expressing the creative wisdom of God. To participate in such a
community, persons must learn to shape their lives towards the
ideal of love, but the consequence of this is that they can fall into
ignorance and egoism. Because they have fallen, on a massive scale,
it has become impossible for them to realize the intended community, the Kingdom of God, the truly just society. That impossibility
is original sin. People in a fallen world still have many choices
between self-determining egoism and openness to a higher creative
power. The former choices cut the world off from the source of its
being, and are inherently self-destructive. The latter choices,
though always partial and imperfect, connect the world to an infinite creative power which can eventually realize the divine goal. In
the meanwhile, the world will remain a mixture of egoism and
imperfect faith. But in it, the mercy of God calls people to turn
from the greed, hatred, and delusion which are so natural to them,
and trust in that personal power which alone can ensure the
intended goal of human life. This is not identical with a pure moral
choice of good or evil, though all the Scriptures emphasize that a
genuine choice for God always entails an intention and an effort to
do what is right. Moralism is always mitigated by the divine mercy,
which calls all to relationship and which makes such relationship
possible for all those who regret the evil they do and trust in God.
The life of human persons with corrupted moral freedom is not one
of striving for individual moral success. It is a life of learning to
accept and mediate freely given divine love in a community of
people bound together in suffering and in compassion.[31]

TRADITIONAL ACCOUNTS OF ORIGINAL SIN

In the Christian tradition, the idea of original sin has often been
merged with that of original guilt and given a moralistic interpretation, as it was in Augustine. Each human child, at the moment it is
born, is then seen as inheriting a sense of guilt, as being deserving
of damnation, before it has even performed any action. Its will is
corrupt and blameworthy, and it is perfectly just of God to punish
it eternally, or to forgive it, if that happens to be the divine pleasure.

---

[31] This is what is known in Christian theology as the 'communion of saints'.

Augustine writes: 'In committing so great a sin their [the first parents'] whole nature, being hereby depraved . . . was so transfused through all their offspring in the same degree of corruption and necessity of death . . . that all would have been cast headlong into the second death . . . had not the undue grace of God acquitted some from it.'[32] All human children are born with a depraved nature, and justly suffer for the sin of their first ancestor.

Calvin, too, speaks of a 'hereditary corruption', whereby 'the sin of the first man passed to all his posterity'.[33] 'Before we behold the light of the sun we are in God's sight defiled and polluted.'[34] So Calvin defines original sin as 'a hereditary corruption and depravity of our nature, extending to all the parts of the soul, which first makes us obnoxious to the wrath of God, and then produces in us works which in Scripture are termed works of the flesh'.[35] This doctrine is in fundamental contrast with Ezekiel's statement that each person should be punished only for their own sin.[36] Whereas one may see how a corrupted nature can be inherited, like some disease, it is impossible to justify the transference of guilt from one person to another by the mere process of generation.

Even the hypothesis of hereditary corruption looks odd, given modern knowledge of genetics, which disallows the inheritance of acquired characteristics, and given an awareness that the whole universe was not corrupted, as Calvin supposed, by the sin of Adam, but that death and passion existed before the arrival of humanity on the cosmic scene. One needs to reject, on moral grounds, the idea that children are born guilty. One needs to reject, on scientific grounds, the ideas that moral fault can be inherited, and that some fundamental genetic change in humans could be caused by a primeval sin.

Nevertheless, the Augustinian tradition was expressing, however misleadingly, an insight into the human condition. Humans do seem to be burdened with weakened and corrupted wills, and this makes it impossible for them to enter into that community of shared experience and action that is God's intention for creation. Moreover, the moralism that concentrates only on the individual's achievement of moral success misses an important dimension of human existence.

[32] Augustine, *City of God*, 14. 1 (London: J. M. Dent, 1945), ii. 26.

[33] John Calvin, *Institutes of the Christian Religion*, 2. 1. 5, trans. H. Beveridge (Grand Rapids, Mich.: Eerdmans, 1989), 214.

[34] Ibid.   [35] Ibid. 217.   [36] Ezek. 18: 20.

It was Nietzsche who saw, more clearly than most, the hidden resentment and self-righteousness that can lie behind a purely moralistic view.[37] The resentment is against the wicked, who flourish unfairly in this world. One's secret desire for vengeance is expressed by the thought that they will suffer beyond measure in the world to come. The self-righteousness lies in the claim that one deserves the due reward for one's moral efforts, since one has, after all, performed very well in the tests put before one throughout life. Wearing the mantle of moralism, vengeance and pride can thus safely flourish. Compassion and humility can be put aside, since the wicked are beyond compassion and the righteous have nothing for which to be ashamed. Moralists, attaining blamelessness, can isolate themselves from their fellow beings, their feelings atrophied, their relationships severed. Penitents, eschewing thoughts of praise or blame, seek to be filled with God, with compassion for all beings, and with hope for authentic fulfilment of life.

Whatever moral reservations one may have about Augustine and Calvin, at least they wholly undermine such a moralistic view of human life. They stress that everyone is destined for eternal punishment, by right. It is not something reserved for others (the wicked), since one belongs to that class oneself. Thus the doctrine of Hell does not express a secret resentment against others. It expresses a fear for oneself, which one might more moderately express as a realization that it is impossible to achieve that relation to God that God had intended, and, left to oneself, one is condemned to isolation and solitude, to a world of greed, hatred, and delusion, for ever. Moreover, salvation is purely by grace, so one can never claim to be worthy of it, or to have achieved it by personal effort. Humility is very much in order, since one does not and never can deserve that God raise one up to eternal fellowship in love.

But if Augustine and Calvin avoid moralism, they do seem to fall into indifferentism, since no reason, other than God's pure will, can be given why some are saved. Perhaps it is Karl Barth who most clearly grasps the implications of the universal love of God, when he insists that God offers salvation to all without exception, so that none stands outside the range of the divine mercy.[38] If humans are

---

[37] Cf. F. Nietzsche, *The Anti-Christ* (1888).

[38] 'There is no one who does not participate in [Christ], in this turning to God', Karl Barth, *Church Dogmatics*, ed. G. W. Bromiley and T. F. Torrance (Edinburgh: T. & T. Clark, 1936–77), iv. 2. 217. This is partly based on the New Testament

in a state of original sin, they are also in a state of universally offered redemption, and it is a mistake to stress one side of this view of human nature without equally stressing the other.

Theologians and church councils have surprisingly often made this mistake, and have given rise to a restrictive and even distressing interpretation of the Christian gospel. It is in some ways surprising that an Augustinian doctrine of original sin developed, given its absence in Jewish belief. Schoonenberg suggests that its development followed from a restrictive interpretation of baptism, especially infant baptism, as being necessary for salvation.[39] Certainly, the biblical basis for it is extremely thin, and in effect lies in one short chapter of the letter to the Romans, and particularly in one verse of that chapter, Romans 5: 12, 'sin came into the world through one man and death through sin, and so death spread to all men because all men sinned'. This has been read as saying that by the sin of the first man, Adam, all human beings have been brought under condemnation, and suffer the penalty of death. The first canon of the Council of Carthage (411 CE) anathematizes those who deny that human physical death is the result of Adam's sin. The Council of Lyons affirmed that unbaptized babies are deprived of the beatific vision, and thus must be seen as going to Hell, even if their punishment there is not as bad as that of murderers.[40] (The idea of Limbo, or a state of natural happiness for the unbaptized, was a later development.) The Council of Trent in its third canon insisted that original sin is transmitted '*propagatione, non imitatione transfusum*'. Babies do not simply imitate sin which is prevalent in their society. They inherit a sinful nature, and this carries guilt with it, a guilt that merits eternal condemnation, and can only be remitted by baptism.[41] By baptism, the guilt of original sin is remitted, but the preternatural gifts which Adam had are not restored.

If one accepts the general scientific view that humans are quite recent arrivals on the biological scene, and have evolved from other forms of organic life, it is impossible not to fall under the anathema of Carthage. Physical death did not come into the world with the

statement that 'as in Adam all die, even so in Christ shall all be made alive', 1 Cor. 15: 22.

[39] Cf. P. Schoonenberg, *Man and Sin*, trans. J. Donceel (London: Sheed & Ward, 1965), 157–68.

[40] 'The souls of those who die . . . with original sin only, immediately descend to hell,' Denzinger, *Enchiridion*, 464.

[41] Ibid. 792.

first human being. The Roman Catholic Dutch New Catechism of 1969 is reticent on the subject of original sin and death. But an appended supplement, prepared by a Commission of Cardinals to explain the Catechism, in a fairly desperate manœuvre, suggests that, whereas animals suffered and died in the natural course of things before the first humans existed, nevertheless if humans had not sinned, they would not have died.[42] It seems a rather arbitrary procedure to exempt humans from the general laws of biological development in this way. Moreover, it is almost impossible to see how the sin of Adam could have so altered the genetic make-up of humanity as to cause both sin and guilt to be passed on by inheritance to all his progeny. It is morally difficult to accept that a God of universal love could permit creatures to come into being who, by their natures and before they have done anything, are guilty and deserving of eternal punishment. It is even more morally difficult to accept that all unbaptized persons—the vast majority of the human race—will actually incur such a punishment.

It is, however, plausible to hold that, because of the early moral failures of many humans, the whole human world has become entrapped in egoism and estranged from a sense of the presence of God.[43] The loss of the vision of God is indeed the natural consequence for individuals born into such a world. In that sense, one may construe the belief that 'humans are born guilty' as the assertion that the natural destiny of ungraced human nature is the punishment of loveless existence, which is Hell. It may be true that the natural human situation falls under divine judgement. But that can only be said when it is equally clearly seen that it also, and from the very first, falls under the divine mercy: 'God has consigned all men to disobedience, that he may have mercy upon all.'[44] If this is so, it cannot be held that by baptism, and only by baptism, 'the guilt of original sin is remitted', as the Council of Trent held.[45] Yet one can say that only by God's grace can relationship to God be restored. This grace is universally available to all, and must be appropriated by personal response. Baptism is the sign that such grace comes as an offer to all, that it is normatively mediated in a community patterned on Christ, and that the church as a community truly

---

[42] *A New Catechism* (London: Search, 1969), suppl. 17–20.
[43] Schoonenberg tentatively suggests this thought, *Man and Sin*, 192–3.
[44] Rom. 11: 32 (RSV).   [45] Denzinger, *Enchiridion*, 792.

mediates the life of Christ, who has opened a new and living way to relationship with God.

The Greek Fathers usually interpreted 'death' primarily, though admittedly not exclusively, as spiritual death, as estrangement from God and lack of the divine spirit.[46] In that sense, death is the consequence of sin. Physical death had always existed in the biological realm, and it was not the result of sin. But one might hold that, in a situation of estrangement from God, physical death took on a new terror, as it carried the threat of final separation from God for ever, and the frustration of all hopes of human fulfilment. The character of death as threat, which is so much part of much human experience of it, is the direct result of sin.

Paul probably regarded Adam as a historical figure, and so he could see Jesus as a second Adam. But the point of his teaching is that estrangement from God, which brings with it a missing of the mark of human life and, ultimately, its spiritual destruction, flows from numerous and repeated conscious and responsible human sins in the past history of the human race. It now characterizes the whole human order, which is accordingly under divine judgement, as unable to fulfil its intended goal. Sin entered into the world by one man,[47] and that led to spiritual death. In so far as the whole world becomes involved in the sinful condition, estrangement from God becomes the human condition. As Romans 5: 14 explicitly says, even those who did not 'sin like Adam' are subject to this death.

The natural way to read this is not to say that the sin of one individual renders millions of other individuals, who had no part in it, guilty. It is rather to say, in Paul's terms, that through the sin of one individual the power of evil has been given entrance into the human world, and by the complicity of many others spiritual estrangement and corruption has come to mark all human life. The parallelism of Romans 5: 19 should be maintained: 'as by one man's disobedience many were made sinners, so by one man's obedience many will be made righteous'. The obedience of Jesus does not actually make everyone good, without their knowledge or consent. Rather, it opens to all persons the possibility of that goodness which can only be the result of complete divine indwelling, just as the disobedience of the first sinner made such goodness impossible, by cutting off the

---

[46] Cf. Vladimir Lossky, *The Mystical Theology of the Eastern Church* (Cambridge: James Clarke, 1957), 130–3.

[47] Rom. 5: 12.

world from the active presence of God. The fifth chapter of the letter to the Romans cannot therefore serve as a basis for any doctrine of universal original guilt, from which baptism is needed to gain exemption. Indeed, its central message is almost the opposite, that humans have not been left in a condition of estrangement from God, but that God has acted to ensure that estrangement can be overcome. 'One man's act of righteousness leads to acquittal and life for all men.'[48]

For all its difficulties, a doctrine of original sin, as an estranged condition of humanity, does express a distinctive and illuminating view of human nature. It warns that a society of true freedom and love will not exist in this world. But it proclaims that a way to it has been opened in this world. The Kingdom is trans-historical, but it fulfils the historical. To live by duty is to strive always to do what is right, in a world that tragically prevents one's acts from achieving the good at which they aim. It is possible to do all that one ought, but it is not possible to achieve a wholly fulfilled human life. To live by faith is to accept the inevitable disorder of this world, to accept the power of divine love to open up a positive relationship to God, to begin to allow oneself to be conformed to the divine image, and to trust in the promise of a new creation which will both cancel and fulfil this one. The doctrine of original sin, even in its revised, soterial interpretation, prevents one from being Utopian about human dreams of a perfect society. It prevents one from falling into despair over the evident moral failures of individuals and societies. It underpins the importance of continued moral striving, while undercutting the moralism which judges all humans on their achieved moral probity. It counsels total reliance on divine forgiveness and mercy for healing human incapacities and granting fulfilment in a life of perfected relationships beyond the ambiguities of this earthly life. It emphasizes the importance of community and relationship, as fundamental features of personal existence. And it leads one to look for a disclosure of divine power to liberate one from egoistic desire into eternal life. Thus it inherently points towards a doctrine of redemption from sin and reconciliation with God, not to an ultimate pessimism or judgementalism but to the affirmation that, 'just as we have borne the image of the man of dust, we shall also bear the image of the man of heaven'.[49]

---

[48] Rom. 5: 18.   [49] 1 Cor. 15: 49.

9

The Doctrine of Atonement

One of the most distinctive doctrines of Christianity is that of atonement, the redemption of humanity by the suffering and death of Christ. Judaism and Islam both emphasize the justice and mercy of God, insisting that God requires obedience to the moral law, but will forgive those who are genuinely penitent for their wrongdoing. They tend to see the Judgement Day as one in which each person will be judged for his or her own conduct, and in which no person can atone for the behaviour of another,[1] and insist that, if God is indeed merciful, there are no conditions for the divine mercy, certainly not the death of an innocent man. So there is a historic tradition of rejection of any doctrine of salvation by the cross in both Judaism and Islam.

On deeper reflection, however, the gulf between Christian doctrines of atonement and Judaeo-Muslim insistence on the accountability of each person before God, and the unconditional nature of the divine mercy, may not seem so great. In considering the idea of a fall from the ideal human state, it turned out that all Abrahamic traditions agree that humans are estranged from God, and are in bondage to egoism. The attainment of the divinely intended goal for human society consequently seems to be impossible without some transformation of human nature by the divine power or grace.

Moreover, the prayers of the righteous are naturally desired and given as ways of helping people to come to the knowledge and love of God. Humans do not live out their moral lives in isolation, but are profoundly helped or harmed by the acts and prayers of others. In particular, an act of renunciation by one person in order to help another can be a powerful force for good, and can be effective in freeing people from egoism.

It is also true that, although God's mercy is conditional only on genuine penitence, the idea that God may freely share the suffer-

---

[1] 'No bearer of burdens can bear the burden of another', Qur'an 6: 164.

ings of creatures, and not remain aloof and untouched by the most extreme human evil and suffering, is one that reveals a sort of mercy that manifests supreme compassion.[2]

In all the main Abrahamic traditions, therefore, there is a natural place for divine grace, human self-sacrifice, and divine sharing in human suffering. When a Christian speaks of redemption through the cross, it is precisely these elements that are of greatest importance. In the life and death of Jesus, Christians maintain, these elements come together in a way that reveals the path to human liberation from sin in a new and powerful way.

The earliest New Testament documents, the Thessalonian letters, do not have a highly developed doctrine of atonement. They simply state that Jesus 'died for us so that whether we wake or sleep we might live with him'.[3] All the emphasis is on hope for coming salvation, seen in terms of deliverance from evil and union with God. Believers can know they are chosen for deliverance, because the Spirit came among them with power, renewing their lives in joy and hope. The death of Jesus is paralleled with the deaths of the prophets and with the persecutions of the early churches.[4] It is his resurrection that gives assurance that he will return. His death is simply the price of his resolute opposition to the hypocrisies of his society. He was prepared to pay that price to demonstrate his utter trust in the love of God. God confirmed the completion of his role as the obedient Son by raising him from death, so that he could return to destroy evil and draw the penitent to himself. Thereby his life of obedient self-giving was established as the pattern of the divinely given path to salvation. Jesus 'died for us', in that his final act of self-giving opened the way for God to raise him from death and deliver humanity from the power of evil.

On this earliest written view of the atonement, Jesus' death on the cross was the condition for his resurrection as the truly faithful Son. The resurrection was the condition for his return in glory to destroy evil and deliver those whom the Spirit has sealed. This is consistent with the Marcan statement that 'The Son of man also came not to be served but to serve, and to give his life as a ransom for many.'[5] Jesus lived out of compassion for humanity, and was faithful to God even when it led to his death. By that self-offering,

---

[2] Cf. the discussion of A. Heschel in K. Ward, *Religion and Creation* (Oxford: Clarendon, 1996), 19–24.

[3] 1 Thess. 5: 10. [4] 1 Thess. 2: 15. [5] Mark 10: 45.

he showed that he was uniquely fitted to be the vehicle by means of which God could deliver humanity from evil. His death is the price of freeing humans from slavery.

There is no thought that the price is paid to anyone, least of all the Devil. Some of the earliest models of atonement developed by theologians think of Jesus' death as a ransom paid by God to the Devil, who is tricked into releasing humanity from his clutches by accepting Jesus' death in return, only to discover that Jesus eludes his clutches at the last moment.[6] This model seems to require that God is an even greater deceiver than the Devil, and so it is quite unsatisfactory. Jesus' death is not a price paid by God to the Devil for a number of human lives.

His death has a twofold aspect. On the one hand, it is the self-giving of perfected martyrdom, of one who gives his life that God's will might be done. On the other hand, it expresses the price paid by God himself for the divine determination to liberate human lives from self-destruction, which requires God's patient sharing in the suffering of creatures and compassionate empathy with the sufferings of the innocent, to open the way of return to God from within the human situation. Jesus suffers and dies simply because perfect love suffers when it confronts the structures of self-regard erected in the human world. Those structures may seem to destroy the one who loves. But Jesus is not destroyed, and will return to destroy self-regard, either by its annihilation or by evoking faith and uniting the faithful to his own universal love.

The deep structure of this Pauline picture is that human self-regard leads to violence, hatred, and destruction. The way of God, in such a world, is a way of service and self-giving, which often seems to be defeated by evil. Yet such a way leads to deliverance from evil, for it leads beyond the self-destroying world to a community of perfected love. Jesus is the one who embodies this path to union with God in his own life. He makes it possible for others by the gift of the Spirit, who brings joy and hope. He will unite all his disciples with himself in God, and in that community evil and suffering will be no more.

The Pauline message is essentially a call to union with the risen Christ, who has revealed the path of unity with God through his faithful witness even to death, and through his divinely empowered

---

[6] Gregory of Nyssa, Great Catechism, ch. 26.

conquest of death. And it is a proclamation of joyful hope in the ultimate triumph of Christ, who has the power to deliver all sentient beings from the evil that entraps them.

The atonement is eternal union with God in Christ, and it is effected by Jesus' life of healing, forgiving, and challenging love, by his final faithful self-offering, by God's raising of his life to glory, by the gift of the Spirit of Christ who co-operates to transform human hearts, and by Christ's final liberation of humanity from evil. The cross is an important part of this fivefold process, as it encapsulates and focuses the depth of Jesus' self-offering. But it should not be made the sole moment or means of redemption. Its main importance is to affirm what sort of person it was that God raised from death to rule the divine Kingdom. It is a person who gives his life in order that God's purpose of redeeming humanity might be fulfilled.

The letter to the Galatians amplifies this general view. Christ 'gave himself for our sins to deliver us from the present evil age, according to the will of our God and Father'.[7] It was God's will that there should be an utterly faithful human life. Though it would be destroyed by the structures of self-regard, that life, precisely because of its faithfulness, would be raised by God to glory, so that it could reveal the path to union with God, and be the means of our liberation from evil. Jesus dies for us, in that his self-abandonment to God in a fallen world reveals the way to immortality for those trapped in that world.

JUSTIFICATION BY FAITH

Just as it is the faithfulness of Jesus which expresses and confirms his union with the Father, so it is our faith-union with Christ that unites us to the Father, in him. In Galatians, Paul introduces the legal terminology which has been so important in subsequent thinking about atonement, but which in some ways has proved to be misleading. Justification—from the verb 'to justify', *dikaiow*—is not, he says, to be obtained by keeping the Torah, but by faith in Christ.[8] Living justly or rightly is not just a matter of keeping some moral rules. The most important command in Torah is to love God with the whole heart. Thus to live justly, in accordance with Torah,

---

[7] Gal. 1: 4.   [8] Gal. 3: 24.

is to live in friendship with God. It is to live in full acceptance and reflection of the divine love, to live in the power of the divine love alone.

It is that which, Paul says, is impossible, because however hard one tries, human estrangement from God cannot be overcome by human effort. It can, however, be overcome by God's establishing relationship with humanity by a divine act of compassion and empowerment. This is what happens in the life of Jesus, which manifests both divine compassion with suffering and divine conquest of death. Believing that Jesus has lived in faithful self-giving and has been raised from death, one believes that victory over self and its structures is possible. Believing that God acted in him to annul self-regard and liberate from death, one believes that God has opened a way to inner freedom for humanity. Believing that Christ is inwardly present in the Spirit—and this belief involves the inner experience of the Spirit—one believes that God is leading one on this way of liberation. Believing that Christ will bring all things to himself, one believes that life's purpose will be fulfilled when God acts finally to eradicate evil and suffering from creation. Salvation, the healing of the estrangement of human existence from its divine ground, is wholly effected in the person of Jesus, partly effected in many who trust in his power, and promised to all who ultimately accept his power. Justification is by faith, in that by living on the basis of these beliefs, friendship with God is established, not by human effort, but by divine power, the power that acted in Christ to face suffering and overcome it.

When 'justification' is taken to mean, 'a declaration of legal innocence', one faces the difficulty that a guilty person has to be declared innocent by God. But, if God is perfectly just, how is this possible? As I have interpreted it, justification means 'establishing the possibility of being rightly related to God'. How can a person whose deepest motives and dispositions are to cause great harm be rightly related to God? Only if those motives and dispositions are wholly changed, by an inward turning of the mind, a *metanoia*. That can be effected by God, if the divine love can work within the human mind itself to transform it. That requires, on the human side, sincere contrition for the harm one has done, desire to make amends and to serve God, and reliance on the divine power to transform one's self. It requires, on the divine side, a way of bringing people to see the harm their self-regard causes, a way of showing what sort of life God requires, a way of beginning to achieve that life, and a promise of its final full achievement.

The cross of Christ shows the suffering that self-regard causes to self, to others, and to God. It shows the life of obedient self-giving that God requires. It shows the possibility of liberation from the power of destruction and death. And it becomes the means by which that liberation takes effect in human lives. Whereas a great saint can teach what one must do to be liberated from suffering, the Christ shows in his life what God does to liberate humanity from suffering. Christ is the vehicle of that divine redemptive action. Men and women, by turning from self-regard and accepting this disclosure of the path to release, receive into their lives the divine power which raises them to immortality. As Paul Fiddes puts it, in a sensitive reinterpretation and defence of the thought of Abelard, 'The cross of Jesus [is] an event which has a unique degree of power to evoke and create human response to the forgiving love of God.'[9] The crucifixion is not just an event which gives an ideal example of how to live, or which exercises some sort of moral influence upon people, as they think of it. It is the historical vehicle of divine power to forgive and heal: 'the Holy Spirit . . . applies to us the renewal of the divine image in Christ's nature'.[10] A similar emphasis on the essential role of the Holy Spirit is found in Colin Gunton: 'It is the "hidden" and "efficacious" power of the Spirit which gives significance to this particular sacrificial self-giving.'[11] The Spirit which empowered Jesus, in his perfected union with the Father, is the same Spirit who shapes many human lives on the pattern of the life of Jesus.

This theme is central to the thinking of St Paul, who constantly speaks of the indwelling power of Christ, and of the shaping of human lives into the image of Christ. But Paul also puts things in a different, more juridical way, by saying that we fall under the curse reserved for those who fail to keep God's law. Our self-regard leads to an estrangement from God that we cannot overcome; but Christ 'becomes a curse for us'.[12] He accepts the suffering of estrangement and death, and because of his obedience he is raised to the

[9] Paul Fiddes, *Past Event and Present Salvation* (London: Darton, Longman, Todd, 1989), 29.

[10] Ibid. 153.

[11] Colin Gunton, *The Actuality of Atonement* (Edinburgh: T. & T. Clark, 1988), 130.

[12] Gal. 3: 13.

presence of God. Thus he becomes the pattern and vehicle for our liberation to union with God. This does not need to be seen as a quasi-mechanical transaction, in which Christ suffers a penalty which we should have paid. Such a view takes too external a view of the inner connection between sin and suffering, and too narrow a view of the free forgiveness and redemptive love of God.

No doubt past wrongdoing needs to be compensated for by self-renouncing action to help others or to compensate them wherever possible, which shows penitence to be genuine. Harmful habits established in oneself need to be eradicated by a long process of self-discipline. There is no sense, however, in which past wrongs can somehow be erased by the infliction of suffering on the wrong-doer, whether this is inflicted by oneself or by others. Past harm cannot be undone, and punishment will certainly not undo it.

Of course, persons who have caused great harm should not be treated as though they have tried hard to help others all their lives. If they do not repent, but continue in evil, it is inevitable and just that their world will become destructive and harmful to them as well as to others. In this way they will reap the effects of their actions. This, I think, is the truth in the retributive theory. But if they repent, the appropriate divine response is to require them to work for the good of others, not simply cause them to suffer pain for its own sake. One should not, therefore, think of God as impos-ing a fixed punishment on penitent wrongdoers. One should rather think of God as encouraging them to work self-renouncingly for the welfare of others, and thereby become capable of accepting and responding to the divine love. One can best think of this as a freely accepted penance.

That penance cannot be borne by anyone else, and it cannot sim-ply be remitted. What, then, is forgiveness? It is accepting the pos-sibility of full personal relationship, on the sole condition that the penance is undertaken sincerely. God can forgive, without requir-ing any fixed penalty from anyone. But relationship with God is effected by God, by a specific act which takes human life into unity with God. God sets us in right relationship with God, while we are incapable of it and estranged from God. God overcomes that estrangement by entering the human situation and transforming it by the power of the divine life.

'Justification' does not mean that I am regarded as innocent by God because another person takes the fixed punishment for my wrongdoing. It means that if I sincerely repent and embark on a course of penitential self-renunciation, God promises full personal relationship with the divine. God justifies me by setting me in right relation to the divine, through the indwelling power of the Spirit of Christ, who was faithful to death and thereby achieved victory over the worst that evil could do to humanity. All I need to do to receive this gift of relationship is to accept the Spirit of the crucified and risen Lord with trust, gratitude, and hope. That is how justification is by faith.

THE DESOLATION OF THE CROSS

It is thus true that Jesus suffers because of my sin, and that his suffering and consequent exaltation opens the path to my reconciliation with God. But this does not have to be interpreted juridically, as if God requires that an innocent man is punished so that I can be declared innocent of crimes I have committed, and can never undo.[13] Such a juridical interpretation strangely skews the justice of God, and can lead to a misinterpretation of the divine–human relationship as one of legal transaction rather than as one of loving personal relationship. The cross is redemptive because it manifests the patient suffering of God, who acts by the persuasion of love to recreate self-imprisoned souls in the image of the liberated humanity of Christ.

There may seem to be an ambiguity in this account. Is Jesus a man who, by his faithful obedience even to death, is raised to God's presence, sends the Spirit and is given authority to return in judgement and liberation? Or is he the eternal Logos, divesting itself of its glory and bliss, to take on itself human suffering and estrangement, in order that humanity should be raised to the life of deity in him? The antithesis is falsely drawn, for Jesus is both the utterly faithful human person and the eternally self-giving Word of God, the two united indissolubly in one transfigured moment of history.

It should be clear that Jesus cannot be simply an ordinary human person, since such a death—and there have been millions—cannot be the means of human redemption. On the other hand, it is not an

---

[13] Though Calvin's account is subtly qualified, it is liable to such a juridical interpretation: 'The punishment to which we were liable was inflicted on that Just One', John Calvin, *Institutes of the Christian Religion*, 2. 16. 5, trans. H. Beveridge (Grand Rapids, Mich.: Eerdmans, 1989), 438.

adequate conception of God's share in the sufferings of creation that it should be limited to just one short human life. God must know, and know by acquaintance, all creaturely suffering. 'Creation involves God in cost and pain from the beginning.'[14] So the meaning of the incarnation cannot adequately be seen as uniquely enabling God to share in the suffering of humanity. God already shares in and experiences all the suffering of creation.

Of course, though God knows what it is like to experience human suffering which is the result of sin, it cannot be regarded as God's own suffering. Could Jesus' suffering be regarded as God's own suffering? It is not the result of Jesus' sin. Whereas God may react to my suffering in sympathy, that sympathy must always be affected by the distancing effect of my selfishness, with which God cannot identify. In the case of Jesus, there is no such divine distancing. This is wholly innocent suffering, perhaps uniquely so,[15] and it is consciously borne by a human person to forward the divine purpose of liberation from self. Thus God can not only experience it with unreserved compassion and empathy, but can unreservedly embrace it, as an expression of the divine will and purpose. Of course, God does not will the suffering, as such. What God wills is the bearing of the suffering, in so far as the suffering is caused by the self-centred wills of humans, precisely for the sake of liberating human wills from bondage to evil. God assents to the commitment of Jesus to bear such suffering, and God wills that such freely accepted bearing of suffering shall be a means to human liberation. In that sense one can speak of Jesus' suffering as God's own suffering, a bearing of suffering that God unreservedly wills and accepts, in all its tragic depth.

It follows that Jesus' cry of dereliction from the cross cannot reflect an attitude of despair, since that would be a sin. It can, however, express a human sense of the absence of God, as Jesus experienced the great barrier that sin erects between the divine love and human life. Could it express a belief that God has abandoned the obedient son?[16] Such a belief would be a false belief, and would reflect a lack of total faith in the divine promises. Both of these are

---

[14] Fiddes, *Past Event*, 22.

[15] Jesus 'in every respect has been tempted as we are, yet without sin', Heb. 4: 15.

[16] Such a proposal seems to be made by Hans Urs von Balthasar: 'the concentration of everything contrary to God in the Son is experienced as being abandoned by the Father', in *The von Balthasar Reader*, ed. M. Kehl and W. Loser (Edinburgh: T. & T. Clark, 1982), 148

difficult to ascribe to a perfect human person. Could it express a *feeling* of abandonment by God? One can say, 'I feel as if I had been abandoned, even though I know I have not.' One might ask, 'Why does God not give me feelings of encouragement or a sense of divine presence and empowerment?' Such feelings, the 'dark night of the soul', are common in the prayers of the saints. It is a sense of divine withdrawal, inaccessibility, and remoteness; a sense that one is cast on one's own resources, without spiritual consolation or joy. To 'forsake' is to leave to one's own resources, and there is a sense in which God does that, in spiritual experience.

God is always present, sustaining one's very existence, working out a purpose for good. But one may lose the consciousness of that fact. Indeed, one may be set by God to work on one's own soul without more than that minimum of divine co-operation which is needed to hold one in being. In loss of the consciousness of the divine presence, and in the quiescence of the divine Spirit, who ceases actively to work in the heart, Jesus could enter into the experience of human estrangement without ever believing that God's purpose could be defeated.

But can the Son lose consciousness of the Father, and be deprived of the perichoretic activity of the Spirit? The classical answer is that he could, but in his human nature only. That is to say, there is a human consciousness which, though without flaw, experiences the absence of a God whose presence had been continuous, intense, and vivid, and a withdrawal of that creative joy of the Spirit which had been the constant accompaniment of his activities. That, more than purely physical pain, is the ultimate suffering of the passion. Jesus dies, and in his passion consciousness of the source of life, wisdom, and joy, the sense of the beloved, is lost. The soul experiences a vast unbroken solitude, in which the springs of love and creativity seem dry and inaccessible, and all the energy of life seems drained away. Jesus, the perfected soul, experienced such a death, after first experiencing at the hands of others the pain and humiliation of torture, abandonment, and betrayal.

Centuries of meditation on the suffering and death of Jesus have given rise to the belief that the passion of Jesus is the seeming reversal of that which marked him out as the Son of God. He had been filled with the healing power of new life. Now he was helpless in the face of death. He had been vividly aware of the presence of God, now he felt no sense of the divine presence. He had been filled with the joy of the Spirit, now he was saddened with the knowledge that all had turned against him, that little had been accomplished by his life and teaching. He had proclaimed human liberation from the power of death, now his short ministry was about to end in ritual execution. How can this dying soul be identified with God?

His whole life had been lived in complete co-operation with God, a co-operation so close that human and divine formed a unique unity in him.[17] God works in him to teach, heal, and forgive. He gives himself wholly to God to be the vehicle of divine action and the medium of an uncorrupted divine experience of finite selfhood. His human consciousness is a vehicle through which the divine life is expressed. He not only shows in his life what God is like, he manifests the healing power of God, and so is God in action. Yet now this divine activity seems to be withdrawn. Jesus' experience leads him into the ultimate wilderness. Jesus foresaw this in Gethsemane, and accepted its necessity. He was faithful not only in the first wilderness of temptation, but also in the last wilderness of desolation.

Jesus, unlike some sages who by their advanced spiritual state are said to be beyond the experience of suffering, experiences both physical suffering and a sense of abandonment by God. Since he is regarded as wholly good, one must suppose that he never loses his faith in God's promise of resurrection, and he never falls prey to self-regard or despair. But he does experience the consequences of self-regard, as far as feelings and awareness go. His faithfulness to God endures the final test, the loss of the sense of the presence of God.

This human consciousness, even in its most extreme feeling of estrangement, is not in fact estranged, since God does not in fact abandon it. Yet the feeling is real and almost overwhelming. It essentially belongs to human consciousness, and cannot be a feeling of the divine nature in itself, cannot belong as such to the divine nature, though it has been suggested that God can accept and will it in a unique sense. One cannot say of Jesus' experience of desolation that it is experienced by the divine nature, or by a divine person which can somehow become alienated from the other persons of a divine triad.[18] It must be the experience of a human subject.

[17] This view is outlined in my *Religion and Revelation* (Oxford: Oxford University Press, 1994), 258–82.

[18] As Moltmann seems to suggest: 'On the cross the Son suffers death in being forsaken by the Father. But the Father suffers the death of the Son, and in it his being forsaken by the Son', Jurgen Moltmann, *History and the Triune God*, trans. J. Bowden (London: SCM, 1991), 24.

Yet that subject and the divine Subject, the Logos, are not related externally, as one finite subject to another. The human subject is the finite image of the divine archetype of love, and the vehicle of the divine love. It is precisely because Jesus is empowered by the divine love that he is prepared to embrace the most extreme consequence of estrangement, in order to plumb the depths of human alienation and, by patient endurance, to assume it to the divine life.

Why should Jesus enter into such an experience of desolation for me? Because it is the ultimate consequence of human sin, and he accepts the vocation of experiencing the ultimate consequence of sin. Only thus will his faithful unity with God have endured and triumphed over every inducement and effect of sin, over every human temptation and every human consequence of sin. Only thus will the ultimate human estrangement be reconciled to the divine life. Jesus is attested as the utterly faithful human person, by his endurance of the worst that sin can do.[19] He is so faithful, of course, because of his empowering unity with God. Even while he lacks a feeling of that unity, it remains. He does not just happen to triumph. God creates a human nature that faces the worst that can befall it, yet remains unscarred and faithful. Human faith must often face the experience of desolation. In Jesus it has done so, and endured.

In this way, the full humanity of Jesus is attested. He experiences what the divine nature alone cannot. Thus he is not an avatar, above suffering and only *appearing* as a human being. He is not one who exists above worldly sufferings in supreme equanimity. He is one who endures worldly sufferings in steadfast faith, hope, and love. God vindicated that faith by demonstrating the unity of humanity and the divine in exaltation. Jesus becomes the way-founder, the liberator in whom humanity and divinity are united. In his birth, human and divine were united. This unity endures, though hidden, through suffering and death. It is fulfilled and revealed in the transfigured life of glory.

But how is that liberation achieved for me? Because it is the means by which I am to be united with God, the event which reveals the path to deification in human history for me and for all sentient persons. In some way, the drama of the passion and resurrection of Christ must be played out in every human life. The uniting, enduring, exalting power of the Spirit which was in the person

---

[19] 'Although he was a Son, he learned obedience through what he suffered', Heb. 5: 8.

of Jesus is given also to me, to begin the work of liberation. God co-operatively acts to form me in the image of Christ and liberate me from self.

If Jesus was a man whose special vocation it was to reveal the divine nature, then his acceptance of suffering and death does that in a telling fashion, for it is revelatory of the universal nature of God as suffering love. But Jesus is united to God in a closer way than that. He is a man who is true to his vocation of expressing the divine nature, as it confronts human self-regard. He is also a man in whom God acts to liberate humanity from self-regard. His whole life is filled with the Spirit, to whose leading he is wholly responsive. Before his passion, he inaugurated a new covenant, to be sealed with his freely accepted death (his blood). In this covenant, the victorious life that was in him is given also to us.

The unity that God effected in Jesus must also be effected in others. Jesus not only shows the pattern of such union, and establishes it as a historical reality. In and through the self-offered life of Jesus, the universal Spirit begins the work of establishing the pattern of divine–human relationship in a new form, one which is to continue in all who accept the Spirit of Christ in repentance and trust. One might say that Christ continues to offer his life in and through us, beginning in us that ascent to perfect knowledge and love of the Father which we are unable to make by our own power.[20] Christ does in and for me what I am unable to do, establishing the relationship with God that has been destroyed by sin. Salvation is by mutual participation, human participation in the glorified life of Christ, and the participation of the Spirit of Christ in transforming human lives.

THE IDEA OF SACRIFICE

The Christian accepts that God has a purpose, or many purposes, for creation, and that God wants created persons to co-operate in realizing these purposes. The divine purpose for creation is that people should grow in creativity, sensitivity, and community by co-operative relationship to God, in realizing many particular values in the universe.[21] These values include caring for the welfare of all sentient beings, shaping natural beauty by careful conservation,

---

[20] 'It is no longer I who live, but Christ who lives in me', Gal. 2: 20.
[21] This view is developed in some detail in my *Religion and Creation*, pt. 3.

and understanding and developing the energy of the material world to express new forms of being and relationship.

When human persons turn from co-operation with God to the pursuit of selfish desire, these purposes are impeded and frustrated. People become destructive, insensitive, and individualistic. They use sentient beings as objects for amusement or investigation. They destroy the environment. They use energy to develop weapons of destruction and means of exploitation. Human life and its environment are defaced and corrupted. People are born estranged and in ignorance of the very source of their life. Such a world can only be condemned by God. When the Bible speaks of the 'anger' of God, it refers to the fact that God must oppose and exclude the fallen world from relationship with the divine Being.

Yet God's love is not destroyed by this corruption of the divine purposes, but continues to will that all should come to know and love God, and share in the divine life of creativity, wisdom, and bliss. While God necessarily condemns sin, God's love is so great that it takes the initiative in seeking to rescue human souls from their own corruption. To do that, God must first of all reveal to the world the fact that it has condemned itself to futility and suffering.[22] God must reveal that it is sin, selfish desire, that inevitably brings with it spiritual death. God must reveal that it is possible to repent—to turn from selfish desire—and to come in time to know God fully. God must reveal that there is a way to overcome selfish desire and attain the goal of perfect love. These are the 'Four Noble Truths' of theism. These things can only be revealed by one who knows them to be true, that is, by God in person, or by a person who has overcome self and attained perfect compassion. Christians assert that they are revealed by one whose freedom from selfish desire enabled him to be the perfect channel of God's self-revealing presence and love.

The theist will naturally believe that it is only God who can bring finite persons to perfect love. For God will need to infuse the divine love into the souls of human beings, so that they are able to respond to the guiding and co-operating love of God. Thus the way to the goal of release or liberation from sin is a way established by God to mediate the divine love to those who will turn from self and trust in the offer of love and the promise of fulfilment. It is not just a way

---

[22] 'The creation was subjected to futility, not by its own will but by the will of him who subjected it in hope', Rom. 8: 20.

of abandoning desire.[23] It is a way of discovering the desire for God within the heart, where only God can place it. So God must not only reveal or teach the way to liberation, but must also provide an appropriate form in which the divine love can be mediated to human beings, establishing in their corrupted souls the possibility of a loving relation to God.

This revelation and this mediative form for the divine love was definitively established in the covenant made through Abraham and then through Moses with the people of Israel. In the commands and ordinances of Torah, God revealed the nature of sin, the penalty of sin, the promise of liberation and the way of faithful obedience which would lead to the fulfilment of that promise. In the sacrificial rituals of Torah, God laid down the mediative form which expresses the right relation between sinful humans and the perfectly loving God, and which makes that relation possible.

The central element of the Temple sacrifices[24] is the offering, at some personal cost, of a gift, usually a perfect animal, to God. In this way a life is given back by those whose own lives are given by God, whose possessions are held in trust from God. There are three main types of sacrifice, all of which parallel the giving of gifts in human society, express the appropriate form of human relationship to God, and mediate the living presence of God to the faithful devotee.[25] To that extent, Tylor's idea, in 'Primitive Culture', that sacrifices are primarily gifts to the gods, expresses an important element of truth.[26] First, in the holocaust or fire-offering, a perfect bull, ram, or goat is wholly burned and its blood sprinkled around the altar.[27] This expresses the dedication of the offerer's life to God, showing that one holds nothing back in acknowlegement of total dependence and devotion. The sacrificial gift is given to honour and acknowledge God as the rightful owner and giver of all good things.

Second, in the fellowship offering, the meat is shared with the offerer and his companions.[28] This expresses a desire for commu-

[23] In this sense, it contrasts with traditions that teach that one should 'avoid delight and aversion' (*Sutta-Nipata*, trans. Saddhatissa (Richmond, Va.: Curzon, 1994), 74). Even so, as I have stressed, this is more a matter of emphasis than of outright contradiction.

[24] The rituals are detailed in Lev. 1–7.

[25] Cf. G. B. Gray, *Sacrifice in the Old Testament* (Oxford: Oxford University Press 1925), 64–5.

[26] E. B. Tylor, *Primitive Culture* (London: John Murray, 1873).

[27] Lev. 1.   [28] Lev. 7: 11–36.

nion, sharing in fellowship with God, and God establishes fellowship and peace between those who eat in the divine presence. This is the element which Robertson Smith stressed,[29] and it is certainly an important element, though not the only one, in the sacrificial cultus of Israel.

Third, in the guilt and sin offerings, a gift is given to express sorrow for past wrongs and ask for forgiveness.[30] With the destruction of the carcass by fire, the sin of the sacrificer is destroyed by God and fellowship is re-established. Sacrifices may also be offered to give thanks to God for the divine goodness, and to implore a favour, either for oneself or, preferably, for others. Thus the sacrifices define and embody the right relationship between creature and creator, one of reverence, gratitude, penitence, communion, and petition. They thereby enable God to relate to humans in Lordship, forgiveness, mercy, and empowerment. They are the mediative form in which God relates appropriately to creatures, symbols and effective channels of the divine covenant.

There is nothing in the intrinsic character of the animal offered which will causally bring this relationship about. One offers the sacrificial gift because God has ordained that way of worship and prayer. Our making the sacrifice in the ordained way shows our trusting obedience in God, and God wills to answer our prayers and deliver us from selfish desire in response to such obedience. As Fiddes puts it, 'Sacrifice is not something human beings do to God (propitiation) but something which God does for humankind (expiation).'[31] Humans cannot invent some rite which will cause God to view them with favour. God ordains a rite by means of which God can begin to remove human selfishness and establish a right relationship to the divine.

The sacrificial ritual came to an end with the destruction of the second Temple. It is just at that point that the disciples of Jesus proclaimed that a new age had begun, with the birth of a community of a new covenant and a new kind of sacrificial mediative form of divine love. They saw Jesus as the embodiment of Torah, the Wisdom of God, in a human person. They saw him as Israel's true King, with the authority to inaugurate a community of universal love and establish a new covenant, open to Jews and Gentiles alike.

[29] Robertson Smith, *Lectures on the Religion of the Semites* (London: A. & C. Black, 1894).
[30] Lev. 4: 1–5, 13.   [31] Fiddes, *Past Event*, 71.

They saw him as one whose death was not a defeat, but a voluntary self-offering to effect God's purpose of transforming the mediative form of the Temple sacrifices into a new mediative form of the spirit of suffering love, identified by its activity in the life of Jesus, which was to be proclaimed throughout the whole earth.

The connection between sacrifice and human liberation is that, in a world of selfish desire, justice can flourish only through the self-sacrifice of those whose goodness exposes the hypocrisies of power and draws the destructive forces of 'the worldly powers' upon themselves. Through such apparent defeat, through obedience to goodness, the secret power of love can begin to operate in those human hearts that turn from self to trust the promise of deliverance from suffering and selfish desire. 'Victory is the refusal of Jesus to exercise power demonically.'[32] So Jesus' sacrifice was the totally obedient offering of his life to God, both in mediating the divine love in healing, forgiving, and teaching, and in remaining true to his vocation in face of imminent and actual death.

The sacrifices of the first covenant were the divinely ordained mediative form in which the divine Spirit begins to transfigure human desire into selfless love. So the voluntary self-offering of Jesus becomes the mediative form of a new covenant, through which the Spirit transfigures us into the image of Christ. In the old covenant, the penitent brought an animal to the priest, to be offered to God so that God could establish a covenant relationship between Creator and creature. In the new covenant, penitents bring their own lives to the 'heavenly High Priest', who lives everlastingly with the Father,[33] offering his own life so that the Spirit of God can begin to form human lives into the image of selfless love. It is as we are able to some degree to crucify ourselves with Christ that we become able, through the power of the Spirit, to be filled with the power of his resurrection life.

It is the life, death, and resurrection of Jesus which becomes the pattern and origin of the Spirit's activity in the community of the new covenant. So it is quite correct to say that the sacrifice of Jesus makes human deliverance from evil and reconciliation to God possible. One can see how this sacrificial model can lead to the idea that Jesus offers a perfect 'sacrifice, oblation and satisfaction' that reconciles the Father to sinful humans. Yet it is important not to

---

[32] Gunton, *Actuality of Atonement*, 75.   [33] Heb. 9: 24.

think of this as God requiring the death of an innocent human being before God can forgive sinners. For it is the Logos of God who dies, who is the sacrificial victim. It is God's own self-sacrifice, not the death of someone else, which appeases or annuls the divine anger against sin. This is a way of saying that, while God wholly opposes evil and suffering, yet God will take the consequences of that evil, if by it humans may be brought to turn from evil and seek eternal life with God. God's anger is not something separate from God's mercy, which needs to be appeased before it disappears. Rather, God is always merciful, but that mercy can only effectively operate when humans turn from that to which anger is the only appropriate response, and trust in the mercy which sacrifices itself in order that all sinners might be saved. God sacrifices bliss by permitting and sharing the sufferings of the world. God the Father ordains and accepts the sacrifice of Jesus, both as expressing the divine self-sacrifice and as establishing in history a new and definitive mediative form of the redemptive activity of the Spirit.

Such a view of atonement sees the cross and resurrection of Jesus as an adequate mediative form, a paradigmatic icon, of the Spirit. The image which is common in the Orthodox tradition of the glorified Jesus stretching out his arms to the world from the cross expresses well some of the main complex elements of this originative event. In that image one sees a perfect human self-offering, and at the same time the divine judgement on human sin. One sees the divine self-sacrifice of the eternal Word, and the transfiguration of humanity to full union with God. One sees the priestly prayer of oblation and the gift of divine life. All this is mediated through the ritual re-presentation of the originative event. The cross of glory is the icon of the Spirit's redemptive action in the world, which annuls the power of selfish desire and makes humanity and divinity 'at-one'.

10

Salvation by Grace

THE IDEA OF SATISFACTION FOR SIN

Traditional reflections on the atonement have to some extent pursued misleading analogies from the rather varied and unsystematic New Testament uses of sacrificial imagery. Anselm sees the misleadingness of some patristic accounts of atonement in terms of 'ransom' and of internal conflict in God. But he in turn falls prey to an over-rationalistic approach which pursues an inadequate view of punishment in terms of Cyprian's concept of 'satisfaction' to its logical conclusion. Anselm begins his great work on the atonement with a preface making the extreme claim to prove 'by absolute reasons, the impossibility that any man should be saved without him [Christ]',[1] and to show that 'immortality could not be fulfilled unless God became man'.[2]

The claim is extreme, since God could presumably enable humans to know and love God in many ways, unimaginable by us. Thomas Aquinas, for example, held that God could have forgiven human sins without the incarnation and crucifixion, if God had so chosen.[3] It is certainly good if God raises a human life to unity with the divine life, thus showing in a human life the nature of God as self-giving love, the nature of human perfection as obedient trust, and the goal of human life as resurrection to eternal life. Incarnation is a peculiarly expressive form of divine self-revelation, manifesting the personal form of God and showing that human and divine can be united in the closest manner. The nature of the divine Spirit who works in us to incorporate us into the divine life is decisively revealed and expressed in the pattern of the human life of Jesus, the mediator and reconciler. The threefold pattern of *kenosis*, the divine self-emptying to serve creatures; *enosis*, the uniting of human and divine; and *theosis*, the raising of creatures to share in

---

[1] Anselm, *Cur Deus Homo*, Preface trans. S. N. Deane, *Basic Writings* (La Salle: Open Court, 1962), 191.

[2] Ibid. 192.   [3] Aquinas, *Summa Theologiae*, III q. 46 a. 2 ad. 3.

the divine life, is well expressed by the incarnation and passion of the divine Word. In all these ways the incarnation is deeply appropriate for bringing humans to know and love God, and to share in God's own love. It is not necessary to claim that this is the only way there could have been.

Anselm's main argument is that humans cannot achieve their purpose, eternal happiness, unless their sins are remitted.[4] 'Sin is nothing else than not to render to God his due.'[5] Sin dishonours God, and one must make some compensation to God to 'pay back the honour of which he has robbed God'. Anselm is here relying on a juridical analogy, and suggesting that wrongdoers should restore what they have taken, and in addition add more in compensation. If I slander you, I must restore your reputation, and also compensate you in some way satisfactory to you. So we ought to compensate God for the dishonour we have done God by disobedience.

Richard Swinburne, in his restatement of an Anselmian view, argues that sinners owe God repentance, apology, reparation and penance.[6] They must be truly sorry, they must apologize publicly, they must make reparation, and must compensate God by some further acts of penance. The difficulty with this is that it is very hard to see what human actions could possibly make compensation to God, to whom all things already properly belong.

It is true that God lays duties on me, and also offers me the gift of friendship. By sinning, I fail in my duty and reject God's friendship. In what way could I compensate God for this failure and rejection? And would a God of perfect love require compensation for a slighting of the divine honour? Our acts cannot cause God to lose anything, and loss of reputation will not harm God. Perhaps one could argue that our sins, in causing creaturely suffering, cause divine experiential knowledge of suffering, and thus impair divine bliss. Moreover, one might suggest that God loses the satisfaction of seeing the divine purposes fully carried out in the world. Perhaps we do, in some sense, cause God to suffer. But how could we compensate God for that suffering? What would be a possible and sufficient satisfaction? If we think of a crime of stealing money, then it is fairly straightforward to think of repaying the money, plus some more for the inconvenience and distress that has been caused. If we

---

[4] Anselm, 12. 10, in *Basic Writings*, 215.   [5] Anselm, 1. 11, ibid. 216.
[6] Richard Swinburne, *Responsibility and Atonement* (Oxford: Clarendon, 1989), ch. 5.

think of slandering someone, then one might think that the slanderer should make a public retraction, and perhaps again pay damages for the loss of public esteem that may have been incurred. If we think of torturing someone, we obviously cannot simply return what we have taken, whether money or reputation. We can never take the pain away. But perhaps the nearest thing to appropriate redress would be to do what we can to procure their happiness, and repay them for the distress we have caused.

Anselm seems to suggest that the slander analogy is the most appropriate for sin against God. We have dishonoured God, so we must make recompense by honouring God to a degree that makes up for the dishonour we have done God. It is obvious that this is impossible, however, since to honour God is to obey God wholly. We can never do more than that, so we can never pay back an excess of honour to God. Not only that, but since we can never obey God wholly anyway, we can never even honour God properly, let alone to excess.[7]

We cannot even give God what we owe, complete reverence and obedience, much less think of any way of compensating for our past failures. We cannot really make reparation to God, since the suffering we have caused can never be undone. We could at best undertake a life of self-renunciation in the service of others. But since we are supposed to do that anyway, it would not constitute compensation. Moreover, we are simply not able to do it perfectly, so we seem to be in an impossible situation. It might be better, therefore, to drop the vocabulary of 'compensating God'. We can still accept Anselm's main point that we are unable to live the life of perfect self-giving service of others, and of obedient trust that God requires.

Christians believe that there is one human life which was so united to the divine life that it was not enslaved by selfish desire, and so was able to give due worship to God. Jesus lived a life which duly honours God, in praise, thanksgiving, and obedient love. That is all very well, but what has it to do with us? Anselm argues that, being divine, Jesus' life had an infinite surplus of merit, which can be given to us.[8] This idea of merit is tied to images of a moral account-book, the surpluses or deficits of which can be moved around among different persons. In matters of morality, how can

---

[7] Anselm, 1. 20, in *Basic Writings*, 239–42.   [8] Anselm, 2. 14, ibid. 275–6.

one person's merit be used to compensate for the misdeeds of someone else?

We can drop that unappealing image, however, and still think that Jesus' life was lived and offered by him as a prayer to God for the sake of others. Jesus offers his life as a prayer to God that humans should be liberated from self. It is a form of sacrifice, pain freely accepted and offered to God in order to bring good to others. The cross is the perfection of prayer in a world opposed to the will and presence of God.

To understand how one person's prayer can bring forgiveness and obedient faith to so many others, one has to consider that Jesus is one whose life is uniquely united to the life of God. Jesus' life is not just a perfect human prayer. It also embodies the act of God which accepts suffering, which unites human and divine nature, and which raises the human to the divine life.

There is a double mutual self-gift of divine and human in the life of Jesus. As Jesus surrenders his life to God, so God acts in and through Jesus to give the divine life to others. It is Jesus' surrender of his humanity which enables God to act in him to liberate from egoism, and establish a healing relation to God. In the first place, that liberation happens in the person of Jesus itself. But it also happens through him, as he is able, through his self-offering, to mediate the liberating power of God. Thus, in his life, Jesus heals, forgives, and exercises power over the forces of chaos and disintegration in human life. His whole surrendered life is filled with the Spirit of God, and that Spirit is mediated through him, as a source of life to his disciples.

What Jesus does for human salvation, in offering his life as a perfect prayer, is to reveal, embody, and mediate the Spirit. Being fully present in him, the Spirit takes the form of his life, in that life's bearing of suffering, its reconciling power, and glorious unification with God in resurrection. As the cosmic Christ is the archetype on which the creative power of the Spirit shapes the intelligible forms of the universe, and the completed pleroma towards which the Spirit shapes all things, so the historical Jesus is the exemplar, the individual human being who gives form to the Spirit who fills his life. Jesus' self-offering is not a masochistic self-denial, but an opening of his humanity to creative energizing by the Spirit. His prayer gives particular form to the Spirit and mediates it to those who turn to him in penitence and faith.

In our case, we may pray for something, and God may subsequently act in response to our prayer. But in Jesus' case, human prayer perfectly channels the divine response. His prayer of self-sacrifice is also and at the same time the historical mediation of the divine action to liberate human lives from the power of egoism. Of course, the prayer of the cross is not sufficient to accomplish human liberation on its own, as though it could be effective without any human response at all. It is necessary for individual persons to ask for the prayer of the cross on their own behalf, and thus to receive the cruciform power of the Spirit, which can heal and liberate them, and relate them positively to the love of God.

If Jesus' prayer was only one event far away in history, limited in time and place, it would be hard to see how all human persons could ask for it on their behalf. It is true that Jesus' sacrificial life of prayer, brought to its culminating moment on the cross, happened once in human history. But what it manifests is the eternal character of God, as sharing in suffering, so as to patiently persuade creatures to return to the divine presence. The cross shows at one moment in time the eternal self-offering and passion of God for human redemption, and it releases the power of God for liberating human lives from evil and death.

It is essential that the cross and the resurrection should be considered together, since the liberating power of God is effected in Jesus' raising from death. The divine response to the self-offering prayer of dereliction from the cross is the raising of that human life into the glorified life of God. Though Jesus' prayer is not for himself, the response to it must first concern him, for it is through his victory over death that divine life flows out to the world.

THE HEALING POWER OF THE SPIRIT

Because of his victory over death, Jesus lives for ever in the spiritual realm, continuing to offer himself as the High Priest of the earth.[9] That is, he continues to pray for the deliverance of humans from evil, as the one who once offered himself as a perfect and voluntary sacrifice. His prayer did not just once take place outside Jerusalem and then cease; it continues without end. God ordains that the people of the new covenant should express their worship, peni-

---

[9] Heb. 6: 19, 20.

tence, and communion by asking the heavenly High Priest to offer his completed earthly life for them. That priestly prayer is effective because it remains the channel of divine liberating action. As it united the humanity of Jesus to the divinity of the Word in glory, so now it can unite our humanity to the divine, by the action of the same Spirit who filled his life and took form from it.

What Jesus prays for is that the redemption of human nature which was effected in him should also be effected in millions of other human lives. The same Spirit who united him to God from the first moment of his life, and whose action in us is patterned on his life, is sent by him to fill our lives and unite us to God. The Spirit does this by making the body and blood of Christ, the substance of his prayer of oblation, present in many communities of disciples throughout space and time.

The body of Christ is the local physical realization of the presence of Christ. This was first fully manifested in the person of Jesus, in a life of self-giving love. Because of that human self-giving, the Christ was able to be fully manifest in and through it. Through the action of the Holy Spirit, Christ is made locally manifest at many times and places, as the life of Jesus is remembered, and its form made present. Here the *kenosis* of the Christ is made present, as he offers himself, an eternal reality but one who was fully manifest in Jesus, and thus in the re-presented form of Jesus. The body of Christ is the making-present of the eternal Christ in a particular form, given its meaning within the whole liturgical presentation of the event of Jesus the Christ. The blood of Christ is the life, the human openness to the eternal life of the Logos, which has opened it to us, in the community formed on the making-present of his human life.

It is important to see that salvation is social and historical. It is easy to say that God will unite everyone to the divine. But for this to happen, they must know what God is, what unity with God is, and how such unity is effected. These things are not by any means universally apparent. God shows what God is, a passionate and merciful God, through revelation by the prophets of Israel. The goal is revealed as a community of individuals related in love. The way is participation in the covenant community. Jesus, in this context, reveals a further aspect of God as suffering, self-emptying, and humble love, reveals the Kingdom to be not an ethnic group but a free association of hearts, and reveals the way as participation, through faith, in his own death and resurrection. If we trust in Jesus we will follow the way of his self-sacrifice, so that he may live in us his resurrection life.

Seen in this light, the major deficiency of Anselm's account of atonement is that the Spirit does not prominently figure in it. All transactions are effected between Father and Son, as if it was a question of debts owed to the Father and rewards owed to the Son, which could be balanced in such a way that the Son's reward could be used to pay all debts owing to the Father. Anselm suggests that God cannot simply ignore sin, since that would be unjust. 'Satisfaction or punishment must needs follow every sin.'[10] Anselm turns the screw, saying 'you make no satisfaction unless you restore something greater than the amount of the obligation.'[11] 'Man as a sinner owes God for his sin what he is unable to pay, and cannot be saved without paying.'[12]

It is true that, in human society, sin cannot just be ignored. We cannot turn a blind eye to people who harm others by their conduct. We do feel that they should do what they can to undo the harm and compensate for it, and also that they should suffer some penalty for their actions. Just as good acts merit some reward, so evil acts merit a deprivation of good. But what sort of deprivation? Perhaps the most appropriate punishment, though it is not possible for humans to arrange it, is for the criminal to feel the degree and sort of suffering that has been caused, to feel the victim's sufferings as his or her own. Evildoers, we feel, should come to understand how their acts cause suffering; should know what it is like to suffer in that way, by suffering the consequences themselves; and should do something to compensate the victims for it.

The difficulty is that, on such a view, the chain of suffering seems virtually unbreakable. Each of us goes on doing evil throughout our lives, failing to understand the harm we do, failing to sympathize properly with others, and failing to work for their good. Thus we bind ourselves more and more firmly to the penalties of evil, the experience of all the suffering we have caused to others.[13]

If that is the penalty of sin, then it is literally true that God bears the penalty for us, since God experiences all the suffering of creatures, including the sufferings that they cause each other. It is also

[10] Anselm, I. 15, in *Basic Writings*, 224.
[11] Anselm, I. 21, ibid. 244.   [12] Anselm, I. 25, ibid. 253.
[13] That is what accounts for the rise of *bhakti* traditions in India, when the impossibility of breaking out of samsara is seen. Cf. Ch. 2 of this volume.

true that we can never 'expiate' our evil by suffering all the suffering we cause. While we desire that wrongdoers should experience the suffering they cause, we would not wish them to be totally destroyed by the weight of such experience. In addition, there is the consideration that the addition of so much suffering to the universe would not improve it. As Plato said, a good man will never cause harm to others.[14] It would be ironic if we showed our disapproval of those who harm others, by harming them.

Of course, it could be held that we are not simply harming people, when we bring home to them the harm they have done by causing them to experience some forms of suffering themselves. But this can only plausibly be said when there is some hope of that suffering leading to good. The goal of the imposition of forensic suffering should be to lead wrongdoers to see the depth of their evil, to get them to try to compensate for it and to change their characters for the better. In other words, the morally acceptable goal of punishment is the compensation of the victim and the reformation of the offender. It is only if offenders refuse to face up to the harm they have done that forms of punishment may continue. Even then, there should always be the hope that repentance and reform may occur, and thus the door must always be open to that.

Thus we are left with a dilemma. On the one hand, wrongdoers should experience the suffering they cause. On the other hand, it is not good to increase the amount of suffering in the universe without hope of good issuing from it, or to place even a wrongdoer beyond the possibility of liberation from suffering. So one might conclude that wrongdoers should have real experience of the sufferings they cause, but not to such a degree that they will never be able to achieve freedom from suffering, if they genuinely seek to compensate in action for their wrongs.

If one accepts this account, then God cannot simply ignore sin. The divine reaction to sin will be to bring sinners to see the nature of the suffering they have caused, in the hope that they will repent and seek reformation and compensating forms of action. But a just and merciful God will not seek some exact amount of 'satisfaction' for each sin committed. That would render the human situation hopeless. Few people could properly atone for their own sins, and it is impossible to see how it would be morally acceptable for one

---

[14] 'It is never right to harm anyone', Plato, *The Republic*, 1. 335, trans. F. M. Cornford (Oxford: Oxford University Press, 1941), 14.

person to make satisfaction for another's sin. *That* would be a case of God simply ignoring sin and individual responsibility for it.

In that sense, the idea of satisfaction should be rejected. God will still be implacably opposed to sin, to all acts which harm and destroy created good. God will require from each person a price for the commission of sin. That price will be some experience of the suffering that has been caused, the acceptance of penitential action to try, however inadequately, to restore good where harm has been done, and a resolution to reform and turn from egoistic acts.

On Anselm's account, the satisfaction that humans cannot make is made by one who is both God and man. There is a perfect human life, through which God can reconcile all humans to the divine. Underlying the unsatisfactory concepts of 'satisfaction' and 'substitution' there is the insight that God's response to sin is not just one of opposition and judgement. God will take into the divine self the consequences of sin, as God shares in the sufferings of creatures. God will, in a way that creatures could not, effectively transfigure the harm done by sin into a process that will lead to an eventual form of goodness. With regard to the sinner, God will act positively to persuade humans to see and feel the harm sin causes, to persuade them to repent, to help them to engage in altruistic acts, and to assure them of the unchangeableness and the eventual victory of the divine love in every penitent life. God does what humans cannot do, in the sense that the life of perfect self-giving love which humans cannot live is formed in them by the action of the Spirit of the Risen Christ. In this way, God patiently suffers all the harm caused by human sin (and thus undergoes the 'penalty due to the sinner', the feeling of the suffering sin has caused). God empowers in Jesus a perfectly selfless life. God acts to form that life in the penitent, through the action of the Spirit.

The heart of Anselm's argument, as he presents it, is that none but God can make satisfaction for sin; none but a man ought to do it; therefore only a God-man can do it.[15] There is, however, an internal weakness in this account. God is able to make satisfaction because God is infinite, and only a being of infinite merit can make satisfaction for the sins of the whole world. But if it is God in person who makes satisfaction, to whom is it made? It does not make sense to suppose that one can make satisfaction to oneself for an

---

[15] Anselm, 2. 6, in *Basic Writings*, 258.

offence someone else has committed against one's own honour. In any case, it is only the human nature of Jesus that suffers; for Anselm, the divine nature remains impassible and immutable. Yet that human nature is finite, so it cannot make infinite satisfaction. The tradition claims that the human nature is possessed by the divine Person, so that the divine Person can truly be said to suffer, though only in human nature. The fact remains, however, that the suffering of the human nature is clearly finite, and indeed rather limited. So the amount that God suffers is not infinite, and cannot make satisfaction for huge numbers of sins. The quasi-mathematical model Anselm sets up simply will not work.

The Anselmian formula is correct, however, in saying that it is human persons who must 'make satisfaction' to God by turning from selfish desire and living lives of selfless love. Yet it is only God who, in a fallen world, can give the power to make such satisfaction. Human nature must be healed of the disease of self, and made whole in the power of the Spirit. In Jesus, by divine power and perfect human response, a whole, integrated, selfless and God-centred love was fully actualized in history. Moreover, Anselm is right in holding that this life, culminating in suffering and death, is offered by Jesus as a prayer for the healing of all humanity, and thereby becomes a mediating form of divine power to all who ask for it. But this is not a matter of the Father substituting one person's infinite merit for our own inadequate offering, by some odd form of moral accountancy. It is a matter of the participation of the believer in the healing power of the Spirit of Christ, which annuls selfish desire, unites the human soul to God, and promises final liberation from self.

THE SOTERIAL VIEW OF ATONEMENT

Instead of 'satisfaction' and 'substitution', it might be better to speak of 'healing' and 'participation'.[16] What God requires of sinners is a transformation of life in penitence and obedient love. This requirement is met by participation in the power of the Spirit, which is luminously expressed in and mediated through the life and self-sacrificial death of Jesus. Jesus' sacrifice gives a particular form to the Spirit's activity, and founds the community of the new

---

[16] Paul Tillich, *Systematic Theology* (Welwyn: Nisbet, 1968), ii. 203: 'Not substitution but free participation is the character of the divine suffering.'

covenant in which the Spirit can transform human lives into the image of cruciform love. It was Schleiermacher who explicitly expanded the Abelardian approach to atonement to include the notion that redemption is 'a continuation of the person-forming divine influence'[17] which was creatively manifest in the person of Jesus. A similar idea is to be found in the Anglican theologian John Macquarrie, who speaks of the church as 'an ever-expanding centre in which Christ's reconciling work continues'.[18]

The theologian who has done most to place the ideas of healing and participation at the centre of a doctrine of liberation from estrangement is Paul Tillich. He brings many powerful insights to the analysis of the human predicament and to the way in which salvation is to be positively construed as participation in 'healing and saving power through the New Being in all history'.[19] His resolute opposition to all forms of 'supernaturalism' or spiritual causality in the temporal world, however, and to any form of theistic personalism, tends to deprive the concepts he uses of content and therefore of ultimate plausibility.

Tillich describes the New Being as 'essential being under the conditions of existence, conquering the gap between essence and existence'.[20] This New Being was fully realized in Jesus, by his 'sacrifice of himself as Jesus to himself as the Christ'.[21] 'The New Being is present in him . . . those who participate in him participate in the New Being, though . . . only fragmentarily and by anticipation.'[22] Tillich rightly sees that, within his system, the appearance of the New Being, of essential being, under the conditions of existence, is an ultimate paradox. In fact, it seems to be an impossibility, since he elsewhere says that 'actualised creation and estranged existence are identical'.[23]

When he speaks of essential being, he describes it as purely potential, a state of 'dreaming innocence'. While the fall into estranged existence is logically distinct from actual existence itself, they are necessarily identical: 'Man's estrangement from his essential being is the universal character of existence.'[24] How, then, can there be a truly human life which is actual and yet not estranged? It

[17] F. D. E. Schleiermacher, *The Christian Faith*, trans. H. R. Mackintosh and J. S. Stewart (Edinburgh: T. & T. Clark, 1928; first pub. 1830), 427.

[18] John Macquarrie, *Principles of Christian Theology* (London: SCM, 1966), 292.

[19] Tillich, *Systematic Theology*, ii. 193.

[20] Ibid. 136.   [21] Ibid. 142.   [22] Ibid. 136.   [23] Ibid. 50.

[24] Ibid. 86.

is hard to see what Tillich means by the life of Jesus being 'non-estranged', since he explicitly denies that Jesus is sinless,[25] and that there is in the life of Jesus 'any supernatural interference in the ordinary course of events'.[26]

If one allowed that God can exercise causal power within history to unite human lives to the divine, then one could see how such power might be uniquely exercised to unite one human life wholly and from the first to the divine life. One might see why this should be a unique event, since it occurs in a unique revelatory context in history, and it makes the divine–human unity in Jesus different in nature from that available to persons born in a condition of estrangement from God. Such a unique divine–human unity, however, would entail sinlessness and supernatural causal influence (one does not have to use the word 'interference'). Indeed, only appeal to a unique, divine causality could render plausible any claim that the New Being is only and fully realized in Jesus.

One might also want to stress that the New Being is not just a mode of being which has overcome the polarities of existence, but one which realizes a full conscious knowledge and love of God. It is not a sort of impersonal Power which realizes itself 'fragmentarily' in history, but a conscious being-in-relationship to a personal Lord, who discloses the divine presence and empowers finite persons to receive the divine love. The sense of 'participation' in New Being that is needed is not the reception of a new power of courage and creativity (though it may include that). It is the inclusion of oneself in a dynamic relationship of love, in which divine and human co-operate and interpenetrate, so that one can speak of 'Christ within, the hope of glory',[27] and also speak of being 'united in Christ',[28] to express the depth and intimacy of the relationship. It is the establishing of that dynamic relationship, effected by divine initiative, that heals the anguish and suffering of estrangement. It is the promise of a fulfilment of that relationship in a consummation of love that replaces existential despair by hope.

Because of his insistence that one should not speak literally of life after death, Tillich is unable to give real content to the Christian hope. Accepting that the New Being is only present very imperfectly and 'by anticipation' in history (except in Jesus), in what sense does he think it will ever be fully realized? When he comes to

---

[25] Ibid. 145.   [26] Ibid. 186.   [27] Col. 1: 27.   [28] Eph. 1: 10.

speak of eternal life, he says that 'eternity is neither timeless identity nor permanent change'.[29] Individual streams of consciousness
will not continue for ever, and yet in some way self-conscious life
'cannot be excluded from Eternal Life'.[30] There is some sort of fulfilment 'beyond the separation of potentiality and actuality', which
he (after Schelling) calls 'essentialisation'. He sees the whole
process of life as a 'way from essence through existential estrangement to essentialisation'.[31] In that process, essence is described as
mere potentiality and essentialization is the removal of the conditions of time, space, and the polarities of existence, the 'creative
synthesis of a being's essential nature with what it has made of it in
its temporal existence',[32] taken up into a trans-temporal eternity.

It seems to me that, for all his protests to the contrary, Tillich
finally capitulates to a non-temporal, non-relational, and therefore
impersonal view of ultimate reality and the ultimate human goal.
The picture of the progress of historical being from an undivided
dreaming innocence, through estranged historical existence to a
trans-temporal, reintegrated consummation—the whole process
being eternally complete—is unmistakably Hegelian. Such a God
does not create others, who relate in freedom to the divine intentions, and whose lives develop in co-operation with (or in resistance
to) God, to find wholeness and the realization of their positive
potentialities within a relationship of mutual love. There is no real
hope of healing, when all the spatio-temporal conditions that make
both suffering and healing possible have been removed. All one
could hope for would be the 'freezing' of the always incomplete into
eternity, not any chance of completion. Perhaps in the very long
run one could envisage a trans-temporal consummation of existence. But before then the average person would want to have a better chance of creating something worth consummating than is often
available on earth. That is what Tillich's view seems to rule out.

In the end, while Tillich is right to look for human healing by
accepting and participating in the self-giving love of God, his view
of God as 'Being-itself', and of healing as participation in 'essential
being', makes it impossible to interpret the divine love in a dynamic
and relational way. He cannot account for the uniqueness and perfection of Jesus—a human person raised to union with the divine
through the power of love, in order to open a historical way to such

---

[29] Tillich, *Systematic Theology*, iii. 446.   [30] Ibid. 441.   [31] Ibid. 450.
[32] Ibid. 427.

union for all human persons—since essential being cannot, in his system, come to actual existence. He cannot account for the relational and personal nature of salvation, since he has no ultimate place for a personal Lord, to whom human persons can relate. He cannot account for a real hope of a future complete healing of estrangement, since there is nothing after death, for him, but the essentialization of completed historical lives, which are always doomed to be partly unhealed. In these respects, Tillich's theology of atonement seems an unsatisfactory interpretation of the Christian tradition. Yet his emphasis on the universal healing activity of the Spirit which was present and effective in a unique way in and through the self-offering of Jesus, and in which human persons can now participate, encapsulates well the shift in theological thinking from a juridical interpretation of redemption, for which a particular event pays a price which propitiates the wrath of God, to a soterial interpretation in terms of healing and unconditional divine love.[33]

THE UNIVERSAL DIVINE ACTION OF REDEMPTIVE LOVE

Anselm's account of atonement presupposes a Platonic view of human nature, according to which individual humans are real because they share in a fully real, intelligible essence of humanity.[34] Jesus' death could 'make satisfaction' for all human sin, because in him essential human nature, which owed an infinite debt of honour to God, itself paid that debt by being possessed by a being of infinite value, the eternal Word. When such a Platonic account is rejected, individual humans are seen as more real than the mere abstraction of 'human nature'. It then becomes hard to see how every individual can literally 'share in' the sin of Adam, which they themselves have not committed. It is hard to see how 'my' sin can be compensated for by the sacrifice of another human individual, when I do not instantiate the very human nature he has redeemed.

Anselm could see each individual human as participating in the responsible fall of essential human nature, and as reconciled to God by participating in the renewed human nature inaugurated by Jesus Christ (though even there the complication existed that only some

[33] This shift was noted and expounded in Chs. 2 and 7 of this volume.
[34] 'Every created substance exists more truly . . . in the intelligence of the Creator, than it does in itself', Anselm, *Monologium*, 36, in *Basic Writings*, 146.

humans participated in redeemed human nature). When Calvin came to formulate a basically Anselmian theory, he had to take account of the new themes of individual responsibility and accountability. For a non-Platonic view, each individual deserves a punishment for sin, but there is no longer an easy way of connecting the individual's sin to the fall of Adam or of connecting the individual's salvation to the self-sacrifice of Jesus. One can no longer plausibly say that one simply has to acknowledge and make historically apparent what has 'really' taken place in the world of essential natures.

Calvin's suggestion was (following Augustine) that Adam's sin was transmitted by procreation, and that Jesus' death was a substitutionary payment of a penalty on behalf of others.[35] This produced a paradoxical triad of individual responsibility, existing alongside the inevitability of sin, and a redemption that did not depend upon personal merit. That suggestion gives a much more severe and morally questionable doctrine than the Anselmian tradition, with its subsumption of individuality under universal human nature. A more radical revision is required before a morally adequate account of atonement can be given in non-Platonic terms.

In that more radical revision, in a world in which individuals are more real than essential natures, divine knowledge will no longer be seen as timeless contemplation of universals. God must know things in their particularity, and must know particular existents as adding a new element of reality to the relatively abstract conception of universal possibilities. Thus God must have a form of knowledge that is closely analogous to experiential knowledge of particulars. God must, for example, have experiential knowledge of the happiness and suffering of finite individuals. In a reversal of the Hellenic tradition, it now seems that an omniscient being must in some sense experience the suffering of the world, and not be wholly untouched by it.[36] The cross becomes an expression of the divine experience of all created suffering. It is not the expression of divine anger against another, but the acceptance by divine love of the suffering that evil causes. It is not the vengeance of God, but the wounding of God.

---

[35] 'Our acquittal is in this—that the guilt which made us liable to punishment was transferred to the head of the Son of God', John Calvin, *Institutes of the Christian Religion*, 2. 16. 5, trans. H. Beveridge (Grand Rapids, Mich.: Eerdmans, 1989), 439.

[36] This case is argued in my *Religion and Creation* (Oxford: Clarendon, 1996), ch. 10.

With such acceptance of the suffering of God goes an acceptance of the temporality of God, who enters into such experiential relationship with a changing and evolving cosmos. Since radically new things come into being within the universe, it is easy to see rational agents as responsible creators of novelty, rather than as players who act out a timelessly ordained role. Creative freedom becomes a fundamental feature of human nature, and in relation to it God plays a co-operating, guiding, persuasive role, rather than an all-determining one. In this perspective, the cross is not plausibly seen as one discrete event which remits all judicial penalties. It comes to express the universal, persuasive love of God, which always and everywhere seeks to draw free human agents into relationship, by its exposure to the destructive powers of evil and its undiminished continuance in love.[37]

Belief in the freedom and creativity of individual agents arises from the emphasis on the reality of the particular, the new, and the temporal, which is generated by the scientific world-view. It could be taken as a threat to belief in God. It certainly does threaten belief in a God who autonomously decrees everything that is to happen, and whose omniscience owes nothing to the actual existence of the physical universe. But it may suggest a view of God which is in some ways more biblical, a view of God as one who participates in the happiness and the suffering of creatures, and who universally seeks to persuade them to co-operate in the realization of some of the distinctive values that are potential in the structure of the created universe.

Because of this stress on universal divine participation and persuasion, it may seem that the uniqueness and importance of the cross is threatened. The cross of Christ may seem to be reduced to a mere symbol of universal divine action. But what the cross symbolizes is precisely the divine activity of healing and redemption, which must always be appropriately related to ever-changing, unique, and particular events in cosmic history. The divine activity will be everywhere the same in its general description (sharing, persuading, loving), but precisely for that reason, it must always be different in its particular actualizations (in particular acts of

---

[37] A powerful expression of the persuasive love of God is found in Whitehead's work: 'The nature of God . . . includes the ideal vision of each actual evil so met with a novel consequent as to issue in the restoration of goodness', A. N. Whitehead, *Religion in the Making* (1926; London: World Publishing, 1960), 148.

persuasion, co-operation, and love). In human history one will then expect to find many new and creative actualizations of divine action, all of them expressing in some particular way the persuasive love of God. Such actualizations will, as co-operative, be responses to particular configurations of human desire and decision, thought and feeling, and evocations of new complexes of human thought and action. Sometimes, in situations of human conflict, self-regard, and obsessive desire, the divine action may be almost wholly hidden, or may take the form of judgement, the opposition of love to everything in human life that opposes love. But there will be other times when some person or group of persons comes near to expressing that selfless love and wisdom that enables the divine action to be disclosed in a fuller and creatively new way.

One such serendipitous time was the flowering of prophecy in Israel and Judah in the eighth century BCE. A combination of a long historical development of prophetic activity, a culture of monotheistic worship, a situation of political and religious crisis, and the birth of a number of charismatic individuals, resulted in a new disclosure of the nature of God as requiring justice and mercy and promising liberation and fulfilment.[38] So, Christians believe, at the time of Jesus a set of unique historical conditions existed which made possible the birth of a teacher, prophet, healer, and mystic, who could at once fulfil and transform the Messianic expectations of a doomed Israel. In and through his death, God was able to act in a new, creative way to make that event the mediative historical form of the divine love. The cross is not just a symbol of an unchanging divine activity. It expresses and mediates a new and creative divine act, through which human estrangement is seen to be overcome in the person of Jesus, and union with the divine life is consummated.

In this context, one does not primarily think of the death of Jesus as an event in which God uniquely shares in human suffering, and which propitiates, once and for all, the anger of God, or which pays the penalty for all human sins. One thinks of it as an event which consummates Jesus' life of self-offering to the Father. Because of that, it is an event in which the Spirit unites humanity to divinity in mutual self-giving love. It is an event through which the Spirit heals estranged, wounded, human lives, in so far as persons participate in

---

[38] 'I hate, I despise your feasts . . . but let justice roll down like waters', Amos 5: 21–4.

the power of the Spirit of Christ. There is a place for participation here, as there was in patristic times, though now participation is interpreted differently. It is not participation in a timeless, immutable nature. It is participation in the dynamic and creative power of the Spirit, which is historically mediated through and patterned on the historical event of Jesus' death and resurrection. The cross of Christ becomes the mediative form through which the grace of God heals human estrangement, in the communities of those who accept it as the source of their life in God.

Does this mean that those who have never heard of Christ are without the redeeming grace of God? There has often been a temptation to say this, out of a misguided desire to emphasize the necessity of Christ's passion to human salvation. Yet the God who is revealed in Christ is precisely a God who goes to any lengths to offer salvation to everyone.[39] If Christ reveals God as universal forgiving love, will God not be at work universally to forgive and reconcile persons to the divine self? But if that is true, what is really so new or important about Christ's historical life and passion?

God always suffers because of human wrongdoing. God is always ready to forgive, always willing to overcome human estrangement and lead humans to fellowship with the divine. But God's actions must be performed in the causal contexts of human history. They cannot be the same everywhere and in every circumstance. God's forgiveness must become known at some particular point in history. Some particular acts must overcome human estrangement in an effective way. God must act in particular ways to begin to persuade humans to prepare themselves for fellowship with the divine. It is when one considers what God might do in particular cases that one must allow for different sorts and degrees of divine action.

There are many human experiences of God, usually corrupted by passions of various sorts. There are many ways of seeking liberation from suffering, usually distorted by cultural and conceptual presuppositions. In this situation, one might suppose that God never becomes truly known, and never establishes in us a form of truly appropriate relation to God. But if God is continually acting, however constrained by causal, cultural, and historical conditions, and however co-operatively with inadequate human responses, to make the divine presence known and establish in us a conscious, loving

[39] 'He is the expiation for our sins, and not for ours only but also for the sins of the whole world', 1 John 2: 2.

relation to God, one might expect that there will be some point or points in history at which God becomes truly known, at least to some extent, and an appropriate, if not perfect, relation to God is established.

One may plausibly hold that every religious tradition will forever carry some cultural distortions and limitations of knowledge. But it is implausible to think that nothing, however general or basic, will ever be accurate in this area, especially when God is trying to get people to see the divine nature better. If God is revealed as perfect, suffering, forgiving, and loving, one might indeed still interpret forgiveness and love in very imperfect ways. But it is hard to see that there could be anything inadequate in the vitally important, if rather general, assertion that God is universally loving.[40] Similarly, if the goal of human life is loving union with God, and if the way to that goal is participation in the divine love, those facts must come to be known at some point in history, but their truth is not just relative to that historical time. There is a sense in which some truths about God must be simply and absolutely true.

God's action to transfigure human lives will always meet with some resistance, except in a case where a human subject is wholly attuned to the divine will. Christians believe that in Jesus there existed a unique point wherein, by divine grace, there is a human experience free of self-regard and wholly attuned to God. Here God's action is not hindered by a resistant self or by such a self's culpable ignorance. In this human life God acts unhindered to manifest the divine love in a uniquely perfect manner. The revelation of the divine nature and the ultimate human goal in relation to it will be much clearer in such a life.

Moreover, this is not a life-pattern which stands as merely an external object to be imitated by human effort. That is the common travesty of Abelard's so-called 'exemplarist' view.[41] Rather, by Jesus' self-offering, the liberating power of God has been transparently realized in history, as humanity and divinity are united in one personal reality. That power is then released into history in a new and dynamic way, as Jesus becomes the icon or image that the

---

[40] It is in that sense that I argued that one might speak of a 'final' revelation, even though it is never finally or fully comprehended, *Religion and Revelation* (Oxford: Clarendon, 1994), 278–82.

[41] Abelard's view is given a much more sympathetic treatment in Paul Fiddes, *Past Event and Present Salvation* (London: Darton, Longman, Todd, 1989), 140–60.

Spirit uses to build human lives towards the pleroma of their ultimate fulfilment in God.

In Jesus, according to Christian belief, God acts in a uniquely clear, unhampered way, to evoke repentance by revealing the divine nature as suffering, redemptive, unitive love. God acts to show the life that is required of us, to establish a community in which such a life can be begun, to show that the human goal of divine–human fellowship is possible, and to draw people into such fellowship. Thus there will be particular, historical acts that establish this community, founded on a primal revelatory event in which divine–human fellowship is archetypally established. The Spirit is the power which made that event possible, as the icon, and formative pattern of the Spirit's continued co-operative action throughout the world.

On this view, atonement, the liberation of human lives by God from selfish desire and their uniting in fellowship with the life of God, is necessary if human nature is to attain its intended fulfilment. Such atonement must involve the disclosure of God's patient bearing of the sufferings of the world (a sacrifice or giving-up of unmixed bliss for the sake of the possible goods of human life). It must involve God's revealing the pattern of perfected human life in God (a life of healing and forgiveness). It must also involve God's effective transformation of humans from self-regard to the love of supreme beauty, in accordance with that pattern (the gift of the Spirit). This revelation must come in a particular history and context that is able to manifest God's particular actions in the world, actions which begin and define the particular process of forgiveness and fulfilment that constitutes the Christian life.

In such a context, one can quite properly speak of the cross as paying a price which releases humanity from sin. This is not, however, a quasi-monetary payment which God pays to God, and which cancels what humans alone ought to pay. Such a transaction is both useless (one cannot meaningfully make a payment to oneself) and unjust (every person must 'pay' for their own sin). The 'price' is the suffering sin causes, that God freely endures. God, in assuming Jesus to the divine life, establishes the way of release from death. The Spirit makes that life which was in Jesus present in other human lives, repeating in a partial and developing way both its self-sacrifice and its transfiguration into the divine. So, living by faith in the cross and risen life of Jesus, by trust in the power of the Spirit who formed that pattern and brought it to completion, and by confidence in the Father in whom this power and pattern are indestructibly grounded, one is made a sharer in the eternal life of God.[42] That is release, and its price is the suffering of God and the self-giving sacrifice of Jesus, in whom God was fully present and active, united in such a way that we may rightly speak of Jesus and the eternal Son as one and the same.

THE PARTICULARITY OF THE ATONEMENT

This view of atonement is in some ways reminiscent of what Gustav Aulen calls the 'dramatic' or classical view of Christ as fighting sin, death, and the devil and winning a victory over them.[43] Aulen, however, stresses the 'contradictory' and unrationalizable aspects of such an idea, deploying the Lutheran imagery of a battle between the divine wrath and the divine love, in which love wins only after a bitter struggle. This idea of a cosmic battle or of a conflict within the being of God itself is too mythological in flavour to be recoverable completely in a scientific age. One can, however, speak plausibly of a rupture between the spiritual ground of nature and the world, corrupted by human self-will. If the spiritual ground is, in its essential nature, the perfection of love, then one can conceive the possibility of divine action to reconcile nature to its true ground. This reconciliation is through the Spirit, fully manifest in the life of a martyr, a faithful witness, who gives his life wholly to the divine will, and thereby founds a community patterned on and empowered by his life, as the manifestation and channel of the divine life. In his self-sacrifice one sees the suffering of God and the transforming action of God to unite natural and divine. There is no battle fought within the being of God. But there is a divine victory over the alienating forces of destructive self-will, a victory not by fighting but by the indestructible power of the persuasive, patient, reconciling love of God. There is no price to be paid to recompense a disgruntled monarch. But there is a cost to the process of reconciliation, a cost borne by God and by the person who consents to be God's agent of reconciliation. We do not offer Christ as an objective reservoir of merit to remit our guilt. Rather, the Spirit enfolds us in the mutual self-offering of divine and human in Jesus, made

---

[42] 2 Pet. 1: 4.
[43] Gustav Aulen, *Christus Victor*, trans. A. G. Hebert (London: SPCK, 1931).

present to us so that we can be included in that life of perfect prayer and in the transfiguring love of God. The Christian idea of redemption thus stands between the notion of a human achieving liberation by strenuous effort and the notion of a purely divine avatar offering humans the divine love. Human and divine are united in the Spirit who continues to be the source of life of the community of the new covenant, a covenant for uniting God and all creation in restored harmony and beauty of being.

It is not open to those who believe in a God of universal redeeming love to hold that with the birth of the historical church, God opens a door to salvation which had been closed until the cross. Jesus teaches, even if in a story, that the redeemed go to 'Abraham's bosom', so that presumably Abraham is among the redeemed.[44]

How could Abraham be redeemed by a Christ of whom he had never heard, and by an atoning death which had not yet happened? These questions only pose difficult problems if one sees Jesus and the death of Jesus as solely historical events, with a historical causality which can only run forwards in time from their occurrence. The problems disappear when one recalls that Jesus is the historical embodiment of the eternal Word of God, whose nature does not change with the incarnation. The nature of the Word is, for the main Christian tradition, fully embodied in Jesus, and the humanity of Jesus is transfigured by its unity with the Word. But the Word is changeless in essential nature and universal in divine omnipresence. Both the Word and the Spirit of God act at every time and place, in appropriate ways, to reconcile persons to their Creator.[45]

The nature of the Word is decisively disclosed in the life of Jesus, and the vicarious suffering of the Word is openly manifested in history and in its true character in the death of Jesus. It follows that Abraham (for example) could not be fully aware of the nature of the Word, or perhaps would not even be able to identify Him as such. The Word would have to act in regard to Abraham in a hidden, not fully recognized, way.[46] He would have come to Abraham in forms that that human mind could formulate and understand. What existed at the time of Abraham was the eternal love of God, which

---

[44] Luke 16: 23.

[45] John 1: 9: '[Christ is] the true light that enlightens every man.'

[46] This is the basis of Karl Rahner's idea that many may be 'anonymous Christians'. If one does not take this to mean that 'they are really Christians, though they do not realize it,' I would think that Christians have to adopt some such belief.

includes the decree and decision to become incarnate and die, in a foreseeable and unavoidable conflict with evil. That irrevocable decision was the cause of Abraham's redemption, because nothing could prevent its later historical actualization.

The crucifixion cannot take effect only on those who have a direct causal link with it, since that would limit the scope of redemption quite unacceptably. One must say that it is the eternal Word who redeems, and who redeems universally. But the manifestation of the character of that Word in history, and the appropriate mediative form for its reception by human hearts, will occur in particular circumstances and at a particular time. God acts in some way to reveal and liberate everywhere. But the adequate revelation and the appropriate form of liberation is and must be actualized at a particular point or points in history. That does not exclude others from the redemptive action of God. But it does mean that an appropriate grasp of God's nature and purpose, and of what it means to attain full union with God, is necessarily limited, in history, to specific places and times. This is not a disadvantage, but a necessary condition of genuine revelation.

Full knowledge of God is the ultimate goal that God wills for human life, but there is a long journey before that goal is reached, and the journey, too, is part of what God wills for human lives. Eventually, and in very many cases that will be after earthly death, God will make the divine being known to all who have prepared themselves for it, and it is God's will that all during their earthly lives will have some chance of preparing themselves.[47] Such preparation will consist in making such progress as is possible in the overcoming of self, some growth in creativity, sensitivity, and compassion, in personal integration and moral action, some openness to relationships that enable personal lives to grow.

Just as human knowledge and understanding in general develops, so one might expect knowledge and understanding of God to develop, in response to self-disclosures of the Divine occurring in cultural contexts that are in many ways limited by imperfect scientific and moral understanding. Revelation can plausibly be seen as universal, partial, and developing. On such a view, one's eternal destiny may depend upon one's innermost attitude to the revelation one encounters personally, on one's response to egoism and to

---

[47] This is entailed by the belief that 'God our Saviour . . . desires all men to be saved and to come to the knowledge of the truth': 1 Tim. 2: 4.

offered love or compassion. For the theist, it will depend on one's inner preparation in such ways for an eventual full revelation of the presence and love of God. It is not true that an honest rejection of religious evidences will lead to damnation, or that an acceptance of religious beliefs on evidential grounds alone will lead to salvation. The key question is whether people now live lives of egoistic desire or of selfless altruism. That is what leads, if persisted in, to eventual damnation or salvation.

It may be said that, if everyone has some chance to prepare themselves for God, there is no need for a special revelation of what God is, or for a special mediation of the divine Spirit as it really is. That is clearly false. What we are all working towards is the revelation of what God is, and the adequate relationship to God that only the Spirit of love can implant. Naturally, then, one would hope for such a revelation during this earthly life, if possible. Indeed, only if there is some such revelation somewhere on earth can one plausibly claim that there is a God of love who wills that all should eventually come to know the divine self.

All that may be *required now*, in a particular case, for eventual salvation is altruistic moral commitment. But that is a very long way from saying what salvation is, or what is sufficient to obtain it, or what is desirable or helpful in obtaining it. If salvation is knowledge and love of God, it would certainly be helpful, even now, to do something more than be generally altruistic to prepare oneself for it. It will eventually be necessary, and it is now desirable, to know God's nature, will, and purpose. In view of this, one would expect God (if there is one) to find some way or ways of disclosing the divine nature, will, and purpose. God will guide humans towards a knowledge of the presence of supreme power and value, the overcoming of egoism, and the possibility of a goal of wisdom, compassion, and bliss. Such disclosures will be conditioned by the nature of particular cultures and partly hidden by obscuring factors due to human egoism. Yet from a Christian point of view, the icon of the crucified and glorified Lord identifies what an encounter with God truly is, and mediates the saving power of God in an undistorted form. Such an adequate form must exist, sooner or later, but that in no way confines the saving power of God to those people who happen to hear of it during their earthly lives. Once the form exists, however, it is part of the vocation of those who receive such a revelation to witness to it throughout the world, in acts of love and service, so that they too can manifest and mediate, however imperfectly, the unconditional love of God.

The community of the new covenant, which is the church, bears the Spirit who shapes all things on the archetypal form of Christ the eternal Word, who shapes human persons in the image of the exemplary form of Jesus the Christ incarnate, and who shapes the cosmos into the pleromic form of the inclusive cosmic Christ. The vocation of this community is to allow the Spirit to liberate human lives from selfish desire, and unite them to God in selfless love. It cannot be said that this vocation is very clearly seen in human history, since all human communities share in the ambiguities of fallen human nature. Yet the vocation exists, and it is in accepting it, Christians believe, that the true nature and destiny of the human self can be discovered and its realization begun.

If the destiny of the self is to be shaped in the image of Christ, to be united in the universal Christic community, and to be selflessly united to God in conscious knowledge and love, that destiny must transcend earthly life. The church will not only be the servant of God on earth, but also the gateway from earth to the life of eternity. One cannot therefore arrive at a true estimate of the Christian view of human nature until one has some idea of its account of the ultimate destiny of the soul. As with the doctrine of atonement, the Christian account of immortality clearly belongs to the Abrahamic religious tradition, but it relates various strands of this tradition in a distinctive way. In the next two chapters, I will try to bring out this distinctiveness by developing a view of the ultimate human goal in relation to Jewish and Muslim beliefs about human destiny.

11

The World to Come

THE HUMAN SOUL AND ITS FULFILMENT

I have suggested that it is proper to speak of a substantial and enduring soul, the continuing subject of actions and experiences in a rational and responsible sentient life. It seems plausible to speak of a continuing subject, because all experiences are 'owned', and are essentially the experiences of a particular self. Experiences are not separate entities, like pearls on a string. Each new experience is received into a complex of formed attitudes, memories, and dispositions, so that its experienced character varies from person to person, according to their past experiences and responses.

Consider the hearing of a particular sound. To one person it may be an uninteresting component of a set of noises, with no pattern or significance. To another it may be part of a beautiful symphony, taking its meaning from the notes which have gone before it to form a tune, and from the way it is expected to form part of a future pattern, as part of a piece of music. In order to have meaning, the sound has to be incorporated into a remembered past and into the expectation of a specific sort of future. The remembering, incorporating, and expecting are all activities, which can be learned, practised, and improved. For this to be so, one has to think of one continuing agent, active even in the apparently passive reception of experience, to give it meaning and significance.

Memory and personality (dispositions to interpret in specific ways, and to take an interest in particular sorts of things) are involved in the having of experience. Human experiencing involves active recall of the past and organization of data into continuing patterns. It involves a continuing agent self, with a growing fund of more or less integrated experience and a growing capacity to perceive, interpret, and create patterns in experience. There is a continuing agent, but it is not separable from the experiences and dispositions which constitute its developing character.

Similarly, when one thinks, it is not just that thoughts succeed one another. An active subject forms the thoughts and entertains them. It must be the same self who completes a thought as the self who started it, otherwise the thought would not hold together as one assertion. In this way, the idea of a continuing and active subject of thought is presupposed by the activity of thinking itself. One must speak of a subject of experiences and actions (including thoughts), who remains the same throughout a succession of experiences and actions. Over time, it realizes many of its innate powers, and in doing so it modifies those powers, forming a responsibly shaped character. It builds up a stock of experiences that governs the way in which each new experience is interpreted, and places new experiences in a unique complex of feelings and ways of understanding, giving them a unique and unrepeatable character. Each person has a unique viewpoint on the world, formed by the internalization of a unique history and culture. So each person is an intentional agent who acts against the background of such uniqueness, and projects its own existence into the future along a partly self-chosen trajectory, who expresses and comes to a more or less explicit awareness of its own nature and possibilities.

Souls are not propertyless entities. They essentially possess dispositions and some experiential content. When fully functional, those dispositions are realized in actions that exhibit a unique and developing form of creativity, and their experiences form a coherent unity of developing understanding and feeling. But souls can be injured and impaired. Their unity and autonomy is fragile and contingent. The soul can be lost in a fragmented sequence of disordered actions, routines in which it becomes trapped, without any ability to take responsibility for itself. It can be lost in misunderstood and disconnected experiences, bound to suffering and despair, without any coherence or meaningful pattern. If a soul becomes wholly disintegrated into fragmented routines of action and incoherent sequences of experience, than it may be said to be lost or dead. All unity, integration, and rational coherence gone, the soul dies, even the bare awareness of one continuing consciousness disappearing in a chaos of unrelated elements of awareness. 'Do not fear those who kill the body . . . rather fear him who can destroy both soul and body in hell.'[1] As the body can be disintegrated into its constituent elements, so the soul can fall apart into

---

[1] Matt. 10: 28.

the elements of routine and disconnected experience. That is true death, and it is the extreme possibility for souls which fail to find some integrating centre of value-directed action and value-enjoying experience.

The resurrection life may in this respect be thought of as the realm of the healing and integration of the soul, its recovery from fragmentation by centring it in God, who alone has power to direct its actions towards creative goodness, and order its experiences in a true perception of the meaning and intellectual beauty of things.[2]

Such an account of the soul as a continuing substance may sound reminiscent of what is often called 'Cartesian dualism'. Indeed, I do not think Descartes was too far wrong when he defined the soul as a 'thinking thing', a subject of thought.[3] But two major qualifications need to be made to what is usually thought to be Descartes's account. One is that the assertion of a continuing conscious subject of experience and action is compatible with what I called 'very soft materialism',[4] for which that subject is identified in a sophisticated sense with the brain. The other is that the soul should not be regarded as a separately existing entity, apart from its physical and social environment. On the contrary, it is embodied in an environment to which its attention is directed, and in which its innate dispositions can be realized. It is essentially intensional and self-expressive, open to objects other than itself, realizing its nature in forms of being beyond itself, and coming to awareness of itself in apprehending the interpretations that others put upon its actions. The personal world is one in which there is a continual reflection of persons upon one another, each reflection incorporating a new and uniquely creative response, which comes to awareness of itself as it is in turn reflected from others.[5] The soul is not locked into some solipsistic world of private thoughts, or strangely linked (through the pineal gland) to an alien world of mechanistic law. It is essentially open to others and self-expressively related to others in a common semiotic world of communicating agents, who express and interpret meaning precisely through the forms of their material embodiment.

[2] Cf. the discussion in Ch. 11.

[3] Descartes, *Méditations*, trans. A. Wollaston (London: Penguin, 1960), Meditation 2, p. 111.

[4] Cf. the discussion in Ch. 7.

[5] Cf. Alistair McFadyen, *The Call to Personhood* (Cambridge: Cambridge University Press, 1990), ch. 3.

People contribute their own creative expression to the sum of relationships, and without a stock of inherent dispositions to express, there would be nothing to relate. In that sense, individuals may be called 'substances', or subjects of properties and dispositions. But people can only flourish in relationships, which make possible particular forms of life in which they can express their nature. They apprehend that nature as it is reflected back to them, in the apprehensions and creative responses of others. Such apprehension flows back into their own creative projections of the future, which also incorporate responses to the self-expressive being of others, evoking ever new forms of action in a continually self-renewing sequence of mutual action and response.

It is characteristic of the existence of this form of personal being that it is by nature contingent and fragile. The capacity for empathy, for interpreting and reflecting the inner lives of others, is inherently capable of distortion. One can come to see others as means to fulfilling one's own desires, and their feelings can come to seem important only as feeding one's own. One can refuse to disclose one's true feelings and intentions to others, and so engender a distorted understanding in them.

The capacity for creativity, for communicating oneself without reserve to others, is inherently capable of corruption and self-interest. One can come to see others as competitors in the attempt of each person to realize their own nature as fully as possible. One can seek to exercise power over others, or engage in aggressive conflict, in the name of realizing one's own creativity. Thus empathy is easily distorted into egoistic desire, and creativity is corrupted into egoistic aggression.[6]

Once this happens, instability is introduced into the interconnected web of social relationships, which can no longer unequivocally support unreserved empathy and creativity. People will need to protect themselves from the aggressive pride and competitive desire of others, and the erection of defences will undermine the openness which should characterize the fully personal society. The community of persons will become an alienated and constitutionally imperfect community.

Karl Marx sought the remedy for this condition in the hope for a society of plenty, without class distinctions or central government,

---

[6] One of the most powerful descriptions of this process is found in the play *Huis Clos* (*No Exit*) by J.-P. Sartre.

where oppression would quietly disappear before the warm fellow-feeling of freely co-operating proletarians.[7] That dream has visibly died in the twentieth century. Religious believers have always proclaimed that a more inward change is necessary, that desire and aggression are corruptions at the heart of personal being, and need to be transformed into that empathy and creativity which is their true and uncorrupted form.

On a generally evolutionary account, desire and aggression are natural inclinations of human beings which have been preferentially selected in the long process of development toward more complex forms of life. Other inclinations, of co-operation leading to empathy, and of curiosity leading to creativity, have also been selected by the same process. Human nature contains a mixture of competitive and co-operative dispositions, and when responsible choice arises it must be made between these dispositions.

Desire and aggression are corrupt only when they are chosen in situations where empathy and creativity could and should have been chosen. It is natural for the theist to think[8] that the presently obervable human condition, in which humans are largely in bondage to desire and aggression, is a corrupted one, which need not have existed and which could still, in principle, be corrected.

For desire to become empathy, one needs to discipline the mind to desire the good for its own sake, and ideally to have some vision of perfect beauty which can re-centre desire outside itself. For aggression to become creativity, one needs to train the mind to become a channel of perfect creative power, an instrument of the divine will to realize goodness in a co-operative community. Selves which are dispersed into egoistic and competing units need to be united in a new compassionate community centred on worship of and obedience to the perfection of the divine Self. The self needs to be opened to a vision of goodness and to be empowered by the will to realize its own unique image of goodness.

From a theistic viewpoint, the most important fact about human beings is that they are essentially related to God. They do not exist as independent entities. At every moment their existence is received from God, in order that they may take responsibility for realizing some state of affairs that can be offered back to God in devotion.

---

[7] Cf. Marx, *Critique of the Gotha Programme* (1875), in *Selected Writings*, ed. Bottomore and Rubel (London: Penguin, 1961), 261–3.

[8] Cf. Ch. 8.

God gives a set of potentialities, from which humans can select some to realize in a uniquely creative way. They actualize in reality and consequently in the being of God itself the experience of those values, as new and creatively actualized elements of being. God could not have unilaterally brought about those values in that form (i.e. as freely actualized by a created agent). Because the values become elements of the divine being, they can be, and should be, offered to God in loving devotion. Human existence is thus essentially a receiving (a unique understanding), shaping (a unique creativity), and returning (a unique communicative expressing) of dependent being.

On this understanding it is natural to think that the human soul is not autonomous, in the sense of being wholly self-legislating, independent of others, and responsible only for its own individual acts.[9] It is a centre of individuality which takes form and realizes itself in a community of selves, ideally united in creative co-operation and shared experience, all attending to the beauty and mediating the activity of the supreme Self. The existential problem from which religious faith begins is that the actual human situation is very far from such an ideal. Even on the most optimistic estimate, there are very few humans who have overcome selfish desire and aggression, who have become aware of a reality of supreme bliss, wisdom, and love, and who have become vehicles of unlimited compassion and creativity in the world. The vast majority are in bondage to desire, in ignorance of God, and in fear and contempt of others.

In such a situation, the danger is that the 'ought' which drives one to seek liberation from self, conscious union with the supreme Self, and universal compassion, becomes disconnected from any goal which can possibly be attained. There is good reason to think that the egoistic self cannot be conquered simply by resolute effort, that the supreme Self cannot be known simply by willing, and that compassion cannot be attained by determination.[10] If one is to be liberated from egoism, there must be a transforming vision of supreme goodness, which can centre attention outside the self. If the supreme Self is to be known, it must make itself known, mak-

---

[9] Cf. Paul Tillich on autonomy and theonomy, in *Systematic Theology* (Welwyn: Nisbet, 1968), i. 92–6.

[10] Rom. 7: 19: 'I do not do the good I want, but the evil I do not want is what I do.'

ing itself vividly present to consciousness. If the heart is to become truly compassionate, it must be renewed by becoming the vehicle of a compassion that has the infinite patience and strength that humans lack. If there is to be any hope of attaining the goal of the truly human life, it must be accomplished by divine self-disclosure and by divine power, that is, by revelation and grace.

If this is the case, the religious life becomes less a programme of self-discipline and more a plea for divine help, and a confession of natural incapacity. We can see, sometimes dimly, what we ought to be. We can see that we cannot realize that state without divine help. Yet the sad truth is that even those human beings who claim to have or to offer such help very often do not seem to have escaped the bondage of self, ignorance, and delusion. Divine help may exist, but it seems to come in an efficacious way to so few that we cannot realistically hope for liberation in this life. It is because of this that the religious imperative, in virtually every tradition, leads to the development of belief in a continued life beyond physical death, where the goal might be fully attained.

Those few who have passed beyond desire to a consciousness of God and a mediation of the divine love, will not, perhaps, demand immortality for themselves. Such a demand would betray precisely that egoism which they must have overcome. They possess a life which is already united to the eternal, 'eternal life'.

Yet those who realize the quality of eternal life in this earthly life regrettably seem to be very few. The vast majority of humans, whose lives are bounded and limited by conditions beyond their control, by suffering, oppression, and early death, cannot realize on earth any real knowledge of God, or any conscious participation in the compassionate and creative activity of God. They cannot even realize the natural potentialities that God has given them, much less actualize those potentialities in a conscious and co-operative way with the supreme Self. They cannot realize the goal that God intends them to realize.

If one believes that human life has a goal, and that a loving God would make the attainment of that goal possible for creatures, one seems compelled to believe that there will be some possibility of growth and development beyond death. When human lives are reasonably fulfilled, and knowledge of God seems widely shared, it may seem unduly greedy to hope for a continuance of life beyond its naturally allotted span. But when human lives are corrupted and destroyed, and knowledge of God seems almost to have disappeared from the earth, any theist must hope, even if only on behalf of others, that there will be some possibility of fulfilment and knowledge of God after earthly death.

THE DEVELOPMENT OF IDEAS OF AN AFTERLIFE IN HEBREW RELIGION

It is significant that belief in life after death only became an important feature of religious life in ancient Israel after the deaths of the Maccabean martyrs had made it difficult to see how God's promise of justice—of a realization of goodness in a community of love—could be fulfilled either in the defeated society of Israel, or in the lives of those who had given their lives to try to obtain it.[11] In this sense, belief in life in a world to come is a result of perceiving the theistic goal of human life, the proper fulfilment of human nature, and of perceiving the apparent inability of earthly life to accommodate the realization of that goal. This might be taken simply as a tragic perception of the impossibility of an ideal human life. But a theist who has a sense of the power and love of God will be virtually compelled to suppose that the Creator must make the attainment of a divinely intended goal, which is also a divinely commanded ideal, possible.

It is for this reason that even those who do not desire immortality for themselves will fervently desire it for others. Those, the vast majority, who cannot escape from desire, ignorance, and indifference, though believing in the divine compassion and love, have reason to hope that the divine help for which they pray may be given after this brief life is over, so that they may obtain the divinely intended goal of liberation from self, and consciously realized knowledge and love of God.

Even those who have ignored or rejected the thought of God or of liberation may have done so out of ignorance, or without reflection or full consciousness of what they are doing. For them, too, anyone who believes in a supreme reality of love will suppose that there will be some way in which they can come to true awareness of the nature of the choices they have made, and have the opportunity to turn their lives in a new and positive direction.

[11] Cf. Bernhard Anderson, *The Living World of the Old Testament* (London: Longman, 1975), 589–91.

Finally, those who have oppressed, hated, and killed without compunction or penalty will, in a morally ordered universe, be brought to see and feel the sufferings their actions have caused. They will, to put it crudely, feel such suffering themselves, in their own consciousness. There is reason to think that the infinite power of God will not permit the unjust to flourish in the long run. An afterlife will exist, not only to make possible the fulfilment of frustrated possibilities, but also to bring the unjust to a full knowledge of, and appropriate punishment for, their actions. The suffering of the unjust, for a morally mature view, will be aimed at turning them to goodness. Whether or not that happens, those who believe in the final power of the love of God will hope for a final elimination of all evil from creation, and the leading of all things which have not finally turned from God to their proper perfection. That would be the fulfilment of the divine purpose, which the divine power must be able to ensure.

Such a view of life after death, at least in the Abrahamic traditions, is prompted by consideration of what is involved in the existence of a perfect God, and by reflection on what would constitute a proper fulfilment of the divine purpose for creation. Just as there is a tension in these traditions between the pressure of the 'ought' and the impossibility of attaining the goal in life, so there is a tension between the fact that God's purpose is to be realized in this material universe, and the fact that human egoism seems to make it impossible of realization.

Different religions might be seen as different attempts to give a coherent account of the disparity between the moral goal of human existence and the foreseeable achievements of human beings. In the Indian traditions one may not always want to speak of a 'moral goal', but one would have some idea of a state free from suffering and having the character of wisdom and bliss.[12] The hypothesis of rebirth seeks to show how such a state is possible for everyone, even though in this life most people are very far from achieving it. In the Semitic traditions, the hypothesis of rebirth was not seriously proposed, probably because of the much greater importance given to particular material bodies and communities, when considering questions of personal identity. For that very reason, it was harder,

---

[12] 'The inquiry into Brahman . . . has for its fruit eternal bliss', Sankara, *Vedanta Sutras*, trans. George Thibaut, in Sacred Books of the East, 34 (Delhi: Motilal Banarsidas, 1962).

in the Semitic traditions, to think of the possibility of life after death at all. How can the frustrated possibilities of a material system be fulfilled in a life after death, which will presumably not be material?

From the earliest times in the Abrahamic faith, one obvious solution to the problem of the disparity between the religious goal and its possible achievment on earth was to adjust the goal to what is actually achievable. It might be unrealistic to aim at complete self-lessness, at vivid and unceasing knowledge of God, or at the attainment of universal compassion. Such idealistic aims might even be seen as harmful, in promoting a sense of inevitable failure and guilt, and lowering proper human self-esteem. It might be said that the supposed ideal of a completely selfless person is likely to lead to a masochistic self-hatred. A desire for total unity with God is a sort of self-deceived mystical egoism. And any pretence of universal compassion simply destroys the natural bonds of kinship and community, which are the only things keeping humans relatively humane and sociable, replacing them with a vacuous 'love of humanity' which has no practical implications.

Instead of pretending to have such impossible and morally destructive ideals, one might aim at keeping such achievable rules as those of not killing, stealing, or lying, at obeying God's commands so far as they are thought to have been revealed, and at being merciful and charitable, especially to one's friends and neighbours, and to a reasonable degree. On such a view, the religious goal is achievable—God does not require the impossible—so one can be accounted righteous before God, and can have done all that one ought.

Some interpretations of the basic laws of Judaism and Islam, Torah and Shari'a, can seem rather like that. The religious goal is obedience to the Law, and such obedience is possible, so that the goal is fully attainable. But things are rather more complex. Within Judaism, the Torah does not simply call for obedience to a set of moral rules. It exists to set apart the people of Israel as a people in covenant with God, and Torah is essentially one part of the covenant that God makes. It is what God requires of the people. The other part of the covenant is that God promises to guard and protect the people of Israel, to give them freedom from their enemies, and a land in which peace and justice will flourish.[13]

---

[13] Deut. 28: 1–14.

There is a goal, which is not just obedience to Law. The goal is the establishing of universal peace and justice, and of Israel as the centre of the worship and praise of God. This is a goal which Israel's disobedience seems to make unrealizable. The prophets attempted to explain Israel's political failures in terms of a failure to keep Torah.[14] In consequence, they deepened the requirements of Torah beyond obedience to a few external rules. Fastening on love of God with all one's heart, and love of neighbour as oneself, they could rightly point out that fully obeying such a law was not, after all, possible for most people, at least not without divine help.

Jewish tradition retains a hope for a future just and peaceful world, but usually posits the need for special divine action, perhaps by mighty historical acts like those of old, perhaps even by recreating the whole universe, before it can come about. But how can one ensure that people will be totally obedient to God in future, if they are not so now? Will human sin not always be liable to recur, and prevent the coming of a perfectly just society? Furthermore, since the goal, in its deepened sense, includes knowledge and love of God, it is not attained by the vast majority of people who live or who have lived on earth, but only by the few who will be alive when the truly just society, the kingdom of God, comes.

Such considerations led to the idea, widely current but not universal at the time of Jesus, that history would end in a great Judgement, after which there would be a new heaven and earth, and a resurrection, perhaps only of the just, in a world from which sin and suffering had been purified. All the just of all ages could share in that kingdom, whereas the unjust would be thrown onto the rubbish heap, Gehenna.

The goal is now seen as the resurrection world, and entry to it is by obedience to Torah. Unfortunately, this will not quite do either. Most Jews have not kept Torah properly, which is why the goal could not be achieved on earth. So it seems that there will be very few resurrected righteous, while most people will find themselves cast into Gehenna. Some tough minds could tolerate such a doctrine, but it does not accord well with the idea of a God who is perfectly loving, and cares for all creatures.

God's original purpose—a righteous earth—was not achieved. But God has a secondary purpose ready, and that is to prepare

[14] Jer. 26: 1–6.

humans for a resurrection world, by their obedience to Torah on earth. Even so, only a tiny number of humans make the grade. At this point the prophets call for repentance, and reliance on the merciful forgiveness of God. God's tertiary purpose, they taught, is to grant resurrection life to all who sincerely repent of their sin and rely on divine mercy.[15] God will make righteous those who turn to the divine mercy in penitence and faith (trust that God will accept them).

Now, however, a further complication looms. One could think of a resurrection to happiness for those who are actually just, and a resurrection to punishment for the unjust. But the vast majority of humans will neither be wholly unjust not wholly just. They will be penitent, and will need to be made righteous by divine help. This 'making righteous' is unlikely to occur in a flash. It seems to require a long process of learning and disciplined response. Where can that occur?

Jewish tradition has never developed a formal doctrine of Purgatory or of an 'intermediate state', between death and resurrection. But if God's purpose is to prepare creatures for life in a perfected resurrection world, continued preparation after death is needed, in addition to an instantaneous judgement and resurrection. The Hebrew Bible has available the concept of Sheol, the underworld place of the dead, where they seem to have some sort of shadowy existence as *rephaim* or image-bodies. In the Book of Job, Sheol is described as 'a land of deep darkness . . . of deepening shadows, lit by no ray of light, dark upon dark.'[16] The dead have a sort of life, but they do not praise God, and it is doubtful whether they even have consciousness. Existence in Sheol is a kind of sleep: 'there is neither doing nor thinking, neither understanding nor wisdom.'[17] There is no thought of preparation or development in such a view. Whatever purposes God has must be realized on earth, before death takes every life into silence.

Belief in a resurrection of the dead is first mentioned in the second century BCE, and the prophet Daniel writes that 'many of those who sleep in the dust of the earth will wake, some to everlasting life, and some to the reproach of eternal abhorrence.'[18] However, there is no official doctrine of resurrection in Judaism. The Sadducees rejected it, the Pharisees mostly held that only the just are resur-

[15] Jer. 31: 31–3.　　[16] Job 10: 4.　　[17] Eccles. 9: 10.
[18] Dan. 12: 2–4.

rected, and the Essenes apparently taught that the soul leaves the body altogether. The apocryphal Book of Enoch speaks of punishments for the wicked after death, followed by a judgement after which there is a division into the bliss of the righteous and the suffering of the wicked in 'an abyss of fire'. There is, however, no specific mention in Enoch of a resurrection of the body.

A twofold concern exists in these traditions, one for the fulfilment of God's purpose for creation, and another for the just treatment of human souls. The former concern leads one to look for some moral fulfilment in this space-time, the latter leads one to beliefs about personal survival of death. The obvious way to hold them together is to posit a resurrection of the just in a renewed and perfected material world, and the exclusion of evil, either by annihilation, or separated existence (in Hell), or by the conversion of the wicked to God and the elimination of conflict and suffering from creation. This in turn implies a two-stage immortality—a first stage, immediately after death, when evil can be purged and understanding developed, leading to a second stage, at the end of human history, when a society of perfect justice in a renewed earth will be instituted.

SHEOL AND HELL

What was not available to the biblical writers was the evolutionary view, which makes it clear that some conflict and development is necessary to this material order. Sentient beings emerge from unconscious matter, with conflict and death having been necessary conditions of their emergence. They are parts of a cosmic process aimed at actualizing communities of self-aware and self-directing material beings, consciously related to the creator. It is not just the end state of a community of perfectly sensitive and creative beings which is of value. The emergent process itself realizes many distinctive sorts of good, even in its struggle with conflict, loss, and death. God intends that such a process should exist, and within it God desires the realization of specific values at particular times and places. History is a value-realizing process, and its temporality and particularity make possible great and distinctive goods, willed by God.

Each soul, when it is born, has a specific set of potentialities, and God desires it to express these creatively, to play its part in advancing the cosmic purpose. Very often, the values that God desires are

not realized. Sometimes, they are wholly frustrated by the actions
of other people. Usually, each human life is a mixture of realized
value and failure to implement the divine will. God's will that distinctive values should be realized is done, and in this sense the cosmic purpose as a whole cannot be frustrated. But there is much
frustration and corruption of the divine will in particular matters.
As long as such corruption continues to exist, there will never exist
the perfectly just and loving community that is the final aim, if not
the only purpose, of creation.

One might therefore think of God as having a twofold purpose.
One divine goal is the continuance of the cosmic process and the
realization of its distinctive values in situations of conflict and a
continual struggle for goodness. The other divine goal is the realization of the final aim of a perfectly just and loving community of
sentient beings. It is possible that the cosmic process will always
remain imperfect, though enabling many forms of goodness to exist
which would otherwise never be realized. Even if it ends with the
establishing of the just community, the vast majority of sentient
beings will never have been members of it. Thus a concern for personal fulfilment leads to the belief that the resurrection world will
be a new creation, with different, non-conflicting laws of being,
when the history of sentient life in this universe has come to an end.

For Judaism such a concept of a new creation could never replace
or undermine the importance of history and moral purpose in this
world. Life after death, even where it exists in Judaism, never
becomes the real life to which this earthly life is only a prelude. A
new heaven and earth may indeed be necessary to express the justice of God and the triumph of the divine sovereign will, but the
most important thing is that God has a definite purpose for this
material universe. It is a human responsibility to help to realize it,
and it is a tragic loss when, through human failure, it is not fully
realized.

For some Jews, it is enough to speak of the moral challenge to
justice and mercy on earth, and to hope that a just society will come
to be sometime in future. For others, the promise of God requires
a perfected resurrection world, a new creation, for all who are penitent and trust in God. And that seems to imply some form of personal existence before the resurrection, in a realm that allows of
development, before the Final Judgement puts an end to all development. The form of that existence remains undefined, though it is

natural to think of it as allowing communication and growth, and thus as being quasi-physical rather than wholly disembodied.

Since, however, it is a realm where the moral consequences of earthly life are worked out, and where souls come to know the truth about the nature of ultimate reality, its form of being must be quite different from that of this physical universe. One of the chief problems with the hypothesis of rebirth is that this material universe is governed by physical laws which have no moral import. Laws of gravity, electro-magnetism, and thermodynamics govern a structure which is perhaps looser and more flexible than strict Newtonians used to think, but which still operates on general mathematically formulatable principles. If souls are reborn into this universe, it is most unlikely that their lives will be able to develop so as to realize the moral and spiritual consequences appropriate to their acts in a past life. Physical laws operate without reference to particular moral and spiritual considerations. Chance and necessity govern the way things go in this universe to an extent which makes any belief in the moral appropriateness of occurrences extremely difficult to sustain.

If there is to be an afterlife in which souls can be prepared for final resurrection, in which they can learn the truth about the full context and consequences of their earthly actions, come to know more clearly the purposes and character of God, and experience the suffering that they caused to others as a punishment intended to bring them to repentance, the structure of that world to come will have to be very different from the structure of this universe.

One may think of it, as the Oxford philosopher Henry Price did, as 'ideoplastic' rather than purely physical.[19] That is, occurrences in it will be caused by ideas rather than by impersonal laws. Things will happen, and will be known to happen, because they enable one to work out new attitudes to past actions, and build those past acts consciously into a reshaping of character, in response to a more clearly known presence of God. It will not be a resurrection world, in the full sense, because it will not be the 'new creation' of this world, in which its hidden potentialities for good are unveiled, and it is transformed to be a visible sacrament of a manifest spiritual reality. It will rather be a realm of preparation, in which personalities are shaped by the reworking of their own earthly memories,

---

[19] H. H. Price, *Essays in the Philosophy of Religion* (Oxford: Clarendon, 1972), 115.

habits, and acquired dispositions, towards a readiness for full participation in the new creation (or towards eternal exclusion). It may be thought of as an image-world, rather like a more coherent and interpersonal dream-world, wherein complexes of desire and unresolved inner conflicts can be worked out. In so far as it is a dream-like world, 'sleep' is an appropriate metaphor for that afterlife state before the resurrection. But the dreams of that sleep are shaped by God to preparing souls for a new life in a renewed resurrection world. Such an idea represents a development of the early Hebrew idea of Sheol, orienting it more clearly towards the attainable goal of the final community of peace and justice, in a renewed and transfigured earth.

It must be said that for some, perhaps for most, Jews this is all too speculative and uncertain to be a matter of required belief. There remains in Judaism a range of views about the ultimate destiny of the human soul. It is possible to believe that there is no personal existence after death, but that a perfectly just society will exist in future, when God's chosen servant, the Messiah, brings peace to the world and liberation for Israel. Such a society, living under the physical laws of this universe, will pass away in time, but it will fully realize the divine goal of a just community, and it is not necessary that a goal lasts for ever.

Most Jews, however, do accept that there is a personal existence after death. The Babylonian Talmud contains graphic descriptions of afterlife states, particularly of Hell (*gehinnom*), where the wicked will be tortured in many horrifying ways.[20] It must be admitted that the idea of a Hell, where sin can be punished, has loomed very large in all the Abrahamic traditions. It may seem from the discussion so far that one might expect an afterlife of discipline and development. But what one gets, very largely, is an afterlife of punishment and retribution.

Many contemporary Jewish writers disclaim any idea of eternal punishment. Chief Rabbi J. H. Hertz, in his Commentary to the Prayer Book, says that 'no eye hath seen, nor can mortal fathom, what awaiteth us in the Hereafter, but even the tarnished souls will not be forever denied spiritual bliss. Judaism rejects the doctrine of eternal damnation.'[21]

[20] Dan Cohn-Sherbok, 'The Jewish Doctrine of Hell', in D. Cohn-Sherbok and C. Lewis (eds.), *Beyond Death* (London: Macmillan, 1995), 56–62.
[21] Ibid. 54.

If that is so, Hell must be seen as redemptive, as preparing souls for eternal bliss. But it is rather hard to see how (just to take one rabbinic image) being stung by gigantic scorpions until one's eyes melt in their sockets can help to prepare the soul for such a destiny. It would certainly cause one to beg for mercy, and do almost anything to escape. But how could it cause one to become truly selfless and loving, which is the only real qualification for entering the world to come?

In much religious thought there is a retributive mentality, that wants to see those who have done evil suffer extreme torment. It is natural to think that, since the consequences of evil are finite, the torment will be finite also. Having been tormented, one will once again have a clean slate, and can choose to do good or evil. If one has the memory of torment vividly in mind, one will certainly choose to do good—to tell the truth, refrain from stealing and adultery, and so on. One will be propelled into Paradise out of fear of Hell, a fear which has now become real and vivid, unlike the rather uncertain fear which exists on earth.

If Hell is seen as a place of punishment, then on release one will presumably enter Paradise, a place of reward and comfort, the abode of the just. But on this scheme, the place of the Last Judgement and Resurrection become obscured. The judgement has already taken place, punishments have been endured, and Paradise has been attained by some at least. All the Last Judgement can do is confirm one's status, and send one back with a body to Hell or Paradise for ever.

A greater difficulty with this view is that, if people are to be propelled into Paradise by fear, God could simply have arranged to terrify people into obedience on earth. Some passages in the Hebrew Bible suggest that God did so, when he destroyed sinners by earthquakes and plagues of various sorts. But it has to be admitted that God is not very consistent in meting out punishments in this way. Earthly punishments seem to fall on good and bad alike, and they are so ambiguous that most people do not even interpret them as punishments, but as natural disasters.

More importantly, for all his hostility to experiential religion, Immanuel Kant at least performed the service of pointing out that morality is a matter of the heart, not just of conformity to outward rules. It matters what one's motives are, and fear is not an acceptable moral motive.[22] If all that matters is obedience to rules, then fear is as good an incentive as any to ensure obedience. But suppose that God desires creatures to share experience and co-operate in creative action, for the sake of realizing distinctive values. Fear is precisely one of these corruptions of co-creativity which need to be eliminated from the human soul. To reinforce fear as a central motive is to corrupt the idea of salvation itself, to make it a matter of outward conformity, not a transformation of the heart.

A deeper religious perception might see that it is only love that can drive out fear.[23] Fear and aggression are constitutive of a fundamentally corrupted relation to others. When one understands how such corrupted relations arise, one can begin to understand how a person could make choices that lead to Hell, even though no rational agent could choose Hell for its own sake.

The evil person takes pleasure in having power over another life. Torturing another person can give pleasure, because one has a great sense of freedom and power, of being able to do whatever one wants, while the other is helpless. The whole point is that other people are not normally helpless, and that one is not in general able to do whatever one wants. It is only in the special situation of the torture-chamber that one rises to this false omnipotence, taking pleasure in the delusion of unlimited power, precisely because in the outside world one has to defer to others, or at least to the uncontrollable power of fate.

The sense of freedom and power is in itself good. It is the sense of successful creative action. But such creativity can be frustrated by inability, lack of self-confidence or recognition, or sheer exhaustion. Then one might seek to restore a sense of self-worth in fantasizing ways, one of which is to dominate others by fear or force, and so compel recognition of one's power and worth.

In a similar way, it is natural to take pleasure in the company of others, as they help one to achieve one's purposes and extend one's understanding. Such natural sociability can be frustrated when others block one's plans, obstruct one's progress, and show disrespect or mockery. Then the fantasizing response is to create special situations in which others are compelled to give one pleasure, by becoming purely instrumental to fulfilling one's own desires.

---

[22] Immanuel Kant, *Kritik der Praktischen Vernunft*, Dialektik 9, ed. Paul Natorp, 2nd edn. (Berlin: Königliche Preussische Akademie der Wissenschaften, 1913), 147.
[23] 'Perfect love casts out fear', 1 John 4: 18.

Instead of taking pleasure in the being of others, one takes pleasure in the contribution of others to one's own desires. Sociability becomes hedonism, and one comes to devalue those who exist only to give one pleasure.

The paradigm case of this fantasizing response is pornography, when one ignores completely the personality of another person, and treats them purely as a stimulus to sexual pleasure. People can become locked into such fantasies, until normal responses become impossible. One sees others simply as objects to dominate or to provide pleasure. They are dehumanized, becoming either instruments or obstacles to one's own sense of power and enjoyment. The world of co-operating creative and empathetic agents breaks down, and is exchanged for an egoistic fantasy world, in which one is a demonic god, seeing the world as a self-creation that exists only for amusement.

Such a world, being a fantasy, cannot survive prolonged contact with reality. Moreover, it is inherently self-destructive. When one has reduced others to instruments of amusement, the pleasure quickly palls. Self-fulfilment depends upon the positive co-operation of others, which can draw out new creative powers and contribute new perspectives. It depends upon the creation and contemplation of intrinsic values, states, and processes which are valued for their own sake. But the egoistic fantasy-world reduces others to ciphers that are not allowed to co-operate or contribute to one's self-understanding in any way. It reduces values to private states of pleasure, with no intrinsic worth, and therefore, ultimately, without enjoyment.

The life of the demonic god-self is ultimately empty and pointless. It seems to give power over others and pleasure in the existence of others, but it does so only in a fantasy world, where the existence of others has actually been denied. The isolated self withdraws from reality. Friendship and compassion become impossible for it. In the end, it collapses into the very self-loathing it had been seeking to avoid, because it realizes that it is incapable of realizing its goals in reality, and is only living a pretence.

This state of alienation from God and from others is the state to which pictures and metaphors of Hell point. It is far from being harmless. It destroys the web of human relationships, it causes pain and suffering to others in pursuit of its fantasies, and it frustrates the purposes of creation, or human existence. It is not just a harmless retreat into a private world of fantasy, but a destruction of the social and personal world, and the cause of immense human suffering. Not only is the egoistic self ultimately powerless. Its temporary and fantasized power destroys and its desires isolate and antagonize. The ego is a destructive and hated god, which ends up hating its own creation, hating its inability to produce a creation of intrinsic worth, and hating itself as the reality which expresses itself in the hateful illusion of creation. Hell is the doomed attempt of the self to stand in the place of God, as controller of its own destiny.

THE FULFILMENT OF THE DIVINE PURPOSE

There are four major questions which a theist needs to raise about this situation. What is the point of allowing such harmful behaviour? What is the appropriate divine reaction to it? How, if at all, can it be remedied? And what will be its final outcome?

The first question itself splits into two. Why should God create a world in which such suffering occurs? And how could anyone choose evil? The hypothesis that best explains the occurrence of suffering is that God, a being of supreme intrinsic value which is essentially self-diffusive being, necessarily generates some temporal universe. Some conflict and suffering are necessarily entailed by the existence of such a universe, which evolves through a dialectical process of conflict and resolution, with a necessary structure which includes a 'random' element, the basis of eventual free and responsible action. God cannot be said to intend suffering, either as a means or as an end, but God is its cause.[24]

This does not decrease the goodness (the supreme intrinsic value) of God. Nor does it limit the power of God by any external constraint. Naturally, we are in no position to discern the internal necessities of the divine Being. But we do know that God has necessary properties, and that no possible being could possess more creative power than God. Thus we may conceive of God as necessarily causing a universe in which suffering exists, and as intending, with the greatest possible power compatible with the necessary structure of such a universe, that the universe should produce conscious agents who can create and share values in community. God co-operates to realize good, within the constraints of law, probabil-

---

[24] 'I form light and create darkness, I make weal and create woe', Isa. 45: 7.

ity, and creaturely freedom which belong by necessity to such a universe as this.

Consistently with this hypothesis, many theists have held that the possibility of evil is implicit in the possibility of human freedom. But it has not always been very clear just how this is. It is not very realistic to imagine someone having a blunt choice between good and evil, and choosing evil. Aristotle was right in thinking that one can only rationally choose what seems to be good.[25] There are, however, different sorts of good. Sensual pleasure is good, and a sense of freedom is good. Aiming at the happiness of others is good, and so is creating a work of art.

Finite souls have a choice of goods. The soul is essentially such that it can choose to share and co-operate, or aim at personal pleasure and the exercise of power. It might seem that the rational and informed soul should see that egoism will lead to suffering in the long run, and so could not choose it. Yet the essence of egoism is the overcoming of reason by passion. One chooses the present pleasure because of its unique intensity, and puts aside thoughts of future pain.

If souls evolve in a largely competitive world, with limited knowledge, it is easy to see how the choice of personal pleasure might easily outweigh such abstract considerations as the general good. It is easy to see how persons frustrated in social life might find pleasure in exercising power over others. The conditions of human existence make egoism understandable. The problem is how anyone can ever make a good choice, in a world of such limited knowledge, strong passions, and evolving nature.

The soul must be brought from a condition of instinctive passion to love goodness for its own sake, and to see that friendship and co-operation are parts of goodness. Evil choice is the choice to resist the difficult transformation from egoistic pleasure to disinterested goodness. That is to resist the vision of possible goodness, when it threatens to undermine a known life of pleasure.

If a soul fails to respond to goodness, and chooses the way of egoism, it will embark on an ultimately self-defeating path. In this situation, an appropriate divine response would be to let its self-defeating nature become clear, to let the soul experience the

---

[25] 'The Good has been rightly defined as that at which all things aim,' Aristotle, *Nicomachean Ethics*, 1094^{a}1–22, trans. J. A. K. Thomson (London: Penguin, 1953), 63.

full consequences of its choice, overcoming all self-deception and ignorance. The soul must come to know the pain it has caused, and the emptiness of egoistic existence. This is, of course, a sort of isolation and of pain, a clear realization of the full consequences of selfish choice. It is not a fixed penalty, arbitrarily assigned to some offence. It is a process of bringing a soul to see what its choices really entail, in the long run, both for itself and for others. That will involve feeling the pains of others and facing up to the emptiness of one's own self. One might call it the experience of Hell.

In this situation, can egoism any longer be seen as good? It will surely be clear that the way of self is the way of death. The question is: will that perception be enough to turn a soul to the love of goodness for its own sake? It would seem not, for it will still be an egoistic perception that egoism is self-defeating, and so it will not release one from egoism! How can a soul be brought to love goodness? It cannot be compelled to do so. What is needed is a change from a self-regarding idea of goodness to a disinterested idea. This needs a true appreciation of the experiences of others, an enlargement of sympathy, a seeing of others as one sees oneself, which can be accomplished if one felt the pains and projects of others as one's own. Such a thing would make egoism impossible, since there would be no reason to choose the pleasure of one person (this one) over that of others. Being identical with everyone (or no one), one would choose disinterestedly, and for the sake of goodness.

For an Advaitin or Vaishnava, this is the ascent from ignorance to knowledge, since one is not actually identical with just one human personality, and wisdom is to see this.[26] For a theist, it is more difficult, since one is an individual self with its own unique experience and projects, and only God sees all disinterestedly, as not being identical with any experiences or projects, yet being inwardly aware of them all. The theist needs to move to God's viewpoint, or, since that is impossible, to accept the divine viewpoint as the true one, which is to obey the divine will rather than one's own. That submission of the soul to God is precisely what is at issue, however. God can make you feel the pains of others, and make you know that you have caused them. But even God cannot make you genuinely feel sorrow for that.

---

[26] 'He who dwells in the body can never be slain. Therefore you need not grieve for any living being', *Gita* 2. 30.

One might surmise that God will try to bring all souls to repentance, by giving them knowledge of the harm they cause to themselves and others, by causing them to experience the sorts of sufferings they have caused to others, and by granting them some vision of the divine goodness and love. That might be the sort of existence possessed by souls in Sheol, beginning immediately after death, and lasting until the decisions of all souls have become irrevocable. It is not a matter of penalty which, once paid, leaves one back where one started, perhaps propelling one into Heaven out of sheer terror. It is an attempt at reformation, partly but not wholly through the experience of pain. It cannot be guaranteed to succeed, because fear of punishment remains an egoistic motivation, and cannot lead to true penitence. Yet the human soul is created to realize and enjoy goodness. It can find fulfilment and health only by attending to objective goodness. And the divine Being is in itself supremely attractive, and enters into the realm of human suffering to help souls escape from bondage. So one may legitimately hope that all souls might finally return to God, as the only source and goal of their lives.

Souls which are or which become penitent, and wish to learn to love goodness for its own sake, will learn obedience to God, growing into conformity with the divine will, until they are ready for entrance into the perfected community of justice. (This 'upper division' of Sheol may be called Paradise.)

Souls which have submitted themselves to the divine will during life, will live in the presence of God, but they too will wait for the coming of the perfected community, when they can be joined by all the penitent and when the history of the human race in this universe is completed. (The presence of God is usually termed Heaven.) Jewish tradition places some souls bodily in heaven, normally naming Elijah, Moses, and Enoch.[27] There they can take some interest in human affairs, but in any case it is clear that they live whole and entire in conscious enjoyment of the divine Presence. Even so, however, the divine purpose of founding a community of the spirit, a Messianic kingdom, has not yet been fulfilled, but must wait for the full number of the redeemed to be raised from Sheol or Paradise.

---

[27] The classic account of Elijah's ascent into heaven is at 2 Kgs. 2: 11. Gen. 5: 24 records that 'God took Enoch', and Moses' tomb has never been found.

Then will come the Last Judgement, dividing the perfected community from those who refuse to enter it, and establishing a new form of creation, the final goal of the evolution of life on earth. All the dead will rise to judgement, and a new heaven and earth, existing without suffering or death, and in full consciousness of the presence and guidance of God, will come to be. It is then that humans will obtain their share in the world to come. Scriptural sources make clear that this world has quite a different character from the present space–time. Lions will eat straw, and no creature will destroy any other.[28] Yet it is a temporal, social world in which individual personalities will continue to exist, not an entrance into some timeless or transpersonal form of being. It might be said that the new creation will be a transfiguring of this spatio-temporal order to make it a transparent sacrament of the spiritual order. it is not, as in some Indian traditions, an ending of the material, but its renewal by being taken up into the divine being, to manifest and express that being fully.

Hell is the exclusion from this renewed universe. It is referred to as *Gehinnon* in rabbinic sources, the name of the valley outside Jerusalem where sacrifices were offered to Moloch. Modern Jewish writers are usually at pains to deny any doctrine of eternal or unending Hell. The idea of a place of unending punishment, without any hope of reformation or repentance, is very hard to reconcile with the concept of a merciful God. Even if one holds that souls have put themselves beyond the possibility of repentance, the existence of unending frustration and agony would seem to entail a permanent diminution of the bliss of God. Can one really accept that God and the saints will be happy to see the justice of God done, in the punishment of sinners, when this entails the existence of unending pain?

Of course, even if all pain and evil is eradicated from creation, it will still have once existed. If the divine memory is perfect, all creaturely suffering will still in some sense be present to God. In that sense, suffering will always be part of the being of God. Yet that suffering can be placed in a wider context, which shows it to be implicit in an overwhelmingly great good. It is not eradicated, but its character may be transformed by the good that surrounds it.

To say that the pains of Hell will never come to an end implies that there are some lives which it would have been better never to

---

[28] Isa. 65: 25.

have lived. There are some things it would have been better never to have done. But to say of a whole human existence that it would have been better had it never been, seems to be an indictment of creation itself.

Can God create for the sake of goodness, and yet create things that it would have been better not to create? One might say that it is good for God to create free souls; it would not have been better not to create them. Yet they might make choices that God opposes, realizing states that God would prefer should not exist. It is consistent to say that God desires to create a free soul, and that God does not desire the states which that soul realizes. A soul may choose a state of itself which would be better not to exist. Opposition to the will of God does exist in creation. Does it make much difference whether it will always exist, or whether it only exists for a finite time?

One may feel that God's will cannot be frustrated for ever, that things that God opposes must eventually be eliminated. If so, in the end the divine purpose will be perfectly realized, though it has not been fully realized in the history of creation. God has, as it were, moved with the universe through conflict and opposition to a state of reconciliation and bliss. If one thinks it important that creation should eventually realize a state in which there exists nothing that opposes the divine will, then the existence of an eternal Hell is ruled out. It is incompatible with the omnipotent will of a merciful God.

What one might suppose is that, since fulfilment only comes by being centred on goodness, souls which are in bondage to egoism will be impaired and diminished in being, and will fall into a state of progressive disintegration, until they cease to exist as personalities. This is still in a sense a failure of divine will, for God wished them to have eternal bliss. But they chose otherwise, and in that case God wills their non-existence, so that in those souls that remain, the divine will can be perfectly fulfilled. Hell becomes the realm of a progressive loss of being, until at last all remnants of coherent agency and experience cease to exist, and only the perfected community of love remains.

The emphasis on doctrines of the world to come in Judaism has always been on the final fulfilment of the soul, for which existence in the intermediate state will be a preparation, and which will be realized in the resurrection world. The most important points to bear in mind are that in so far as Hell exists, it is the consequence of the choices of its inhabitants, that release is assured on condition of repentance, and that the divine purpose of human fulfilment will eventually be fully realized. Hell is a possibility for human souls, but God exhorts, persuades, and enables all created souls to choose life, and it is for this reason that God offers them a share in the world to come.

12
Human Destiny in Judaism and Islam

THE COMING OF MESSIAH

Speculation about the details of life after death are not frequent in Jewish writers. As Maimonides says, 'They do not lead to the fear or love of God; nor should one attempt to calculate the End.'[1] Nevertheless, Maimonides includes in his list of basic beliefs important to Judaism a belief in the resurrection of the dead. He sees the ultimate aim of Torah as perfecting souls to enjoy eternal bliss in the world to come. The main concerns are that righteousness and wickedness should somehow be requited, and that souls might find fulfilment in relation to God. The main division that is made is between those who 'have a share in the world to come' (those who keep Torah or, for *goyyim*, the *sheva mitzvot*) and those who do not (unrepentant sinners). There are plenty of visions, poetic fantasies, and warnings about the destiny of human souls in rabbinic literature, but no official doctrine or specific interpretation of such material exists.

More important to rabbinic Judaism than such speculations about the nature of the afterlife is the idea of the coming Messiah, the anointed servant of God, who will usher in an age of peace and restore Israel to a place of spiritual, and maybe political, leadership among the nations. There are many Rabbinic interpretations of the Messiah, ranging from an almost entirely political interpretation that he will deliver Israel from subjection, and allow the Torah to be studied and observed fully, to a belief that the material world will be transformed into 'a new heaven and a new earth',[2] with the coming of the Messiah, who is a pre-existent being (though not a fully divine being).

---

[1] Maimonides, *Mishneh Torah, Melakhim*, 12, in *The Code of Maimonides* (New Haven: Yale University Press, 1951–).

[2] Isa. 66: 22.

Some Rabbis have held that the time when the Messiah is to come is predetermined (the author of the Book of Jubilees), but others insist on the penitence of all Israel as a precondition for redemption, and hold that it may not take place at all.[3] The statement, 'May those who calculate the End of Days perish' is attributed to Jonathan ben Eleazer,[4] and it has occasionally been held either that the Messiah has been delayed because of the sins of the people, or that the Messianic age has in fact begun, but has yet to be completed (Rav Kook has applied such an argument to the state of Israel, to explain why peace has not come, after the founding of the state).

The political interpretation may construe the Messiah, not as an individual, but as a sort of 'golden age', and Rabbi Norman Solomon hints that either the Messiah will be an individual with a spiritual teaching for all humanity, or that it is a personification of an ideal age, which will never be wholly realized in history.[5] Hermann Cohen held that talk of the Messiah really refers to the progress of the human race towards perfect justice: 'the idea of Man—that is the messianic idea'.[6]

The supernatural interpretation includes midrash such as that predicting the slaying of the *yetzer ha-ra* (evil inclination): 'The Holy One, blessed be he, will bring the evil inclination and slay it in the presence of both the righteous and the wicked.'[7] This entails that in the Messianic age people will be so transformed that they no longer feel the inclination to evil. They will obey Torah naturally and easily.

It is possible that everyone will repent and obey the Messiah: 'In days to come, the king Messiah will be told, "Such and such a nation has rebelled against you". He will say, "Let locusts come and destroy it" . . . When the people see what great distress they are in they will come and do him homage.'[8] This is suggestive of the view that the experience of suffering will in the end bring all to repentance.

---

[3] Rabbi Eliezer, Babylonian Talmud, *Sanhedrin*, 97*b*.

[4] Norman Solomon, *Judaism and World Religion* (London: Macmillan, 1991), 139.

[5] Ibid. 158–69.

[6] Hermann Cohen, *Jüdische Schriften*, ed. F. Rosenzweig (Berlin: C. A. Schwetschke, 1924), 124.

[7] Babylonian Talmud, *Sukka*, fo. 52*a*.

[8] *Midrash Shohar Tov* on Ps. 107, trans. G. Friedlander (London: Kegan Paul, 1916).

On the other hand, some sources speak of destruction for those who oppose the Messiah in the last battle: 'All the nations who have humiliated and oppressed Israel will see the good that Israel enjoys, and will then revert to dust and never live again . . . but those who have not humiliated nor oppressed Israel will be present in the days of the Messiah.'[9] There is no talk of everlasting torture, but there is a destruction for those who oppose the purposes of God for Israel.

The Jewish New Year liturgy is capable of being interpreted in either way. It asks God to impose dread upon all creatures, so that 'all creatures prostrate themselves before thee'. But it also prays that 'all wickedness shall be wholly consumed like smoke'.[10] Either way, whether the wicked repent or are consumed, the liturgy looks forward to a time when only righteousness will exist, and all creatures will be united in the praise of God. Even that, of course, as Norman Solomon points out, can be interpreted in a strong or weak sense. In the strong sense, there will be a sudden divine intervention into history, establishing a Messianic kingdom centred on Jerusalem, and the acceptance by all nations of God's rule. In the weak sense, if and when Israel repents, she will achieve political independence and become a centre of spiritual teaching for the world.

For the weak sense, the Messianic kingdom is clearly distinct from the world to come, which is open to people of all ages, and is not a future historical society on earth. Thus Maimonides looks forward to the Messianic age as one in which the Temple is rebuilt, there will be no hunger or war, and Torah can be studied in peace, as a preparation of souls for life in the world to come. In that day, 'the whole earth will be full of the knowledge of the Lord as the waters cover the sea' (Isa. 11: 9).[11]

For the strong sense, however, it may be doubted whether one is speaking of a historical future at all. A world in which the evil inclination no longer exists, in which lions and lambs lie down together, and in which there is no war, hardly seems a possible future on earth. If one also speaks of the dimming of the sun and stars, and of a new heaven and earth, it seems that one must be speaking of a radically transformed creation. In that case, just as the wars of Gog and Magog have been interpreted, not as literal wars on earth, but

[9] *Tanna Debe Elijah, trans. Friedlander,* Yalqut Shimoni, Exodus, 212.
[10] *Authorised Daily Prayer Book* (London, 1941), 327.
[11] Maimonides, *Mishneh Torah: Melakhim,* 12.

as symbols of the triumph of truth over error,[12] so virtually all references to Jerusalem, the return of exiles, the reinstitution of the Temple sacrifices, and the perfect understanding of the mysteries of Torah, must be given a symbolic interpretation. They will refer to the heavenly city beyond this space-time, the gathering there of all people to God, the final revelation of the true meaning of sacrifice, of the true vocation of Israel, and of the divine will for humanity.

The Messianic kingdom, at the extreme of this interpretation, becomes synonymous with the resurrection world, and the coming of Messiah to institute it coincides with the end of history and the last great judgement on all of humanity. The flowering of this sort of cosmic symbolism in late Jewish apocalyptic thought provides the context in which the Christian faith took form, as a belief that the Messiah had come to inaugurate on earth a foreshadowing, a prolepsis, of the spiritual kingdom which would fully dawn only with the resurrection of all humanity at the end of history.

The Christian 'spiritualization' of the Messiah is normally rejected in Judaism, and stock Jewish argument against Christian claims is that Jesus cannot be Messiah, since he plainly did not usher in an age of peace and security for Israel. In view of the great variety of possible Messianic interpretations within Judaism, however, it may be truer to say that the Christian interpretation of Messiah lies at or near one extreme of the range of possibilities for Judaism. The provision of a symbolic or spiritualizing interpretation for the biblical imagery is standard in rabbinic thought. Even the distinctive idea that the Messiah has already come in a hidden form, to establish an earthly prefiguring of either a future historical or a truly eternal kingdom, recurs in Judaism from time to time. Some members of the Lubavitch movement have proposed that their Rebbe will return after his death to found the Messianic kingdom. This is indeed a rather extreme form of Messianism, but it is a possibility within Judaism, and not just an anti-Jewish idea.

The idea of a Messiah is certainly present in Judaism, though there exist many variant interpretations of it, and most would admit that it has become quite problematic in modern times. Rabbi Norman Solomon lists four changed insights in the modern world which render the traditional idea difficult. One is that the biblical

[12] M. M. Kasher, *Ha-Tequfah ha-Gedolah* (Jerusalem: Shelemah Institute, 1968), 519.

time-scale for humanity is only about 6,000 years in total. The immanent advent of a Davidic king, who would fulfil God's promises of peace for Israel and play a major part in God's re-establishment of the Adamic state of friendship with God, does not look unreasonable in such a time-scale. But if the earth is to exist for another thousand million years, it may seem more reasonable to stretch out the Messianic idea so that it looks to the development of a truly just and loving humanity over many years.

Another factor is that the Messianic idea is confined to the Israelites, and says very little about the vast majority of the world's peoples, the *goyyim*. Rabbi Solomon suggests that the imagery of a conflict between Israel and 'the nations' can best be taken, in this extended context, as a 'prototype or symbol' of the general conflicts between good and evil throughout history. That does not mean that Israel has no special role to play in history. It does mean that the role might be seen in terms of spiritual leadership or moral service, rather than political domination.

Then, we might best see Bible and Talmud as guides to life, aids to enlarged insight and challenges to new response to God, in changing situations. The development of diverse traditions of Talmudic interpretation, the fact that Torah needs constantly to be applied to new situations, and the character of rabbinic exegesis as allowing for argument and extrapolation, all suggest that the Messianic idea should be seen as containing many different spiritual insights, but no definitive literal mapping onto reality. It is a permanent resource for prayerful reflection about the nature of true humanity in relation to God, not a list of facts which puts an end to further independent thought.

Finally, Solomon suggests, the general perspective of biological and social evolution makes it difficult to accept any doctrine about a final and permanent state of society, which will put an end to evil for ever.[13] One might add that, if freedom is an important feature of human nature, and if its development always allows for evil choice, one cannot expect any historical state to exist which can be guaranteed to remain perfect.

One might think this would lead Rabbi Solomon to locate the Messianic kingdom beyond history, in the new earth in which the evil inclination has been destroyed. But, while not denying that

---

[13] Solomon, *Judaism and World Religion*, 158–9.

possibility, he prefers to find a view of Messiah which will apply in this always ambiguous realm of human history and freedom. He rejects 'all theories that offer to cure the world's ills by bringing about some undefined "new order" '.[14] One can think of the Messianic age as an idea that will never fully be realized, but which offers hope in times of hardship. It seems to me that if this is to be a real hope, then one is committed to some sort of realization of the kingdom. If that cannot be expected in history, then one is committed to a trans-historical kingdom. It remains a hope for this world, in the sense that individuals will only enter the kingdom as a result of a ceaseless striving for justice and reconciliation in history.

In Judaism, the tension remains unresolved between a hope for evolution towards a perfected society, and the recognition that the kingdom can only exist beyond history, between the call for all individuals to work for justice, and the recognition that they will always fail to achieve it, between the declaration of judgement on all who are unrighteous, and the admission that the divine mercy wills to deliver all humanity from sin. These tensions can be, and are, resolved in various ways. But one can see the forces that lead to the positing of a world to come, in which the divine mercy can find a way of bringing all who will respond into the joy of the divine presence, and the insistence that what is of primary importance for humans is the pursuit of justice and deliverance from oppression on earth. Though Judaism makes no claim to be a universal religion, these beliefs are of universal significance, and the Jewish people can make a fair claim that their historical vocation has been, and still is, to bring this significance before the attention of the world.

THE AFTERLIFE IN ISLAMIC THOUGHT

Belief in life after death is much more central in Islam than it is in Judaism. 'The fear of the Last Judgment and the Lord of the Day—that is the most fundamental motif of this new religion that underlies all its aspects and determines its basic mood.'[15] Prophet Muhammad constantly reiterates the theme of judgement and the resurrection to Heaven and Hell. While one can be a Jew without

---

[14] Solomon, *Judaism and World Religion*, 160.
[15] Toshihiko Izutsu, *Ethico-Religious Concepts in the Qur'an* (Montreal: McGill University Press, 1966), 17.

believing in the resurrection of the dead, it would be impossible to be a Muslim and deny the resurrection. The thought of judgement is determinative of the life of every believing Muslim.

There is, not surprisingly, no belief in the coming of a Messiah who will redeem Israel and give her primacy among the nations. Muhammad was aware of Christian claims that Jesus was the Messiah, but the Qur'an has a very different interpretation of such claims from the Christian one. The Qur'an refers to Jesus as 'the Messiah',[16] though the term is never used in the sense of a coming deliverer of Israel. In one verse he is associated with the Day of Judgement: 'And (Jesus) shall be a Sign (for the coming of) the Hour (of Judgment).'[17] It is not wholly clear that this verse refers to Jesus at all, for the parenthesised 'Jesus' in Yusuf Ali's translation actually reads 'he' or even 'it' in Arabic (*inna-hu la-'ilmun li '-sa'ati*), and some commentators take the pronoun to refer to the Qur'an. Nevertheless, Muslim tradition is that Jesus will personally return before the Day of Judgement, and there is a hadith that Jesus will return to kill *Dajjal*, whom Christians call the Antichrist. Jesus will then go to Jerusalem to pray in accordance with Shari'a, kill pigs, break crucifixes and demolish churches.[18] He will not be the Judge of good and evil, since that is reserved for God alone. He will take his proper place as a prophet, giving precedence to Muhammed.[19] He will, after having seen the defeat of *Dajjal*, and the coming of a time of peace, die and be buried. This account of the Messianic coming or return has little in common either with Jewish hope for a deliverer of Israel or with Christian hope for an inaugurator of a transformed creation. In Muslim thought, everything is subordinated to the advent of the Last Judgement, and there is no role for a Messianic figure to play. Israel no longer has any spiritual role to play in the world, since the first (and last) truly universal world prophet, Muhammad, has ushered in the final form of religion: 'This day I have perfected your religion.'[20] There will be a new creation, a new heaven and earth following the final judgement, as Christians believe, but there is no human being, not even Muhammad, who will be the universal judge and ruler of Paradise. In this, as in all other things, God has no human partners.

[16] Qur'an 3: 45.   [17] Qur'an 43: 61.

[18] al-Zamakhshari, *al-Kashshaf* (Beirut: Dar al-Fikr, n.d.), iii. 494, ll. 20–7.

[19] Cf. the discussion in Neal Robinson, *Christ in Islam and Christianity* (London: Macmillan, 1991), 103–5.

[20] Qur'an 5: 4.

After death, each soul enters into an intermediate state, *barzakh*, where it waits for the Day of Judgement. Little is said in the Qur'an about this state. It is compared to sleep: 'O woe to us! Who has raised us up from our sleeping place?.'[21] On the other hand, it is written: 'Reckon not those who are killed in Allah's way as dead; nay, they are alive, being given sustenance from their Lord; rejoicing in what Allah has given them.'[22] Here, the dead are represented as being conscious and joyful. There are apparently rewards in *Barzakh*, and punishments, too: 'They (Pharaoh's people) shall be brought before [the fire] every morning and evening and on the day when the hour shall come to pass.'[23] Even before 'the hour', the day of resurrection, the wicked feel the fire of punishment.

Barzakh can be compared to a state of semi-consciousness, compared to the full consciousness of the resurrection life. Yet it has been said that 'the bliss of the Grave is better than any delight that this world can offer'.[24] Some think that there may be progress in it, as souls prepare themselves for judgement. No specific doctrines have developed around the idea, such as that of Purgatory in Catholic Christianity, but prayers for the dead are common in many Muslim communities.

From the state of *barzakh*, also referred to as 'the grave', the dead are raised to judgement, and then sent to Paradise or Hell. In Paradise 'there will be for them therein all that they wish—and more besides in Our presence'.[25] In Hell there are many sorts of terrible torments. In its fire 'as often as their skins are roasted through, we shall change them for fresh skins'.[26] The states of Paradise and Hell are described in what may seem to be very literal terms. In Paradise there are gardens, rivers, and trees, and 'companions of the right hand', *hur*, of virginal purity, grace, and beauty. Since there is to be a resurrection of the body, it is only reasonable to think that there will be a pleasant environment in which bodies can exist. But the Qur'an is fairly clear that resurrection bodies will not be exactly the same as earthly bodies: 'We are not to be frustrated from changing your forms and creating you (again) in (Forms) that ye know not.'[27] The Garden, its rivers and its shade

---

[21] Qur'an 36: 52.   [22] Qur'an 3: 168.   [23] Qur'an 40: 45.

[24] Lazla Mabrouk, *The Soul's Journey after Death*, an abridgement of Ibn al-Qayyim, *Kitab al-ruh* (Birmingham: Al-Hidayah Publishing, 1996), 15.

[25] Qur'an 50: 35.   [26] Qur'an 4: 56.   [27] Qur'an 56: 60, 61.

are said to be 'a parable' or likeness (*mathal*).[28] And it is expressly said that the delights of Paradise are not known, and are therefore not literally like those of earth: 'Now no person knows what delights of the eye are kept hidden (in reserve) for them—as a reward for their (good) deeds.'[29] After the Day of Resurrection, there will be a new earth, with quite different laws of being: 'the earth will be changed to a different earth, and so will be the heavens'.[30]

On the one hand, the delights of Paradise are not those of disembodied existence. They are, in some sense, temporal, social, and material. Yet the nature of that materiality is entirely different from this. It is expressive of spiritual realities in an immediate way, which is inconceivable by us, though the Qur'an speaks of it in parables. Some critics have mocked the Qur'anic teaching that there will be *hur* in Paradise, interpreting it to mean that there will be young, beautiful maidens who can provide sensual pleasures, while always remaining virgins. This is not borne out by the text. Chapter 56, verses 15 to 38, depicts the blessed in Paradise as sitting on golden thrones in gardens of bliss, being served by youths with beakers of clear water and bowls of fruit, and having wide-eyed companions 'like Pearls'. The picture is one of rustic delight, in which the delights of taste, smell, and sight are enhanced and transformed to give a higher spiritual joy. It is certainly not a picture of riotous sensuality. There will be no intoxication, and 'No frivolity will they hear therein, nor any taint of ill—only the saying "Peace! Peace!".'[31] It is a garden of restrained delight, and in it the overwhelming good is the presence of God: 'God hath promised to Believers, men and women, gardens under which rivers flow, to dwell therein, and beautiful mansions in gardens of everlasting bliss. But the greatest bliss is the good pleasure of God.'[32] There is no suggestion of sexual activity, and the 'companions' are said to be loving, undefiled, and virgin-pure. Any sympathetic commentator would take them to symbolize the beauty and purity of love and companionship, which are to characterize the life of Paradise.

The emphasis of the Qur'an on the life beyond death is quite remarkable, given the general lack of interest in that topic in most of the Hebrew Bible. The ultimate reason for it is the general Qur'anic view of human life as a first stage in an infinite journey of spiritual development. The ultimate object of human life is *liqa'*

---

[28] Qur'an 13: 35.   [29] Qur'an 22: 17.   [30] Qur'an 14: 48.
[31] Qur'an 56: 25.   [32] Qur'an 9: 72.

Allah, meeting with God. What, for believers, gives to human life
its real and enduring purpose is 'the certainty that they are to meet
their Lord, and that they are to return to Him'.[33] Human souls are
born in this world, where the presence of God is obscured and
veiled. Here they begin a pilgrimage which will never end, seeking
to unfold what is within them, for good or evil. They may choose
the goods of the material order: 'Those who rest not their hope on
their meeting with Us, but are pleased and satisfied with the life of
the present . . . their abode is the Fire.'[34] The life of ambition, sensuality and power offers attractions to souls which have no strong
sense of their own true nature and the purpose for which they were
created. But the real nature of those attractions is revealed after
death, when the soul takes on a form which its own desires have
shaped. The chains of Hell are the chains which bind the soul to
physical attachments, now impossible to realize, and which prevent
the soul from rising to the realm of the spirit. The fire is the burning of frustrated desire, and the food that chokes the eater is the
realization that one has centred one's life on things that separate
one from the only thing that can satisfy one's deepest longings.

The life which turns, however waveringly, towards the light of
God, is set on a course of endless spiritual progress. 'It is for those
who fear their Lord, that lofty mansions, one about another, have
been built.'[35] Immediately after death, in *barzakh*, one takes on a
form which begins to make possible the realization of higher spiritual forms of being. After this time of preparation, at the Day of
Resurrection, there is the full awakening to higher spiritual life, and
the further pilgrimage of the soul begins. The gardens wherein
rivers flow are realms where the seeds of future forms of being can
grow. The waters are those of trust in God, bringing refreshment
and purity. The shade is the veil which still protects the young soul
from the full vision of the light of God, which lies far ahead on its
journey.

Thus one can form a dynamic view of the life of Paradise, as an
infinite journey towards the ultimate meeting of the soul with God.
We can only grasp the next stage, and even then only in material
parables and images. But it does not have to be thought that there
is just one short life on earth, followed by an endless, rather disap-
pointingly sensual and rather boringly passive life lying on couches

---

[33] Qur'an 2: 46.   [34] Qur'an 10: 7, 8.   [35] Qur'an 39: 20.

in a garden, surrounded by beautiful young girls. Such a conception would undermine the deepest spiritual teaching of Islam, which is the unity of all things in God, and the human quest as one of coming to realize that unity. Human life is a seeking to return to the unity of God from the diversity, impersonality, and conflictual oppositions of material existence in which humans are born. That journey is endless, and its goal is far beyond the imagination of every human mind, except that, perhaps, of the greatest prophets. It is because the goal is so exalted and unimaginable that Islam proclaims the life to come as infinitely better than and different from this life. Yet, so as not to leave humans in vague dreams of some far-off consummation, it lays down a specific law for the beginning of the journey in this life, proclaims an hour of inexorable Judgement at the ending of this life, and provides vivid parables of the Fire and the Garden to show the consequences of human actions in this life.

The Qur'anic teaching leaves a great deal of room for human reflection and interpretation. What it teaches unequivocally is that human beings are constituted by their total dependence upon a God who is 'the cherisher and sustainer of all worlds, most gracious, most merciful, the master of the Day of Judgment'.[36] They will find their true destiny in worshipping that God alone, and living by divine grace. That is the goal at which every Muslim aims. If it can be partly glimpsed in this life, it is in the world to come that it can be fully realized. Belief in the resurrection is the natural consequence of an intense longing for God. That is why the doctrine of the world to come plays such a central part in Muslim belief. Yet the doctrine does not in any way detract from the importance and seriousness of life in this world. For it is in this life that one determines one's status before God at the Day of Judgement.

PERSONAL RESPONSIBILITY AND THE MERCY OF GOD

Some Qur'anic verses offer a very severe doctrine of personal responsibility for good and evil: 'If one heavily laden should call another to (bear) his load, not the least portion of it can be carried (by the other).'[37] Islam has no doctrine of 'original sin' or guilt, and so it is generally held that it is possible to lead a sinless life. Indeed,

---

[36] Qur'an 1: 2–4.   [37] Qur'an 35: 18.

all the prophets are said to have lived sinless lives: 'no prophet could (ever) be false to his trust',[38] and Muhammad is described as *Al-amin*, completely faithful to God. Thus it is possible for souls to be adjudged wholly righteous at the Day of Judgement. Nevertheless, any idea of a rigorous assignment of exact penalties is heavily qualified by the basic doctrine that God can forgive all sins, and that God will give the righteous much more than they deserve. No Muslim believes that every soul will get just what it deserves, since the mercy of God wills to draw all souls into the infinite bliss which is life with God in Paradise.

There is a tension here between the justice of God and the mercy of God, and one could by using isolated verses from the Qur'an develop a doctrine either of a vengeful and punitive God or a doctrine of a merciful and forgiving God. There is no doubt, however, that the doctrine of mercy is the determinative one.

It is a logical point that mercy can only be exercised after the verdict of justice has been pronounced. God cares about human goodness and evil, about upholding the moral order of the universe. Therefore just penalties must be declared, and just verdicts must be pronounced—perhaps even by souls themselves, who see the true character of their deeds, at Judgement Day ('Read thine (own) record: sufficient is thy soul this day to make out an account against thee'[39]). But then the overwhelming goodness of God will far outrun the limits of justice: 'He that doeth good shall have ten times as much to his credit.'[40] The righteous will receive far more than they deserve. Similarly, the evil, as soon as they repent, will experience the goodness of God in such a way that sin is actually removed: 'Turn to God with sincere repentance; in the hope that your Lord will remove from you your ills and admit you to gardens beneath which rivers flows.'[41]

There is no account of how God will remove ills, but it seems plausible to think that awareness of the sufferings one has caused, through the experience of personal suffering together with the awareness that one is oneself its cause, and the knowledge of the divine presence, will purify the soul and fill it with the pure compassion of the divine. 'Their Light will run forward before them and by their right hands, while they say, "Our Lord! Perfect our Light for us, and grant us forgiveness." '[42] Perhaps one can find here the

---

[38] Qur'an 3: 161.   [39] Qur'an 17: 14.   [40] Qur'an 6: 160.
[41] Qur'an 66: 8.   [42] Qur'an 55: 8.

thought that, as souls gradually free themselves from the obscuring darkness of sin, the light of God grows brighter for them and in them, and makes their lives transparent to the action and bliss of God. They come to shine with the divine light, though it never becomes their own possession. So they grow continually in perfection.

The verse in fact refers to those in Paradise, and so 'forgiveness' is not the best rendering of the word *istighfar*, which means 'a protection against sin'. The prayer of the righteous is to be continually protected against the possibility of sin, and brought to ever higher stages of spiritual perfection by divine help. There is such a stress in the Qur'an on the need for continual resort to God for protection and guidance, and on the complete sovereignty of the will of God, that no one should think that Islam is simply a matter of doing good works or evil works by one's own efforts and then being properly rewarded or punished for eternity. Even the sinless, who are wholly faithful to God's law, can progress infinitely in spiritual perfection, and they will do so only by divine help. Even the sinful, who will be assigned their due penalty for sin at the Judgement Day, can be brought to Paradise by the infinite mercy and compassion of God, and by the prayers of believers who share in the divine compassion.

There is, it must be said, dispute about the eternity of Hell among Muslims. Some hold that there is no release from Hell, once Judgement has been declared: 'Nor will there be a way for them out of the Fire.'[43] However, Jusuf Ali, in his note to this verse, simply says, 'Our deeds are irrevocable and we must pass through the Fire of repentance and regrets.'[44] There is no escape from the penalty of sin. But nothing is said about that penalty lasting for ever. Nor is it denied that God may deliver sinners whenever God pleases, though they will not be able to escape whenever they please. An especially telling verse is, 'They will dwell therein for all the time that the heavens and the earth endure, except as thy Lord willeth.'[45] In this verse the word *khalidin* is used. This comes from *khulud*, which can take the sense of 'eternal' or 'unending'. It can also, however, like the Greek work *aeonios*, used in the New Testament, mean 'a long time'. Many, perhaps most, Muslim theologians accept eternal

---

[43] Qur'an 2: 167.
[44] Yusuf Ali, *Commentary on the Holy Qur'an* (Introduction to the Qur'an), 65.
[45] Qur'an 11: 107.

punishment in Hell, assuming that the phrase 'the heavens and the earth' will include the new heaven and earth of the resurrection world. But the phrase *illa ma sha'a Allah*, 'except as God wills', clearly leaves it open that God may will to deliver sinners from Hell. Some Muslim theologians have held that Muslim sinners can be redeemed from Hell, whereas non-Muslim sinners cannot be. But the belief that all will eventually be taken from Hell, even if it is a minority view, is more firmly rooted in Muslim tradition than it is in Christian, though it proceeds from the same sorts of arguments about the mercy of God that some Christian theologians increasingly use.

Intercession (*shafa'ah*) is an important part of Muslim prayer. According to a hadith recorded by Bukhari, generally regarded as the most reliable transmitter of the sayings of the Prophet,[46] those in Paradise will plead for those in Hell, and will be allowed to bring out those they recognize. Angels, prophets, and believers will all intercede for those in Hell whose lives contained even an atom of good. Then God himself will bring out those who never did good, and have been turned into charcoal, and cast them into the River of Life, from whence they will emerge like pearls. It seems that, while those in Hell can see no end to their suffering, there is an end, and all souls will at last return, through the overwhelming mercy of God, to Paradise. What has to be burned away is the transient self, immersed in sensuality and desire. The true self can never be satisfied until it rests in the presence of God, which is its true home, and for which it is inevitably destined. Earthly life is an exile from God, and Hell is the furthermost extent of such exile. From both, there is a return to God, when the soul recognizes the only reality that can fulfil its deepest nature, and the self-destructive nature of selfish desire.

The Qur'an states that God, the all-compassionate and merciful, is the only ultimate intercessor: 'Except for Him they will have no protector nor intercessor.'[47] God's mercy is sufficient for all. It is the divine help which enables sinners to escape from the evil consequences of what they have done, when all other means have failed. But this does not mean that intercession is forbidden: 'No intercessor (can plead with Him) except after His leave.'[48] The

---

[46] Cf. al-Hafiz Abu Abd-Allah Muhammad ibn Ismail al-Bukhari, *al-Sahih al-Bukhari* (Cairo: al-Miriyah Press, n.d.), 97: 24.

[47] Qur'an 6: 51.   [48] Qur'an 10: 3.

meaning is that there are no intercessors independent of God, who might be able to relieve a person of responsibility for evil, without turning to God in penitence.

By God's permission, however, the angels intercede: 'How many so ever be the angels in the heavens, their intercession will avail nothing except after God has given leave.'[49] They intercede that humans may be kept from evil deeds, and they 'pray for forgiveness for (all) beings on earth'.[50] Prophets and believers can also intercede, by God's permission. Muhammad prayed constantly for his followers, and of his prayers the Qur'an says, 'Verily thy prayers are a source of security for them.'[51] In Muslim tradition, Muhammad will be the first to pray on the Day of Resurrection, and his intercessions will be accepted by God.

Although God's mercy is sufficient for all, and will perhaps finally rescue all from Hell, God wills this mercy to be channelled through the prayers of angels, prophets, and believers. In particular, Muhammad, who faced great trials and opposition and came near to death as he began to take up his prophetic call, but who was vindicated by God, is so closely aligned to God that his intercessions on the Day of Resurrection will be immediately accepted by God, and thus will be wholly efficacious.

Such a belief modifies considerably the teaching that each person must bear the burden of their own sin. Indeed, that teaching is misunderstood if it is taken to rule out all effective intercession and divine forgiveness. First of all, mercy is freely offered during earthly life: 'God forgives all sins; for He is oft forgiving, most merciful. Turn ye to your Lord (in repentance) and bow to his (will), before the Penalty comes on you: after that ye shall not be helped.'[52] At the Judgement Day itself, each person stands alone, all their good and evil deeds are weighed, and their souls judged accordingly. But after that, just as one may suppose that in the unending life in Paradise liberated souls help one another, so they may help those in Hell by their intercessions. The help must be freely accepted, but there is no doctrine in Islam that every soul must pay the full penalty for its sin. On the contrary, there is forgiveness for all sin, and there is a tradition that, even in the world to come, there is help for every sin, both directly from God, and through the prayers of the angels, prophets, and believers.

[49] Qur'an 53: 26.   [50] Qur'an 42: 5.   [51] Qur'an 9: 103.
[52] Qur'an 39: 53, 54.

It is an unresolved question within Islam whether there is release from Hell, which the prayers of the faithful can help to obtain. What is unequivocally clear is that God will judge justly, and yet give unlimited mercy to those who repent while they can. The unequivocal belief is that God is both just and merciful. The disagreement is about what the combination of justice and mercy implies for the ultimate destiny of human souls. Within Christianity there is a similar clarity about divine justice and mercy, and a similar set of disagreements about the consequences for human destiny. But in Christian thought, the crucial element is the belief that in Christ, God has acted decisively to accomplish human redemption from the demands of strict justice. This belief involves a transformation of the Messianic hopes of Judaism, putting upon them a trans-historical interpretation. How this affects Christian views of ultimate human destiny is the topic of the following chapter.

13
Human Destiny in Christianity

The idea of a world to come is not essential to Judaism (though very central to it, historically). The same cannot be said of its major heresy, Christianity. There is no sense in giving Messianic status to Jesus of Nazareth, unless he is to return to complete the Messianic mission of eradicating evil and establishing the kingdom of peace among all people. The disciples of Jesus revised the Messianic idea by uniting it with the originally quite distinct idea of 'the suffering servant',[1] by giving the Messiah divine status, and by crediting him with the authority to institute a new covenant and a new Israel. The latter claim, in particular, is enough to place the new group outside the historic people of Israel, though it is not clear that Jesus himself or the disciples at first intended such a radical move. The Gospel accounts suggest that Jesus saw his mission as almost exclusively to the people of Israel.[2] It was only when it had failed that there is talk of extending discipleship to Gentiles, and even then, after the death of Jesus, there was much dispute among the apostles as to how far, and on what terms, this should be permitted.

It is very important to locate the beginning of the Jesus movement in its historical context, with its extremely varied, highly symbolic, and politically charged versions of Messianic belief. It is highly unlikely that there is just one view of the Messiah which was applied to Jesus in the early church. It is much more likely that a wide variety of views coexisted, and were used to give insight into the sort of divine revelation that was felt to have occurred in the life of Jesus.

One thing, however, was obvious. If Jesus was Messiah, then the anointed Davidic king of Israel had been rejected by his own people, and had been executed as a criminal. This left a twofold problem. How was he to deliver Israel, who had rejected him? And

---

[1] Isa. 53: 4–12.
[2] 'I was sent only to the lost sheep of the house of Israel', Matt. 15: 24.

how was he to bring peace to the world when he was dead? The solution offered by the apostolic community was to say that he had instituted a new Israel (the church), which would become the spiritual teacher of the nations, and that he would return at some future time to usher in the age of peace. These beliefs give the framework within which Christian views of post-historical life could be worked out.

If Jesus had really died, he had presumably entered Sheol, the world of the dead. On one account, he said to a penitent thief, crucified with him, 'Today you will be with me in Paradise.'[3] The Gospels record that after three days he rose from the world of the dead, and appeared to the disciples at various times over a period of forty days, in bodily form. Then he ascended to the presence (the 'right hand') of God, until his return, leaving the Spirit as the witness to and mediator of his presence. One New Testament letter records an early belief that in Sheol he preached to the dead.[4] The dead to whom he preached are referred to as 'spirits in prison', and are specifically described as those who were disobedient in the time of Noah. At that time, 'all flesh had corrupted their way upon the earth',[5] and God had determined to destroy them.

If one divides the underworld into Paradise, for just or penitent souls, and Sheol, for disobedient sinners, then it seems clear that the author of this letter believed that Jesus preached to some of those who had been sinners on earth, and had been destroyed by God in judgement. This is in accordance with the view that Sheol can be a time of learning and development, and with a widespread Jewish view that, after a time of suffering, sinners can repent and turn again to God. The revelation that God in human form had died for the sake of bringing sinners to repentance, and had even entered the world of the dead to seek and save the lost, would manifest the utmost that a God of love could do to bring all human souls to penitence and faith. It is thus a natural extension of the insight that in Jesus God does everything possible to accomplish human salvation.

It is, in my view, deeply unfortunate that in later Catholic tradition the possibility of penitence after death is denied. Thus Jesus was held to have preached only to the just who have died, and what came to be called 'the harrowing of Hell' was seen as the release of

---

[3] Luke 23: 43.   [4] 1 Pet. 3: 19, 20.   [5] Gen. 6: 12.

those holy souls who were already eagerly awaiting their Redeemer into the presence of God and the life of Heaven.[6] For this later view, all people before the time of Jesus are in the prison of Sheol. When Jesus descends to Sheol, he at that time divides it into Heaven, for the just, and Hell, for the unjust. From that time, all souls pass to Heaven or Hell immediately at death, or (for the later Latin Catholic tradition) to a state of purification before entering Heaven, known as Purgatory. All the Final Judgement can do is confirm the judgement which has already been passed at the point of death, beyond which even the power of God can produce no repentance or liberation.

This is contrary to the natural reading of 1 Peter, which is that Jesus' preaching is to the disobedient, and that preaching is meant to lead to penitence.[7] More importantly, it undermines the justice of God to say that no repentance is possible after death, it undermines the power of God to say that God cannot permit such repentance to be possible, and it undermines the love of God to say that God would not do everything possible to seek and save all souls, whether living or dead. The divine presence in Sheol, manifested in Jesus, is, as it always is, a redemptive presence of suffering and unitive love. It never closes the door on any sinner who is still capable of turning from self to the objective source of universal love.

It is an inescapable truth that there are millions of humans who never hear, on earth, the name or teaching of Jesus. There are millions who must die with radically false beliefs about the nature of the world and the life beyond. It seems, then, that there will be millions of souls which have not truly known of the redemptive love of God, shown in Christ, and who will therefore not have had a genuine chance of penitence, following from a genuine knowledge of God and of the nature of sin.

One could, of course, always suppose that every human soul has some sort of ultimate choice, even though it was not recognized as such, between good and evil during its life, and that it will be somehow regarded as 'penitent by desire', if it dies without actually

---

[6] *Catechism of the Catholic Church* (London: Geoffrey Chapman, 1994), 144, 'It is precisely those holy souls, who awaited their Saviour in Abraham's bosom, whom Christ the Lord delivered when he descended into Hell.'

[7] The recent interpretation of the passage as referring to Jesus' condemnation of fallen angels, imprisoned between heaven and earth, strikes me as very forced and weakly evidenced. It can be found in W. J. Dalton, *Christ's Proclamation to the Spirits* (Rome, 1965).

confessing its sins before God.[8] One might say that every soul will make some choice between good and evil, and that is what it will be judged on after death. But that is not very satisfactory for the usual Christian view of the severity of sin and the impossibility of natural human goodness. It sounds very much like a doctrine of salvation by good works, which is contrary to traditional Christian teaching.

It does not seem very realistic to suppose that every human soul has somehow made an absolute decision of love for God, or of closing itself against God, before death. The most one could suppose is that all souls have acted in a way which will, if persisted in, lead to the love or rejection of God. It is difficult to see what such actions could be, since their character is completely hidden from observation. In any case, many thousands of souls will have only had the choice for one or two responsible actions, in lives cut short by disease or handicapped by mental illness. Others will have acted wrongly through petulance or misjudgement, and died before they had time to reflect. With what confidence could we then say that 'death puts an end to human life as the time open to either accepting or rejecting the divine grace manifested in Christ'?[9]

Belief in unlimited divine love requires that every possible thing will be done to bring souls to penitence and reliance on God's help. To close the possibility of penitence with death seems to deny the obvious possibility of seeking to draw souls back to God after death, and thus limits the divine love unacceptably. It seems more consistent with biblical revelation to think of each soul entering the world of the dead, to a disclosure of the true nature and consequences of its earthly acts and attitudes. This may take the form of pain (a reflection of the pain caused to others), of a realization of the injury done to oneself through selfish desire, and of the torment of self-exclusion from the love of God (having become unable to give or accept love). It may take the form of happiness (a reflection of the happiness caused to others), of a clearer knowledge of one's own nature and potentialities, and of delight in the experience of the divine presence (love accepted to the degree one can share it).

---

[8] Cf. Karl Rahner, *Foundations of Christian Faith*, trans. William Dych (New York: Crossroad, 1995), 440, 'Wherever a person . . . risks himself in freedom . . . he is gathering time into a validity which is ultimately incommensurable with the merely external experience of time.' That is, such a person, however unconsciously, makes a decision for or against eternity.

[9] *Catechism*, 233.

The former state might be thought of as Hell (*Gehenna*), where
the fires of passion burn fiercely. But those fires can also burn away
desire, and have a purifying function, which can lead one to turn
away from the self-destructive path of greed, hatred, and desire.
The appearing of Christ in Hell is the manifestation of the self-
giving love of God in the shadow-world of pain and isolation which
is the world of injured souls. God is always present in Sheol,[10]
though God may be experienced by egoistic souls as burning fire
and stern judge of evil (which is a major reason why one may think
that Sheol cannot be permament, since it would then be true that
the divine Being itself was always experiencing unredeemed Hell).
Jesus manifests God on earth in a particular historical expression of
divine love, with distinctive consequences. So Jesus' manifestation
in Sheol is a particular temporal event in the life of the dead, which
makes clearer to them the character and particularity of the divine
love. As, on earth, the manifestation of Christ is the origin and pattern of the proclamation of God's forgiveness and unitive love, so
in Sheol all the dead will hear this gospel, as Jesus' manifestation in
Sheol, as the way of salvation from the darkness of ignorance and
desire, comes to be proclaimed to all who have died. It would be
tragic if the only purpose or consequence of the manifestation of
the Saviour in Sheol was to confirm the unending torment of the
lost, as if to increase their suffering even further. Its purpose must
be the release of souls from the prison of their own desires, by offering to them the power of selfless love.

Paradise is referred to in the Gospels at one point as 'Abraham's
bosom', where the just recline.[11] For them, there is no punishment,
but it would be odd to think that there is also no further progress
possible in knowledge and perfection. There is much for most, perhaps for all, souls to learn about the nature of God and the divine
purpose for the world. It is unlikely that one will be magically made
perfect in the twinkling of an eye, so this will not be a realm of actually perfected souls.

It might be better to think of there being a continuum from the
deepest Hell to the most blissful Paradise, with many worlds
between, between which souls can progress in greater knowledge
of their true nature and relation to God, still enduring conflict
and frustration to varying degrees. We have seen that H. H. Price

[10] Ps. 139: 8.   [11] Luke 16: 22.

conceived of this intermediary state as an image or dream world, in which desires and aspirations would work themselves out in an environment more controlled by morally ordered laws than our present material environment. Jesus' saying: 'In my Father's house there are many resting places,' fits such a picture rather well.[12] In the paradisal worlds, Jesus appears to confirm the personal love of God for every soul, and to encourage souls on their own journey towards the divine light.

From this point of view, souls do not pass at death to eternal Hell, to the presence of God in Heaven, or to Purgatory, where they are cleansed and purified until they pass to Heaven. They enter the dream-worlds of death, a whole continuum of worlds, from worlds of apparently endless suffering to worlds of apparently timeless bliss. They enter the world which best expresses their spiritual state at death, and they then progress through these worlds, or remain in them, in accordance with their own continuing spiritual development.[13]

It would not be correct to think of existence in these worlds as disembodied, but one may think of the bodies that exist there as dream-bodies, to a certain extent insubstantial and subject to imperfections of various kinds. Such bodies exist to express states of spirit, and they carry all the imperfections and limitations of the souls whose bodies they are. After his death, Jesus appeared in the intermediate realms, to confirm and manifest the divine presence, and to mediate divine grace in a particular way to all the dead.

According to the Gospels, Jesus returned from the worlds of the dead after three days, and appeared to many disciples. Then he 'ascended to the right hand of God'. That is, his human reality was united immediately with the being of God, becoming for ever a clear and evident manifestation of the divine glory in human form. It may well be, though we do not know, that there are many, perhaps infinitely many, other manifestations of a divine glory that is, after all, itself infinite. But Jesus will, according to Christian belief, always remain a true manifestation of God in human form, and will always be the paradigm, the pattern, of the mediation of divine grace to all humanity. He takes his place 'above the heavens',[14]

[12] Cf. William Temple, *Readings in St. John's Gospel* (London: Macmillan, 1963), 218.

[13] Cf. John Hick, *Death and Eternal Life* (London: Macmillan, 1976).

[14] Heb. 7: 26.

above even the highest paradisal world, as the express image of the invisible God.

THE NEW TESTAMENT APOCALYPSE

The disciples of Jesus believed from the first that the Lord would return from his place in heaven to establish the Messianic kingdom in its fullness. The particular forms which this belief took were no doubt almost as varied as the forms of Messianic expectation in Jewish tradition. Early records of some traditions of interpretation can be found in the New Testament, especially in the so-called apocalypses of the synoptic Gospels.[15] At least some disciples thought that Jesus would return to the earth in the near future, within their lifetimes.[16] They thought that they and the dead would meet Christ 'in the air', and that the wicked would be destroyed. They looked for the return of the Lord, coming 'like a thief in the night', and they prayed for the new age to dawn soon, when the dead would rise to judgement, evil would be eradicated from creation in a great and final battle, and the faithful would enter eternal life.

The imagery used in expressing these beliefs is that of the Jewish apocalyptic literature of the time, and we have seen how many varied interpretations of that imagery there are. No reflective Christian can, or ever could, take this imagery literally, as though it gave a literal consecutive narrative of specific future events. It is a great theological error to try to do so. The hermeneutical problem is therefore to decide which images are to be determinative for one's own thinking about these matters.

The basic Messianic belief is that the Christ is to return and transform the material world into its spiritual form, and this ultimate transformation begins, at least in part, in the lives of his disciples. The New Testament writers adapt various strands of the Apocalyptic genre to express this belief. Thus the prediction of the 'Messianic woes', of war, earthquake, and famine, builds on the prophecies of Isaiah,[17] which refer to the defeat of the tyranny of Egypt and a future political and religious ascendancy for Israel. The Lord will 'smite and heal' the Egyptians,[18] and they will turn to the Lord, offering sacrifices in his name. So God's judgement on

---

[15] Matt. 24; Mark 13; Luke 21.
[16] Cf. 1 Thess. 4: 16–17.
[17] Cf. Isa. 19: 2, developed in Matt. 24: 7.
[18] Isa. 19: 22.

the political powers of the earth is a preliminary to their healing, and to a new age of justice and peace.

Judgement is a major theme of apocalyptic writing, which takes up and even intensifies themes in Ezekiel and Daniel.[19] 'The end' is not the end of the world, but the end of Israel's age of apostasy and idolatry, and the end will be bloodshed and disaster for the oppressive nations of the earth. But judgement is never the final word. On the contrary, it always functions as a warning, and is never without hope for those who turn in penitence to God. On the Day of the Lord 'the sun will be dark at its rising and the moon will not shed its light'.[20] Yet this prophecy of utter doom is followed by the assurance that 'the Lord will have compassion on Jacob and will again choose Israel . . . and aliens will join them and will cleave to the house of Jacob'.[21] Again, the emphasis is not on the ending of the whole universe, though that is what it literally says ('the host of heaven shall rot away and the skies roll up like a scroll').[22] The emphasis is on the ending of a corrupt age and the beginning of a new age, when 'the ransomed of the Lord shall return and come to Zion with singing'.[23]

The central figure in Christian apocalyptic is the 'Son of Man', who comes 'with the clouds of heaven' to have 'an everlasting dominion'.[24] His rule follows that of the beasts who have dominated world history, and it brings an age in which 'the saints of the Most High' will rule in justice. At that time, a 'great trumpet will be blown',[25] and all the scattered people of the tribes of Israel will be gathered from the 'four winds'[26]—'if your outcasts are in the uttermost parts of heaven, from there the Lord your God will gather you'.[27] God will 'circumcise their hearts', so that they will love the Lord their God with all their hearts.

It is important, if one is not to fall into a naïve literalism, to read the apocalypse in the context of prophetic thought, and to trace its imagery back to the primal Jewish concern with judgement on 'the nations', the restoration of Israel, and the eventual fulfilment of the divine purpose for humanity. In the Christian case, as has been noted, the Messianic idea was already changed so that it was no longer concerned with establishing a national state of Israel. It is therefore to be expected that the 'coming of the Son of Man' would

---

[19] Ezek. 7: 2, 'An end has come upon the four corners of the land.'
[20] Isa. 13: 10.   [21] Isa. 14: 1.   [22] Isa. 34: 4.   [23] Isa. 35: 10.
[24] Dan. 7: 13, 14.   [25] Isa. 27: 13.   [26] Zech. 2: 6.   [27] Deut. 30: 4.

not be identified with the restoration of Israel as a state. It is concerned with judgement on evil, with a call to repentance, with the promise of a new age and a new covenant with God, and with the eventual fulfilment of God's purpose. But how exactly these things are to be understood is left to the sensitivity and understanding of the hearer.[28]

In general, one may perhaps say that the genre of New Testament apocalyptic has three main levels of interpretation. First, there is a historical dimension, usually pointing to some imminent social catastrophe, but holding out hope for the future. In the New Testament case, the catastrophe was the collapse of the civilization of the ancient world, and an ensuing age of barbarism and anarchy. The military power of the Roman Empire would collapse, Jerusalem, the Temple and the old covenant would be destroyed, and the state of Israel would cease to exist. The hope was the existence of a community of the new covenant, the church of the new age, as a growing company of those gathered to God through Christ (gathered by angels from the corners of the earth to the presence of the Son of Man, clothed with the *shekinah* of God), and enduring to the birth of a new era.

There is also a cosmic dimension which uses temporal symbols to look beyond historical time altogether. In this respect, the whole universe is so transfigured that evil and suffering are eliminated, and a new creation comes into being, with Christ as its centre. Such transfiguration cannot occur until the last freely choosing human being has been born, and until the present laws of nature, which entail suffering to some degree, are changed. In other words, one is looking beyond historical time altogether, to a different realm of being. What is being said is that Christ, the cosmic Lord, rules in a Kingdom beyond suffering and self-regard, and all who are faithful to him will find their lives fulfilled by their completed and conscious union with him.

The third dimension is the existential, for which the symbols are internalized, and one views each moment as one of judgement on evil and election to eternal life in Christ. The judgement is not on other people sometime in the near future. It is on oneself, now. The rapture and union with Christ is not in historical time at all. It is a process begun now, as Christ comes at each moment in judgement

---

[28] A good discussion of apocalyptic imagery can be found in: G. B. Caird, *The Language and Imagery of the Bible* (London: Duckworth, 1980), esp. ch. 14.

but also, and primarily, in forgiving love. But its completion is beyond history, and on a different plane of spiritual existence.

Apocalyptic imagery further exemplifies three noteworthy characteristics—a foreshortening of time, a cosmic amplification of events, and a physical objectification of spiritual realities. Thus the ultimate goal of the universe is portrayed as breaking into present reality, as already 'at hand'. It is thereby transformed from a vague hope for some far future generation into an immediate goal which calls for action and response in the present. Events in the societies and history of the one small planet Earth are given cosmic significance, so that even the sun and the stars become signs of human destiny. Historical events take on eternal significance, and are related to the purposes of God for the universe itself. The battle of good and evil which takes place in human hearts and lives is presented as a war between spirit powers, between Satan and Michael the archangel. The struggle to overcome egoism and desire and establish a community of justice and peace, is represented by the struggle of the mythic powers of darkness and light, to bring about the final triumph of goodness over chaos, ignorance, and selfish desire.

This is the genre used by some of the letters to young churches that have been included in the New Testament, such as the letters to the Thessalonians, which speak of a short time of increasing conflict between good and evil, culminating in the rule of Antichrist, a malign militaristic power. Then the Temple in Jerusalem will be desecrated and destroyed, and the sky will be emptied of the light of stars, sun, and moon, bringing the age to an end. Then the 'Son of Man' will return with all the dead. The faithful will meet him in the clouds, and the age of injustice will come to an end. In this account, the different dimensions of apocalyptic are woven together and presented in a highly symbolic form, with many layers of possible meaning, some of which remain unknown to us. To interpret them for a very different age requires both poetic sensibility and a sensitivity to the enduring spiritual meaning which may be almost hidden by the culturally limited world-view of the time.

If Jesus is truly human, with all the limitations of knowledge that implies, one will not be surprised if he did not give clear, precise, and infallible teaching about the future. His knowledge is limited to that of human personality, though a personality which is deeply united with God. Such a personality, looking to the future, will see both bad and good possibilities. It is quite possible that he would be able to foresee the rejection of God's purpose for Israel, culminating in his own death. He might also see the promise of God's Spirit, manifest in his own life. He may have felt and proclaimed the beginning of the rule of God in his own person. He could have foreseen the rejection of that rule, and the impossibility of any sort of political liberation for Israel. He could have envisaged the extension of God's promise to the whole earth, and founded a 'new Israel', probably composed of a 'remnant' chosen from the Jewish people, with the twelve as its rulers, to proclaim that promise.

It would be possible for a great saint and prophet to come to such beliefs, to foresee a great cataclysm coming on Israel, together with the flowering of the divine promise in the founding of a spiritual kingdom, and a new and dynamic outpouring of the Spirit. This is the end of the age of the old covenant, and the beginning of a new, more inward covenant. These are the historical and spiritual realities of which apocalyptic images speak, in many obscure and fantastic forms. It would not be surprising if, in their main outlines, they go back to the teachings of Jesus himself. It seems clear, however, that they were elaborated by various early groups of disciples, and it is these varied, composite, and elaborated forms that we possess in the New Testament.

THE TIME OF THE PAROUSIA

Belief in an imminent return of Jesus and the closure of the age are quite natural, but heavily culture-bound, beliefs. They find a parallel in the many millenial movements which spring up when people despair of social and political reform, and look for a destruction of the powers of brutality and oppression which seem to govern the world, and the dawn of a new age of spiritual enlightenment. The early Christians were faced with sporadic persecution from the militarist empire of Rome, with ejection from the synagogues, and with a world in which the only alternative to military dictatorship seemed to be barbarian anarchy. Jesus was believed to have predicted the destruction of the Jerusalem Temple, and thus, apparently, the end of the age of the covenant with Israel, as a nation state. He had been raised from death, and through him the Spirit had been poured out on the apostles. It looked as though the general resurrection of the dead was already dawning. It was natural for early Christians to hope for an imminent end to the brutal world order, and the raising of all the dead to usher in the Messianic kingdom.

At the same time, there are many strands of early Christian thought that present a different picture. Paul found that his vision of a glorified Jesus and his preaching of the dying and rising Christ appealed to Gentiles more than to Jews. He came to see the gospel as one of freedom from the rules of Torah, and salvation by trust in God and new life in the Spirit. So his concern was not just to call a remnant of Israel to repentance, but to preach the gospel to Gentiles throughout the whole world. Whereas in his first letter to the Thessalonians, he speaks of Christ returning very soon, in the letter to the Romans he expresses the view that 'a hardening has come upon part of Israel, until the full number of the Gentiles come in'.[29] A new vision of the church's mission to the whole inhabited world clearly modifies any belief in an imminent end of the world.

Similarly, the visions of Peter, recorded in Acts 10 and 11, brought him to believe that the gospel was to be preached to the whole Gentile world. In Acts 15, the first Council of the church recommended the abolition of part of Torah for Christians, and this again shows a growing awareness that the church has a missionary task, which can only be completed if the return of Christ is delayed. It is only now, two thousand years later, that one might plausibly claim that the missionary task of preaching 'to the ends of the earth'[30] has been accomplished. And even now it is not plausible to think either that the gospel has been presented in a positive and challenging way to all people, or that we have properly understood what is implicit in the call for justice and mercy which the gospel contains. It took over a thousand years for the church to condemn slavery, and it has not yet unequivocally managed to see what is involved in the equality of men and women in Christ. One may well think that there is much for it yet to learn and to do, before the gospel has properly been preached to all.

Another important and related strand of thought in the New Testament is the teaching of John and Paul about the cosmic Christ, and the building up of the body of Christ in the physical universe. This might be called the 'mystical theology' of the New Testament, for it speaks of the uniting of the material to the spiri-

---

[29] Rom. 11: 25.   [30] Acts 1: 8.

tual, in a way which enables the material to become the true manifestation and mediation (the 'image') of the spiritual. The letter to
the Colossians speaks of Christ as the 'first-born of all creation; for
in him all things were created, in heaven and on earth . . . in him all
things hold together'.[31] Here Christ is seen as vastly greater than
the human Jesus. Christ is the wisdom and archetype of the whole
universe. That universe exists in him, held together 'by his word of
power'.[32] Moreover, the 'mystery of the divine will' which was
revealed in Jesus, is that God will, in the fullness of time, 'unite all
things in him, things in heaven and things on earth'.[33]

This gives a cosmic perspective very different from that of a
human Messiah returning to save a tiny number of Christians from
a doomed pagan world. It is the perspective of a universe patterned
on Christ, existing in Christ, and being united in Christ, to fulfil the
divine purpose for the whole universe. 'The creation itself will be
set free from its bondage to decay and obtain the glorious liberty of
the sons of God.'[34] Though Paul had not thought of the theory of
evolution, he sketches a picture which comes vividly to life in an
evolutionary perspective. The whole material universe is striving to
realize a freedom from decay, a unity and beauty, which is to be
brought about by the actualization of the Christ-life in the material
structures of being, by 'the manifestation of the sons of God',
beings which bear Christ within themselves. As, in human beings,
the universe consciously realizes its calling to be formed in the
image of Christ, so the Spirit of Christ begins to form that image,
and bring the physical realm itself to a share in eternal glory.

In such a perspective, the contracted time of apocalyptic writing,
which symbolizes vast cosmic processes by speaking of particular
catastrophic events around Jerusalem, is once again expanded to
embrace the whole universe ('everything in heaven and earth').
God's purpose for the earth is that evil will be destroyed, Christ, the
cosmic archetype, exemplar, and pleroma of all creation, will be
manifest on earth, and the natural order itself will be changed and
renewed. This purpose has cosmic implications, for it will play an
important, though to us unimaginable, part in the renewal of the
whole cosmos: '[The heavens] will perish . . . like a mantle thou wilt
roll them up, and they will be changed.'[35] How these things will
happen, we do not know. But this perspective preserves a central

---

[31] Col. 1: 15–20.   [32] Heb. 1: 2.   [33] Eph. 1: 10.
[34] Rom. 8: 21.   [35] Heb. 1: 11.

Jewish belief that God has a purpose for this material creation, and that the renewal of the cosmos is put into the hands of creatures, as a responsibility that they bear under God.

We can now see that the expectation of some early Christians that the world would end at any moment embodied a myopia which saw only a few Mediterranean peoples as the whole human world, and which saw only the planet Earth as the whole universe. Such myopia is understandable, in a culture in which it was generally thought that the whole universe had been created only four thousand years ago, with humanity as its sole centre, and would not change radically in the future. But it is not excusable for a culture such as that of the modern world, which believes that the evolution of life extends over millions of years, and sees Earth as only one planet out of billions (though we have no idea if other life-forms exist in this universe).

It appears that Jesus would not say when the final purpose of God was to be accomplished: 'Of that day or that hour no one knows.'[36] Yet he called the disciples to watch and keep awake, lest they were caught unprepared. The existential import of this teaching is that God is always at hand, in judgement and in glory. Each moment is a confrontation with a God whose command and whose promise is inexorable and immediate. Saying that Jesus sits at God's right hand is a metaphor which refers to the closest form of union between Jesus and God. So saying that 'the Lord is at hand' is a metaphor which refers to the immediate relation of every moment to its future in God, the God who has been revealed in Christ Jesus. The Messianic kingdom will come, and we must act as if it dawns in each moment, because each moment in fact determines our eternal relation to it. But the time and the exact manner of its coming is in the hands of God, who works out the divine purpose through the activity of the Spirit in the lives of creatures, and who wills the whole universe to be united in Christ.

As a warning against an over-literal expectation of an imminent end of the world, the second letter of Peter reminds its readers that a thousand human years is as one day with God.[37] It is a sad and futile activity to try to work out the timetable of redemption. What must be held together are the beliefs that God will realize his purpose for the fulfilment of all creation, and that our personal relation

---

[36] Mark 13: 32.   [37] 2 Pet. 3: 8.

to that fulfilment depends upon our response to our immediate future as the making-present of God in the form of Christ and the power of the Spirit. All the imagery of apocalypse and of mystical theology exists in order to provide an imaginative framework which can preserve and give life and power to those beliefs. If both traditions, each itself richly diverse, are held together, the deepest insights of early Christian teaching can be retrieved and elucidated in the very different context of the modern scientific world-view.

One major type of interpretation of Christian apocalyptic thought was, and still is, to see the Messiah as establishing a society of peace and justice in the future of the earth. When these beliefs are translated into the different context of scientific belief in an evolutionary universe, one natural way to interpret them is to see them as embodying a hope for human progress towards the perfectly just society on earth, or perhaps somewhere in space. On such a view, Jesus, as Messiah, is the exemplar of the just life, and inaugurates the church as a community of the Spirit, whose task it is to bring the world to eventual renewal in justice. The church is the Israel of the new covenant, and its task is to be the priestly servant of the world, leading it to the eventual establishment of the Messianic kingdom. At that time, Christ will return, as the *parousia*, the being-present, of the cosmic archetype and pleroma of all creation. Evil and conflict will be eliminated, and a new form of human being, no longer subject to suffering and individualistic selfishness, will be realized.

The Messianic expectations of Christianity are not containable within the purely political interpretation of some Jewish hopes that the Messiah is to establish the nation of Israel as the spiritual teacher of the world. Christians accepted that Jesus had instituted a new Israel, which was not a political state (though its relations with the old Israel were the subject of agonizing reflection, of the sort expressed in the letter to the Romans). Jesus had taught that his kingdom was not of this world.[38] He now lived a transfigured life in the presence of God, and his return would be to judge the whole world. This could not be merely a change of political leadership. It had to be the ending of world history in its present form, and the transformation of the universe into a new and spiritualized nature. If this is the future of the earth, it is a future in which it will be quite radically transformed.

[38] John 18: 36.

The Christian expectation has usually been that God will act decisively to transform the universe. A cosmic interpretation is forced on Messianic imagery, and thus from the very beginning it implicitly contained a teaching which compels a revision of early hopes for an imminent end of the universe—hopes which would in fact have cut short the realization of much of the divine purpose for human history. The writers of the New Testament letters did not conceive of these purposes, and it is hard to see how they could possibly have dreamed how much human history would change.

Yet one need not think of the eschatalogical act of God as a discontinuous interruption of the course of history. Just as one might see creation as a long and continuing process of the emergence of new forms of being, so one might see the consummation of all things as spread out over a long process of continuous evolutionary emergence. Disease and warfare might be gradually eliminated, and a new sort of human, or suprahuman nature might evolve, over a very long period of time. Eventually, the whole material universe, or at least the part of it bearing human consciousness, might so develop that its material basis is transfused into a different form of conscious or spiritual being. The 'coming of the Christ in glory' will be the full manifestation of all things united in Christ and transfigured by the beauty of the divine being, so as to enter into a new form of life in God, free of the forces of conflict and decay which are essential to material existence. In this perspective, the destiny of the whole material universe is to generate from itself a new and distinctive form of spiritual existence, and its purpose will be realized only when it does so.

COSMIC OPTIMISM: TEILHARD DE CHARDIN

The best-known advocate of this type of Messianic interpretation is Teilhard de Chardin, who sees life on earth in terms of an emergence of consciousness from the material order, moving towards the total spiritualization, or Christification, of matter itself. Humanity is, for him, 'the axis and leading shoot of evolution'.[39] It is the place, on this planet, where hominization—the progressive spiritualization of all the forces contained in the animal world—begins. With humans, a noosphere, or 'thinking layer', is added to

---

[39] Pierre Teilhard de Chardin, *The Phenomenon of Man*, trans. Bernard Wall (New York: Harper, 1959), 36.

the biosphere, and a new stage of evolution begins, in which the earth 'finds its soul'.[40]

Teilhard finds the thought that evolution has stopped with *homo sapiens* unduly pessimistic. It would, he thinks, make 'thought, the fruit of millions of years of effort, stifled, still-born in a self-abortive and absurd universe'.[41] So he tries to extrapolate from the evolutionary past the direction in which the process seems to be heading, if it is indeed a meaningful, God-directed process. The process is, he thinks, one of the emergence of fuller consciousness, fuller unity and fuller intentional control of being. One might then begin to think of a 'super-soul above our souls'.[42] 'Evolution is an ascent towards consciousness . . . therefore it should culminate forwards in some sort of supreme consciousness.'[43] This he calls the Omega Point, when all consciousnesses will be united in one supreme hyperconsciousness. This will not be a loss of individual consciousness. He speaks of 'Each particular consciousness becoming still more itself . . . the closer it gets to [other consciousnesses] in Omega.'[44]

It can sound as though Teilhard is thinking of the merging of all individuality into one superconsciousness, but he is at pains to deny that. He denies that the Omega Point can only come into existence at an extremely distant future. It sounds like that, when he seems to suggest that 'some Soul of souls should be developing at the summit of the world'.[45] But he insists that the whole process of evolution must be initiated and maintained by Omega, which accordingly must be thought of as 'supremely present'. It must be 'a distinct Centre radiating at the core of a system of centres', the core of a system of 'harmonized complexity'.[46]

Omega cannot be dependent on the chance outcomes of impersonal physical laws, for it must also be conceived as the originator and sustainer of those laws. It must be transcendent of evolutionary space and time, not something that comes into existence at the last stages of time. Teilhard says, 'Autonomy, actuality, irreversibility, and thus finally transcendence are the four attributes of Omega.'[47] The Omega Point is thus the ascent of souls to integral union with an eternally existing Omega, not the emergent creating of Omega itself.

In this process, Omega is changed, in so far as it comes to include in itself the whole emergent and convergent history of the universe.

---

[40] Ibid. 182.   [41] Ibid. 233.   [42] Ibid.   [43] Ibid. 258.
[44] Ibid. 262.   [45] Ibid. 268.   [46] Ibid. 269, 262.   [47] Ibid. 271.

It may seem that this evolutionist vision still lacks one vital characteristic of traditional belief about the end of all things. Is it true that only those who are alive at the time of that final self-transcending point of evolution will share its glory? What has happened to the countless millions of the dead, who have never seen that moment of consummation? What about the resurrection of the dead?

Teilhard's suggestion is that at the Omega Point, matter and time are decisively transcended. Many forms of consciousness, during the long evolutionary process, have not just passed into nonexistence, but into the image-worlds of death, where they exist, until they too are brought into the final transfiguration of the material universe. At the end of the world, the transfigured order will include within itself all the souls of persons long dead, since the universe has been ' a collector and conservator . . . of persons'.[48] The ultimate evolution of humanity, then, is to transcend space-time. It will create a collective and spiritual form of life, having come to understand and control all the forces of its material nature and origin, and having entered into conscious relation with 'a supremely attractive centre which has personality'.[49] In that form of life, all the souls the universe has generated will be brought to fulfilment—or perhaps to that 'eternal destruction from the face of God',[50] which is the ultimate destruction and death of all that binds itself irrevocably to the perishing order of the material.

Teilhard speaks of the end of the world as 'the wholesale internal introversion upon itself of the noosphere',[51] and of 'detaching the mind, fulfilled at last, from its material matrix'. He is clearly not speaking of a just society in a world which remains materially very much as it is now. He is thinking of an immense duration of time— millions of years—into the human future, and of a transformation of the material conditions of existence through scientific understanding. Disease and hunger will be conquered by science. Human nature will be perfected by genetic control, replacing 'the crude forces of natural selection'.[52] There is undoubtedly an ultimate cosmic optimism in Teilhard, which is founded on his belief that the purposes of God cannot ultimately fail: 'However improbable it might seem, [humanity] must reach the goal.'[53]

[48] Pierre Teilhard de Chardin, *The Phenomenon of Man*, trans. Bernard Wall (New York: Harper, 1959), 272.

[49] Ibid. 284.   [50] I Thess. I: 9.   [51] Chardin, *Phenomenon of Man*, 288.

[52] Ibid. 282.   [53] Ibid. 276.

Teilhard seems to be committed to the thought of inevitable progress in evolution, and of an immensely long time-scale in which this progress can be made. He does not, however, think of the progress as culminating simply in a perfect society on earth, or as giving birth to a cosmic supermind, which would be God. On the contrary, he thinks of it as prompted by an ever-existing God, as always in relation to God, and as culminating in a complex and harmonious society of selves, centred on God. This will not be during historical time, but at the end of historical time, and so it will be the ending of time as we experience it.

Teilhard's evolutionary vision of the Christification of the cosmos has been criticized as unduly optimistic, in view of such events as the Holocaust, and the seemingly ineradicable evil in human lives. But the evolutionary perspective is a very long one, and the present stage of human evolution must be regarded as only just beginning. If we can see the million years of human existence as just the first fraction of a future which stretches ahead for thousands of millions of years, it may seem unduly pessimistic to suppose that human nature cannot change or improve in any way in all that time.

In any case, Teilhard does allow for another possibility. 'Evil', he says, 'may go on growing alongside good.'[54] Alongside the unifying and harmonizing tendencies of the noosphere, there may also be a growth of discordant energy, seeking to impose its will by brute force, and refusing to centre life on God-Omega. In that case, he suggests, there will be the sort of final paroxysm envisaged in the New Testament apocalyptic imagery of a final battle with Gog and Magog.

There may be a part of the noosphere which decides to 'cross the threshold' into Omega, leaving behind a part which remains locked into its own dying materiality. When the materially exhausted planet dies, all will die with it, except those in the noosphere who are liberated in 'an ecstasy transcending the dimensions and the framework of the visible universe'.[55] The dead who have, across the immensities of space and time, centred themselves in Omega, will rise into a transfigured world beyond historical time. Those, if there are any, who have refused transfiguration to the last, will rise to find themselves finally locked into the death of the planet, in the searing fire of the expanding sun, the fire of ultimate destruction, when 'the

---

[54] Ibid. 288.   [55] Ibid. 289.

elements will be dissolved with fire, and the earth and the works that are upon it will be burned up'.[56]

Teilhard is a very long way from a simple political Utopianism, which sees everything on earth getting better and better until the perfect society comes into being. His form of cosmic optimism allows for terrible conflicts of good and evil, but insists that the good will be conserved for eternity, while the evil is destined for destruction by fire. The material universe itself will be transfigured into a sacramental form of being, in which it manifests community, individuality, and the open manifestation of the glory of God. All the souls which it has produced in its long history, which have not finally and in full awareness refused to respond to the attracting power of the divine love, will be gathered into the immortal society which centres on God-Omega. But as for the stuff of matter itself, once it has become the empty husk from which the fruit of immortality has been drawn by the light of God, it will cease to be. The laws of thermodynamics will finally drain it of all life, and it will pass away, its purpose completed, its long history of emergence, convergence, and self-transcendence at an end.

COSMIC PESSIMISM: JURGEN MOLTMANN

Teilhard achieved a remarkable and visionary synthesis of New Testament imagery about the coming Day of the Lord, and an evolutionary view of the universe. The main difficulty which both scientists and theologians have felt about it is precisely that it seems, like all futurology, to more resemble poetic vision than either a sober scientific estimate or a highly probable conclusion from the biblical sources. There are scientists who are prepared to speculate along evolutionary lines, and who do see cosmic history as an inevitable progress towards spiritual realization. John Barrow and Frank Tipler are among the best-known.[57] But their views on these matters are widely regarded as on the fringes of scientific respectability or credibility. The biblical sources, too, are much more ambiguous about the possibility of universal progress towards perfection than is Teilhard. So many theologians feel that one might rather expect a more sudden, even cataclysmic, end to the

---

[56] 2 Pet. 3: 10.

[57] Cf. John Barrow and Frank Tipler, *The Anthropic Cosmological Principle* (Oxford: Clarendon, 1986), ch. 10.

history of the earth. This would be followed, on a Christian view, by the total recreation of the earth, probably in some other physical order, since it will be free of suffering, conflict, and decay, and thus its physical laws must be quite different from the laws which govern this spatio-temporal universe.

In this vein, Jurgen Moltmann objects that Teilhard overlooks the ambiguity of the process of evolution itself, which works on the principle of the survival of the fittest, and thus casts aside the weak and helpless in its 'progress' towards greater intelligence and control of the environment.[58] Evolution, Moltmann claims, has no redemptive efficacy, and cannot promise any protection for the weak and suffering, or anything like a resurrection of nature or of the dead. Moltmann also complains that Teilhard 'brushed aside the possibility that humanity could ever suffer a nuclear catastrophe',[59] and did not see that time is running out for life on earth, because of the ecological disasters which progress is preparing. Moreover, the immense time-scale of millions of years which Teilhard proposes would, it seems to Moltmann, leave the historical Jesus far behind in early human history, eventually to be completely forgotten and replaced by some form of 'cosmic gnosticism'.[60]

These objections, though fairly made, are of rather unequal weight. It is not entirely plausible for a theologian to regard evolution purely in terms of blind mechanisms of natural selection, if the whole process has been intentionally created by God. The emergence of molecular complexity, replicatory ability, the formation of central nervous systems, and consequently of consciousness, are highly improbable on principles of natural selection alone.[61] It is reasonable for a theist to suppose that God, who plans for the existence of conscious life in the universe, will not leave evolution wholly to chance, but will guide the process in a non-invasive way which leaves the relative autonomy of emergent creatures unimpaired. If God guides the processes of evolution, one must suppose that its goals will be achieved. Evolution is not out of divine control, and it is not a neutral or malign process. It is under the guidance of divine providence, and thus it must have redemptive

---

[58] Jurgen Moltmann, *The Way of Jesus Christ*, trans. Margaret Kohl (London: SCM, 1990), 294.

[59] Ibid. 295.   [60] Ibid. 296.

[61] Cf. K. Ward, *God, Chance and Necessity* (Oxford: Oneworld, 1996), ch. 4.

efficacy, in the sense that it is intended to, and will, make possible redemption for all conscious beings. The processes of evolution by themselves will not effect the resurrection of the dead or the spiritual transfiguration of the universe. But Teilhard does not suppose that they will. He only hypothesises that the material universe will evolve to a stage at which it will become so open to the guiding action of God that its renewal will be a divine act continuous with the processes which have preceded it.

It is the consideration that the world is under divine providence which also gave Teilhard the confidence to say that God would not allow the earth to be destroyed, whether by nuclear holocaust or by some other ecological disaster. However, it must be conceded that we do not know what the goals of God for creation really are, or what limits God has placed on the divine providential rule. Before the theory of evolution was ever thought of, people believed that God had a purpose in creation. The divine purpose was to generate a community of creatively loving persons. Human evil had corrupted that purpose, and so God consigned the world to its own self-destruction, ensuring only that those who showed penitence and faith would be saved from the world, for life in a new creation.

For such a picture, the ending of the world in fire will not be a final frustration of the divine purpose, which will have been fulfilled by the generation of souls destined for the Messianic kingdom. Humans might not be the growing-point of a long process of evolution to come. On the contrary, biologists seem agreed that the physical evolution of humanity has stopped, and it may be that the purpose of the earth has already been achieved by the generation of souls capable of relation with God. Whether this planet ends in some humanly formed disaster, or in immolation by the sun, it is, it may be thought, humans who will be recreated in the image of Christ, and not some superhuman form of life, far ahead in the cosmic future, of which we can imagine little or nothing.

This is a more cataclysmic view of the end of human existence. If one is not to allow for a gradual spiritualization (or Christification) of matter itself, it is certain that human existence will come to an end. Other space-times may come to be, and may already exist in abundance, for all we know. But this one will end, and its end will either be a long-drawn out and gradual exhausting of all available resources of energy, a slow and enervating dying, or a more sudden catastrophe on earth, perhaps caused by human evil or stupidity.

Moltmann seems committed to the latter possibility, because of his argument that Christ would be forgotten over a very long time-scale. That argument does not seem very strong. One of the most evident developments in modern culture is the ability to retrieve the past and to record information with much greater reliability. Electronic resources already enable us to know more about ancient history than almost any previous generation, and current events can now be recorded for posterity in ways previously undreamed of. If progress continues, it is to be expected that the data of the past will become more, not less, accessible over time.

Of course, over millions of years the sheer amount of material may seem daunting. A great deal of selectivity will be needed. Yet it will be possible to arrange materials in patterns which illuminate their significance, and that significance will become greater rather than less for events that prove to be turning-points which change the whole course of history. Even millions of years in the future, the name of Isaac Newton will not be forgotten, as the discoverer of the basic laws of mechanics. Much less will Jesus of Nazareth, the originator of a world-wide church and of a spiritual movement that changed the world, be forgotten.

In addition, Jesus never has been a merely historical figure for the church. He is a figure around whom has developed a particular human understanding, or range of understandings, of the cosmic archetypal Christ. Whatever happens to religion in the future, it is very likely that the Christian Church will continue to exist, however much modified in form. It will therefore continue to relate to God through the image of the cosmic Christ, an image which originated with the life, death, and resurrection of Jesus of Nazareth, and which always seeks to reproduce the pattern of reconciling love which was seen to be manifested in that life.

We may be sure, therefore, that the historical Jesus will be remembered to the end of human history, as the matrix (the historical origin and pattern) of the church's relationship to and life in God through the cosmic Wisdom, the Christ. Moreover, the final disclosure or *parousia* of that Wisdom will always lie ahead, in the future consummation of all things. What Moltmann overlooks, in his fear that Jesus may be forgotten under the sheer weight of years, is that the church will always continue to be the body of Christ. It will exist in Christ and move towards greater fullness of life in Christ. It is true that the cosmic dimensions of Christ are so vast that we can scarcely comprehend them. It is true that our individual conceptions of the historical Jesus may be quite a long way from the truth in many respects. Yet the living and creative Spirit which forms the life of the cosmic Christ within humanity will never become divorced from its historical manifestation in the life of Jesus of Nazareth. The story of that life, and therefore the historical life which underlies it, will always be the founding narrative which outlines an always contemporary spiritual way of relation to God, understood as redemptive and unitive love, and lived in the power of the universal and creative Spirit of love.

Nevertheless, it has to be conceded that earth's history may end in catastrophe. If so, it is not a catastrophe anyone should pray for. When early Christians prayed that the Lord should come soon, they were praying for divine deliverance from evil. They were not praying that the earth should be destroyed by human evil. They were ecstatically aware that the resurrection life had begun in them, so that the kingdom was already present embryonically within them. It was natural for them to think that its full birth could not be long delayed. They could not foresee the possibilities for progress in culture and technology that lay ahead. They could not see (we Christians still cannot properly see) the greater task of the church—to them, a small and marginal sect on the borders of the Roman Empire—to make the material world the sacrament of spirit. They could not see the vast cosmic implications of their belief that all things in heaven and earth were to be united in the life of Christ. We can see these things, and so realize the real tragedy of a sudden and violent end to human history. But we can also see the possibility of tragedy, in a world where every advance in technology seems to be also an advance in the capacity to destroy the earth.

Christian prayer for the contemporary world should perhaps be that the world should not end soon, but should realize the will of God 'on earth as in heaven'.[62] But it should also be that, whenever the world ends, the perfected Messianic kingdom should make present the pleroma of the cosmic Wisdom, in the Spirit-filled community of a transfigured earth, which can fully manifest the glory of the creator God. If the end of history is soon, the Christian belief is

---

[62] Matt. 6: 10.

that even that tragedy is not unredeemable. The world of humanity will not simply cease to be. Christ will 'come again', in the form
of his cosmic glory, and in a transfigured world, to usher in the
Messianic kingdom in a new earth. Whether late or soon, the
ultimate hope is for the resurrection of the natural order, and
the participation of all the souls which have ever been created in a
divine and incorruptible life.

14
The Ultimate End of All Things

Karl Rahner does not seem to me to be correct when he says that 'eschatological statements about man, about the immortality of the soul, about the resurrection of the flesh, about an interval, and about the relationship between individual eschatology and universal, collective eschatology . . . cannot be synthesized into a neat conceptual model'.[1] The model of souls as taking image-embodiments in the afterlife, of the cosmos as moving towards the emergence of a unified community of self-aware and self-directing spirits, of the ultimate liberation of that community from the realm of transient and dying matter, and of the creation of an incorruptible resurrection-world in which all responsive souls will share at the end of this historical space-time, seems to me a coherent one. It is plausible, in being a possible extrapolation from an evolutionary view of the cosmos, and in so far as it is based on a genuine apostolic experience of the resurrection and ascension of Jesus.

The idea of resurrection in a different form of space is fairly clearly presented in the main New Testament passage dealing with resurrection, 1 Corinthians 15: 35–50. Oddly enough, this passage did not play a large part in developing the classical Christian tradition. There, Paul makes it clear that the physical body (*soma psychikon*, lit. the mind-body) dies, and what is resurrected is a spiritual body (*soma pneumatikon*), as different from the physical as wheat is from the seed from which it springs. He explains that it is impossible to envisage what this body will be like. But it will be incorruptible and glorious, and thus not subject to the laws of this space-time. It will be fully part of the 'body of Christ', and thus be a part of God, wholly devoted to the divine will and expressive of the divine action. It will not be in this material realm, but in 'a new creation', which has no need of any sun for light and heat, and in

---

[1] Karl Rahner, *Foundations of Christian Faith*, trans. William Dych (New York: Crossroad, 1995), 443.

which there is no more sea.[2] It will live with other resurrected bodies in a community of creative understanding and love.

One might think of the mind-body as the body that is immersed in this physical world, its attention focused on physical realities and its actions directed to the mastery of nature and the gratification of feelings. The spirit-body will be a body constituted by its intimate relation with God. It's attention is focused solely on the supreme Lord, and it's actions will shape nature to endless forms of beauty and happiness, under the direction of the supreme Lord. It is useless to ask about its form or shape. Nevertheless, it will be perfectly suited to enable the soul to actualize those sorts of capacity which had a largely frustrated expression in the material world.

In one passage, Paul writes that as the physical body decays, the spirit body begins to take shape, even during this mortal life.[3] Eternal life, for Christians, is not just something that begins after death. It is the quality of life seen in relation to the eternal God. So the spirit-body exists even during life. Paul typically speaks of humans as made up of body, soul, and spirit.[4] In this context, one can interpret the soul as the mind oriented solely towards the material world (the 'false ego'), and the spirit as the personal subject interpenetrated and empowered by the Spirit of God (the true self). For those who are 'in Christ', the Kingdom in a sense exists on earth. Yet it does not exist fully, since it still confronts and is not free from the evil and conflict that mark all human affairs. As long as freedom, conflict, and suffering exist, the Kingdom cannot exist in its fullness. This material world, even if it once could, cannot now fully actualize the Kingdom of God.

On this view, the material world comes to have the function of generating souls, subjects of thinking and willing. In a fallen material realm of conflict and suffering, they have responsibility for fighting evil and striving for justice and the flourishing of the natural order, for the coming of the Kingdom of God. However, the Kingdom can only be fully established in the spiritual realm, in which evil is eradicated and all created life shares in the divine life. In that kingdom, the Bible supposes, the natural order will be beautiful and pleasing, animals will take their proper place in the community of sentient beings without conflict,[5] people will live in

---

[2] Rev. 21: 1, 23.   [3] 2 Cor. 4: 16–5: 5.   [4] 1 Thess. 5: 23.
[5] Isa. 11: 6.

creative communion, and God will be present in and through all things.

The Christian view of the self is that it emerges from the material order, but it is destined for a spiritual order. It is born in a 'body of death', oriented to the desires of the senses and the pride of the mind, doomed to frustration and the ultimate failure of its earthly hopes. But it is destined to receive a 'resurrection' body of spirit, and for Christians that is the teaching Christ comes to inaugurate. The apostles saw Jesus after the death of his material body in his spirit-body. They believed that they received the Spirit in a new and powerfully transforming way through loving devotion to him. The Divine Spirit began to shape their spirit-bodies, so that they would become 'like Christ', and would eventually be wholly united to God through and in him. At the end of historical time, they believed, Christ would return and transform the whole material realm into its true spiritual form, wherein all humans, living and dead, could achieve their true destiny.

The Gospel accounts of the resurrection appearances of Jesus corroborate the general Pauline picture. After appearing in the world of the dead, the Gospels claim that Jesus was manifested to the apostles. The resurrection appearances were discontinuous, and occurred over a period of time, symbolized as 'forty days'. It cannot be supposed that the physical body of Jesus left the tomb and lived in hiding somewhere in Jerusalem or Galilee, suddenly appearing to some of his followers from time to time and disappearing as abruptly. Indeed, Matthew's Gospel asserts that a great stone had closed the entrance to Jesus' tomb, which was only rolled away by an angel after the resurrection.[6] Matthew did not think that Jesus had simply got up and walked out of the tomb. His body was not found in the tomb, so one must suppose that it had ceased to exist in the physical realm.

Where, then, did it exist during the time of the earthly appearances? It had in fact so changed in kind that it was no longer subject to the laws of this spatial realm. Not only did it leave a sealed tomb: it appeared in a room whose doors were locked,[7] and it vanished suddenly at will;[8] it manifested in different forms,[9] so that Jesus was unrecognized by two disciples on a seven-mile walk to Emmaus,[10] by Mary Magdalene in the garden,[11] and by a group of

---

[6] Matt. 28: 2.   [7] John 20: 26.   [8] Luke 24: 31.   [9] Mark 16: 12.
[10] Luke 24: 16.   [11] John 20: 14.

disciples on the beach.[12] Matthew records that when the eleven disciples saw him on a mountain in Galilee, some of them doubted that it was Jesus.[13]

These accounts suggest that Jesus did not continuously exist in this spatial world, but in a paradisal world, from whence he appeared in visionary forms to various groups of disciples (but, tellingly, not to unbelievers or to the world at large, as if to prove he was alive beyond doubt). Such visions were, however, substantial.[14] In Luke's account, Jesus assured the disciples that he was not a spirit, and said, 'a spirit has not flesh and bones as you see that I have', and he ate fish.[15] He invited Thomas to place his finger in the marks of the nails in his hands.[16] Luke and John both stress that Jesus' body was solid, recognizable, and capable of ingesting matter.

One might think that one has here two Gospel traditions, one more visionary and the other more material in the understanding of Jesus' resurrection body. Yet there is no insuperable difficulty in supposing that a physical body could materialize and dematerialize in space, under the influence of a higher spiritual power. Visions are normally visual or aural in character. But there is no reason why they could not be also tactual and capable of causal interaction with the environment in which they occur. Such an account of the resurrection appearances as a number of substantial and veridical visions is most coherent with the Gospel testimonies.

It would mean that Jesus' resurrection body existed in Paradise, in a different form from that of any physical body, but was able to manifest on earth at intervals over a period of time. This account also has the advantage of being wholly consistent with Paul's account of the resurrection body as being quite different from the material body, with his insistence that 'flesh and blood cannot inherit the kingdom of God',[17] and with his claim that he had seen the risen Lord in the form, not of a physical body, but of blinding light.[18]

Jesus, after his death, took embodiment in the image-forms of Sheol and Paradise, where the dead work out the consequences of

---

[12] John 21: 4.   [13] Matt. 28: 17.

[14] Augustine distinguishes visions into corporeal (seen with the senses), imaginative, and intellectual. The resurrection appearances seem to be an especially substantial form of corporeal vision. Cf. Augustine, *The Literal Meaning of Genesis* (New York: Newman, 1982), 12. 6. 15.

[15] Luke 24: 39–42.   [16] John 20: 27.   [17] 1 Cor. 15: 50.
[18] Acts 22: 6.

their earthly lives and are prepared for the Final Judgement and creation of the resurrection world. But he also possessed the glorified form of resurrection body which will be the inheritance of all at that Day, and in that sense was 'the first fruits of those who have fallen asleep'.[19] It was that glorified body that appeared in visionary forms to the apostles. The 'ascension' of Christ into heaven[20] is the cessation of those appearances, and the the assumption of the glorified body to the direct presence of God. It is certainly not a matter of a physical body going somewhere far away in this space-time—which confirms the belief that Jesus' resurrection body is not properly part of this space-time, and is therefore not 'physical' in the usual sense.

For the earliest strands of Christian belief to which we have access, Christ's body of glory now exists beyond even the highest paradisal world, enfolded wholly in the divine life, 'having become . . . superior to angels'.[21] Of its activities and emanations we have been given virtually no information. But Christian belief is that at the end of historical time it will become present to all humanity, and inaugurate the resurrection world, in which 'we shall be changed', and 'bear the image of the man of heaven'.[22] That is what is sometimes misleadingly called the Second Coming, properly the *Parousia*, or the universal presence of Christ in glory to all creation.

The New Testament thus suggests that the resurrection world is a form of reality which is in no spatial relation to this world. Many, perhaps all humans will enter it at the ending of the history of this space-time. But some humans, and certainly Jesus, live such an embodied existence now, though in a very different, glorified form of embodiment. The post-death appearances of Jesus were an affirmation that the power of divine love is stronger than death, and a promise that the ultimate destiny of humanity is to be united in the glory of God for ever. Before the fulfilment of that resurrection life, the dead live in different forms and degrees of embodiment, in Sheol or Paradise. They are not spatially related to the earth, but they do have a certain temporal relation to earthly life.

THE LOGICAL COHERENCE OF RESURRECTION

It may be thought that I have spoken rather blithely of the possibility of bodily resurrection. Bernard Williams has argued that with-

---

[19] 1 Cor. 15: 20. [20] Luke 24: 51. [21] Heb. 1: 4.
[22] 1 Cor. 15: 49–52.

out bodily continuity, any alleged resurrection of the same person would in fact only be the creation of a replica person.[23] But a replica is not me, as we can see by imagining that many replicas may be created, even while I am still alive. So, Williams argues, it is not possible for 'me' to survive the death of my body. To use Dennett's analogy, any insertion of a programme for a particular person into a new piece of hardware could, at best, produce a replica, and not a resurrection of the very same person.

The same programme could be inserted simultaneously into many computers, producing many coexisting replicas of me. Personal identity, the argument goes, is, however, transitive—that is, if person A is identical with person B, and B is identical with C, then, necessarily, A is identical with C. Suppose that person A dies and is resurrected as person B. But A is also resurrected, perhaps by mistake, as person C. In this case persons B and C, the two coexisting replicas, cannot be the same person as each other. They are clearly two different bodies, with different, even if entirely similar, personalities and sets of memories, and their life histories from the point of their replication will be different. But B is supposed to be the same person as A, and C is supposed to be the same person as A. On the hypothesis, however, A cannot be identical with both B and C, if B and C are not identical with each other. Williams suggests that, in this case, none of these persons are identical with the others. Therefore A, having once died, can never be resurrected. There could at best be a future copy of A, and that will not be the same thing.

This argument, if it works at all, is much too strong for what Williams wants. He wants it to show that a person can survive only if a particular body or brain is continuously existent in space and time. So no person can survive the death of their body. The continuous existence in space of a particular physical body is, he says, a necessary condition of personal survival. This is a very arbitrary condition. One can easily think of physical bodies splitting into two, three, or more. One can think of bodies ceasing to exist for two seconds, and then reappearing in the same place. One can think of bodies changing completely in character—like Kafka's beetle—and then changing back again after a few seconds. One can think of a body jumping in space from one point to another, thus undermining strict spatial continuity, but otherwise remaining just the same.

[23] Bernard Williams, 'Personal Identity and Individuation', in *Problems of the Self* (Cambridge: Cambridge University Press, 1973).

In all these cases, identity of person, according to Williams, would be destroyed. But it is implausible to suppose that a slight change in the laws of nature—so that atoms 'flicker' in and out of existence, thus causing small gaps of physical continuity—could wholly destroy personal identity.

Suppose a body is wholly destroyed, but in the very same moment, or a micro-second later a different, but qualitatively identical body is created in the same space. That would also destroy personal identity, according to Williams. It seems that, for Williams, one will only survive as the same person if one's body remains strictly continuous in space and time. But one can never be sure that it has not been changed while one sleeps. So one can never be sure whether one is the same person or not, even if one has what seems to be the same body. All one can be sure of is that one has a very similar body. In fact, the smallest physical components of one's body are transient in existence, and the most one can hope for is that there will be overlaps of continuity.

Such a notion of personal identity is unrealistically restricted. We would surely be quite happy to say we have survived, even if there has been a tiny temporal or spatial gap in the continuity of our bodies. The existence of a much bigger temporal gap, between death and resurrection, is not different in principle. It will be disconcerting if many copies of me are resurrected, just as it will be disconcerting if many copies of me are lying in the same bed when I wake up tomorrow morning. Yet I am confident there will be only one of me in bed tomorrow. Theists are equally confident that there will only be one of each person who gets resurrected, since God will ensure that is the case.

I think we should therefore say that an exact replica of me *is* me, as long as I cease to exist and there is only one replica.[24] The situation is more complicated if I continue to exist, or there are many replicas of me. If this happens, we might find it most convenient to say that a person has divided. What originated and developed as one person has split into many. In such an imaginary case, personal identity will not be transitive over time, for the causal routes taken by divided people can be quite different from each other, while being continuous with the originating pre-divided person. Indeed,

---

[24] Thus I agree with Parfit when he says, 'Being destroyed and replicated is about as good as ordinary survival', Derek Parfit, *Reasons and Persons* (Oxford; Clarendon, 1984), 201.

people can divide and merge again, and change their identities by degrees until one might not be sure whether one is—to take a well-known example—Derek Parfit or Greta Garbo.[25] That curious case is one in which a being, Parfit, has its memories and personality slowly changed, until eventually it comes to have half of Parfit's memories, and personality, and half of Garbo's, which have been inserted into it.

That, like excessive replication, would be extremely disconcerting, and a theist would not believe that God would intentionally create and resurrect Parfit-Garbos. Nevertheless, it does seem that continued personhood can be a matter of degree, in principle, just as the continued identity of any physical object is. Is there any reason why a theist should object to that? It may be thought that each person has, or is, just one unique soul, which is a separate entity, either present or absent in its entirety, and that making personhood a matter of degree would undermine that belief. Parfit, it may be said, has such a unique substantial soul, and there must be some point at which it ceases to exist, as his memories and personality are replaced by those of Garbo. The difficulty, it is said, is that it seems arbitrary to pick any such specific point. If so, Parfit suggests, personal identity cannot be determinate, and one cannot speak of the soul as a 'separately existing entity'.[26]

In trying to decide what one might say about this, we may try to imagine what would happen to a subject if its memories were gradually eliminated. That happens to some extent anyway in life, but fortunately it rarely extends to the whole background of attitudes and feelings which have been built up or modified over many years. Even people who lose their memories usually retain a general knowledge of how to read, walk, and speak, and rely on a background of feelings and beliefs, even if of a rather general character. If large stretches of memory were wholly eliminated, the unity and continuity of experience would certainly be disrupted. If memory was wholly eliminated, it does seem that one would start again as a subject of experience, even if one's dispositions to act remained the same.

A person can be injured or destroyed in this way, and in this sense such disorders as senility do destroy the person. The ability of the subject to interpret its experience in the light of its past

[25] Cf. ibid. chs. 10–13, esp. pp. 237–43, for the Greta Garbo example.
[26] Ibid. 216–17.

experiences and responses to them is undermined, and moral responsibility is diminished. Just as people develop in childhood, so they may disintegrate under the impact of disease. The theist will believe that God will restore experience fully to resurrected persons (though there are important complications about painful or disordered experiences), and that is part of the resurrection hope. On this view, the proper response to Williams's puzzle case of a person who is told that they will be tortured, but only after their memories have been wiped out,[27] is that it is not they who will be tortured at all. They will die, and a person closely causally connected with them—closer than a child, for example—will be tortured. That is, however, cause enough for fear.

Similarly, if all a person's dispositions are wiped out by some dreadful experiment, their personal existence will be destroyed. All the habits and practices they have shaped over the years will be destroyed, and they will be effectively dead. If only some dispositions are wiped out, it seems most plausible to think of them as being injured, to a greater or lesser degree. Such injury is possible, and happens in cases of severe brain injury. In cases of paralysis, for example, the dispositions are not destroyed, but the capacity for realizing them is destroyed. Thus they cannot develop properly, and this is a severe impairment of personhood. At the resurrection, one may think that bodies will be able to realize all dispositions fully (though again there are complications about the realization of dispositions to evil or destructive actions). The resurrected person will, nevertheless, be able to build on the habits and practices that result from the realization of powers while in the earthly body.

I am thus inclined to say that one should think of a continuing self as the subject of experience and agency, and in that sense that personal identity is determinate. It may be misleading, however, to think of such a subject as a 'separately existing entity', since there is no question of it existing without any experiences or dispositions. Moreover, in extreme situations subjects may be severely injured, merged, or divided. The Parfit who loses half his memory and character still exists, but is a severely injured individual. The more memories and character he loses, the more severe is the injury to his soul. The limiting case is the loss of all memory and character, when the soul is destroyed. But it is possible in principle for a soul

---

[27] Williams, 'The Self and the Future', in *Problems of the Self*, 46–63.

just to hang on to existence by a hair's breadth, with a few memories and dispositions left.

The theist can admit this theoretical possibility, but insist that the destiny of souls is in fact in the hands of God. That being so, no soul will be injured beyond the point at which it is able to respond to God and grow eventually to its proper maturity. No soul will be destroyed, unless it knowingly and responsibly rejects God, the only source of its life. When souls are injured, through severe amnesia or change of character, God will restore to them, in resurrection, the memories and dispositions which were properly theirs. In the case of infant souls, which have had no chance to accumulate experience or realize capacities, the appropriate hope would seem to be that God will provide for them an opportunity for experience and action, which will allow the potential of their lives, frustrated on earth, to find some fulfilment.

The theist therefore has good reason to hope that Parfit-Garbo cases will not arise in fact. A Parfit severely injured by scientific experimentation will, at the resurrection, be restored to his original state of remembrance and character. But what would happen if a Parfit-Garbo were, by some disastrously immoral experiment, to come into being? Parfit loses half his memory and character, and gains half of Garbo's, perhaps by the removal of one hemisphere of Parfit's brain, and the transplant of one hemisphere of Garbo's brain into the vacated space. If two brain hemispheres are put together, each may truly believe it has done and experienced many things in the past, but each will now suffer a severe impairment in its ability to act as an autonomous and responsible individual. Parfit-Garbo is a merger of two injured and impaired individuals. But the question is, what has happened to Parfit's soul, and to Garbo's?

One is inclined to say that Parfit is still there, until the last memory or disposition is wiped out, but more and more severely impaired. The same must be true of Garbo. So we have a combination of two impaired persons. They are now compelled to act as one, with a new total set of dispositions and a confusing mixture of past experiences, which will govern how new experiences are interpreted and responded to. If all this is possible (and it is not clear that it is, since the interconnection of experiences may be such that they cannot simply be separated off in this way), then souls can be merged, since what constitutes a soul is a certain unity of experiences and dispositions to act. Parfit and Garbo may well both say,

'I am an injured shadow of my former self. Indeed, my responsible action as an individual stopped when I merged brains with somebody else. Then a new agent began to exist, whose responsibilities must be calculated anew.'

Parfit and Garbo do not die in the merger, but their responsibility is diminished to an incalculable degree. It might be better to think of a new responsible agent as coming into being, which could be resurrected as Parfit-Garbo, oddly born with a set of completed experiences and habits. Then Parfit and Garbo (up to the merger) could be resurrected as separate individuals. This would have the strange consequence that Parfit and Garbo did not die, but were injured. Yet they are resurrected as three individuals, a pre-injury Parfit, a pre-injury Garbo, and a post-injury Parfit-Garbo. Perhaps only in this type of case would God be rational in implementing the logically possible manœuvre of resurrecting two copies of one individual. But it is a very special case, and one hopes that it will never in fact arise. The only reason for even thinking of it is that it has been used (by the real earthly Derek Parfit) in an attempt to undermine the idea of one continuing substantial soul. I am inclined to think that this alarming thought-experiment does not undermine such an idea of the soul, but simply shows the possibility of extreme injury to a soul, and the possibility of its death and possible reconstitution (when the original memories and dispositions are restored).

Of course, most people who believe in bodily resurrection do not think of it as the creation of strict replicas at all. They think of the resurrection body as a different kind of body in a different kind of space, so physical similarity as well as physical continuity is broken. What this means is that it is psychic continuity which is truly important to the survival of a person, the continuity of experiences and dispositions, which can be re-embodied in a new and hopefully more expansive form. I have suggested that it is a reasonable implication of Christian belief to think of there being two different forms of afterlife embodiment, one in the intermediate 'image world', followed by final embodiment in a resurrection world. Neither form will be a strict replication of earthly bodies, but in both forms of existence there will be a continuation of the experience and dispositions of individual persons.

In the image-world of the intermediate state, the consequences of human habits and desires can be worked out, to prepare souls for their final destiny. But in that state, even the just will continue to anticipate the resurrection world, in the hope that the whole material cosmos will ultimately be transfigured by the unambiguous presence and power of God. Those who hope for resurrection hope that there will be a perfect recovery of the memory of all they have done. At the same time, this will not be a simple vivid reliving of experience, which would undesirably recreate all the suffering and distress of earthly life. Memory will be so transformed that suffering is set within a wider context of learning and development, and even earthly joy is relativized by a deeper consciousness of the presence of God. Yet it is important to personal survival that the memories remain, however transformed, so that people who enter into eternal bliss will always know themselves to be the same people who suffered, enjoyed, sinned and repented, learned and developed, on the long journey towards God.

The resurrection hope is also that the dispositions which were so partially and inadequately manifested on earth will be enabled to develop in a new and more pliable environment. Capacities and talents which were never realized will be able to grow, and habits and skills which were formed on earth will either be strengthened or reshaped into more creative forms. If this is so, the resurrection world will be one in which new forms of experience and action are possible, but in which nothing of earthly life will be forgotten or useless.

The conclusion is that the continuity of a physical body, and even the creation of an exact replica of such a body, is not necessary to the continuance of the same person. Yet the soul, the bearer of memories, experiences, and dispositions, is properly embodied in some form which allows those dispositions to be expressed and those experiences to be added to and reshaped in an environment not wholly dissimilar to that of earth. If this is so, the resurrection will be to some form of existence which in important ways resembles that of the planet earth, but it will be an earth and a universe which is in a real sense a new creation.

THE TEMPORALITY OF THE AFTERLIFE

On such an account as this, temporality continues after death, both in the intermediate world, where time is needed for souls to progress (or regress) in understanding and purification, and in the resurrection world, where people live in social relationships, in enjoyment of a changing environment, and in growing and endless contemplation and love of God. The idea of a temporally continuous human life after death, generally accepted by classical theologians, has, however, been rejected by many contemporary theologians. It is not surprising that classical models of immortality lead to insuperable problems when an attempt is made to interpret them in a non-temporal way.

These problems surface in the work of a number of recent theologians. Reinhold Niebuhr offers an interesting case, since his attitude to human history is quite different from that of Teilhard de Chardin. Niebuhr is adamant that there will never be an establishing of the Messianic kingdom in history: 'Where there is history at all there is freedom; and where there is freedom there is sin.'[28] The supposition that the world might gradually move towards a perfectly just society, or that it is inevitably progressing in morality, is undermined by the reality of human freedom. As long as humans are genuinely free, some of them will sin, and no society will be free of the tragic consequences of sin.

For Niebuhr, there is no necessary development in history, no great plan culminating in a world-historical goal. If there is a consummation of the world, beyond suffering, conflict, and evil, it must lie beyond history, that is, in eternity. The disagreement between Teilhard and Niebuhr is not so much about the ultimate goal, which both agree to be trans-historical, but about the path to that goal. It is about whether the cosmos evolves towards it, or whether history will continue to its end, whether late or soon, without dramatic changes in human nature or society.

Yet there is a further level of complexity in Niebuhr's account. It may seem that the 'new creation', in which living and dead exist together, will at any rate succeed the first creation, and therefore be temporally continuous with it. However, Niebuhr asserts that the new creation is in eternity, and insists that this eternity is neither a continuation of history and time, nor a timeless, static blankness in which history has no significance.

Eternity is not a continuation of time, because, as Rahner puts it, 'A time which spins on into infinity . . . is really unintelligible, and indeed would be more terrible than hell.'[29] So, Rahner says, 'It is

[28] Reinhold Niebuhr, *The Nature and Destiny of Man* (London: Nisbet, 1945), ii. 83.
[29] Rahner, *Foundations*, 437.

necessary to avoid clearly and from the very beginning the impression that we are dealing with a linear continuation of man's empirical temporality beyond death.'[30] There are two main problems with this sort of account. One is the psychological question of whether endless time really is 'more terrible than hell'. The other is the conceptual question of whether one can coherently conceive eternal life for humans as anything other than a linear continuation of temporality.

Psychologically, many people do find the idea of endless life unappealing. Simon Tugwell says, 'I am not sure that I would have the patience endlessly to pursue an ever-receding goal.'[31] The thought that patience is required to endure interminable lengths of time is a very odd idea of an endless life of companionship and bliss. Fr. Tugwell has in mind Gregory of Nyssa's idea that, since God is infinite, the soul can progress infinitely in knowledge and love of God, without ever being exhausted. The point he surely misses is that God is not, for Gregory, an ever-receding goal, but an enduring yet inexhaustible presence. It is not that one is always travelling to meet someone who never actually appears, but that one is always in the presence of God (one has always arrived, in some sense), and yet there is always more to learn about God.

Among the things that give meaning and value to human life are the contemplation of beauty, the deeper understanding of truth, the expression of personal creativity, and the sharing of experience with loved ones. When one is immersed in these things, time may seem to stand still. In fact, however, the continuance of time is what allows one to contemplate and create, since even simple, changeless enduring is a form of temporality. In so far as one is totally engaged in worthwhile experience and activity, one has no sense of the passing of time, and so no sense of exhaustion.

If one adds to this the knowledge that, beyond the present experience, which one has no desire to end, there are none the less new and greater values; that ahead of one there lie no dangers to fear or boredoms and depressions to endure; that the present will not pass into forgetfulness, but will be conserved in a renewed and strengthened memory, as vivid and fresh as every present moment; then why should endless time be anything like hell? Every moment will

---

[30] Ibid. 436.
[31] Simon Tugwell, *Human Immortality and the Redemption of Death* (London: Darton, Longman, Todd, 1990), 40.

be filled with the conscious delight of the presence of God. The possibility of responding to that delight in creative ways, in company with millions of other souls whose histories are of endless interest, can only enhance the joy of God's Kingdom.

I am even tempted to say that the question of whether one can anticipate with eager longing an endless learning about other persons, an endless engagement with new co-operative and creative concerns, and an endless exploration into the infinite mystery of God, is a good test of whether one has learned what it is to love. If eternal life is the consummation of love, it seems to involve precisely that learning about others, sharing with others, and interaction with others, that involves temporal existence.

Everlasting time will be different in quality to the time humans experience on earth. Earthly time always carries with it an anxiety that suffering or despair may be yet to come, that the future is not under our control. In the Kingdom, God controls all future time, so that there is nothing to fear. Earthly time carries a sense of transience, of constant passing, and thus, for some people, of unsatisfactoriness. In the Kingdom, this transience will have the positive feature (as it can do on earth) of ever-renewed freshness and intensity, which will make boredom or ingratitude unthinkable. Earthly time carries constant forgetfulness, and the eventual death of all memories, however cherished. In the Kingdom, the past is perfectly conserved in God, and always open to souls who desire to know it, with all the vividness of its first experience. Earthly time is shot through with all those failures to understand, to love, and to act virtuously (creatively and well), which make human experience unsatisfactory. In the Kingdom, we will know as we are known, we will be filled with divine love, and we will be empowered by the creative Spirit, which will make our lives an unbroken sharing in endless bliss.

If one believes that the being of God is, in one main aspect, temporal, then it is natural to think that eternal life will be a sharing in the divine temporality, or at least in those minuscule parts of it which are available to our finite minds. Fr. Tugwell suspects that the prospect of such endless life may somehow deprive our earthly lives and individualities of significance. 'A life that simply stretches on and on indefinitely could never constitute a real story.'[32] It

[32] Simon Tugwell, *Human Immortality and the Redemption of Death* (London: Darton, Longman, Todd, 1990), 43.

would be 'shapeless and aimless'. It is importantly true that, if one really accepts the possibility of endless life, the few years spent on earth will be the merest fraction of our real lives. Our troubles and sufferings will indeed pale into insignificance: 'The sufferings of this present time are not worth comparing with the glory that is to be revealed to us.'[33] This life is the infinitesimal prelude to the real life which awaits in the world to come.

Yet this life has a decisive importance. Each earthly life has a unique shape and story, and that will not be lost in eternity. Its endless growth in God is not a development into a different sort of being, but the continuing renewal of experience of a person who was born at such a time in such a place on earth, and who remains recognizably that person for ever. Is 'forever' not too long to be the same person? To think that it is, is to judge by the standards of earthbound experience, for which time can stretch ahead as a blank space, needing to be filled with ultimately futile diversions. One should rather seek to conceive of an experience which is in itself of supreme value, so that it fills the moment with happiness and a sense of fulfilment. Then one should imagine this moment as being continually renewed, with the same quality and intensity, and as being succeeded, without being replaced, by other moments of equal value.

Such a sense is, perhaps, what Boethius was seeking to convey in speaking of 'a good thing which once obtained leaves nothing more to be desired'.[34] Boethius's only mistake was to suppose that such a perfectly fulfilled experience was changeless and timeless. The mistake is to think that we can coherently conceive of any human experience as not even enduring for a moment. All experience takes time, though one need not wish, or be able to, measure that time. One certainly would not wish such an experience to come to an end, and in that sense the enduring must be endless as well as immeasurable. It is a small step to see that an endless and immeasurable moment of supreme beatitude may well contain within itself an infinity of sub-moments, each perfectly fulfilling in itself. It may contain the possibility of change, in so far as personal creativity continues to be of great value, so that eternity may be conceived as a process more than as an immutable state. But this process is

33 Rom. 8: 18.
34 Boethius, *The Consolation of Philosophy*, trans. V. E. Watts (London: Penguin, 1969), bk. 3, prose 2, p. 79.

also one of endless and immeasurable activity, in which contemplation and creative action are closely interwoven. If some form of creative change was not possible, talk of the 'resurrection of the body' seems to be an unnecessary complication. One can timelessly contemplate God very well without a body, and the whole point of a body is to enable one to move, act, and experience in new ways. All such bodily activity, however, would in heaven be filled with a vivid sense of the presence of the unlimited God. In this way, one may have the idea of unending time, without the disadvantage of having to imagine a permanently unsatisfied journey towards an always unattained goal by a constantly changing personality.

We have now passed from the psychological point to the conceptual. Not only must eternal life take time, and in fact exist endlessly. It must also come into being *after* earthly life has been completed, and must therefore stand in an ordinary temporal relation to earthly time. This is clear from the fact that the quality of one's eternal life is causally dependent, at least to some extent, upon one's acts on earth. Since causes must precede, or be not later than, their effects, one can only be judged for one's actions after they have all been completed. It is a matter of simple logic that the Day of Judgement comes after the completion of earthly life. It is therefore a continuation of time.

Since the quality of this time is different from that of earthly time, it is intelligible to speak of it as trans-historical. It comes into existence after the ending of the time of human history on earth, and also after the ending of the time of the intermediate state, wherein (I have suggested) all souls still have the opportunity to progress and to repent.

Rahner says that 'the single, concrete person reaches fulfillment when he is fulfilled in God as a concrete spirit and as a corporeal person'.[35] This sounds like an unequivocal declaration of the creation of a new time after the ending of historical time. However, he also says that 'death marks an end for the whole person',[36] and 'The achieved final validity of human existence which has grown to maturity in freedom comes to be *through* death, not *after* it.' Death itself is seen as a moment in which a person is fixed in a state, either of 'entrance into God's presence', or of 'closing oneself against' God. If this state is not temporal, however, it is impossible to see

---

[35] Rahner, *Foundations*, 436.   [36] Ibid. 437.

how people could know what state they were in. It is implausible
that they realize this at the point of death, or at the last moment of
consciousness. It must therefore, despite Rahner's disclaimer, be
conceived of as a conscious moment after death.

Rahner himself is forced to concede this when he tries to give an
account of Purgatory, which speaks of purification after death.
When, however, does the purification take place? He is compelled
to admit that the full glorification of the person does not come at
death for most people,[37] so, he says, there is a sense in which 'temporal categories can still be applied here'. This exposes the real
problem with 'eternalist' accounts of immortality. They allow no
time for progress in understanding, for the development of potentialities which may have been frustrated on earth, or for a new and
more vivid experience of God than was ever possible on earth.

This is particularly difficult for Rahner, who wishes to allow for
the possibility that all human beings may be saved by Jesus Christ.
His well-known thesis of 'anonymous Christianity' holds that
people may in fact be saved by Jesus, though they never realize that
fact during their lives. If that is so, however, the eternalization of
their lives in God cannot simply be some sort of assumption of their
earthly lives into the eternal being of God. To enter into salvation,
they will have to have some new experience which brings them to
know their Saviour. Otherwise, the idea of salvation is empty of
content. The logic of his argument should lead him to posit some
time of development after death. The reason that it does not is
Rahner's belief in the timelessness of God, and his belief that
eternal life is a sharing in the life of God. The difficulty would
be resolved by accepting that there is a divine temporality, so that
eternal life is a sharing in an appropriate way in the everlasting life
of God.

THE REDEMPTION OF THE PAST

Paul Tillich's eschatology shares a similar fate. Tillich is reluctant
to associate himself too closely with what he calls the 'philosophers
of becoming'. Yet he sees the importance of temporality to the
being of God. He therefore tries to get the best of both worlds, and
say that God 'has neither the timelessness of absolute identity nor

[37] Ibid. 442.

the endlessness of mere process'.[38] This concept of God, the union of two contradictory positions, together with their negations, is wholly vacuous. There is a way of rescuing it from sheer incoherence. That is to distinguish a timeless aspect from a temporal aspect of God. It is his refusal to take this way that leaves Tillich's concept of eternal life in confusion, since it shares the incoherence of his idea of God.

Tillich traces a threefold pattern in the relation of the eternal divine life to the temporal creation. It is, he says, 'the way from essence through existential estrangement to essentialization'.[39] First of all, creation exists as essence, or possibility, in God. Then, in the 'fall' from essence to existence, creation exists in total dependence upon, but estranged from, its ground of being. Finally, all creation is fulfilled in God, is 'essentialized', in a state 'beyond the separation of potentiality and actuality'.[40] For this model, God is not complete in the divine essence, without creation. 'The world process means something for God', and God 'finds fulfilment only through the other'.[41] Yet God is eternally fulfilled, and is never just on the way to fulfilment in serial time. Eternal life is the transtemporal fulfilment of individual life in time, the 'elevation of the positive within existence into eternity'.[42] Thus 'the eternal is not a future state of things. It is always present.'[43]

The idea of a timeless God containing all essences and actualizing some of them, in a single timeless act, is a coherent idea. It is, however, incompatible with the belief that God is in any way changed by creation. A timeless being cannot be changed in any way. In what sense, then, is God 'fulfilled' by relation to the other in time? Only in the sense that creation expresses something of the being of God that would otherwise be unexpressed.

One can think of the temporal proceeding from, and depending upon, the timeless, if one thinks of the whole of time as caused and known in the same act by a timeless God. But can one think of the whole of time as being 'liberated from the negative' and fulfilled in God? One cannot be thinking here of anything caused in God by the temporal. Even divine knowledge of the temporal must not be dependent upon it, but be coincident with the divine will to create. One can only be thinking of all the good things of creation, timelessly actualized and timelessly known by God as not only possible,

---

[38] Paul Tillich, *Systematic Theology* (Welwyn: Nisbet, 1968), iii. 449.
[39] Ibid. 450.   [40] Ibid.   [41] Ibid. 451.   [42] Ibid. 434.   [43] Ibid. 426.

but actual. In other words, one is thinking of God's timeless knowledge of the actuality of the world. But in what sense is that a fulfilment for individuals in the world? It leaves them exactly as they are, in their subjective consciousness. Who, then, experiences eternal life? Only God, it would seem, who alone can 'essentialize' the actual in the divine knowledge, simply by knowing it in the act of willing it. But if God does that, the nature of estranged existence is being falsified. It exists precisely as estranged, and if God is to know it as non-estranged, God will have to overlook all the negative elements of suffering, conflict, and pain that are important parts of its nature.

The only coherent account to be given is a fully temporal account (and Tillich continually uses temporal terms in giving his account), for which events in time really do change God by causing new consequential states of divine knowledge and response. Individuals can themselves experience their fulfilment, but only by living another form of life when the negative elements have truly been eliminated, and by knowing God more fully—and therefore in a future state. Divine knowledge of the present will always be a knowledge of suffering as well as of goodness. Tillich says that the negative 'is present in the eternal memory as that which is conquered'.[44] But again, it is only too obviously not actually conquered in every present moment. If evil is to be conquered, it must be by being eliminated and overwhelmed by the goodness of the creation, of which it is an undesirable part. Goodness does not triumph in every present, even from God's viewpoint. Thus, if one is to speak meaningfully of a fulfilment of individual life in eternity, there must be future state in which individuals can experience the victory of positive elements in their being, in which conflict has been decisively superseded by the 'Sabbath rest' of God's peace.

It is not enough to say, with Reinhold Niebuhr, that 'the contradictions of human existence . . . are swallowed up in the life of God'.[45] Since individuals suffer those contradictions, they are not 'swallowed up' until those individuals find a way out of alienation and conflict. It is not enough, though it is important, to say that 'eternal significance belongs to each moment of our existence, and to historical existence taken as a whole'.[46] We will need, at some

---

[44] Ibid. 426.
[45] Reinhold Niebuhr, *Beyond Tragedy* (New York: Scribner, 1937), 19.
[46] Niebuhr, *Nature and Destiny*, ii. 305.

future time, to realize the significance each moment had, to see it in the framework of God's purposes for all creation, to find some way of coming to terms with our failures to utilize the opportunities we had, and to build the significance we then perceive towards the realization of values which may have been frustrated during life. Indeed, many moments may take on their real significance only when it becomes possible, in some future, to use them in realizing values to which they were always directed, but which were never actualized.

The Christian hope thus requires a temporal future after the resurrection of the dead. It is a different sort of temporality, however, a sharing in the divine temporality, without loss, instability, absence, or anxiety. And it is a future which, though without end, will never lose touch with the individualities and the events of this womb of souls, this space-time universe. For it is the inner significance of the history of this world that will be worked out, contemplatively and creatively, in the world to come, in immeasurable and unending time.

It is important for the Abrahamic tradition that nothing will be lost of the past. That past cannot be changed. It can, however, be reinterpreted, seen in different contexts, and it can be continually reused as a resource for explorations of possibilities that the past closed off. It is rather like seeing a film of one's past life, from a number of points of view, and in a number of different contexts, and seeing possibilities from the past that can be brought to life to reorient one's present actions and attitudes. Yet it is more than that. For if that past is to be redeemed, each moment that was lived in estrangement from God, must be consciously relived and related to God.

Suppose I killed someone. That moment can never become good, in any context. But it can be redeemed, if I relive it in full consciousness of the suffering and loss of my victim, in full awareness of the destruction of God's purposes and of the alienation from God it causes, and in genuine sorrow for what I have done. It would be pointless to relive that suffering, alienation and sorrow over and over again. Indeed, Hell might be seen as the continual reliving of the felt knowledge of the suffering and alienation, no doubt with regret but without the sorrow of penitence.

What I will know in eternity is that, on condition only of penitence, God forgives me and reconciles me to the divine life. If I have subsequently done all that I can to make amends and to return to God, then my sorrow at that act is placed in a broader context, in which it becomes the prelude to full acceptance by the gracious love of God. I cannot, therefore, relive such moments in isolation (again, Hell might be the disintegration of life into isolated moments of suffering and anguish). I can relive the moment as a moment of grace, in which the forgiving love of God is freely given even to one wholly undeserving of it. All the emphasis goes onto the grace of God, none onto my corrupt will. The redemption of that moment of the past comes, not when I can justify it in terms of some alleged greater good it produced, but when I can relive it as a moment of the unmerited acceptance of freely given grace, of total dependence on God. Part of the broader context, too, may be the knowledge that my victim has entered into the life of grace, and shares in the divine forgiveness. Thus a new reconciliation between old enemies would also transform the way in which this past is seen, setting it within a story of enmity overcome and community restored which does not remove its tragic dimension, but transfigures it by setting it within a wider reality of love and reconciliation which has finally conquered evil. To relive that moment redemptively is not just to watch an old film of a violent event. It is to surrender the moment completely to the mercy of God, and to recognize that such surrender is a part and condition of that sharing in the divine beatitude that is eternal life. The past is redeemed by being fully known, and relived within the consciousness of the infinite love, mercy, and beatitude of God.

In experiencing the past, as it has been received into the life of God, moments of joy will be intensified by the clear knowledge of the divine commendation of and sharing in that joy. Times of suffering or sadness will be muted and transformed by the clear knowledge that God heals and forgives, sets those times within a pattern wherein the necessity of evil becomes clear, wherein distinctive goods are realized, and removes the past pain from the present experience of it by the consciousness of overwhelming love. No one will ever experience again the pain of a million deaths. One will not forget that such an experience occurred, and it will always remain horrifying. Yet it will not be contemplated in its original intensity and horror. It will be seen as taken up into the suffering of God, and there transfigured by victorious love. In the divine glory to come there will always be the remembrance of pain—the cross set in the heart of God for eternity. But the present experience will be of mercy, of reconciliation, and of love triumphant—the everlasting life of glory raised from the threshold of death.

Moltmann seeks to express this by saying that 'the parousia comes to all times simultaneously in a single instant'.[47] It is not just an added event at the end of time, which leaves the past unredeemed. When Christ comes in judgement, each moment of every life will be opened up, to be relived in the light of the ultimate response of each soul to God, a response perhaps long fashioned in *barzakh*, and now perfect and finalized. One should nevertheless unequivocally say that there will be a time beyond historical (this cosmic) time, in which the redemption of the past can take place, and God can be experienced in a more vivid and interior way. Moltmann's own notion that time itself will end, that 'once death is no more, there will be no more time either, neither the time of transience nor the time of futurity',[48] does not allow for that newness of truly human experience that the resurrection world must afford.

THE LAST JUDGEMENT

If historical time can be redeemed in this way, what is the fate of those who, perhaps for ever, refuse to accept love and reconciliation? If Christ comes in judgement, does this not imply a division between those who are accepted and those who are found wanting? One major image in the New Testament of the Last Judgement, the parable of the sheep and the goats, speaks of the sending away of the goats to 'eternal punishment'.[49] Belief in everlasting torment in Hell has played a prominent part in much Christian teaching, despite the fact that it seems a standing affront to the central Christian teaching of the unlimited mercy of God. The division, however, is a division between life and death, between living forever before the face of God, and being destroyed for ever from before the face of God. Just as the ultimate punishment for crime in ancient Israel was death, so the ultimate punishment for sin is the everlasting loss of God by a death from which there is no return, an

---

[47] Jurgen Moltmann, *The Way of Jesus Christ* trans. Margaret Kohl (London: SCM, 1990), 317.
[48] Jurgen Moltmann, *The Coming of God* (London: SCM, 1996), 294.
[49] Matt. 25: 31–46.

unending destruction, a truly eternal punishment. This is a terrible loss, and the pain of Hell is the knowledge of that loss. But it is not unending torture. Unlike eternal life, it has an end, and that end is death.

The doctrine of everlasting torment has no place in the gospel of a God who will even descend to Sheol to bring souls to repentance, and who takes upon himself the sufferings of the whole world. Even the casual reader of the New Testament must be struck by the vivid contrast between two different doctrines of divine justice which can be found in stark juxtaposition. Having said that God 'will render to every man according to his works',[50] Paul almost at once adds that 'no human being will be justified in [God's] sight by works of the law'.[51] Similarly, having said that 'we must all appear before the judgment seat of Christ, so that each may receive good or evil, according to what he has done in the body',[52] Paul almost immediately continues, 'In Christ God was reconciling the world to himself, not counting their trespasses against them'.[53]

The first doctrine is that divine justice is retributive. Each person receives different rewards and punishments for what they have done. Justice looks to the past, and clears the moral account-book by assigning a balancing sum of good and evil. The second doctrine is that divine justice is redemptive. No one is good enough to claim any reward, but God will freely give. No one can free themselves from the grip of egoism, but God will freely forgive. Justice looks to the future, and creates the capacity for goodness in all who will receive it.

It is not oversight or accident that these two doctrines stand together in the New Testament. The fact is that justice and mercy go together, but always 'mercy triumphs over judgment'.[54] There is judgement, when the secrets of all hearts will be disclosed, when humans will see the harm they have done to others and the corruption of soul they have brought upon themselves. 'Jesus is revealed from heaven with his mighty angels in flaming fire, inflicting vengeance'.[55] The fire of destruction burns up and destroys all those who oppose the way of love, because nothing can stand in the Messianic kingdom which obstructs or impedes love in any way.

Yet the paradox of this statement is that the judge of the world is Jesus, who taught that the perfection of love is to love even one's

---

[50] Rom. 2: 6.   [51] Rom. 3: 20.   [52] 2 Cor. 5: 10.   [53] 2 Cor. 5: 18.
[54] Jas. 2: 13.   [55] 2 Thess. 1: 7.

enemies, and to give one's life for sinners, who himself bore the sins of the world in his own person, and who came not 'to judge the world but to save the world'.[56] How can such love destroy even the wicked? Karl Barth claimed that 'In the Biblical world of thought the judge is not primarily the one who rewards some and punishes the others; he is the man who creates order and restores what has been destroyed.'[57] If the revelation of the glory of God in the face of Jesus Christ is genuine, God's love will never aim simply at retribution. God wills the fulfilment of all sentient creatures: 'The Lord is . . . forbearing . . . not wishing that any should perish, but that all should reach repentance.'[58] But creatures can set themselves against God's love, seeking in their pursuit of self to destroy creation. Love itself must set a barrier against their activities, frustrating their actual desires for the sake of the rest of creation, and in the hope that they may yet turn to accept love.

That which frustrates the desires of the self is felt as fire. Thwarted desires turn inwards, to rage and burn within the self. Full knowledge of the glory of God, and of the joy of the kingdom from which one has excluded oneself, is both darkness and fire. Darkness, because it is exclusion from the light. Fire, because excluded souls torment one another incessantly, and feel God's presence as an ultimately destructive threat to the world of hatred they have shaped.

This is the world to which all will travel, as long as they turn from God. Christian teaching is clear, that such is the natural destination for all human lives: 'If we say that we have no sin, we deceive ourselves'.[59] Such deceit will be burned away by the light, which is searing fire to those who seek to conceal their motives in darkness. If, then, we are to be judged by our works, we will find ourselves thrown into *Gehenna,* that rubbish-pit whose fire never goes out, and destroyed for ever. We will not divide into the good and the evil—the moralistic version of Judgement Day—for 'the whole world is in the power of the evil one'.[60] If we are judged by works alone, our destiny is the fire of destruction.

God's will, however, is not destruction, but life: 'As in Adam all die, so in Christ shall all be made alive.'[61] This 'all' is not to be dis-

---

[56] John 12: 47.

[57] Karl Barth, *Dogmatics in Outline*, trans. G. T. Thomson (London: SCM, 1960), 135.

[58] 2 Pet. 3: 4.   [59] 1 John 1: 8.   [60] 1 John 5: 19.   [61] 1 Cor. 15: 22.

missed lightly. It sets up a correspondence between the universal estrangement of humanity, from which none are exempt, and the universal reconciliation of humanity, which similarly refers to human nature as such, and therefore includes all individuals who share human nature. Elsewhere, Paul stresses the same theme: 'One man's act of righteousness leads to acquittal and life for all men.'[62] It may seem unfair for one man's trespass to lead to death for all, a real death, a real destruction of the flesh. But the picture is transformed if one believes that one man's act of goodness brings about life for all, a real life, a rising from death.

In this picture, there is no arbitrary selection of some people for eternal life. On the contrary, 'God has consigned all men to disobedience, that he may have mercy upon all.'[63] This statement follows from the long discussion about the place of the people of the Old Covenant in the purpose of God, and from Paul's conclusion that they were 'broken off', or destroyed, to allow the Gentiles to come to knowledge of God's salvation in Jesus. But 'If they do not persist in their unbelief, they will be grafted in' once more, so that finally 'all Israel will be saved'.[64]

The obvious interpretation is that divine judgement brings destruction, but that destruction is not final, and will be succeeded by the reconciliation of the whole of Israel to God. This prefigures or is part of the final realization of the greatest mystery of all, 'the reconciliation of all things' to God.[65] When the Day of Judgement comes, the judge is the one who 'is the Saviour of all men',[66] and who freely gave his life to be 'the expiation . . . for the sins of the whole world'.[67] Barth writes, 'The Judge who puts some on the left and the others on the right, is in fact He who has yielded Himself to the judgment of God for me and has taken away all malediction from me.'[68] The Last Judgement is the final declaration of God's universally reconciling mercy. It is the transfiguration of Sheol itself, 'the pits of nether gloom'[69] where, according to Jude 1: 6, the 'eternal chains' which bind the fallen angels are not literally unending, but 'age-long', enduring in the age until the Judgement. At that Judgement, all are condemned, but the condemnation having been borne by the Judge himself, the only word pronounced on that day is the word of mercy.

---

[62] Rom. 5: 18. [63] Rom. 11: 32. [64] Rom. 11: 26.
[65] Col. 1: 20. [66] 1 Tim. 4: 10. [67] 1 John 2: 2.
[68] Barth, *Dogmatics in Outline*, 136. [69] 2 Pet. 2: 4.

What, then, of our efforts, or lack of efforts, after goodness? Will they all have been vain, unconnected with God's treatment of us in the world to come? That would evacuate the juxtaposition of retributive and redemptive justice of significance. Divine justice is primarily redemptive. It is concerned with bringing out in us some of the positive potentiality with which we were created. It aims to transform our estranged lives by the dynamism of the Spirit, by whom we 'are being changed into [Christ's] likeness from one degree of glory to another'.[70] But there are degrees of glory. There are various levels of reward and loss, even for those who 'will be saved, but only as through fire'.[71]

God wills to bring all to salvation, but God must begin to shape our lives from what we have made of them on earth. Thus there will be purification by the fires of Sheol, or the rewards of Paradise. These will not be arbitrarily assigned punishments, but appropriate ways of reshaping our characters into the unique forms of manifesting the Spirit of Christ which God wills them to be. God's justice must first be retributive, in the sense that it must treat our characters in the most appropriate way for bringing them to repentance or growth in the Spirit. But it will in its deepest character be redemptive, for it is always directed towards helping us to make amends for our sins, and it offers, far beyond what anyone could deserve, the infinite gift of everlasting divine love.

Still, mercy does not compel. Jesus Christ is 'our wisdom, our righteousness and sanctification and redemption'.[72] But the possibility of the ultimate refusal of God exists. If any actualize that possibility, then the coming of Christ in glory to recreate heaven and earth, the final transfiguration of creation, the Christification of the cosmos, will also be the making-present of the ultimate division between life and death, health and corruption, creation and destruction. In the vivid symbolism of the Apocalypse, in his vision of the Final Judgement, the saint saw that 'Death and Hades were thrown into the lake of fire. This is the second death.'[73] From the first death, the death of the body, there is resurrection. From the second death, the death of the soul, there is no return. At that time, God shall be all in all (*panta en pasin*)[74] and 'there shall no more be anything accursed'.[75] Evil will be destroyed, and those who refuse to repent, having suffered all that they have caused any sentient

[70] 2 Cor. 3: 18.   [71] 1 Cor. 6: 3.   [72] 1 Cor. 1: 30.   [73] Rev. 20: 14.
[74] 1 Cor. 15: 28.   [75] Rev. 22: 3.

being to suffer, will lose for ever the infinite joy of God, an infinite loss of infinite good.

We may pray that the teaching of the reality of Hell has been a skilful (not always very skilful) means for bringing sinners to repentance. We may pray that no one will suffer the second death. All that Christians are encouraged to affirm positively is that God wills the salvation of all, that God can accomplish it, and that God has entered the deepest 'pits of gloom' to realize it. The form in which God has done this is, Christians believe, the form of Jesus Christ. He lived and taught as a young Jewish prophet. He gave his life as a prayer that the Messianic kingdom might be manifest. He walked in the world of the dead to proclaim the unlimited mercy of God. He appeared to the disciples to assure them of resurrection life. He will be manifested in a form of immeasurable glory when this cosmos ends and a new creation comes into being, one where there will be no night and no sun, for all the souls that have ever lived will live again in a new and incorruptible world where 'the Lord God will be their light',[76] and they will live for ever. So Christians pray that Christ will come, secretly in every moment and openly at the end of time, bringing not the tortures of everlasting Hell, but the final transfiguration of the cosmos into the full manifestation of the glory of God.

[76] Rev. 22: 5.

15
Conclusion

The differences between religious traditions are nowhere clearer than in their views of human nature. I have considered four main religious views, and one non-religious view. It is clear that there are a number of variant positions that can be taken of the place of human life in the universe, and it seems that every possible position has been filled by some world-view. Since these views span the whole spectrum of possibilities, it would be absurd to say that they all really agree. They are best seen as explorations of alternative possibilities for understanding human being in the world.

Yet it is not implausible to suggest that there are common features of religious views. They all see the material world, as it is now constituted, as inherently unsatisfactory. They all propose some better, or truer, form of existence, which can be attained through religious practice. And they all construe that practice in terms of a rather ascetic or disciplined attitude to the material world, and the cultivation of conscious states of bliss, wisdom, and compassion. They all seek liberation from selfish greed, and experience of a self-less and blissful state or condition.

Such disagreements and convergences can be mapped by regarding religious views at different degrees of generality. At the most general level, a wide range of religious views seek liberation from self and the attainment of blissful and compassionate experience. They thus consider that such experience can be attained, and that its attainment is the highest human goal. If one remains at this level of generality, one can discern a common purpose and practice in religious traditions of many different sorts. It is even plausible to suggest that this is the most important feature of religious belief, its spiritual heart. A great deal can be accomplished by pursuing the implications of the belief that such a purpose is the true goal for all humanity, and by exploring how it might best be made easier to realize for all.

At a slightly less general level, there are differences about the nature of the self and about the specific character of the desired goal. Here, the Semitic faiths are distinguished by viewing selves as substantially embodied in the material world, and perhaps as emergent from and always properly parts of such a world. They view the goal in terms of relation to a substantial personal being of wisdom, creativity, and compassion. It is clearly possible, in contrast to these emphases, to view the self as a non-substantial series of events (Buddhism), as an essentially immaterial substance (various forms of dualistic Hinduism), or as an appearance of a deeper unitary reality (non-dualism). Correlatively, the goal might be construed as existence beyond all conditions, as communion with a supreme personal Lord, or as recognition of an ultimate non-dual reality. These are conflicting truth-claims. None of them is theoretically certain, but the choice between them is, as William James used to say, a 'forced' one. One has to take some view, in practice, and this will force a choice, so far as choice is possible, between beliefs. But the practical aim of transcending self in conscious relation to a state of supreme intrinsic value can be pursued on any such view. Moreover, I have pointed out how, within traditions, there are many varieties of interpretation possible, some of which converge with other traditions. No tradition contains a completely closed and immutable set of interpretations, even when it claims to do so.

At an even more particular level, interpretations of the relationship between the self and the goal differ. Christians see the supreme personal being, God, as entering into the suffering of creatures, and uniting them in a communion of love in the divine Being itself. God is seen as acting in one series of historical events, grouped around the person of Jesus, to disclose the divine nature and purpose, and draw creatures into unity with that nature and purpose. Out of the historical disclosure of God as suffering, kenotic love, arises a faith community committed to realizing universal fellowship, creativity, and compassion for all beings, a community that prefigures and inaugurates the perfected communion of love which is seen in this tradition as the goal of creation.

Judaism and Islam are not able to accept these events as disclosive of God, and tend to see Christianity as a more negative tradition that condemns all who do not believe in Jesus as Messiah, and tries to impose the hierarchical authority of the church on everyone. They see their primary and constitutive disclosures of God in the existence of a divine Law, which protects and emphasizes the unity and transcendent sovereignty of God, and the absolute demand for justice and mercy that God makes of every individual. Though there are important strands in each which qualify the rigour of these beliefs, as general traditions of disclosure they stress the moral freedom of the individual soul and its absolute distinction from the Divine. The Christian tradition stresses, by contrast, the bondage of the human soul, its deliverance by grace, and its union with the Divine in Christ.

There are further levels of particular disagreement, as Christians, for example, differ among themselves as to whether salvation is by faith alone, or by faith and works, and about particular ways in which grace is mediated to humans. Religious views continually fragment and diversify as they become more particular. It is easy to suspect that, in the end, each person who presses religious questions as far as they can will end up with a view which is uniquely personal in many respects. What hope or need is there, then, for any sort of unity of religions?

The need arises from the fact that truth is one. It is not satisfactory to remain in a situation in which everyone has a different belief about what is true, for then it follows that almost everyone must be mistaken. That may be inevitable, but it is not as such desirable. So one must continually seek to bring people to agreement in the truth.

Moreover, religious faith is not just a matter of holding specific beliefs. It embodies a commitment to a tradition of disclosure, grounded in an originative person or teaching, which provides a set of symbols capable of being interpreted in a number of changing ways. Faith communities are communities of reflective response to such originative disclosures, and part of their richness is that they can hold together people of quite diverse beliefs on many particular matters. If one holds that many such traditions are likely to contain authentic, if incomplete, disclosures of the ultimate reality and goal, one has a strong motivation to seek for a wider unity which can include that measure of authenticity.

In such a search, however, one cannot simply ignore the disagreements about human nature which exist. In everyday factual matters, the more particular one gets, the more chance there is of getting agreed truth. This is because particular truths are usually about specific matters of fact which can be observed by everyone. In religion, however, the more particular one gets, the less chance there is of agreement. This is because particular truths in religion are usually about matters that cannot be neutrally observed or tested. Arguments multiply precisely because observations cannot settle the matter, and because human reasoning is so weak, changeable, and subject to cultural pressures of many kinds.

This must lead one to question the reliability one can place on arguments to precise conclusions, in religion. It would seem judicious not to place too much confidence on arguments about which there is a high degree of informed dispute. The trouble is that there is dispute even about the most general statements in religion, so one cannot solve the problem by confining opinion solely to the universally agreed. The rational course seems to be to accept the weakness and uncertainty of human thought on such matters, but to remain true to the disclosure one finds in one's own experience. One should neither insist that one's own beliefs are obviously the only or unrevisably true ones, nor pretend that all differences of belief are unimportant, nor that one can live comfortably without having any beliefs in this area at all. This requires the resolute pursuit of truth from whatever standpoint one finds oneself beginning from (which may well involve a deeper realization of what that standpoint really is), together with a preparedness to understand as sympathetically as possible alternative views, and learn from them as far as possible.

Given the fact of human finitude, partiality, and obstinacy, views of human nature will probably remain diverse as long as humans continue to think about such matters. Being informed about them, and avoiding caricatures of them, offers the best hope of pursuing truth responsibly from within one's own tradition. I have expounded a view of human nature from within a Christian tradition which has been positively shaped by encounter with, and sometimes by reaction to, alternative views. An assured grasp of final truth in such matters may elude us, yet it remains important to pursue truth as fairly and comprehensively as possible. In that task, the attempt to come to some coherent and plausible view of human nature and its proper fulfilment must play an important part. That is the modest yet extraordinarily difficult goal of the sort of comparative theology that I have tried to present.

AUTHOR INDEX

SUBJECT INDEX